The Last
Wrestlers

In memory of Uncle Alan. Um abração.

The Last Wrestlers

A Far-flung Journey in Search of a Manly Art

MARCUS TROWER

EBURY
PRESS

1 3 5 7 9 10 8 6 4 2

Published in 2007 by Ebury Press, an imprint of Ebury Publishing

Ebury Publishing is a division of the Random House Group

The Random House Group Limited Reg. No. 954009

Addresses for companies within the Random House Group
can be found at
www.randomhouse.co.uk

A CIP catalogue record for this book is available from
the British Library

The Random House Group Limited makes every effort to ensure
that the papers used in our books are made from trees that have
been legally sourced from well-managed and credibly certified
forests. Our paper procurement policy can be found on
www.randomhouse.co.uk

Printed and bound in Great Britain by Mackays of Chatham Plc

ISBN 9780091910679

'There is no greater fame for a man than that which he wins with his footwork or the skill of his hands.'

Homer, *The Odyssey*

Note

There are simple glossaries of terms at the end of country sections, and notes are provided from p. 360.

Contents

PART 1

India

October to April, 1998–1999

Chapter I

Kushti *Man*

The alleys of Varanasi are like an alternative system of rivulets leading remorselessly to the River Ganga. Whenever I enter the streets, I am flushed down to the *ghats*, the huge flights of stone steps on the riverbank, by the current of people walking with purpose behind me, and have little chance to linger and look for wrestling schools that may be hidden behind the walls and doors either side on the way. My attention pinballs from one signifier of Indian life to another – from the *paan* sellers to the silver buckets to the shrines and *chai* stalls, and the cows and dogs dozing on the edges of the traffic as peacefully as holidaymakers swinging in hammocks. Soon I have to remind myself why I'm here in the first place.

I have no idea what an Indian wrestling school will look like, though I hope I'll recognise one when I see it. I know traditional Indian wrestling is called *kushti* and Indians wrestle outside on earth, but I don't know whether schools will be indicated by a sign or symbol, or hidden behind anonymous façades. I keep an eye out for likely looking pockets of open ground but don't see any, and wonder whether I'm searching at the wrong time of day. Indian wrestlers traditionally get up very early to train – at five or even four o'clock – times at which, jet-lagged, I'm not yet prepared to rise. Perhaps a whole shift of wrestling ends before I'm even out of bed, and broad-shouldered wrestlers turn sideways to pass each other in the narrow streets before disappearing into the camouflage of their daytime lives.

After a few days spent searching without success I give up and ask for help from Masheem, the world-weary manager of the Vishnu Guest House, which is where I'm staying.

'Masheem, do you know any wrestlers?'

'Yes, yes,' he says, 'but first you must visit my friend's silk house.'

'But Masheem, I don't need any silk. Why don't you just introduce me to a wrestler now?'

'Yes, yes. I will arrange for you to meet a wrestler at my friend's silk house.'

Clearly Masheem takes commission from the silk merchant for arranging introductions to foreigners. Before he will do me a favour, I have to do him a favour and visit his friend's shop. At the nearby Poonam Textile House, I sit on a white cushion and drink *chai* while Binod, the salesman, unfurls what seems like every silk in stock.

'What about this one?' he says. 'And this one? This one? And this one?'

While I choose, a wiry man in his twenties enters the room and sits silently: Rajan, my wrestling contact. I settle for a mandala-pattern brocade and buy it partly out of sympathy for whoever has to refold and stack all the cloth afterwards. When the transaction is complete, Rajan leads me, along with Binod and his brothers, to a nearby park, Kali Bari, which is hidden by a wall from a main road I have passed along many times during unsuccessful solitary searches. From the other side of the wall there is no clue to let you know that Kali Bari exists. On that side, there is a gutter of stinking urine where men squat to pee at broken porcelain urinals that look like huge bad teeth. Women cover their noses with their saris as they pass in rickshaws. But this side is a world away from the filth and noise of the street. Here, there are eddies of tended rosebushes, and there is peace and quiet.

We take off our shoes and sandals and approach an exercise area. A small shrine to Hanuman, the monkey god, is built into the wall next to a rectangle of earth, which constitutes the wrestling arena. A collection of enigmatic exercise stones lies nearby. Each is shaped like a ring doughnut, but has a diametrical handle. Some are huge – as big as millstones, truck tyres and lifebelts. The largest has to weigh about 200kg. It defies belief that anyone could lift it. This is exercise equipment for giants.

'How do you lift the stones?' I ask Binod.

Binod asks a shaven-headed man to demonstrate. Bending forwards, he balances one of the smaller stones on the back of his neck. But what he is doing looks totally wrong. His posture is bad, and there is no way he could rest one of the large stones on his neck like that.

Rajan strips down to a white loincloth and scampers around like a monkey. He demonstrates wrestling techniques, which I repeat to show my recognition – to show that, in wrestling, we share a common language. A small crowd gathers. A man wearing white *kurta-pyjamas* steps forward and addresses me in English.

'These men are *sadhus*, holy men,' he says. 'You, a wrestler, are a holy man. This is a holy place.'

He points to a tree next to the exercise area. 'The tree is a pipal tree. It is the tree Buddha sat under at Bodh Gaya.' He gestures to the road beyond the wall. 'There, traffic. Here, the air 100 per cent oxygen. It is clean, relaxing. You exercise here, you never have fever, and your hair will grow thick and black. If you wrestle and do exercises you will have a small penis.'

He must have said that wrong. Surely he is making some kind of macho pronouncement. Surely he means 'large penis'.

'*Small* penis?' I repeat.

'Yes, it is good,' he says.

Afterwards, on a high, I walk back to the Vishnu Guest House. Not only have I located my first wrestling place in a hidden park, but I'm also excited by what the man in the white *kurta-pyjamas* has just said. Wrestlers are somehow holy men – and I, a wrestler, am in some way a holy man too. His words suggest a spiritual depth to wrestling, which is something I came to India hoping to find. I later repeat what he said to Rakesh, a bearded young graduate who works at the Harmony Bookshop, a social and intellectual hub for foreigners on Assi Ghat. Rakesh scoffs at the idea that wrestling has spiritual depth.

'Wrestlers are holy men?' he repeats, caustically. 'It is shit. It is the type of thing people in India say to try to impress you.'

Rajan says he used to be a good wrestler and now teaches children, which is good karma, though he complains about the pay – which must be bad karma. Over the next few days he guides me to more wrestling schools hidden in the folds of the city. Every time we meet he is dressed conservatively in the same *kurta-pyjamas* and black waistcoat, and has a fresh sandalwood-paste *puja* mark across his forehead that flags him as a devotee of Shiva. He walks the alleys with his hands behind his back, proud and surly like a *gunda*, an Indian gangster, while I, the newcomer to these streets, trail a few paces behind in his wake. He imperiously orders boys to go on errands to buy him *paan*, and asks me for money to buy *chai* only to keep the change. We communicate using gestures and basic English. Were we to fully share a language, I know I'd like him even less than I do.

Rajan's gym, Pandey Babua, overlooks the Ganga from the top of a *ghat*. Had you permission to build a wrestling school anywhere in the world, you would be hard pushed to find a better location than the one where Pandey Babua already stands. When you sit on the parapet and look out it is as if you are at the top of a castle battlement; or as though the huge river and the life at the river's edge are a performance within a stadium and you have the best seat in the best stand. The gym itself – called an *akhara* – consists of a square of earth under a corrugated iron roof, a shrine to Hanuman and a couple of equipment rooms. A pipal tree provides shade.

I meet Rajan at Pandey Babua for an early morning wrestling session. He has been eager to challenge me ever since we met – and I've been eager to get a taste of Indian wrestling, even though my health isn't too good. Rajan prepares by performing cartwheels in his white nappy-like loincloth and works himself up into a fervour. I strip down to a pair of boxer shorts, and stretch and try to loosen my stiff back. We spar. Rajan makes fast but reckless dives for my legs. I counter by kicking my legs back and grinding my hips into his head to drive him into the ground. He wrestles with his head too low, so I snap it down with one hand, wedge it in the crook of an arm and squeeze on a front-headlock. I linger a moment longer than strictly necessary for the sake of retribution, then slip behind him. Given that I weigh about 20kg more than Rajan, it is understandable that he cannot do anything with me.

Gopal, Pandey Babua's wrestling instructor, is also eager to challenge me, and is nearer my weight. His attacks are reckless too. He attempts a sacrifice throw by falling back and trying to pull me down with him, but I feel the move instantly and pin him instead. Like Rajan, he wrestles with his head low, so I snap it down and get behind him. When I am accustomed to the way Gopal takes hold, I launch an attack and shoot for a takedown, but he crossfaces me wickedly by rubbing his fist and forearm across my nose and eyes. Exhausted, I have to stop. I lie face down while Rajan gives me a massage. He violently cracks my spine and pounds my head with his fists as though he has just read my diary and found out what I really think of him. Afterwards the three of us sit on the parapet and cool down. Cracks echo from below. Washermen are whipping their wash-stones with spiralled-up sheets at the river's edge.

'You are lucky to be at this *akhara* with its view of the Ganga,' says Gopal. 'Up on the road very traffic: busy, *boop-boop*! Here you can find peace.'

Covered in earth, we look like miners who've just finished a shift. I point to a bucket and tap, as if to say, 'Should we wash there?'

'No,' says Gopal, 'we bathe in the Ganga.'

The idea makes me feel uneasy. To start with, I have a vague idea that the river is polluted. I have also seen vultures boat downriver on bloated corpses of cattle, pecking at the flesh, and seen carcasses, garlanded with their own entrails, bobbing like buoys near groups of bathers. But I know, too, that Hindus regard the Ganga as a holy river, a goddess, and that to refer to her as polluted or refuse to bathe in her waters may cause offence. Pilgrims come from all over the country to bathe from the *ghats*. Washing in the river is believed to wash away sins.

I nervously join Gopal and Rajan as they descend the steps to the river's edge. Marigolds and broken toothbrushes are washed up on the shoreline. Rajan wets his toothbrush with water emerging from a crack in a step and cleans his teeth. Gopal and I wade into the water. The mud feels soft and gooey underfoot. I rub my arms, legs and back with water, but keep my head dry, not wanting to swallow. A nearby youth laughs at my attempts to wash without dunking my head.

'Hello! Your face mud!' he shouts.

I feel found out. Gopal shows me what to do. He plugs his ears with his little fingers then squats underwater and quickly resurfaces three times. I copy him and quickly get out of the water afterwards. The three of us climb the steps back to the *akhara* and get changed. I hang my boxer shorts on a line to dry, and leave.

Early the following morning I return to the *akhara* and wait for Gopal to arrive. Washermen are descending the stone staircase that leads to the riverside. They transport dirty clothes and sheets on the backs of donkeys, or slide bags of laundry down an incline to the base. Then they stand in the river and scrub and dunk the laundry and slap their wash-stones with it as hard as if it had insulted them. But when the sheets are laid out to dry you can see that they are still grubby and dirty. The Ganga may wash away sins, but it is ineffective at dealing with stains at low temperatures.

Gopal still hasn't turned up after an hour. The only other person at the gym is a *chai* shop owner who stands doing wayward bicep curls. Between sets he asks me why I'm here.

'To meet Gopal, but he is late.'

He misunderstands. He thinks I'm saying that I'm the one who's late.

'Yes,' he says. 'You are late. There is only wrestling here for three months: April, May and June. It is the rule at this *akhara*.'

Gopal never arrives. I notice, too, that my boxer shorts have been taken from the line.

Chapter 2

The Fall

If you had known me at that time you would have known all about it. Wrestling, my obsession. It erupted from me, constantly. Seats or no seats, I would stand on trains and Tubes to develop balance, surfing the points, shifting my weight from one foot to the other and dropping my centre of gravity to take the bends. If I saw a couple hugging in the street, without thinking about it – it embarrasses me to remember now – I would analyse their position in wrestling terms, judge who had the better hold and compute what technique they should use next. While I stood and chatted in bars, I would absentmindedly practise wrestling grips – the butterfly, the butcher's, the Gene LeBell special.

If we had spoken at that time, say in 1995, when I was 28 and living in London, I would have told you all about wrestling. I would have told you that it is mentioned in the *Iliad*, *Beowulf* and the *Mahabharata*, and that a wall of a 4,000-year-old tomb in Egypt is painted with a procession of wrestling positions that wouldn't be out of place in a

contemporary instruction manual. I would have related that
Plato wrestled, as did Henry VIII, that Cornwall has its own
indigenous style, and wrestling matches were once used to
settle fishing disputes between the Cornish and Bretons. With
assorted facts such as these, I would have hoped to establish
the pedigree of wrestling to counterbalance the low esteem in
which I'd assume you held the sport.

Wrestling had a great past but its present was painful to
witness. It had fallen into obscurity and dereliction in England,
like a boarded-up old mansion at the end of the street that
everyone says has always been like that. What it was before the
wreckers stole the slates from the roof and ripped out the
fireplaces, what wrestling really is, was difficult to say for
certain, but it was clear who some of those wreckers were: men
who called themselves professional wrestlers but did amateur
dramatics. For my generation, they were the grapplers on TV's
World of Sport – clowns like Giant Haystacks, Big Daddy and
Mick McManus who acted out matches using techniques, such
as the clothesline and drop kick, which belong only in comic
books. The circus performers for a later generation would go by
names like Stone Cold Steve Austen, The Undertaker and The
Rock. When the modern era of faked matches began about a
hundred years or so ago, many professional wrestlers could
wrestle for real but decided not to; most of today's couldn't
wrestle if their lives depended on it, which is why it's
unfortunate they don't.

I had brushes with some of the people who were prostituting
and using wrestling after I naively placed an ad in the sports
section of *Time Out* in the hope of finding people to train with,
only to stumble around in a strange, alien world as a
consequence. I sweated over the wording to make sure the ad
didn't read like a cryptic pick-up message. It said:

Martial arts training partner needed who's interested
in wrestling and grappling

but I got calls that suggested the ad had been edited so that
'sexual' had been substituted for the first three words while
'wrestling' and 'grappling' had been printed in inverted
commas.

A lot of people responded. Every evening I came home from work to an answerphone message light-indicator winking at me flirtatiously. A John from North London claimed he was a brown belt in judo who had learnt some real pro wrestling from an old man next door. I couldn't work out whether he was for real or not, but was suspicious enough not to meet him. He phoned back a few weeks later as Paul from Brighton – I recognised the voice – and put the phone down when I confronted him. Pro wrestlers like to isolate and crank a particular limb or part of their opponent's body to force them to submit; however, it dawned on me that when John/Paul had said he 'preferred to work on his opponent's back' he was choosing his words carefully for their ambiguity. Some time later I discovered that wrestling was on the fringes of the gay S&M scene, and that conversation with John/Paul and a number of others suddenly made a lot more sense.

Adrian, a genuine wrestler who called, set up a small club in a scout hut in Horley, partly on the strength of my enthusiasm. There, I wrestled a slightly built librarian who styled himself 'Leopard Man'. He changed in the toilet cubicle, like a home-video superhero, from black motorbike leathers into a leopard-skin print singlet and tall boots, and growled and clawed the air with his hands before stepping onto the mat. I didn't know whether to wrestle him or shoot him and call a taxidermist. When we sparred, he quickly tired. I turned him onto his back and carefully levered his right arm into a straight armlock. Before the armlock started to come on, Leopard Man cried out in pain, his face screwed up like a paper ball. I was confused. I hadn't yet straightened his arm to the point where he should feel pain. Concerned that I might have injured him without realising, I asked Leopard Man whether he was OK.

'Fine,' he said. 'I just like to give the audience their money's worth.'

There were only two others in the scout hut that evening.

But when I wrestled for real against real wrestlers, I saw that this was something with soul – that it was wide and deep and went all the way down.

Before wrestling, my passion was judo; before judo it was martial arts, and in the beginning there were the weights. Like a series of excellent girlfriends, I cared for all of them – I kept in touch with them all – but the current relationship was always an improvement on the last: in each I found a greater refinement, a greater flowering, of the strong feelings I had valued in the one before.

I was introduced to the weights while at Leeds University. In the uni gym I learnt how to squat, bench-press, butterfly-curl and spot for others. The gym was a masculine place – nothing like the deluge of feminised fitness centres that was to come, with their carpeting, machines for solitary exercisers, Lycra, TV monitors and emphasis on hygiene – places where you feel you're in a cross between an office, a show kitchen and a nightclub where everyone dances alone. The uni gym had the real essentials: a squat rack, chin-up bar, benches, dumbbells, Olympic bars, EZ bars and Olympic plates and ears, plus an upright rowing machine (machine is too elaborate a term – it was more a T bar with plates) to be treated with suspicion because it could easily do your back in.

I took to the weights in part as a reaction against the bookishness of student life. Studying history was all reading and talking about other people who did things, but body-building was a form of action. When I quivered under a heavy weight on the bench-press and tried to squeeze the bar up to full extension for one more rep, I learnt more about who I was and what I could do than in a year of history tutorials. My degree was poorly supervised and lacked a disciplined structure, but the weights gave my life order and certainty, as martial arts and wrestling would later, and a timetable I stuck to without question. At least three mornings a week I put in hard two-hour-plus shifts, alternating body-parts in the standard way. I became a body-building fundamentalist, a weight-training evangelist, feeling nothing but respect towards the other gym regulars for the sincerity of their contests with the weights, and feeling nothing but disdain – like all ideologues, I was very judgemental – for the pencil-necks in Chemistry Soc T-shirts who gatecrashed our fraternity to buzz and clatter around the multi-gym. They had no rhythm, no concentration, no capacity for enduring righteous pain, no pecs.

Mesmerised by the gymnasticism of the spinning kick, I joined the university Tae Kwon Do club. After I moved to

London to work, I dropped Tae Kwon Do for Wing Chun kung fu, which was supposed to be more street-effective; then, because the instructor battered new students, I traded kung fu for a combination of Filipino stick-fighting and boxing, after which I took up Thai boxing. Weights fell into the background. Body-building was too one-dimensional in comparison with martial arts.

When I bench-pressed, I was in a world of predictability, familiarity and control. I knew how heavy the load was, because I put the plates on the bar myself. I knew my capabilities, because I had done the same exercise a few days ago or last week. But martial arts had variety and were more involving: they required movement, footwork, reflexes, balance and co-ordination – all at the same time. At a martial arts seminar the instructor asked the class whether they wanted to try grappling on the ground. I had a go, and held my opponent in the crook of an arm and squeezed on a headlock – the most basic, instinctive hold – while he remained impassive on all-fours, unthreatened and unmoved, yet afterwards I was exhilarated. Everything changed in that moment: without my having realised, this was what I'd been searching for all along. The instructor suggested that those who enjoyed grappling should take up judo.

Combat sport is about establishing rank and status in the same way that sex is about having children. That is not necessarily the thought that is first and foremost on your mind, or the reason you would give for enjoying it, and there may be other refined feelings that motivate you, but it's in there somewhere: you compete to see who is the better man. Martial arts had given me an unreliable idea of my status. I wanted to be able to fight, to defend myself, but never had a real confrontation. We practised punches and kicks with pads and gloves, and never kicked or punched a real opponent with full power and contact without protective equipment. I was never really tested and because I was never tested, I was uncertain of my place in the food chain. But judo began from another point. After a few lessons in how to break a fall without getting hurt, I began to spar full-on. Either I threw someone or not, or they threw me. Outcomes were clear-cut. Judo was frank, as wrestling would be later, and candidly told me what I could do and my place in the scheme of things.

The club I joined, the Judokan in Hammersmith, consisted of two old squash courts turned into a *dojo*, and was overseen by Percy Sekine, sixth Dan. When you opened the front door, you set a bell ringing, like at an old haberdasher's shop, and just kept going back in time from there. Percy was in his seventies, a small, slight man who called everyone by their surname and taught the classic, elegant standing throws of judo. He would stand in the doorway between the two matted courts with his hands behind his back, watching, tutoring, checking the clock to time the bouts during *randori* (free sparring). He would relate, over a whisky at the bar afterwards, that he had already been a black belt when he was shot down over Germany during the war, and that judo stood him in good stead at his PoW camp. You had to know how to handle yourself, said Percy. Judo kept him in smokes too. Camp life could be grindingly dull, and fellow PoWs used to pay him cigarettes to strangle them unconscious. Just before you go under you feel a moment of profound peace.

Like all beginners I started at the bottom, a white belt. The sessions were physically harder than anything I had done before. You constantly tugged, resisted, lifted and moved. Sparring for an hour or so, with a change of opponent every few minutes, was incredibly tiring. Every judo player had a different personality, different ways of taking grip and different pet throws; each posed a new problem. Judo was tough, but it rewarded effort through an uncomplicated transaction that congratulated hard work.

One particular judo player, who was in his fifties but had the body of a 25-year-old, would hold my jacket with his arms stiffened, and leave me spitted on his knuckles whenever I tried to close and make a throw. To begin with, I thought it would be impossible to ever throw him, but eventually I learnt how to get past the sentries of those two arms and put him down on the mat. In moments like those, when I threw someone who had appeared immovable before, I felt like someone new, someone better, as though I had stepped out of the body of the person who went to judo that evening and into another.

Very occasionally hard work was rewarded with a moment of transcendent perfection. One night I sparred with a good, heavy black belt and caught him with *tomoe-nage*, a throw where you fall back, pull your opponent down, spear him in the midsection with your foot, and use your leg and momentum to throw him over and backwards. As I felt him push forward, in harmony with his motion I used *tomoe-nage* so spontaneously that for a second I had no idea what I had just done.

'Did you see that?' the black belt asked Percy, impressed. And to me he said, 'Did you do that on purpose?'

Percy wasn't impressed – *tomoe-nage* was not one of his favourite throws – and I didn't know how to reply, as the move had felt effortless and illusory, like pitchforking a cloud.

I thought judo was destined to be the love of my life – then I met wrestling. I was not monogamous at first but kept intimate relations with both. A book – a scrawny little pamphlet really with a torn-off cover that cost 50 pence – changed my life.

Written by EJ Harrison and published in 1934, *Wrestling* sat waiting for me on a basement shelf of a secondhand bookshop on the Fulham Road. The plates attracted me first – looks are always important at the outset – pictures of wrestlers knotted in esoteric, impossible-looking holds I had never seen the like of in judo: the half nelson and body squeeze, the short-arm scissor, the splits. I swooned for the arcane English. Throws were 'chips', a beginner was a 'young tyro', a good manoeuvre 'a really effective and promising trick'. The techniques were illustrated with pencil drawings and enacted by wholesome youths with side-partings, wearing trunks. The muscular concerns were unusual and intriguing, with EJ railing against the 'scrawny throats of far too many young Englishmen'.

I wanted more dispatches from this lost world, so I went to the British Library and methodically read virtually all its wrestling books. Many were manuals of the same age or older that spoke of a time, distinct from the present, when wrestling was widely practised, understood and valued. They were books that had been ignored and unread. Each was like a survivor of a collapsed mine, gulping for air and ranting about the others left below; each made it clear in so many words that they were counting on me to resuscitate wrestling. I let their authors become my tutors, and read their instructions at a desk under the dome of the old Reading Room, where the clock had stopped, which was either poignant or a poor reflection on a major public service, depending on which way you looked at it.

EJ wrote in 1934: 'There can indeed be very few countries whose active menfolk have not for centuries indulged in some form of wrestling'. He could not have foreseen the inactivity of our current menfolk. Wrestling is probably the most widely practised traditional sport. The Naga tribes in the remote jungles bordering north-east India and Burma wrestle, the Canary Islanders wrestle, Iceland has its own traditional style, wrestling is the Iranian national sport, the Koreans wrestle and so do the Nuba of Sudan and the Dagestanis, yet wrestling literally had no place in the England where I lived. Wrestling comes naturally to men. The fact that men in England had stopped wrestling was a natural disaster – a natural disaster without historical precedent, like the hole in the ozone layer. The practical legacy of its fall was that I could find little proper coaching, few sports centres with mats to use and only a handful of clubs, all of which met infrequently. There was no existing structure, so I tried to create my own, and searched for places where I could train and people to train with – at first by placing the ad in *Time Out*.

'Most styles of wrestling can be practised on the greensward,' wrote EJ, so after having looked up in the dictionary what 'greensward' meant, in summer, at his suggestion, I solved the venue problem by going to the local park to train with Daniel, a musician who answered my ad and became my regular workout partner. Wrestling on grass is traditional. I'd seen photographs of Cumberland & Westmorland wrestlers taking hold in rolling countryside while watched by an audience of cows, but the experience wasn't so idyllic for us.

We went to Bishop's Park in Fulham, where fortunately dogs were banned so there was no chance of being thrown into dog excrement. Unfortunately two dangers persisted: first, we had to be careful not to forget ourselves in the heat of sparring only to roll into the stone birdbath; secondly, we had to take care not to die of embarrassment. It was difficult to wrestle unselfconsciously in a public park in London, though the only people who actually said anything to us were three cocky kids, about ten years old, who told us we were useless.

'That's crap,' said one. 'That's just rolling around.'

He said he did kickboxing himself and demonstrated by screwing up his face and becoming hyperactive. I offered to show him a little wrestling and he threatened to kill me if I hurt him.

But when I was able to wrestle without inhibition, I revelled in it. Wrestling had the same virtues as judo but none of the failings. Though I loved judo, what I liked about it was refracted through a formal, foreign culture: we bowed before and after we sparred and we called throws and holds by Japanese names, such as *ippon-seio-nage* and *kata-guruma*, which sounded as abstract as chemical terms. But wrestling used familiar, folky names for the same throws – the flying mare and fireman's carry – and we shook hands before and after a bout. Sparring without jackets and trousers felt more natural and instinctive, and wrestling had less of the counterintuitive rules that dog and limit judo. It felt familiar in every way, as though it came not from abroad but from within. Learning to wrestle felt like remembering something I'd known all along.

I thrived on the unrestricted drama of wrestling, the fact that, like chess, it combined prescribed moves with unrepeatable positions. Wrestling requires an alive form of physical intelligence. When a wrestler is good he has wit, variety and cards up his sleeve. Wrestlers in Ancient Greece worshipped Hermes, who is commonly known as the messenger of the gods but was also a god of cunning and thieves, and stealing has a lot in common with wrestling: both combine dexterity with trickery. A wrestler tries to pickpocket his opponent's feet from under him.

The best indoor venue I found was a matted, windowless basement, nicknamed the Sweatbox, at the Queen Mother Sports Centre near Victoria Station. There, Daniel and I learnt from EJ's book, from notes I made at the British Library and from books and videos from the States. We took from various styles – the old English disciplines of Catch-As-Catch-Can and Cumberland & Westmorland, the modern Olympic sports of Freestyle and Greco-Roman – but concentrated on submission wrestling, in which the aim is to make your opponent give in, to submit, with an armlock, leglock, strangle or choke. Daniel and I met at the Sweatbox a few times a week. After a warm-up we

ran through throws, takedowns (techniques where you go for
your opponent's legs), practised shots (the motion of going for
the legs), worked on sprawls (a counter to a shot in which you
force your opponent's head down with your hips), then drilled
groundwork manoeuvres, pins, pin-counters like the bridge-
and-roll, and armlocks, leglocks and chokes – anything and
everything that might be useful. Afterwards we sparred,
sometimes for a couple of hours. We fought hard bouts until we
were utterly exhausted and collapsed on our backs, chests
heaving, forearms pumped and numb.

All bareskin wrestling styles are incredibly tough and
scrutinise you with their intense stare. You literally have to strip
down. There is no artifice, there are no props: you are the
equipment. There are no rackets, bats, balls, pitches or
goalposts and you are not part of a team. The team is made up
of you – your mind, legs, arms, hands, hips, back and neck. You
are the goalie, defenders, midfield players, strikers, half the
pitch and one set of goalposts. Everything is on you, your body
and your wits. If you are beaten outright in wrestling you are
completely beaten. In most wrestling styles the aim is to score a
fall, the old term for a throw or pin. If you are pinned or
thrown you have been incapacitated. In other sports you can
walk away when you lose, but the whole aim of wrestling is to
take away your freedom of movement, to take away your
independence. Submission wrestling took that intensity, that
game of pure physical dominance, even further. It was
wrestling at its most primal, with few rules and prohibitions
and no points system to mediate the struggle.

In my masculine fundamentalism, I literally reached a
breaking point. If I straightened out Daniel's extended leg and
used my hips to lock his knee so that the leg was on the point of
snapping, he had no choice but to submit. If Daniel got behind
me on the ground, clung to my back with his feet hooked in so
I couldn't shake him off, and used his bicep and forearm to
squeeze the carotid arteries either side of my neck so that my
eardrums started to pound and I was on the verge of passing
out, again there was no choice but to give in. (It sounds
dangerous, but as long as you go no further than the point of
pain or the threshold of unconsciousness, no one is hurt: it's
like pointing a loaded gun at someone with no real intention of

firing because you have a prior agreement that at that moment they will raise their arms and give in.) Everything, all the time, was difficult: I had to research wrestling, motivate myself, coach myself, coach Daniel, motivate Daniel, negotiate with indifferent sports centres to use their mats, fit myself around their class schedules, train at home, and remember to eat properly. Submission wrestling was unforgiving. I had to face all the problems associated with trying to wrestle in England and at the end of it I had to face someone who wanted to strangle me.

Often, when Daniel and I descended the steps to the basement to wrestle, I felt like we were about to revive a precious lost art – as if we were a combination of anthropologists and athletes re-establishing a long-buried tradition. But sometimes it felt like the end of a tragedy, as though wrestling was a shameful secret, an unwanted child chained in a cellar, half-blind and left to starve.

After university I fell into working as a journalist on magazines and newspapers. I started out as a music journalist, then became a film writer and critic. I also worked shifts as a freelance sub-editor, and would sit at desks in library-like silence while I carved into journalists' copy to make it read properly and fit space. Sub-editing felt like it had the status of a cleaning job. Writers went out, interacted with real people, enjoyed themselves, ran up expenses, then left you to tidy up their work while they went on to the next thing. I intended to give up sub-editing once I'd established enough momentum as a writer, but as my wrestling obsession grew I needed to buy time to train. I found it easier to stick with sub-editing work, which was quite well paid and simple to find, than hustle around for writing, which was always harder to come by.

I began to withdraw from office life anyway and reject the ladder of aspiration predicated on work. I wanted to live through my body as a wrestler, not through computer software, and came to work only two weeks a month, or a few days a week, so that I could spend as much time as possible training. It struck me that it didn't matter what job you did in office world – whether you were a sub-editor or did something more interesting – because on a physical level it amounted to the same thing: sitting at a desk for the best hours of the day. Consequently I had little ambition in office world. I made no effort to network or endear myself to bosses or apply for better jobs. I couldn't really believe that people took office world seriously, that this was where they really wanted to be and what they fundamentally wanted to do.

Success as a wrestler gave me a deep sense of satisfaction that could never be equalled through work. I thought everyone knew the real route to happiness was through the body, and was surprised and disappointed whenever I discovered how wrong I was. I became obsessed with wrestling partly because I preferred the way it defined me to the me defined by the office. This other me was cerebral, sedentary and deskbound, but on the mats I shared things in common with characters in myth and folk tales, not accountants and lawyers. I went through trials and learnt about myself through experience – about how much I could endure and what I could really do under pressure.

My training schedule snowballed. I began to train for up to four or six hours a day, sometimes five or six days a week, and combined wrestling with running, sprint training, plyometrics, weights, T'ai Chi, yoga and bag work – and still kept up judo and Thai boxing. When I wasn't actually training or wrestling, I was thinking about it or practising useful attributes such as grips and balance on the Tube, the train, in the street, the pub. I had big plans for the future. I wanted to open a wrestling club and make a serious attempt to win the British amateur championships and compete in Japan. Like someone who holidays in a place they love overseas until they decide they want to move there, I wanted to give up office life completely and live in me, the wrestler.

While practising martial arts I absorbed Buddhist ideas that wash around them to the core. I believed that to be good you had to embrace the Buddhist concept of being in the moment, or mindfulness. You had to be totally present in your senses, to react and respond immediately to your opponent's movements. The aim was to train so hard that the correct responses were ingrained within you and the thinking mind was bypassed – it was too slow – while you just simply did the right thing in a split-second.

I applied the same beliefs to wrestling. I wanted to develop a type of calm and poise during the chaos and stress of sparring and thought that if I could deal with the intense nervousness I sometimes felt before a bout, I'd be able to handle the stress and anxieties of everyday life. I believed that the primary emotions and feelings that cropped up in daily life were present in wrestling in a more intense and concentrated form, and if I could wrestle with calm and poise I would be able to live with calm and poise too. I wanted to engineer moments of perfection during wrestling, then let them expand until they filled the rest of my world.

I didn't want winning to be everything. Though it felt bad to lose, I wanted the spiritual aspects to be more important than winning and losing. The fact that I competed hard was a given, an incontrovertible rule, but the important part was the inner struggle – in my case learning how to ride the anxiety I felt before a bout and develop that meditative state of calm and poise. Other people, I reasoned, would have other aims, other issues to resolve, but whatever they were, they could fix themselves through wrestling. In my idealism, I wanted wrestling to be pure and uncontaminated. I thought that, beyond the desire to beat one another, as wrestlers we could find common purpose – to improve technically but also to develop as people. Winning had to be defined in these wider terms.

This was OK in theory, but not always possible in practice. To begin with, I was a bad loser whether I liked it or not. If, while wrestling Daniel, he got a strangle on and I tapped the mat twice, the signal for submission, I would be subdued for the rest of the day. Loss felt like it was the few steps away from being murdered that it sometimes was. I dealt with losing by training so hard that it didn't happen often, but that was essentially a way of avoiding the issue. Another problem was that the people I wrestled didn't necessarily think about wrestling in the same terms. Sometimes I could feel my opponent using me as a dummy, and directing their frustration, anger or hostility into my body.

I set up a small club at the Sweatbox. Matt, a tall and volatile skinhead, came to learn. He did Thai boxing and had a large panther tattoo. It was clear he wanted to asset-strip me for technical knowledge, which made me wary. During one bout he foot-swept my lead leg, kicking me hard – in fact it was more of a Thai boxing kick than a sweep. Uncontrollably I grinned and half laughed, embarrassed for him, more than anything else, because of the violence of his technique. He thought I was laughing at him, and threw me aggressively with a trip that I would never have been caught with had I not been standing there a little stunned, expecting an apology. I felt his anger as we wrestled on the ground, but contained him until we reached a stalemate.

'Not bad for a beginner, eh!' he said, venomously, as we both got up afterwards. I tried to calm him down, and told him that we should be friends on the mat and that it was not a place for anger.

'I'm not angry!' he boomed, clearly incensed. 'If I was fucking angry I'd be fucking shouting!'

He should have made up with me afterwards, but instead I, as someone who disliked conflict, made a point of making up with him, and went out of my way to shake his hand while looking him in the eye as we parted on the concourse of Victoria Station. I knew that an incident like that could unsettle me for days if it was left unresolved.

My idealism was rarely matched by reality, which added a philosophical frustration to the practical problems of trying to wrestle in England. Eventually I decided I'd had enough and made plans to go somewhere where I didn't have to work so hard to wrestle – where there were clubs with mats and throwing dummies and instructors and timetabled lessons. I planned to train at a club in Budapest, then go overland to Bulgaria, Turkey and perhaps Iran, all countries with strong wrestling cultures, but when I reached Hungary, with my wrestling boots, kneepads, singlet and judo kit packed, I realised that my heart wasn't in it and turned back. What I really needed was a break from all the intensity, from my obsession with wrestling, so I backpacked through Asia for six months as a prelude to going to live and train in Australia, but my intensity followed me and I became addicted to Thai boxing at a camp in Chiang Mai. I trained as hard, if not harder, than ever before and was billed to fight in the ring until I tore a hamstring and couldn't walk.

That was the last time I ever trained seriously. I realised something was profoundly wrong with my health after I reached Sydney and had recuperated from the hamstring injury. A fatigue unlike normal tiredness would set in after exercise. In the hours following any amount of training, I would feel distant, detached and fuzzy-minded; total physical and emotional annihilation followed the next morning. The symptoms were like a hangover: there was nothing I could do except wait for them to pass.

At first I thought I was simply out of shape and the answer was to exercise more until fit again, but the symptoms just became worse when I did that. I used to be able to train for four or six hours a day, but now a ten-minute jog destroyed me for 36 hours. I saw doctors and had the standard blood tests but they revealed nothing. I tried herbalism, acupuncture and Chinese medicine, yet though each approach briefly helped me feel better on a day-to-day basis, the post-exercise symptoms remained rigid and implacable. I tried to continue wrestling, but it was just too painful. Because my body didn't recover properly, I couldn't train very often; because I couldn't train very often, I couldn't develop endurance or keep my wrestling skills intact; because I was rusty and out of shape, I performed badly, which made me feel despondent. The feeling of despondency was exacerbated by the fatigue and depression that came with biochemical inevitability after exercise. I had no choice but to largely withdraw from wrestling. Without it, I felt isolated, abandoned and left behind. I'd lost my place in the world.

I returned to London and stayed at Daniel's flat. I had the run of the place because he spent most of his time living with his girlfriend. Now and then I went for a short jog to see whether a new therapy or dietary approach had solved my health problem, but afterwards the same symptoms returned and set up the same cycle of disappointment and dejection. Whatever my problem was exactly, it appeared to fall in a diagnostic no-man's land between conventional medicine and alternative medicine, and I became increasingly sceptical that either side would ever come to the rescue.

For money reasons I returned to the job I disliked, sub-editing, this time for a car manufacturer's magazine full of gush about the optimal driving experience and sat nav. Now that I couldn't wrestle it was twice as hard to endure office life as there was no reward for going through the pain. I felt like an outsider in London: I didn't own a place to live, I wasn't in a relationship, and there was no career path I wanted to follow. I'd wanted to be a wrestler and didn't have a plan B.

By 1998 it had been two years since I wrestled seriously. I was 31. That year was supposed to have been a peak year for me as a competitor, but instead I was out of the game. I found it difficult to accept. Sometimes I slid into anger and depression. I would catch myself resenting people passing by in the street who had healthy bodies but clearly weren't putting them to good use. They let their bodies go to waste, I thought, while I, someone who wanted to do something exceptional with theirs, had to live in one that wouldn't function properly.

Deep down I knew my health breakdown was partly my fault. Perhaps 'fault' was too strong a word, but I knew that, were my body a car, I would have to bear a lot of the responsibility for crashing it, because I didn't heed warning signals to slow down. I remembered how, about a year or so before my health deteriorated, I used to complain to my then girlfriend about feeling profound tiredness after our weight-training sessions together, and how I'd have to sleep straight afterwards but still felt groggy when I woke up.

I was still obsessed with wrestling, whether or not I could actually train. Whenever I thought about wrestling, I felt a deep sense of injustice. I couldn't stand how it was languishing. Its character had been assassinated by the Lycra-clad lobster-tan body-builders who acted out bouts for every 'wrestling' organisation that promoted vaudeville, yet no one seemed to notice or care. Wrestling had sunk into obscurity and silly rumours about it were routinely believed.

An accusation that really smarted was that it was a form of violence. A red-haired middle-aged woman I spoke to at a café once said so with great conviction. She hated wrestling, she said, because it was violent – like her ex-husband. I evangelised about wrestling, and told her that its beauty lay in the fact that, unlike boxing, the aim was not to hurt your opponent but to score a fall with a throw or pin. Which didn't mean that wrestling wasn't tough, or being thrown didn't sometimes hurt, or that you didn't get injured occasionally, but in the normal course of wrestling the intention was never to injure, knock out or damage – so, no, wrestling wasn't violent. She regarded me in a way that said she knew wrestling was a form of violence for certain and no one was going to change her mind. To her, I imagined, masculine sports and violence mulched into one: wrestling was the same as boxing, was the same as street-fighting, was the same as a rugby maul, was just like wife-beating and perhaps even rape. I would have passed it off as a maverick opinion but I heard the same thing said a few times. It was an attitude symptomatic of a wider trend in which combative, masculine sports were misunderstood and under-valued, a trend in which the virtues they develop – such as physical intelligence, craft, bravery and strength – were ignored by people who would find it difficult to differentiate between a half nelson, an uppercut and a bottle in the face.

Perhaps frustration at having been stopped from wrestling fuelled my bitterness, yet I couldn't but help feel angry. The sport I loved had had its reputation ruined by professional wrestlers, was hijacked by the S&M scene, faced routine accusations of violence, and generally received no respect. Though wrestling itself was hard and tough, as a culture it was abused and exploited – yet so far it had proven incapable of speaking up for itself. Like an abandoned and mute child, it deserved a full investigation to establish its true identity and real inheritance. Wrestling had lost its place in England and no one even knew what place it used to have. It had been forgotten and the fact that it has been forgotten had been forgotten too.

Something had gone badly wrong in England – and the decline of wrestling was only one symptom. Our culture was curbing our natural masculine exuberance, our urge to express ourselves as males through action, adventure and sport – through the body. I saw it all around. My senses had become supersensitive to it, like teeth sensitised to ice cream and sugary tea. I felt in pain every time I came into contact with the ice cream and sugary tea of 'no ball games' signs, the ice cream and sugary tea of the lobby who wanted to ban boxing, the ice cream and sugary tea of another sports field turned into housing.

One day I felt the same pain as I went for a walk in Clissold Park in Stoke Newington. What looked like a couple of families were taking a stroll together. The parents took the path, but a boy of about ten years old took off his shoes, held each in a hand, and walked over the grass. Inwardly I cheered this flicker of a spirit of adventure and exploration. The boy's mother, on the other hand, harangued him.

'If you cut your feet. . . Stuart, there's broken glass and dog's mess on the grass, Stuart.'

A whine entered her voice: 'People walk their dogs there, Stuart!'

I hoped Stuart would ignore her. Not only ignore her but also fashion a spear from a stick, use it to kill a squirrel, and skin it and eat it raw while he was at it. One of the men in the party began to whine at him loudly too: '*Stuart!*' They all started to call his name and whine. Predictably, Stuart did what he was told and returned to the path.

Stuart's barefoot walk on the grass was at one point of the compass, my wrestling was at another: it was all part of the same thing – us being what we were. His mother's whining, and the lack of wrestling places, were part of the same response: our culture discouraging us from being what we were. The path I was expected to follow was office life, the mediocrity of a middle-class existence as a professional, a computer decorated with Post-it notes, poor posture and ultimately lower back pain.

Through wrestling I had been wandering from that path and there was no going back now, not even if my health wouldn't let me train any more. There was no way I was going to return to the path – two fingers to the path. I resolved to keep wandering from the path, from office world, from England, from sub-editing and Stuart's mother, and to let my deep sense of injustice at the mistreatment of wrestling guide me. I wanted to restore wrestling's integrity and give it back its dignity. I wanted to find active menfolk in other countries who still wrestled, and places where wrestling was celebrated. I wanted to get to the bottom of this thing that had come to mean so much to me and to know what kind of hole was left in England through its absence. I would go wandering, shoes in hand, for however long it took, and I didn't care if I stepped on glass or in dog excrement.

Wrestling needed respect. It needed to be valued again. Whenever I pondered how wrestling might prove itself to have significance and value, my mind inevitably returned to thinking about how I conceived of it as having spiritual value, and how I'd tried to develop that meditative state of calm and poise – how wrestling helped me try to become a better person. Yet the truth was that though wrestling had profound spiritual value for me, I had no idea whether it was valued in those terms by entire cultures. There was no culture of wrestling in England and in that vacuum I had cobbled together an eclectic mix of Buddhist concepts taken from martial arts with a masculine fundamentalism that was, in part, a reaction against the mundanity of modern life. Perhaps I was just as guilty of using wrestling for my own purposes as John/Paul and Leopard Man.

I wondered whether a whole culture regarded wrestling as having spiritual value. When I considered where I might find such a culture, India appeared to be the obvious place to look. After all, India gave the world yoga, a system that unified spiritual development with physical exercises, and many martial artists believed that martial arts originated there. Everything had a religious dimension in India, but was wrestling big there? From having got to know a wrestler called Imran I suspected that it might be.

Imran taught me Freestyle, an honest amateur style in which the aim is to pin your opponent, though you can also win on points scored by executing successful throws, takedowns and groundwork manoeuvres. When I met Imran, he was in his early thirties but looked ten years younger. He was humble and unassuming, wore glasses, had a painterly goatee, didn't drink or smoke, and would wear earplugs because he disliked city noise. You would never guess that he was a former national champion – until you wrestled him. Imran's family came from Pakistan and India before that, and his father was a wrestler, as his father's father had been before him. Imran said that all his grandfather did up until he was 40 was wrestle, eat ghee and drink milk. His own life echoed that structure. Wrestling came first. He would go to the gym or wrestle in the mornings, start work at midday, then train again in the evenings.

His family restaurant on Brick Lane was the only place I knew of in London where wrestling was given a dignified place. On the walls were Pakistani fight posters that showed frowning wrestlers holding golden maces, as well as a painting Imran did of two wrestlers, one of whom was bridging to stop his shoulders touching the mat. I interpreted Imran's and his family's dedication to wrestling to mean it had to retain an important place in Pakistani and Indian culture. Under the circumstances, you had to have a special kind of momentum to wrestle in England, a momentum that had to come from somewhere other than where you were. Mine came from beneath ground and before – from EJ and my mentors at the British Library; Imran's came from abroad – through his family, from India via Pakistan.

And something Imran's father once said stuck in my mind for a long time afterwards.

I travelled with Imran to watch him compete at a Freestyle tournament in Manchester. Afterwards we stopped off at a motorway service station where his dad – always 'Mr Butt' to me – magnanimously bought us fish and chips. Imran was disappointed by his performance at the tournament, particularly as he had lost his second bout by being pinned. His father was disappointed too and told Imran he should have tried other techniques. Mr Butt had never really spoken directly to me before, but when we went back to the car he asked what interest I took in wrestling.

'I wrestle myself.'

'But you are not a wrestler,' he said. 'You are a sportsman who wrestles. You play sports like football and cricket and you wrestle, right? A sportsman who wrestles but not a wrestler.'

The put-down hurt. At the time I devoted all my energy to the sport. Yet as an ex-wrestler himself from a wrestling family, whatever Mr Butt said about the subject warranted respect. He had the aura of an older man who knew what he was talking about. The conversation moved on. A filing cabinet had slammed shut in his mind with what felt like my fingers in it. I felt insulted, yet when I thought about it afterwards I realised that Mr Butt had probably put me down as a way of redirecting the frustration he felt at what he saw as Imran's failure. And I also realised his enigmatic words amounted to a fascinating riddle: what was a wrestler if not simply someone who wrestled? The answer had to amount to an expanded definition of what it is to be a wrestler. Mr Butt's definitions came from Pakistan and India, so wrestling on the subcontinent had to mean something big – and this something big had to be beyond the imagination of someone like myself who knew only the dying culture of wrestling in England.

Going to India was the only sure way to find out about this big something. That's where the wandering would start.

Chapter 3

The Whole World Loses Something

Training at Swaminath *akhara* commences at about seven. I sit on the steps of a *ghat* nearby and wait. Men wrapped in shawls repeat mantras to steel themselves against the cold as they rattle by on bicycles. Goats dressed in pullovers and cows wearing sacking loiter about. Bent-legged *sadhus* climb the steps carrying holy Ganga water. The wrestlers arrive. I join them inside the *akhara* and sit on a low wall. A well-built wrestler smiles and comes over to lay down a piece of cloth for me to sit on. I'm surprised and touched by his hospitality in this, a wrestling school, a place of competition and rivalry.

A wrestler with feminine eyelashes and a podgy belly interrogates me in basic English. How many brothers and sisters do I have? Do I have a girlfriend? Who is my favourite actor? Am I a national wrestling champion? A county champion? A town champion? To my disappointment – and probably his – I admit that I am none of the last three things. The Talker points to some of the others at the *akhara* and catalogues their livestock ownership. He says the well-built wrestler owns twelve water buffalo; he points to someone else who has four cows. I'm puzzled but assume this is like bonding back home by talking about the car you own. I tell the Talker I don't own livestock – or a car for that matter.

There are about twenty wrestlers present. Many of them have mustard oil, which they use to massage their legs, torsos and arms. One of them prepares the arena using a hoe with a short shank and wide blade to chop up and loosen the earth. The instructor arrives on a bicycle. Everyone immediately streams up to him to touch his feet. The ensuing lesson follows the universal pattern: warm-up exercises followed by sparring. I leave before the end but return a couple of days later – this time to take part. I strip down to a pair of shorts, oil my body like the others and wait. When the instructor arrives, I feel awkward and self-conscious. I want to follow proper etiquette but can't bring myself to touch his feet. Instead I stand back and hope no one notices – or if they do that they will think I have a special dispensation as a foreigner to ignore what appears to be a deeply subservient gesture.

We stretch and warm up, then spar. The instructor motions for me to go first. Everyone crowds round. My opponent steps forward – Palu, the *akhara* champion. Palu has a ballooning chest, a big block of a neck and large, muscular legs. A forklift truck would be needed to budge him. He pulls my head down with both hands. I push up his wrists to release the grip. He lunges for my legs. I counter by wiping my forearm across his face then shoot for his legs, but he catches my head, squeezes it in the crook of his arm, crunches me down and gets behind me. Somehow I stand, but Palu picks up my leg, takes me down again and pins me with a rudimentary hold. I smile in embarrassment at being pinned so easily and publicly. Palu notices how tired I am and gestures that we should stop.

The others take turns to spar. After they have finished, we all sit awhile to cool down. Two boys knead Palu's back and arms, while a middle-aged, balding wrestler gives me a massage too. He rubs earth into my back, wrings my arms, and pulls and cracks the joints of my fingers and toes. I try not to wince and look ungrateful as he snags and tugs the jungle of hair all over my body, but what makes me feel more uncomfortable is the idea that he might ask to be paid for the service.

'Swimming?' asks the Talker. By which he means bathing in the river.

We descend the steps to the mud bank at the river's edge.

'First go toilet,' instructs the Talker. He points to a gully. The *ghat* is busy with pilgrims, travellers, tourists and bathers. There is no way I am going to go to the toilet in front of everyone. I walk to the gully, squat with my back to the wrestlers, mime taking a pee, return, and sheepishly bathe in the river, dunking my body underwater three times. I get out as quickly as possible and dry myself on the bank. A man squatting nearby speaks to me in good English.

'I am worse than a beggar,' he says. 'I do not even have a bowl to beg with.'

He wears a grubby *lunghi* and a cheap pair of flip-flops. An aura of grime outlines his toes. His lips are vampire's lips, red from chewing *paan* that has blackened his teeth and left yellow blotches. A scarf covers the bristle of his shaved head. He is perhaps in his mid-forties.

'I have only one meal a day that the ashram provides. That is all. Drinking water from the Ganga keeps me alive. It has vitamins and minerals.'

He takes off his flip-flops and shows the soles of his feet, which are black and cracked like charred wood. He says a doctor has told him he needs proper shoes otherwise he will have foot problems. He sleeps rough in an arcade on the *ghats*.

'All night I am not sleeping because I am shivering. I need a blanket and a *lunghi*. The police came and took my little home. They are corrupt. There is so much corruption here.'

He looks downriver, beyond the wrestlers, who are chatting and laughing in dissonance with his sombre story; he looks well beyond them to the crescent of *ghats* where the Ganga changes course northward and where the older quarters of the city are built. He takes it all in and says, 'India is burning.' While he relates the details of how he was cheated out of his home, I decide to give him some money. Concerned that I'll be mobbed by beggars if seen giving someone a big handout, I fold a 50 rupee note into a little square and shake the man's hand with the money hidden in my palm. He instantly unravels the subterfuge by taking the note and unfolding it in full view. He says nothing. I turn to rejoin the wrestlers, but they have gone.

*

I've journeyed to India from London partly because of a wrestler who made a trip in the opposite direction nearly ninety years ago: Gama. Before wrestling fell – before Gorgeous George, Big Daddy, the shamsters, the fatsters, the masked wrestlers, the wrestling ballet dancers, the midget wrestlers, the tag teams, the Indian deathlock, clothesline and lobster-tan body-builders – buried under every indignity of the last ninety years is an era when professional wrestling had some self-respect. The great wrestlers of that period, the decade or so before the First World War – George Hackenschmidt, Paul Pons, Ivan Podubney, Frank Gotch, Stanislaus Zbyszko – have been forgotten, but some were household names, front-page news, at the time. No doubt there were sham bouts even then, but these were real athletes who really wrestled.

In 1910 a brilliant Indian wrestler called Gama travelled to London to challenge the top Europeans and Americans. Zbyszko accepted and faced Gama across a matted platform in Shepherd's Bush, in front of an audience of perhaps 8,000, on a Saturday afternoon in September. Described by one newspaper as a 'gigantic Galician', Zbyszko was much heavier than Gama, who was at a disadvantage stylistically too as he was used to wrestling on earth under different rules: then, as now, to win a bout of *kushti* you had to 'show your opponent the sky' – in other words turn him so that his back was towards the ground and he faced upwards – whereas to win under the rules of Catch-As-Catch-Can, within which the match was fought, you had to pin your opponent twice. Yet, despite these disadvantages, Gama was the dominant wrestler by far and threw Zbyszko at will. Zbyszko realised he had no chance of winning and every chance of losing if he stood and fought, as sooner or later he would be thrown on his back and pinned, so he played for a stalemate by hugging the mat and crawling around. Gama didn't pin Zbyszko – his victory came not within the rules of Catch-As-Catch-Can but within the wider precepts of masculine dignity. Zbyszko could not stand and wrestle like a man and instead crawled around the ring like a baby around a living-room floor until time ran out. Gama was pronounced the winner after Zbyszko failed to turn up for a rematch the following Saturday. He returned to a hero's welcome in India and became the focus of national pride. His victory suggested that, at a time when wrestling in the West was going through a golden age, wrestling in India was so vastly superior that an Indian wrestler could make a baby out of one of the best Europeans.

I first came across the story of the Gama–Zbyszko fight back in England when I read a book called *Comprehensive Asian Fighting Arts*, written by Donn Draeger and Robert Smith. Gama became a talismanic figure – a name to conjure when I needed inspiration, when I needed to imagine what was achievable as a wrestler and know that the answer was anything. One reason for his success was obvious: Indians trained supernaturally hard. *Comprehensive Asian Fighting Arts* included a brief outline of an Indian wrestler's daily schedule. The amount of exercise catalogued was incredible. Each day, said the book, wrestlers trained for hours on end and performed two exercises, *bethaks* and *dands* – the first a simple squat without weight, the second a cousin of the press-up – in their thousands.

Always on the lookout for esoteric training ideas that might give an advantage, I decided to practise *bethaks* and *dands* in the vague hope that I'd be alchemically transformed into a wrestler in the mould of Gama as a result. To begin with, my legs wobbled and turned to jelly after about 50 *bethaks*, but given time I could do sets of 200 to 250 without a break. In between sets of *bethaks* I did sets of *dands*. To perform a *dand*, you start with your hands and legs in the press-up position, but with your hands a little wider apart than normal and your backside in the air. You glide forwards and down until you reach the line of your hands, then look up and arch back. Finally, you return to the backside-in-the-air position and start again. At first I could do about 30 *dands* without a rest, but soon I was able to do sets of 40 or 50. After a couple of months of daily practice, I was performing 750 *bethaks* and 250 *dands* each morning.

At which point I gave up. Not because I couldn't physically do any more *bethaks* and *dands*, but because I didn't have good enough reasons to continue. In order for me to push myself harder and perform thousands of these two exercises a day, there would have to have been the motivating forces of a coach, wrestling partners, a wrestling club, competitions and prizes, yet there was none of these things in England because England did not want me to wrestle. On the other hand, I concluded, India must have wanted Indians to wrestle: to create the motivation to do exercises so difficult, repetitive and boring as thousands of *bethaks* and *dands* a day there must have been a huge passion for wrestling in India. Wrestlers would train this hard because they wanted to be better than rivals who were also training incredibly hard.

If Indian wrestlers went to these lengths to keep ahead of each other, it obviously said something about the strength of the field. And *bethaks* and *dands* were only ancillary exercises. According to *Comprehensive Asian Fighting Arts* wrestlers also ran five miles, swam, exercised with weights and sparred for hours a day. Clearly they must have been professional in the sense that they wrestled for a living, otherwise they would not have been able to train all day, every day, and surely they would have devoted themselves so completely to wrestling only if there were big rewards – money, garlands, self-esteem, fame and status certainly, but perhaps spiritual rewards too.

There must have once been a huge culture of wrestling in India. I'm here now to see whether it's still alive and to pay homage to the Indian wrestlers who either went, or still go, to such lengths. Wrestlers such as Gama who trained super-humanly hard were defining the outer limits of physical capability. They set what are surely records for the use of a piece of universal equipment, the male body. Here, in India, men did more of what men can do than seems feasible. Yet their incredibleness has gone largely unacknowledged in the West.

I fall ill the day after wrestling at Swaminath: fever, diarrhoea, loss of appetite. The sickness could be caused by something I ate or drank, but I fear I've picked up a bug while bathing in the Ganga. I rest in my room for a couple of days then see James Hetherington, an American Christian, at his bakery and restaurant, The Bread of Life. James has told me that if I ever have a problem I should come and see him. We sit at a small table. James extends his long legs alongside. I relate my symptoms.

'It could be the food or water, but I think it might be because I bathed in the Ganga,' I say.

'Well, pray to God if you do,' says James. 'That is the most polluted river in anywhere. They put sewage in it and cremated bodies. They've got research teams from all over the world trying to figure out how to clean it up. The Mother Teresa mission, just up from here, ties diseased bodies to stones and just throws them in there.'

James notices a scab on my arm. 'You can get skin diseases and all kinds of things from it. Make sure you never go in there with cuts.'

He takes me to see a doctor nearby.

'Good luck,' he says, ominously, as he shakes my hand and leaves.

The doctor listens to my abdomen with a stethoscope and prods it for tenderness. He advises me to eat boiled rice, ripe bananas or plantains, curd, and avoid spicy food, and to make sure all drinking water is boiled and that I don't drink *chai* from glasses or tumblers. I sheepishly admit that I have bathed in the Ganga, but say I don't think I actually swallowed any water. The doctor politely tells me that bathing in the Ganga isn't a good idea, especially for foreigners, who are not adapted to the water. He prescribes antibiotics.

A couple of evenings later, I run into the rough sleeper I met on the *ghat* after wrestling. He materialises on the street in front of me. There is a power cut, and I'm not wearing contact lenses because of an eye infection, so can't see very well.

'I was remembering you,' he says, excited. 'Just now you were in my thoughts. Our meeting is not by chance. It is predetermined. We will have met many times from birth to birth going back to ancient times.'

He tells me to call him 'Swami', a name given to *sadhus*, men who have renounced the world – though in his case it's more the other way round. He asks how I am. I tell him I have a stomach bug.

'I will take you to my guru. He is two kilometres away. We can go now.'

I guess there will be a price to pay. My reticence shows.

'He performs miracles, which is very rare these days,' persists Swami. 'Surely you will come?'

'How much does he charge?'

'It is free.'

'Why should he want to help me for free? Why me?'

'It's not only you, he helps anyone.'

Part of me feels uneasy about the idea of going to meet this guru with a stranger. It may be a set-up. As a relatively wealthy foreigner, I'm an obvious target for con artists and robbers. But then again, maybe the guru is genuine, and if he can help me with my stomach problem perhaps he can also help me with my underlying health problem. I arrange to meet Swami at Tulsi Ghat the following morning, and then visit his guru.

'Surely, you will be coming?' says Swami, clearly unconvinced that I'll actually turn up.

I say I will, though I'm not sure either.

'All night I was not sleeping because I was thinking about you and your problem,' says Swami, as we sit wedged together in the back of a rickshaw. 'When a man walks part of the way with another man he becomes a friend and his problem becomes your problem. That is our Hindu culture. If you are a wrestler and cannot wrestle the whole world loses something.'

His words cut right into me: the whole world loses something if you are a wrestler and cannot wrestle. He means in the context of my stomach problem, but I hear the words as though he is talking about my life as a whole: I'm a wrestler who cannot wrestle because of a health problem that can't be diagnosed and treated, and it feels like I've lost the world; but maybe it's the other way round too – the world has lost me, a wrestler. The whole world loses something whenever someone is stopped from doing what it is they are here to do.

The rickshaw-wallah bicycles away from the Ganga, away from the area I am familiar with, where I feel safest, and into an unfamiliar suburb. We pass through a busy fruit and vegetable market, and squalid shacks and mud houses. Unkempt pigs root around in rubbish. A small girl squats to take a dump in the road with her dress hitched up and each foot on a brick. A telegraph line coughs sparks. It troubles me that Swami drinks dirty river water, especially considering there are handpumps in the streets. I ask him why he does it.

'Ganga water comes from the head of Shiva,' he says. 'It has spiritual power. If you drink it, it helps your creativity and improves your clarity of mind. After bathing in it you can go into deep meditation very quickly.'

'But you must know how polluted it is?'

'The Ganga is not polluted. Factories, they put waste into the river – that is pollution. But the Ganga herself is not polluted.'

We stop at an alley and walk the rest of the way to the guru's house. He sits cross-legged on the floor next to dusty plastic pots, containers and school exercise books. He is in his sixties and wears thick glasses with square frames. Two whiskery old men sit beside him. One has no teeth. His cheeks and mouth suck in and out like a fish's. The two attendants pass pieces of paper to the guru, who draws symbols on them. These he carefully folds and places in a pile. The guru motions for me to sit on the floor in front of him.

'What is he going to do?' I ask Swami, apprehensively.

'He is a Muslim tantra man who practises acupressure.'

The Muslim Tantra Man gestures for me to hold out my palms. He takes a pen, which he dips in a Quink pot of dark blue ink, and draws two sets of parallel lines along the creases of my little finger and ring finger. He looks at the ink lines and shows them to the others in a way that suggests a suspicion confirmed.

'What does he see?' I ask Swami.

'The lines. They do not align properly from finger to finger. Your veins are displaced.'

The guru pulls and cracks my knuckles, pulls my little fingers and shakes my arms. He looks at the ink lines again. This time he is satisfied that they align. He tells me to lie on my back and raise my knees to my chest, one at a time, hands clasped around the knee. I should do this every day, he says. He swings his arms out like an aerobics instructor. That as well. He swings them up and down. This too.

'If you do these exercises every morning, in three days your stomach problem will disappear,' says Swami.

I feel relief – mental not physical. Nothing untoward has happened. At the worst I'm going to come away from the experience with a mild case of ink poisoning and a repertoire of familiar floor exercises to be used in the new context of diarrhoea management.

'So now we go back?' I ask Swami.

'No. This man is not my guru. He is another man. I thought the help of two men would be better than one.'

Swami's actual guru lives nearby in a block of flats a few storeys high. We go up the stairway to a small room with a wooden bed on which sits a young guy wearing a baseball cap. He says the guru is on the roof. We head upstairs. Two men are standing on the roof reading the same Hindi broadsheet. Swami quickly goes over to the younger man and touches his leg. This is Dr Prashand, his guru. He is in his thirties, and has a kind and intelligent face and hair that curls in all directions. He continues to read the paper for a minute or so, then puts it down. The four of us stand on the rooftop, folding and unfolding our arms, like people who have nothing in common save the fact that they are on the same platform waiting for the same train. It feels like we are waiting for something to arrive that is not yet present – familiarity perhaps.

Swami tells Dr Prashand that I need his help. He nods and looks at me, asks where I'm from, whether I'm married, how many brothers I have, how many sisters. We stand around some more. The other man says he recognises me. He is a wrestler and has seen me at Ram Singh *akhara*, which I've visited with Rajan. His name is Vijay Yadav and he is a Congress Party local politician. Something changes, something is decided. Together we go downstairs to Dr Prashand's room.

Swami asks me, as interpreter, what my symptoms are.

'Diarrhoea.'

He does not recognise the word. I make a gesture with my hand to mime a repeated flow from my backside.

'Ah! Loose motions.'

He tells Dr Prashand.

'What method does Dr Prashand use?' I ask.

'He is a tantric yogi. He will pollute the water with his tantra and give it to you.'

'Hypnotise the water,' corrects Dr Prashand in English.

Vijay Yadav says something to Swami, which Swami translates.

'He says I'm taking a risk being with you. The police could harass me. He also says you should join him on his campaign platform. It will be good publicity to have an English wrestler supporting him.'

Dr Prashand goes into a small room and comes out a

moment later with a silver beaker. He tells me to tip back my
head and pours the hypnotised water into my mouth. I look
around the small room in a part of a city I do not know. I look
at the others, one of whom is well built, a wrestler. I look at
Swami. Perhaps, as he said himself, we did not meet by
accident the evening before. Perhaps everything has been
orchestrated. Perhaps the water is drugged. Maybe they are
going to rob me. I feel a surge of anxiety. The five others just sit
there, saying nothing, focusing on me, waiting for something to
happen. For me to pass out, I fear. To mask my anxiety, I smile.
But nothing happens. Vijay gives me the name of a wrestling
teacher, AN Yadav, who he says can help and gives Swami
directions to his school at Sigra Stadium. Swami touches Dr
Prashand's feet as we leave. Afterwards, he is excited.

'The water will take effect instantly!' he says. 'By tonight you
will feel great joy! You will never in your life be troubled by your
stomach again! Dr Prashand's power comes direct from Shiva.
Shiva power is right now working in your stomach!'

Sigra Stadium is a concrete oval skirted by rusty barbed wire.
Swami and I circumnavigate the concrete seats until we reach
an ugly building from which smacking noises are coming.
Inside, Mr Yadav sits behind a desk, like an examiner, with a
wrestling mat in front of him. The class is ending. Before they
stream out the doors, the wrestlers touch Mr Yadav's leg. A few
linger or do exercises. Swami introduces himself as my
interpreter. I catch Mr Yadav look him up and down, at his stale
clothes and lotioned feet, but he doesn't say anything. He
sends a boy out for *paan*, which Swami shares.

Mr Yadav turns out to speak English well. He has heard on
the grapevine that I am in Varanasi to research Indian wrestling
and asks what particular interest I take.

'I want to know what value it holds in India.'

He gets up to fetch a fat hardback book. It is his PhD thesis,
The Contribution of Wrestling to Social Integration in India. He is
a postgraduate in sociology, politics and physical education, he
says.

'What conclusion did you reach in your thesis?'

'Wrestling integrates communities. At the *akhara* you have

Hindu and Muslim, and all castes wrestling together without divisions or friction. The Hindu prays to Hanuman and the Muslim to Ali. Yet many Muslims in the *akhara* like the Hindu gods and goddesses, and they touch the foot of the guru and senior wrestlers, which is a Hindu gesture of respect. There is no difference, proof that wrestling integrates communities. So during trouble between different communities, Hindu–Muslim riots and quarrels, wrestlers become the mediators. They are very popular figures, respected by all. They also send the sick to hospital and help the poor.'

This sounds a little grandiose, but I don't air my scepticism. While Mr Yadav speaks, three wrestlers massage his back, arms and legs.

'It is our tradition,' he explains, when he notices my quizzical look.

Mr Yadav gives the address of Goverdhan Das Malhotra, a wrestling journalist who he says will be better able to help with my research. He seems to be deferring to Goverdhan Das, as though it is only right that I speak to him before he commits himself to talking further about the subject. As we part, I shake his hand. It feels like a slice of warm toast.

The early evening air outside has a cooling effect. Now that Swami has taken me to see his gurus and acted as a translator, I anticipate he will want something in return. I find out exactly what soon enough.

'This world is very troublesome,' he says, breaking the silence during the rickshaw ride home. 'Truthfulness is very cruel. The cold comes and I am shivering. In that room it was warm. Three days I have not slept for shivering. I need a blanket. The doctor says I also need shoes and a new *lunghi*.'

Without anything having to be said, it is decided between us that I will buy him a blanket. After we're dropped off by the rickshaw, we walk towards a market and enter a blanket shop.

'What about this one?' I ask Swami, pointing to one that costs 425 rupees.

'It is OK, but I am thinking it is too heavy to carry. I need one I can port.'

I pick it up.

'The weight feels OK to me.'

'For you perhaps, but I am only eating once a day.'

He discusses the blanket at length with the shop assistant.
'He says it will be warm enough for the winter, but he can
only guarantee for indoor use,' explains Swami. 'He has no
experience of sleeping outdoors.'

Swami's heart is set on a red-check merino blanket. At 525
rupees, it is one of the more expensive ones. I tell Swami to
bargain, and he gets a reduction of 50 rupees. I give the shop
assistant five 100 rupee notes. He slowly turns each so that
Gandhi faces the same way. After we have left the shop, Swami
walks slowly as though weighed down by a heavy meal.

'Now my lifetime can go on,' he says.

The following morning I sit on the toilet knowing that
whatever happens next will be a test of the powers of Dr
Prashand and Shiva. What emerges feels solid at first, but then
there is a telltale splutter and the toilet bowl fills with a brown
soupy liquid. There has been no miracle. Reluctantly, I take the
antibiotics.

James later relays a conversation he had with the doctor.
They discussed the fact that I'd bathed in the Ganga.

'These foreigners are crazy,' said the doctor. 'They think they
can come here and do anything.'

I see Swami on the *ghats* again a few days later. He doesn't
have his new blanket any more and says a madman burnt it in
the night for fuel. I don't believe him and suspect he took it
back to the shop for a refund, which would explain why he
wanted one of the most expensive ones.

The first time I wrestle at Swaminath *akhara* after getting
better, I wear a loincloth, which the Talker has said is com-
pulsory. An Indian loincloth, or *langota*, consists of a triangular
piece of cotton with two ties and a long tongue of material, and
sets a cryptic puzzle. I've practised tying and wrapping one at
home and wear it ready-tied under my trousers to the *akhara*,
but a wrestler takes one look, proclaims the loincloth is too
loose and instructs a couple of boys to help him retie it. He
pulls the tongue of material tight around my crutch, doubles it
back, and tucks it tightly at the rear, while I stand with my arms
out, totally embarrassed, like an adult having his shoelaces
done up by his mother in public. The Talker notices I have a

small bottle of coconut oil. He points at it, laughs and shouts
'Ice!' I open the bottle. The coconut oil has congealed into a
white paste in the morning cold. I thought any oil would do
and didn't realise wrestlers only use mustard. Palu gives me
some of his to use instead.

When the time comes to spar, I am paired off with Palu
again. He beats me but doesn't have everything his own way.
Twice I shoot for his legs and successfully jack him up off the
ground, though I can do nothing to stop him from turning
onto his front to avoid the pin. Yet for a few moments I am in
control, which is enough to salvage some pride. After sparring,
Palu demonstrates the correct way to do *bethaks*. The high
speed at which he performs them surprises me. He stands on
the balls of his feet and basketballs up and down. He springs a
few inches forward when he rises and a few inches backwards
when he squats. Performed at this speed, the exercise develops
cardiovascular endurance as well as leg strength. Palu then
demonstrates *dands*, which are also executed at speed.

I keep visiting the *akhara* for morning sessions. Given time
I realise that a lot of the awkwardness I initially felt was borne
out of misunderstanding. To touch the feet of an instructor or
guru is not a purely subservient act, as it is understood that you
receive a blessing in return. I am never asked to pay for a
massage either. My fear that I would be was the understandable misconception of someone who comes from a
country where men never give each other massages simply
because they need them. Innocent, uncomplicated and
physically intimate transactions like that never occur between
men at home. But here massage is given as a form of hospitality, and senior wrestlers are massaged by juniors as a matter
of course. Massage is good for the health of the receiver and
considered to bring merit to the giver. Giving massage also
develops a better grip, and strong hands are important to a
wrestler.

When I learn to see the *akhara* for what it is, I see a place of
dignity, tradition and robust beauty. Rituals are followed that
give wrestling a precious aura. You bathe and go to the toilet
before practice. Shoes are not worn inside the *akhara*. Before
stepping onto the earth of the wrestling arena you touch the
soil and then your forehead, which amounts to a kind of

apology for touching the earth, considered a mother, with your feet, which are thought of as base. Then you make *puja* to the shrine, in this case a small Shiva lingam, by throwing a little earth beside it and offering a prayer. Qualities of acknowledgement and respect pervade *akhara* life – acknowledgement and respect for the instructor, senior wrestlers, the god that helps you wrestle, the earth on which you stand. How these feelings can endure is made clear one morning when a man in his eighties enters the *akhara* and sprinkles flowers on the earth arena. It is deeply moving to watch. This is a wrestling school, a deeply masculine place, yet it welcomes a fragile old man who has brought flowers with which to honour the place where he learnt to wrestle, a debt not forgotten in old age.

Having become accustomed to wrestling on artificial mats in airless halls, it is exhilarating to wrestle outside in the fresh air on soft earth. I like the natural simplicity of the *akhara*, the fact that it convenes earth, water and shade. It may be a simple place, but it is not mundane. The earth is mixed with tumeric, curd and other ingredients supposed to be good for health. Shade is provided by a pipal tree, which is considered sacred. The water used for washing is a holy river, a goddess. Yet that element, the Ganga, is polluted. I thought the wrestlers would be offended if I didn't join them to bathe in the sacred river, but they don't mind when I slope off for bucket-baths back at the guest house. It is saddening, though, that the idyll of wrestling in Varanasi is tainted – that the simple desire to wash yourself in the Ganga after wrestling has been complicated by the dirty legacy of India's modernisation.

It is disappointing, too, that there is no evidence of the kind of devotion to wrestling catalogued in *Comprehensive Asian Fighting Arts* at Swaminath and the other *akharas* in Varanasi I've visited. None of the wrestlers performs thousands of *bethaks* and *dands*. None wrestles for hours, or runs miles every day. None is a professional, as Gama must have been. If these *akharas* are representative of wrestling in India as a whole, clearly it has gone into steep decline. I'm disappointed, too, by my health. I hoped it might improve in India, that relaxation and sunshine would do me a world of good, but there has been no real change, and fatigue makes it difficult to continue to train. I crash after each session and have to spend the rest of the day and half the next in recovery. It's too high a price to pay, and I reluctantly accept that I will have to stop.

But at least I find out what happened to my missing boxer shorts. By chance I meet Rajan. We sit and eat pizza at the Pizzeria Vaatika on Assi Ghat. Rajan pulls his *pyjamas* down partway to reveal he is wearing my underwear. Obviously he took the boxers from the washing line.

'Problem?' he asks.

I can't quite believe he has had the audacity to both annex my underwear and let me know about it. I contain my anger and tell him that no, it's not a problem in the sense that I don't mind him wearing my boxer shorts for now, but yes it is a problem in the sense that I would like them back. He grins, and I realise all he's understood is the phrase 'not a problem'. I've made the mistake of being too elaborate with someone with limited English. He thinks I think it's OK. The conversation moves on.

After my final wrestling session, I walk along the *ghats* on a post-exercise high – until I run into Rajan yet again. He is carrying my boxer shorts scrunched up in his hand, and has just bathed and washed in the river. He lays the boxers out to dry while we drink *chai* together. Afterwards, he makes the mistake of standing with his back towards me while he has his fingernails cut. I put the boxers in my holdall and quickly walk away without looking back. Strangely, I feel a little guilt, as though it's me who's the thief. Later I think about the providence involved in our meeting like that and wonder whether, as Swami would say, it was predetermined – and whether the Shiva power that failed to work in my stomach has nevertheless been tirelessly labouring to secure the liberation of my underwear.

Chapter 4

5,000 Bethaks *and* 3,000 Dands

Goverdhan Das Malhotra lives near Gaya Ghat within the old walls of the city and his centre of gravity is in the old India of duty, ethics and obligation. He sits on the other side of a small table in a den of a room at his home, surrounded by photos and trophies from his wrestling career. On a wall is a picture of him as a younger man, his hair thick and black, showing a wrestling book to Indira Gandhi; now he is 65, his moustache is silvery and he walks with a stick. He is defensive and edgy, perhaps because he is worried that I will misconstrue and misrepresent Indian wrestling, which is clearly precious to him. I feel uneasy too. An English lecturer called Mr Kesri is acting as interpreter, and he talks fast and translates what Goverdhan Das says into convoluted sentences that are sometimes difficult to understand.

I ask Goverdhan Das what wrestling means to people in Varanasi. He says it is an ancient local tradition. As Varanasi is on a bank of the Ganga, it is a congenial place in which to pursue the sport, he adds.

'The reason why people started wrestling was because it was supposed to be a good thing for the body and mind. For disciplining the mind and building character.'

He says 'character' in English. The way he slits the air with the 'K' sounds suggests this is a subject close to his heart.

'What do you mean by building character?'

'If you have to keep your body healthy, you have to keep yourself balanced, not having sexual escapades here and there,' he replies. 'Sex is the most normal thing in Europe, but when you are a wrestler you keep away from it, and in India. . . '

An ageing journalist is sitting with us. He interjects in booming English. 'To avoid sexual relations with women! This is one of the points to build character! So many people are there in the *akhara*, so they are influenced by the wrestler! He is off sexual relations! He is making body very strong! So this is one of the pillars to build character.'

I don't understand what wrestling has to do with sex. Mr Kesri explains that Indians believe sex makes you weak. Goverdhan Das gets up and walks out.

'Was it something I said?' I ask Mr Kesri.

'No, monkey hassles,' he replies, much to my relief.

Goverdhan Das heard clumps on the roof. Unless you see them off with sticks, gangs of monkeys climb down into houses to steal food.

Goverdhan Das returns. I ask him whether it is a romantic notion that differences based on caste and creed dissolve at the *akhara*. Something is lost in translation. He thinks I'm asking whether it is a romantic notion that wrestlers avoid sex. He sits forward, frowns and waves both hands in front of him, fingers splayed, as energetically as a cheerleader shaking pommels, thundering 'No! No! No!' in Hindi. I sit back, pinned to the chair by the force of his outburst.

'This is not fiction, it is a fact!'

Mr Kesri translates what follows into a landslide of confusing clauses. Goverdhan Das appears to be giving the example of a man, possibly a wrestler, who controlled his sexual desire so completely that at the end of his life, or possibly after he died, semen was 'emitted'. What is meant by 'emitted' I do not know. I am dumbfounded. This is India, a conservative culture, and I am talking to two old men with conservative attitudes, yet they want to discuss sex and semen with me, a stranger. It's perverse, like discussing porn over tea and cake with grandparents at their old folks' home.

Embarrassed, I change the subject and ask Goverdhan Das to outline how wrestling has changed since the days of Gama. He says that the maharajahs were fond of wrestling and were its patrons. You need to eat a lot of food if you want to be a wrestler. Maharajahs paid for wrestlers' prodigious diets. But now the maharajahs are no more and modern businessmen are not interested in sponsoring wrestling. Goverdhan Das complains that the government does not support it either, though it supports other sports. Consequently, wrestling has declined. There used to be few sports in India and wrestling was the most important of the few that there were, but now there are many and it has lost its pre-eminence.

My own experiences have prepared me for this depressing news. The only consolatory thought is that even if the huge culture of wrestling that produced men such as Gama has gone, there may still be old wrestlers alive today who were active when that culture flourished. I ask Goverdhan Das whether any of those wrestlers, any of the men who did thousands of *bethaks* and *dands* a day, who wrestled for hours at a time, who defined the outer limits of human capability, are still alive. He says that some are. I feel a boyish eagerness to meet one as soon as possible – the same eagerness I felt when I visited seaside towns as a child and wanted to see the sea as soon as possible. I want to be in the presence of someone of the same calibre as Gama, to confirm immediately that the incredible wrestlers I read about and imagined back home really did exist.

Goverdhan Das takes my notebook and writes the names of nine wrestlers in the back. Some live in the surrounding villages. Only one has a phone. The greatest of the nine, he says, is Sadho Pehalwan.

The three-wheeler turns off the airport road. We drive along potholed dirt tracks without signposts – roads down which it would be easy to become lost – yet the driver asks for directions at forks, houses and stalls, and everyone asked instantly makes an arrow with their arm to point the way to where Sadho

Pehalwan lives, as though, through his stature as a great wrestler, he has transcended being a man and become a place.

Sadho is sleeping on a bed outside his village home. My new interpreter, a tall 23-year-old economics student nicknamed Pinku, rouses him. Sadho sits up, puts his glasses on awry so that they magnify an eyebrow, and tells me to sit on a bed next to him. Nearby, a water buffalo with sad eyes is tied by a short leash to a bamboo stump. Women wash at a water pump. Music blares from a radio.

Sadho says he is old and sick and might not remember much about his life. He believes he is 80 years old, but can't be sure. He places his hand a few feet off the ground to indicate how tall he had been when he started wrestling. His father and grandfather were also wrestlers, he says. As a child he would go with them and the other boys of his age to the village *akhara* near the banks of the River Varuna.

'Everyone wanted to be a big wrestler in my day. Everyone had the same feeling: they wanted to wrestle. But whether you became a big wrestler or not depended on what diet you were taking. I drank milk and ate ghee, cashew nuts, almonds, sultanas and fruit. I ate whenever I had the chance. Each day I drank five kilograms of milk' – he says kilograms, as Indians commonly do, but means litres – 'and ate half a kilo of ghee, half a kilo of almonds, and fruit.'

'What type of wrestler were you – fast, clever, aggressive?'

'I was all of those things. I knew all the ways. I was strong also. If you were weak, you couldn't apply your tricks.'

I ask how many *dands* and *bethaks* he used to do and how much he weighed. Either he is unsure, or too modest to boast, or both. He tells his grandson to go into the house and fetch an article written about him. Pinku translates. The piece says Sadho was six foot five and a half inches tall and weighed 135kg. Every day he wrestled all the wrestlers at the *akhara*. Every day he did 5,000 *bethaks* and 3,000 *dands*, which is an incredible amount. He also ran nearly five miles daily, and developed powerful arms and shoulders by practising *jori*, a traditional Indian body-building exercise performed with a pair of wooden clubs. Each club is dropped behind the back, then lifted and powered over each shoulder in turn. The ones Sadho used weighed 40kg each.

I am awed by the description of Sadho's training schedule and physique. He must have been a resplendent figure – over 20 stone of wrestling-adapted muscle. He says he went to the *akhara* from 6am to 9am, then 5pm till 9pm every day. Life was a constant round of exercise, wrestling, eating and rest. He did nothing else. He didn't want to do anything else either.

'Did wrestling give you a lot of status?'

'Yes, after becoming a champion, I gained a lot of respect. Everyone knows my address. They always come and ask me how I am. You came all the way from England to meet me. Everyone knows where I live.'

'Were women impressed by your strength?'

He laughs. 'Yes, women really loved me. Everyone wanted to marry me, but what could I do? I could only marry once.'

Pinku continues to translate the article. It lists wrestlers whom Sadho defeated, whom I assume were well known in their day. I ask Sadho to comment on some of the bouts, but all he will say is things like, 'He was fat' or 'I defeated him in about six minutes'.

Agitated by the brevity of his answers, I ask him whether he ever lost.

'No, I was never defeated, I always won,' he says.

His body language tells another story. He corrects himself: 'I drew a few times.'

Pinku reads on: 'Actually, it's written here that there was one time he was defeated.'

Sadho folds his arms and looks down.

'My loincloth started to tear and I was afraid everyone would see me exposed. I went to adjust my loincloth, and as I did so my opponent cheated and threw me to the ground. He cheated. I was trying to adjust my loincloth at the time and was not wrestling, yet he threw me.'

Sadho is too infirm to take us to see his *akhara*. A middle-aged nephew leads us there instead. We walk on paths that finger their way through pea and sugar cane fields until we reach a beautiful spot shaded by a mango tree. This is the *akhara*. A mound of earth crowned with a marigold garland serves as a simple shrine to Hanuman. There is no stone border to enclose the earth of the wrestling arena, like at *akharas* in the city. The only way to tell where the arena begins is by a change in the shade of soil, which is a little lighter inside than out. Before the nephew steps across the border into the wrestling area, he goes to wash at a nearby handpump. He returns, touches the soil then his forehead, sprinkles a little earth on the shrine, prays, crosses his arms in front of his body, cups a hand and pats his elbow with it to produce a clopping sound.

'Never have I seen devotion like this,' says Pinku, impressed.

We return to sit with Sadho. His grandson empties a bag of ball-shaped sweets made from sugar cane onto a plate on a tray. I presume he is about to offer them to Pinku and me, and rehearse a couple of regal lines in my head to thank him for his generosity. The grandson brings the tray over. He has bruises like smoke stains on his head and a cauliflower ear. Obviously wrestling continues to run in the family. He takes a sweet from the plate, breaks it in two, gives half to me and half to Pinku – then feeds the rest of the sweets to the water buffalo with sad eyes.

'It makes them give sweet milk,' explains Sadho.

Sadho gets out of bed to have his photo taken. He stands proudly with his chest out, arms thrown back a little and chin slightly raised. He is still a big, hulking man.

'People used to pay to take my photo,' he says.

Moved by the depth of Sadho's devotion to wrestling, Pinku touches his feet as we leave. Were I Hindu, I would do the same.

The riddle set by Imran's father at the motorway service station in England is easy to solve after a few weeks spent interviewing more of the wrestlers on Goverdhan Das's list, along with others whom Pinku tracks down. To be called a wrestler in India, you have to be committed to a whole way of life. You can wrestle but not be a wrestler in the same way that you can play football but not be a footballer: it's the difference between a casual pastime and a serious vocation. Old wrestlers describe the same tough daily schedule, the same exercises, the same diet, recounting a life so well-defined it almost materialises into physical form in front of me.

Wrestlers of standing like Sadho are given the title

Pehalwan, and the wrestler's training regimen is known as *pehalwani*. Like an element in the Periodic Table, *pehalwani* is always *pehalwani* wherever you encounter it, whoever's life it is embedded in. During the heyday of Indian wrestling, which it transpires ended roughly fifty years ago, a wrestler would visit his *akhara* once or twice a day. There would be a morning session and a session in the late afternoon. The morning session was devoted to exercises and wrestling, the afternoon session sometimes to exercises only.

Often a wrestler would rise very early to start training – at four or even three in the morning. His exercise regime centred upon doing thousands of *dands* and *bethaks*. Many wrestlers ran as well. Those who lived in Varanasi might row to the sandbanks on the other side of the Ganga and go running there in the early morning. Wrestlers might also practise *jori*, like Sadho Pehalwan, though this was often frowned upon because it was believed to tighten the shoulders. They might also exercise with a *gada*, which consists of a shaft with a large bulb of stone at one end. The weight is dropped behind the back and powered onto each shoulder in turn.

It was crucial to secure a good diet. A wrestler would eat as much as possible, partly because *kushti*, like most traditional styles, has no weight categories, so being big was – and is – an advantage. Wrestlers drank a lot of milk and ate a lot of ghee, both of which are considered to be potent foods. If they could afford almonds, which are also considered to be powerful, they might grind these into a paste, mix the paste with milk and drink the mixture. If they couldn't afford almonds they might eat chickpeas instead. This was on top of normal meals. It was taken for granted that wrestlers did not drink alcohol – or smoke for that matter.

Discipline at the *akhara* used to be strict. Wrestlers obeyed their guru without question. Gurus carried a *lathi*, or bamboo stick, with which to beat anyone who transgressed the rules or was lazy. Such harsh discipline used to be characteristic of Indian culture as a whole. Old wrestlers remember their gurus fondly, and sometimes break down in tears as they talk about them. One, Keshav Shonkar, who used to train at Swaminath, says that at first he trained hard because he was frightened of his guru, but after a while hard training became a habit he enjoyed. At some point the stick became inner – the motivating force switched from fear to passion, to love from the avoidance of pain.

Hanuman, the monkey god, was – and is – worshipped by all wrestlers and cited as the perfect role model. He is the epitome of strength and bravery, and also celibate. Every *akhara* in Varanasi has a Hanuman shrine except for Swaminath, which has four situated just outside that wrestlers use. At his shrines, Hanuman is often depicted carrying a mountain with one finger, a famous feat described in the *Ramayana*. Wrestlers make *puja* to Hanuman and ask him to help them win matches.

As Goverdhan Das said, celibacy is fundamental to *pehalwani*. This may come as a surprise to me, but it is common knowledge in India – like the name of the prime minister and the colours of the national flag – that wrestlers must be celibate to maintain strength. I soon learn to relax about discussing semen with people I have just met. In Varanasi circles a celibate wrestler is said to 'keep a tight loincloth'. The phrase has both a literal and metaphorical meaning: wrestlers genuinely believe that wearing a loincloth tight represses sexual desire, and a loincloth is a badge of moral propriety for both wrestlers and Banarsis – inhabitants of Banaras, another name for Varanasi – in general. There is a common belief that your penis will shrivel if you are celibate, so people sometimes boast about having a small penis, which explains what the man wearing *kurta-pyjamas* at Kali Bari was talking about.

Wrestling ability is so closely identified with celibacy that wrestlers commonly relate how their powers went into decline once they began living with their wives. The old wrestlers I meet often had their marriages arranged while they were in their teens, but their wives were only expected to come to live with them years later. The wives of serious wrestlers would frequently join them a few years later than normal so that their future husbands could draw out the years in which they were free to devote themselves completely to *pehalwani* without having to shoulder the responsibilities of a householder and without losing strength as a result of having sex. Some of the great wrestlers of the past never married at all. They believed it was impossible to both marry and be a great wrestler at the same time.

Together, *bethaks*, *dands*, devotion to Hanuman, devotion to your guru, drinking milk, eating *ghee*, celibacy, exercises and of course wrestling itself were the foundations of an Indian wrestler's life. It is reassuring to hear that wrestling used to be taken so seriously in India that men devoted either all, or large chunks, of their lives to it. Here wrestling had – and still has – a dignity it does not have back home. It is self-assured, and does not need to justify its existence or convince anyone of its value. Time spent wrestling is time well spent. *Kushti* has the aura of a venerable ancient tradition. It was – still is – a significant part of Indian culture. Like Goverdhan Das said, *kushti* used to be the most important sport in India, something I never read or heard stated back in England, which is odd considering India used to be part of the British Empire and wrestling was in its heyday during British rule. But then indifference to wrestling is hardly anything new.

Yet though wrestling holds real weight in India, I can't find any evidence of spiritual significance. Whenever wrestlers talk about their motivation, they invariably say they wrestled to 'increase their name' as Pinku translates it – in other words to make their reputation, to enhance their status, become famous. None of them talks about wrestling in the terms I think about it, as a path with spiritual value in which the aim is to develop a meditative state of calm and poise. Of course I can't expect India to think about wrestling in the same terms as mine, but if wrestling is understood to have spiritual value in terms distinct from mine, I can't yet see what they are.

Pinku is both grown up and not quite grown up at one and the same time. He talks in a deep, commanding voice and often frowns when he speaks, yet he is too thin and spindly and his moustache is too bum-fluffy and unmanly for him to project a real presence of authority. He acts as both an interpreter and a knowledgeable guide to Indian culture, and I provide the same service for him concerning the West. Pinku is obsessed with clothes and appeals for information about Western style. In particular, he wants to know the correct name for cargo pants, a mysterious style of trouser that is new to the Varanasi fashion scene. He and his student friends have been discussing the trousers after seeing travellers and tourists wearing them. While they wait to find out their proper name, they are using their own interim label, 'six-pocket denim pants'. I tell Pinku that they are called cargo pants. He gratefully accepts the information, but has a supplementary question the next day: are cargo pants called cargo pants because they are worn by people who work on ships?

Through working closely together, Pinku and I get to know one other well. He suggests I move into his home, which is down a narrow alleyway behind Assi Ghat. His parents have two simple upstairs rooms for rent. I take one, while a Dutchman, Rene, who is learning the traditional Indian weapon art of *boneti*, has the other. Downstairs, in the family home, the hall passageway opens out to a lounge area that leads in turn to a yard without a separating wall. In the mornings, Pinku's father sits on his bed in the lounge with one leg crossed over the other, and stares out to the yard in a daily before-work trance while Pinku's mother, Mamaji (-ji is a respectful suffix), warms his socks in front of a bucket-fire. Mr Pandey never appears to be in a great rush to get to work. He is a lab technician at the pathology department of Banaras Hindu University. A *senior* lab technician, stresses Pinku. The Pandeys' eldest son, Bablu, has two rooms at the back of the yard that he shares with his new wife, who cooks for the family. For no particular reason, I only exchange a few words with him. Pinku and Bablu also have a 17-year-old sister, Poonam, who is sweet, pretty and child-thin.

The Pandeys are Brahmin, from the priests' caste, and within the priests' caste their particular caste ranks highly. Mamaji likes the family to adhere closely to caste rules. While we sit relaxing together upstairs, Rene and I swap stories about points of caste law we observe in the household below. We try to understand the world alive beneath us with the same enthusiasm, yet acknowledgement of insurmountable distance, as marine biologists trying to comprehend the ecosystem of a coral reef from a glass-bottomed boat. Probably all interested foreigners who live in India for any period of time do the same – something about India brings out the anthropologist in everyone.

Most of the things Rene and I notice relate to purity and

cleanliness. Rene once sees Mamaji struggle to carry a container of water and instinctively goes to help, which upsets her – and puzzles Rene. It turns out to be a Brahmin thing. Rene has inadvertently polluted the water by touching the container. When our upstairs squat-toilet has to be cleaned, the Pandeys go to the *ghats* and hire someone from the Untouchables caste to do it, which is a Brahmin thing too. Most Indian families serve guests hand and foot, but after we've eaten, Rene and I actually have to place our dishes next to the washing-up bowl in the yard ourselves – another Brahmin moment.

To someone ignorant of the meaning and importance of caste strictures, the rules can appear wilfully idiosyncratic. I notice that Pinku is not wearing the sacred thread one day and ask him why. He explains that the thread became polluted because he spoke while going to the toilet. He now has to get a new one. The Pandeys appear to be strict about caste law, but Pinku says that on the contrary they are fairly lax.

Goverdhan Das leads the way through the alleys. He taps the cobbles with his red-headed walking stick as he goes, and calls out 'This way' whenever we turn down a side alley. Pinku and I have difficulty keeping up.

'Truly he is a master of the alleys,' says Pinku, impressed.

We stop outside a *chai* shop where Goverdhan Das introduces Nate, who wrestled at his *akhara*. Nate stands and grins while Goverdhan Das tells an anecdote about him.

'Nate once served Mahatma Gandhi. Gandhi was on a train that stopped at Mughalserai, near Varanasi. A businessman asked Nate to go and give Gandhi some milk. He went to Mughalserai, where a large crowd was mobbing the train, and made his way through. He found Gandhi's compartment and went in. Gandhi noticed a little earth on Nate's head and arms, and asked him whether he was a wrestler. Nate said he was. Gandhi admired his physique and felt his muscles, and offered Nate the milk first out of respect. Gandhi drank his milk after Nate.'

We walk the short distance to the *akhara* where Goverdhan Das wrestled when he was ten years old. Like Padney Babua, it overlooks the Ganga. The earth arena is hard and compact: no

one trains here any more. When Goverdhan Das was older, he
wrestled nearby at Pani Pandey *akhara*. It, too, is in decay. All
that remains is a cratered square of earth bordered by bricks. A
railing that once protected wrestlers from a sheer drop is
broken. It was my idea to come to these *akharas*. I hoped that
visiting them would provoke Goverdhan Das into reminiscing
about his time at them, and anticipated that he would become
a little sad when faced with the ruins of these childhood places.
But he does not linger or seem upset. In fact I am the one
depressed. I come from a country where wrestling literally has
no place, where I had to make do with stuffy basements and
public parks, while Varanasi has impossibly idyllic venues such
as these, *akharas* shaded by sacred trees looking out over a
great river, and the irony is that hardly anyone uses them any
more.

We return to Goverdhan Das's home. He takes a pile of
articles from a cupboard in his den and drops them on the seat
next to me. They fall with a satisfying thud, as if Goverdhan
Das wishes to make clear his authority on the subject of Indian
wrestling through the weight of the articles. As if to punctuate
this moment of surrender: his journalist friend recommended
that he should not share his research, but he says he's
developed an affection for Pinku and me during the handful of
times we've met following that first bizarre conversation, and
has therefore decided to help us as much as he can.

I sift through the articles, which are typed in double-spaced
Hindi. Most are biographies of wrestlers from Goverdhan
Das's generation, or the generations before. Many are now
dead. Photographs accompany some of the pieces. With their
excellent physiques and fine moustaches, the wrestlers stare
out from another era. Some hold an ornamental silver *gada*
won as a prize; one stands triumphantly with his foot on the
head of a tiger-skin rug. The articles represent a huge amount
of work: Goverdhan Das doesn't have a tape-recorder with
which to record interviews, neither does he have a typewriter or
computer. He makes notes longhand then goes to the market
to type up his pieces, which he submits to a local paper. He is
probably one of only a handful of people in India who are
recording an important yet dying tradition, yet he lacks even
basic resources.

I borrow a few articles and take them home for Pinku to translate. Each unfolds into a fable that follows the same pattern: the wrestler succeeded through devotion, hard work and respect for his elders and guru. Goverdhan Das catalogues the thousands of *dands* and *bethaks* and other exercises performed daily, and describes the wrestler's diet, particularly how much milk he drank and ghee he ate. He uses stock phrases. To express devotion, he writes, 'He made wrestling his bed and blankets.' To relate physical growth: 'He grew once during the day and twice in the night'; or 'He increased in size [*all over*] by the width of a sesame seed a day.' Through his articles, Goverdhan Das wants to inspire young wrestlers to be clean-living, self-disciplined and hard-working. His mission is to transmit these values to the young and the local newspaper is his pulpit.

I'm attracted by the fact that Goverdhan Das sees wrestling schools as places of significance and value – ethical value – but am turned off by his disciplinarian approach. He comes across as an old-fashioned authoritarian, and the way I see it, hard discipline at the wrestling school will create fear. If a youth is scared into behaving a certain way, his actions lack the real ethical value that comes when he chooses to act that way of his own accord. At the heart of Goverdhan Das's promotion of wrestling is an advocacy of celibacy. If a woman is older than a wrestler, he should regard her as though she is his mother, he says; if she is younger or about the same age, he should treat her like a sister. Goverdhan Das compares this attitude with what he sees as the moral bankruptcy of the West – which he has never visited, which he knows only from media reports – where sexual relationships before marriage are condoned and where, he scalds, schools give sex education. In contrast, he boasts, he and his fellow wrestlers had no idea about sex until they were in their twenties. He appears to be obsessed with the subject of sex and its avoidance. Sometimes I'm not sure whether his primary interest is wrestling or stopping young people from having sex. Whatever the case, he is using wrestling to fight the slide towards Western values and promote the values of his generation, his India.

Through gaining an understanding of Goverdhan Das and other old wrestlers, I come to see how wrestling is tangled up in a generational dispute between, on the one hand, the emerging youth who look to the West and want to own scooters and televisions, wear jeans and baseball caps and perhaps marry someone of their choice and, on the other hand, the older generation, which looks to the past and laments the decline of a belief in duty and obligation, alongside a decline in sincere religious devotion. The increase in the influence of the West, with its concomitant promotion of materialism, is commonly given as a reason for wrestling's fall. The older generation say that the youth of today are soft and don't want to follow tradition. They don't have any discipline and are not capable of the self-sacrifice necessary to become a great wrestler. Yes, they want to have a good physique, but no, they don't want to earn it by doing thousands of *dands* and *bethaks*. If they have the opportunity, they prefer the easier alternative of what is referred to as 'English body-building' – working out with weights, like at gyms in the West. But, say old wrestlers, a physique gained this way is superficial, and both earned and lost quickly.

Old wrestlers complain that the younger generation do a bit of exercise, nothing compared with what they used to do, then hang around in the street wearing Western clothes, trying to look cool. They view the decline of traditional Indian clothes like *dhoti-kurta* and the accompanying rise of Western-style trousers and shirts as visible manifestations of the rift separating them from their grandchildren. In the battle between Western materialism and traditional Indian values, wrestling is the conservatives' ally. Wrestling schools are capsules of tradition where respect and total obedience for your guru and elders, along with devotion, hard work and worship of a god, are practised and encouraged. When I wrestled in London I felt like I was part of a subversive masculine fundamentalist group, but here wrestling is regarded as a conservative force.

Our meetings with Goverdhan Das are having a strong effect on Pinku. He is right out there in the middle of the generational disagreement, torn between traditional Hindu values on the one hand, which are particularly important to a Brahmin, but attracted to Western culture on the other, particularly its cars and fashion. Goverdhan Das's lectures on the virtues of celibacy are making a definite impact on Pinku. When I first met him, I'd catch him ogling the jiggling breasts of Western travellers and tourists, sometimes in an open way that Indians don't realise Western women find offensive. He would talk about how his student friends discussed how many Western women they'd 'had' – whatever they meant by that. Now he says he is 'not that type of boy'. He considers Goverdhan Das a role model and wants to emulate him. He has even taken to wearing a loincloth. Though his sport is cricket, he has even been inspired to flirt with wrestlers' exercises. He wants to be in better shape, he says, and compares my physique favourably with his own, which lacks muscle. Over six foot tall, Pinku weighs only about 55kg.

'I looks like bamboo,' he complains.

Late one afternoon I go out onto the roof and find Pinku there. He says he wants to develop a physique that women will find attractive and asks me how to go about it.

'English body-building would be best.'

'But that is too expensive. The gym is costing three hundred rupees a month.'

'Then you will have to do *dands* and *bethaks*, but it will take you a long time.'

Given the volume in which Pinku proceeds to do these two exercises, my forecast is over-optimistic. He performs a total of seven *dands* and ten *bethaks*.

'At that rate, it really will take you a long, long time,' I say, with a lot of understatement.

A few weeks later, I ask Pinku whether he is still body-building. He says he is and flexes a bicep to prove it. I feel the muscle.

'If I closed my eyes, I would think I was holding the arm of a woman. What body-building are you doing exactly?'

'Actually, I am taking the bananas with my food.'

The theatre of life at Assi Ghat is a fair substitute for television. Small boys play with simple kites that butterfly high above the Ganga. Goats stand around on the steps and casually chew like football managers. They leave pellets of dung around them, which you don't see in football. Children sell postcards of

deities or ask for a few rupees. Early in the morning there is
traffic of pilgrims, bathers and *sadhus*. Stalls cater to their
needs: *neem* twigs for brushing teeth, containers in which to
collect holy Ganga water, marigolds. Men bathe in the river
wearing loincloths, women bathe wearing saris and young
children go naked. Silk merchants, boatmen and would-be
guides hustle for trade among the pilgrims, tourists and
travellers. Students shell peanuts, drink *chai* and gossip as the
sun goes down.

Swami is often on the *ghats*. I have made the mistake of
telling him I work as a journalist back home. He clearly
believes that being a journalist in England is only a rung below
being prime minister, because he has been pestering me ever
since to approach Queen Elizabeth and the United Nations to
discuss the case of how his home was taken from him. He also
demands that I call a press conference to publicise the injustice
straight away. I keep telling him I don't have that type of
influence either back home or here, but agree to help in a more
mundane way by photocopying documents that relate to his
case.

Together we go to a photocopying shop. Swami reaches into
his sack and pulls out a pile of papers and scraps. He sorts
through them with a care that suggests he considers these
documents to be his lifeline. They are bad photocopies,
speckled photocopies of photocopies, but his only hope.
Among them is a list of names and addresses of travellers who
support Swami's case – people, like me, that he must have
sucked into helping him. We get the photocopies done and
afterwards I pay. As we leave the shop, Swami asks me again to
call a press conference and talk to Queen Elizabeth on his
behalf. I tell him for the nth time that I don't have that type of
leverage and walk off, irritated. I sense someone is following
me and turn to see that it is him.

'You will fax the UN straight away?'

Swami changes tack the next time we meet. He wants us to
go into partnership as diamond miners. He says we could buy
a plot of land for 5,000 rupees in Madyar Pradesh and quickly
make the money back plus a lot more. By 'we', of course,
Swami means me. Asking me to buy clothes, food and pay for
photocopying is one thing, but asking for the equivalent of over

$100 to finance some dodgy diamond-mining scheme is going too far.

'We have a saying in England: "If it sounds too good to be true, it probably is." You understand?'

'Yes, that is a contradiction,' says Swami. 'But actually the stars are saying it is a good time.'

'The stars?'

'Yes, the stars, the astrology. We could share the business. If the stars are right, you can turn mud into gold. If not, gold can be turned into mud. Dr Prashand has also been saying I will be lucky – and a sufi told me that it was a good time for me.'

'Look, I've helped you out enough already,' I say, and walk off.

A week later I see Swami again – this time standing outside the Harmony Bookshop.

'I am thinking you are much disturbed with me,' he says, correctly.

I explain that I am angry with him because he took me for a fool with his diamond-mining proposal, which is probably a scam. He seems to accept this, but again requests that I call a press conference straight away to highlight his case. I repeat once again that I don't have any influence in India, and tell him not to keep asking me to do something I can't. He says he has no parents, insinuating that I am his only hope. He notices how unmoved I am.

'I love you!' he blurts out.

I look away, embarrassed.

'I will suicide,' he says. 'I haven't eaten for two days.'

He shivers melodramatically to underline his hopelessness. For a moment I remain impassive, but I can't stop myself from giving in and handing over 50 rupees.

We haven't spoken since – I'm trying to avoid Swami. Sometimes I see him without his seeing me. Once I saw him drinking *chai* and talking and laughing with a friend. He looked like an actor relaxing backstage between performances.

Men of the Yadav caste are easy to recognise: neat, short hair and moustaches; *kurtas* and check *lunghis*. In the daytime they cycle by with milk churns hanging from the handlebars; in the late afternoon they rinse their churns in the Ganga and scrub them clean with straw. Traditionally, the Yadav are cattle herders. In Varanasi and the surrounding villages they often own cows and water buffalo, and run milk businesses and businesses associated with milk such as *chai* stalls and traditional Indian sweet shops.

Wrestling is a tradition among the Yadav, as are the body-building disciplines of *jori* and *gada*. Often wrestling goes back generations in the male line. Because I am not used to thinking about the world in terms of caste, it has taken me a while to notice the connection between the Yadav and wrestling, but it too is common knowledge in India, like the name of the prime minister and the colours of the national flag. Many of the wrestlers I've encountered in Varanasi so far are Yadav: Rajan is Yadav, so is Gopal; Vijay Yadav is obviously Yadav, as is Mr AN Yadav; and Sadho Pehalwan is also Yadav. It's probable that the Talker at Swaminath *akhara* recounted how many water buffalo and cows wrestlers owned because he – and they – were Yadav as well.

Pinku knows an old Yadav wrestler, Kedar Nath, who used to train at Swaminath. We locate his family's *chai* stall in the pinball machine of alleys and ask for directions to his home. Kedar Nath's place turns out to be close. We find him sitting on his bed in his room, which opens onto the street. He is an old man, 85, with a salt-coloured beard bushing from his chin and slack skin around his Adam's apple. Next to his bed is a bowl of ash topped with betel nut and foamy spittle. I notice a tinted picture of a familiar figure, Gama, on the wall above Kedar Nath's bed and instantly feel a connection with him – we share an idol.

'I kept this picture to inspire me, because I wanted to wrestle like Gama, but I never became like him,' he says. 'I didn't have that much ability, but I tried to be like him. Whenever I looked at the photo it inspired me and I started to exercise. It gave me courage. I really admired him.'

He is old enough to have seen Gama wrestle. I ask whether he ever did.

'Yes, I saw him.'

Kedar Nath says he competed at wrestling competitions, called *dangals*, all over India and saw Gama there – along with his younger brother Imam Bux, who was also a great wrestler.

Both Gama and Imam Bux also spent some time at Sijuara Estate in Gaya, near Varanasi, where they wrestled under the patronage of a Brahmin, and Kedar Nath saw them there too when he visited for work reasons.

'They had so much muscle – they were really very big. When you see beautiful things you like them. When you saw their legs, their thighs, biceps, chests, it was great. I saw Imam Bux fight in Banaras at a *dangal* at the town hall that was organised by the government. He wrestled Adalat, who was very fast and sharp. Bux was very strong and powerful – stronger than Adalat – and he could pick him up whenever he wanted. But Adalat always escaped by jumping out and would come back to standing on his feet. That match lasted half an hour. Imam Bux couldn't defeat Adalat because he was so fast. Afterwards Adalat challenged Gama. "Come and try to defeat me!" he said. "If you beat me I will shave off my moustache with your urine!" Gama didn't accept the challenge. He was world champion and considered it would be beneath him.'

'How is today's wrestling different from the way it was when you were a young man?'

'The amount of exercise we did was completely different. My daily routine was that at four in the morning I would get up and perform around 2,000 *bethaks* and 1,600 *dands* in my home, then I would go to the other side of the river to run. When I came back my mother would already have ground almonds for me to drink and after that I would go to the *akhara* to wrestle.'

'You must have been very tired by the time you started wrestling.'

'No. After doing those exercises we'd feel our muscles tighten and think: *Now* I have a leg, *now* I have hands. Otherwise we felt like we didn't have a leg or a hand. That's why we did the exercises first and then wrestled.

'Me and my brother wrestled and my mother took care of us. My father died when I was young. That is a painting of my brother in front of you.'

Kedar Nath gets up and pulls apart curtains of washing that hang across the room on a line. A large painting is revealed on a cabinet door.

'My brother died in 1951.'

Over 40 years ago, but his presence still dominates the room.

A girl comes in to get something from the cabinet. She opens the door and the painting swings out. It seems an indignity for the dead man, like casually opening and closing the lid of someone's coffin.

'My mother took care of everything. She supervised our food, and checked whether we were doing exercise or not. After wrestling she would give us a snack, like buttermilk to drink or *malai*. Then we would work in the shop, because at that time, at about twelve o'clock, the milk came from the villages, and we'd start to make sweets from it. At four I would go to Kali Bari to do *jori* and *gada* after going to the toilet and washing, and my mother would take care of the shop. Nowadays the boys can't do as much exercise as we did. Wrestling is that type of bowl: you have to fill it every day to drink from it. You have to exercise every day to get the benefit.'

A wrestler's job was to exercise, eat and sleep, says Kedar Nath. He had no other work to do.

'My mother wanted me to come back so tired that I would lie on my bed and my eyes would close. At that time parents didn't want their daughters to marry men who were weak. "How is he going to feed our girl?" they'd ask. They wanted to give their daughters to boys who were strong and powerful and could work hard to feed a wife. So they didn't give girls to boys who weren't good wrestlers or didn't have a good physique.'

A wolf whistle comes from outside – a bird in a neighbour's cage.

'In my time you could find a wrestler in each household. Some of them were really big wrestlers, and wrestling was all that they did. When we sat anywhere we would start to talk about wrestling and *dangals*. We'd talk about where we had been, or what prizes were being offered at which competitions – if you go there you will win a *lota* [*a wide-rimmed pot*]; if you go there they will give you respect and tie a turban around your head. I competed in a lot of *dangals* in my time.'

Kedar Nath says he and a group of wrestlers from Varanasi made a tour of *dangals*. They had a planned schedule. If they made enough money, such as a 1,000 or 2,000 rupees, then they might return home. Sometimes, says Kedar Nath, he

would be away from home for as long as eight months, or
sometimes six, four, three or two.

'If you are a wrestler, you cannot live on the money of your
household alone because you will not be able to afford to buy
all the food you need to eat, so therefore you have to find a way
of making some money – therefore we entered the *dangals*.'

'How old were you when you were doing this?'

'From the age of eighteen to forty-five.'

I feel twinges of jealousy. For over twenty-five years of his
adult life Kedar Nath was allowed and encouraged to wrestle
and compete full-time – which is exactly the course I would
have liked my life to have taken.

'You spent all those years travelling and competing around
India?'

'Yes. We really enjoyed going to other parts of India. In our
time there were a lot of *akharas* in the cities. We'd put our things
in the *akhara*, we'd cook our own food in the *akhara*, and eat,
exercise and sleep there. We did everything in the *akhara*.'

'Which bout gave you the most satisfaction?'

'There was a wrestler called Raj Narayan. He was very
famous in his time – he had shown a lot of wrestlers the sky. He
came to Varanasi and I wanted to wrestle him, but his uncle
said I was not eligible to do so, as I was not strong enough. I
felt dishonoured and angry, so I searched for him at *dangals*
and found out that he was wrestling in Hyderabad. I went there
to wrestle him and beat him in two minutes. We took hold and
I suddenly put the *dahk* on him.' A hip throw.

'How do you spend your time now?'

'I rest nowadays. I stay here, eat, take a shower. My sons take
care of the shop.'

During the walk home I tell Pinku that I wish that I, too, had
been given the opportunity to spend my life wrestling, like
Kedar Nath.

'Then you will have to do some good deeds in this life and
come back as a Yadav,' says Pinku. 'But not too many good
deeds, otherwise you will come back as a Brahmin.'

Back in my room, I get out a map of India in order to find
out how far Kedar Nath travelled to challenge Raj Narayan.
Hyderabad is in the state of Andhra Pradesh and nearly 750
miles away to the south. I'm amazed. I imagined Kedar Nath

touring a competition circuit in northern India, not travelling across the whole subcontinent. The lengths to which he went to compete were vast, and he was not even a top-flight wrestler like, say, Sadho Pehalwan.

I feel envious of the licence and encouragement that Kedar Nath was given to wrestle by his mother, caste and culture. My culture didn't encourage me to wrestle. But maybe I wouldn't have embraced wrestling so strongly had I been born into a caste and country in which it was actively encouraged. Perhaps its aura of subversion was part of its appeal.

Chapter 5

A Tight Loincloth

The sound of Pinku in motion comes from the passageway outside – the languid scrape of sandals crossing the floor and the slaps of his feet against the sandals. The high temperature has entered his rhythm. At the end of January, the days became abruptly hotter. Now, mid-February, they are like the busy roads: you don't want to be out in the middle of them – only on either side. Pinku halts at my door and knocks.

'May I come in?' he says.

'Of course.'

He has letters written in longhand that he wants me to type and print. One, he says, is to his dad.

'But Pinku, your father is probably downstairs right at this moment. Why would you want to write him a letter?'

'You don't understand. In India we are having a *dharma* father – I am writing a letter to my *dharma* dad.'

I read the letter. It begins: 'Hi Dad (Sweden)'.

'I'll change that to "Hi, Swedish Dad".'

It continues: 'I don't know whether you know me or not. . . '

'Pinku, I thought you said he was your *dharma* dad. I thought you knew him.'

'I am good friends with his wife. She was here two years ago. She is my *dharma* mother, so he is my *dharma* dad.'

The letter goes on: 'I am sending you an Indian undergarment which we use much in Varanasi. I hope you like it. Signed, your son (not seen) Pinku.'

'You're sending him a loincloth?'

'Yes.'

I imagine the scene in Sweden. It's a winter's day. A man receives a package in the post. He opens it. Inside is a letter from someone in India he has never met who claims to be his son, plus a flimsy item of underwear. I smile to myself as I picture the quizzical look on his face. Moments such as this, when the roles are reversed and Pinku becomes the one full of misunderstanding about my culture, are some of my favourite. I think about how the same things have different meanings in different contexts. In Varanasi a loincloth is a proclamation of moral hygiene, of traditional values, but in Europe it will only amount to an unfathomable-to-bind piece of cotton. In fact Rene says he gave loincloths to friends back home in Holland and they hung them on the wall as art.

Pinku's next letter begins: 'Hello my brothers (Swedish)'.

He has never met these brothers either. This time I leave 'Swedish' in brackets. Whether 'Swedish' is in brackets or not should be the least of Pinku's concerns.

A wrestling teacher tells me that an even greater wrestler than Gama used to live in the village of Kundeshar. He says that in every respect, in every possible way, this man went off the scale. His name was Hari Narayan Singh, and he weighed eight *quintels*, or 800kg, and wore a *kurta* three large people could fit into. He owned 60 cows and 40 water buffalo, and every day he drank nearly all the milk produced by all 60 cows in one milking. He drank from a 10-litre pot and ate 5kg of ghee with breakfast. He exercised with a stone weight of 14 *man* (560kg) and pulled an elephant backwards by the tail just for exercise. When he was angry he would punch the elephant, which would run away in fear. He even killed a lion. The description sounds like a mixture of truth, exaggeration, folklore and myth. I'm eager to discover which element is which and whether Hari Narayan Singh, who is unknown outside India – unknown perhaps outside Uttar Pradesh – redefines the outer limits of physical capability.

Goverdhan Das has heard about Hari Narayan Singh too and would like to write an article about him. I arrange for Anjay, a friend of Pinku, to drive us both to Kundeshar, which is deep in the countryside, so that we can meet Hari Narayan Singh's descendants. One morning Pinku and I get in Anjay's Suzuki Maruti, and we head across town towards Gaya Ghat. Pinku is excited to be going on a road-trip. He sits in the passenger's seat and plays with the stereo.

'Would you like to listen to Michael George?' he asks.

'George Michael? Not really.'

Pinku puts on another tape.

'This music is really fantastic. I'm sure you will be liking it. It is Dr Alban from Sweden.'

'It's My Life' plays. I ask Pinku to put on a Paul Oakenfold tape instead.

'But this is just music, no singing,' he complains.

Pinku respectfully ends the session of Western music when we pick up Goverdhan Das. Anjay navigates the cholesterol of traffic clogging the city streets. We pass a fruit and vegetable market on the outskirts of town, take the bridge across the River Varuna and drive into the countryside. Men pushing barrows of vegetables and orange Tata trucks with eyes painted on their front fenders are heading in the opposite direction. The landscape settles into the tranquil, repetitive groove of mud and brick houses, fields with huge cones of drying dung laid out like haystacks, and cows and bony water buffalo. In Kundeshar we ask after Hari Narayan Singh's family and discover that his grandson, Mahendra, is a doctor with a practice next to a school.

At his surgery, Mahendra is lying cross-legged on a bed with his elbow propped on a bolster. He is a huge man with great forearms, a thick neck and tubby belly. He looks like he comes from another species, one closely related to humans but instantly distinguishable from us by their larger size. Vouching as it does for the family's genetics, his physique opens the case

for believing the fantastic claims made about his grandfather.
At one end of the room is a cabinet of homoeopathic remedies
in dusty bottles, and on the wall behind the dispensing counter
is a painting of Mahendra's grandfather, Hari Narayan Singh
the lion-killer, as an old man. He stands erect and proud, with
his chest out. I ask Mahendra to talk about him. While
Mahendra speaks, patients come in, touch his leg, sit, wait and
approach him when he is ready, at which point he breaks off
from our conversation to take their pulse in the Ayurvedic way
and to make notes. He wears the sacred thread under his *kurta*:
his family is Brahmin.

Mahendra says there was a tradition of both music and
wrestling in his family, and his grandfather was a great player of
the *mirdung*, a drum. Mahendra was 13 years old when his
grandfather died, aged 95 or 96, on 6 June 1949 – he knows
the exact date.

'I didn't know my grandfather that long. When he was old, I
was young, but I have heard a lot about him. My grandfather was
an outstanding man. He memorised all the *Bhagavad Gita*. Early
each morning he would get up and read the *Gita*. Afterwards, he
would intonate, speak, the sounds of the drums, the rhythm of
the *mirdung*: *dada-tee, dada-tee.* When we were young and heard
this we would laugh. We were too young to understand what he
was doing. We thought he was just having fun.'

Mahendra coughs. He has a thick smoker's cough. He takes
a cigarette from a packet and lights it. Trucks drive by with
their klaxons blaring. Goverdhan Das shoos away a couple of
shouting children and sits taking notes.

'Once my grandfather went to his father-in-law's place, and
his sister-in-law played a trick on him. There was a coin with
the head of King Edward on it – a one peisa coin. That family
was also very strong in both wrestling and music. His sister-in-
law took the coin in her hand and folded it in two and said to
Hari Narayan Singh, "I heard you killed a lion. Can you
straighten out this coin?" He was eating and there was a *lota*
nearby. In response, he lifted the *lota* by the rim and squeezed
and folded it, and gave it to her and said, "Can you straighten
this?"

'He used to visit his father's sister's house because that
family was also fond of wrestling and music, and he enjoyed

staying there. He would stay for a month sometimes. There was a place in that village where they tied their animals to stakes in the ground. One stake was really a tree. The upper part of the tree had been cut off and animals were tethered to it. Some villagers decided to play a trick on my grandfather. They said to him, "This stake is not in the proper place, we want to move it," and they started to try to shake it and attempted to lift it out after throwing water on it, but they couldn't. They challenged Hari Narayan Singh – "You have killed a lion, but can you pull this stake out of the ground?" He didn't know it was a tree with roots, but he pulled it out. When he realised it was a tree he told them, "What you have asked of me, I have done, but I will not come to this village again." They had challenged him without his knowing, and he was very angry about it. He made an oath not to visit that village and he never did.'

I ask Mahendra to relate how his grandfather came to kill a lion. He says that when Hari Narayan Singh was in his twenties he set off to compete at a wrestling tournament in Tumkhui, near Gorakhpur. He wanted to wrestle Ghulam, who was the best wrestler in India at the time – this was a generation before Gama. He did not tell his father what he was about to do. When his father found out, he sent a message instructing his son to return home. The family were wealthy Brahmin landowners, and Hari Narayan's father considered it would be shameful for his son to compete for money. Hari Narayan obeyed and came home, but he was frustrated and upset. He journeyed to his wife's place from where he went on pilgrimage by foot to Dwarka, a holy city sacred to Krishna, about a thousand miles away to the west on the Gujarati coast. A servant and a man from his wife's house joined him. They encountered the lion while on the Baroda estate in Gujarat.

'They didn't want to go the long way, which was by road, and decided to take a shortcut through the jungle. However there was a man-eating lion in the jungle, and no one was allowed to enter. Guards stopped them, but at night they took the shortcut anyway. In the jungle they met a *sadhu* called Hari Krishna Das, and the four of them came across the lion together. Hari Narayan told the others to climb trees. When they had done so he threw a stone that hit the lion on its head.

The lion jumped at him. He caught it by both paws and they started to grapple and force each other's limbs back.

'When my grandfather told me this story he used to say, "I would have killed the lion sooner but the problem was it had bad breath." The fight lasted three or four hours until the lion tired and my grandfather threw it to the ground. He put his knee on the lion's chest with so much force that it entered its chest and broke its bones and internal organs. When he took his knee out there were pieces of bone on his leg. Before the lion died it roared in pain. My grandfather was injured and cut too.

'Afterwards he slept. Army guards and others came to the place where it had happened. The other travellers told them not to wake Hari Narayan Singh. The Maharajah of Baroda took him to his palace, and fed and looked after him. He honoured him. The maharajah wanted to reward my grandfather, but he asked for just one thing. "There are a lot of guest houses on your estate," he said. "Please instruct them to give pilgrims free salt for their food." He finished his pilgrimage and came home. That lion was nine feet and seven inches long.'

The story has a neat, satisfying shape. Hari Narayan's father forbade him from challenging Ghulam, India's greatest wrestler, but by chance he was given the opportunity to make his reputation by wrestling a lion, a greater opponent than any human. Serendipity found a way for him to prove himself.

'Did your grandfather say he was frightened by the lion?'

'He told us he wasn't frightened. He said, "The mother of that lion had fed him and my mother had fed me, so it was a case of let's see who was strongest and bravest."'

'What happened to its corpse?'

'The maharajah had it stuffed and sent it to Hari Narayan Singh some time later. He donated it to a Naga Baba from Allahabad who has also passed away.'

'I heard your grandfather pulled an elephant by the tail for exercise.'

'I do not agree with that. That was something different. There was a dispute between relatives. He went to the river to bathe and saw relatives coming on an elephant to attack his family. He ran from the river and caught the elephant by the tail and forced it to sit down. Later, people told the story you have told me and others said that he pulled so strongly that the elephant died soon after, but that is not true.'

Mahendra describes his grandfather's exercise regime.

'You won't believe this,' says Pinku, excited, before he has translated the details. 'He did 10,000 *dands* and 10,000 *bethaks* a day.'

'His wooden slippers are like that,' says Mahendra, using both hands to indicate the length of a giant foot. 'When my sons see his exercise equipment, they don't believe it's possible he could have lifted it. Every day he got up and went to the *akhara* at four in the morning, and came back at ten after bathing, making *puja* and exercising. In the evening he exercised with equipment at home. His hands, shoulders and thighs were very big. His ankles were the same size as his wrists in old age, so you can get an idea of how big his physique was.

'My grandfather was very tall. I myself am six foot two and people say that my grandfather was a foot taller than me – seven feet or something. We saw him in old age. He was really very tall. I can give you an idea of Hari Narayan Singh's weight. When he died we used a special type of bier to carry him to the cremation ground. Usually four people would carry it on their shoulders, but he was very heavy so eight people were needed, and after ten minutes they would become very tired and put it down. They were always putting the bier down. When he was young he weighed five *man* [*200kg*].

'In the last days of his life he presented a wish to be taken to Varanasi. My father took him there. He lived in Varanasi for nineteen days before he died. He died in Assi and they took him to Harischandra Ghat to be cremated. On the day of his death he said to his son, "Go and bathe and then go to the Vishwanath Temple [*an important Shiva temple*] and bring the holy water from the leg of Lord Shiva." My father bathed, went to the Vishwanath Temple and brought the water for my grandfather. Then my grandfather instructed him to change his clothes for him and place him on the ground. My grandfather drank the holy water and then gave up his life. Through the *sadhana* of wrestling he knew he was about to die and that is why he requested to go to Varanasi. He knew he would die that day, so that was why he asked for holy water from the Vishwanath Temple.'

The conversation has wandered into profound territory. According to Hinduism, if you die in Varanasi you attain *moksha*, or liberation from the cycle of rebirths. In effect Mahendra is saying that his grandfather found salvation because through wrestling he developed a remarkable understanding of his body and destiny. Wrestling brought him *moksha*. However, presumably Hari Narayan Singh did not set out to attain liberation through wrestling. Presumably it was only a by-product.

I want to know what Mahendra means when he refers to wrestling as a *sadhana*. The word *sadhana* is part of the vocabulary of religious devotion, so its use in the context of wrestling perhaps indicates a spiritual dimension. I ask Pinku what *sadhana* means exactly. He says 'practice', which is hardly a precise definition. I try, through Pinku, to ask Mahendra about wrestling as a *sadhana*, but we are dealing with ideas and terms that do not literally translate from one language and culture to another, and it is difficult to compose a question properly. We go around in circles for a while.

Mahendra breaks off from our conversation to take a pre-lunch bath behind the surgery – a traditional Indian thing. He takes a large silver bowl with him. He returns a little later with wet hair and adopts the same reclining posture on the bed as before. He gives a consultation then returns to the subject of his grandfather. I try again to find out about wrestling as a *sadhana*.

'The body is not powerful,' says Mahendra. 'Only *atma* [*the soul*] is powerful. Your power comes from the power of *atma*. Look at daily life. You say, "Now I will sleep." When you sleep, first your power of action and desire end. So where has the power of your body gone? It is the *atma* in you that gives you power. Until your *atma* is powerful you cannot realise God. Those who know all the *Gita* know all about *atma*. This is our spirituality. We believe that this body also has a body. So what maintains the body inside the body? *Atma*.'

Before I can clarify what he means by this, Mahendra leaves to have lunch at home. While he is gone, a woman cooks us rice and peas, then eats her lunch on her own. She squats in the small adjoining kitchen among vegetable peelings and plates. After we have eaten and Mahendra has returned, Goverdhan

Das, who has been waiting patiently for his turn to conduct an interview, asks his questions. Though the conversation is in Hindi, I can tell the mood is deteriorating. Goverdhan Das brusquely asks curt questions and Mahendra gives curt answers. Once Goverdhan Das has run through his list, I ask Mahendra again about how *atma* relates to wrestling, but he isn't in the mood to say much now.

'Only *atma* is powerful,' says Mahendra. 'If you don't have strong *atma* in your body then it is useless. All power comes from *atma*. From the power of *atma* I sit, I speak, I stand. You are as powerful as the amount of *atma* you have.'

'How do you make your *atma* strong?'

'Through religious and physical *sadhana*.'

I still don't understand how wrestling builds *atma*, but change the subject anyway. I tell Mahendra that I've heard his grandfather wore a huge *kurta* that three people would fit into.

'If I gave my *kurta* to him, what will happen?' replies Mahendra, as he points to Anjay, who is slightly built.

The stone weight that Hari Narayan Singh used to lift is still in the family. Mahendra leads us to his home, a short walk away, to see it. The stone is behind plastic pipes in a walled garden. A family retainer wipes some hay off it. Hari Narayan Singh's name is inscribed. Mahendra says it weighs 180kg, but it looks about half that weight to me.

We drive back to Varanasi. After we have dropped off Goverdhan Das, Pinku and Anjay fall about laughing.

'Typical frank Banarsi!' says Pinku. He laughs and slaps his thigh. 'Typical frank Banarsi!'

He explains that when we ate rice and peas in the surgery, Goverdhan Das said to the woman who prepared the food, 'We have come to this big kingdom so we are hoping to get something substantial to eat.' By which he meant he expected to be fed more than rice and peas by such a prestigious and wealthy family. Which explains why Goverdhan Das was brusque and surly after lunch. Every time Pinku thinks about it again he cracks into gales of laughter.

The gate to Kali Bari is unlocked. I slip into the park, take off my sandals and sit next to the exercise area and the stone weights. Three schoolboys walk by. When they see me sitting near the *akhara*, they laugh and slap their thighs like wrestlers – entertained by the sight of the foreigner taking an interest in *kushti*.

I like to come to Kali Bari to think. Today I'm feeling the frustration that comes from having to settle for talking to people about events that happened a long time ago – about wrestlers who are now dead – or to people who are old about what they did when they were young, and not being able to witness anything first-hand. There is no way to verify the information I'm being given. Wrestlers leave no hard physical evidence as corroboration. They and their feats live on in memory only. In particular, the stories Mahendra told about his grandfather have been playing on my mind.

Mahendra came across as a credible source. He was a Brahmin doctor and a respected man. He knew the precise length of the lion. He curbed exaggerations. Yet can the details of how Hari Narayan Singh killed the lion really be believed? Could he really have pierced its body with his knee? And could he really have weighed 200kg? Indians routinely misjudge weight, and Mahendra certainly exaggerated the size of his grandfather's stone weight, so it would not be surprising if the figure of 200kg was inaccurate, but then again if Hari Narayan Singh was seven feet tall, perhaps he did weigh that much. However it is almost impossible to believe that Hari Narayan Singh did 10,000 *dands* and 10,000 *bethaks* a day. The figure 10,000 sounds rhetorical and unrealistic, like a conveniently high and round number you'd give in casual conversation in order to impress. No doubt Hari Narayan Singh performed *bethaks* and *dands* in their thousands, but it strains credibility to think that he did 10,000 of each every day. On the other hand, the fact that it's unlikely doesn't necessarily mean it isn't true.

I contemplate the stone weights laid out in front of me. Their immense size grounds the stories I've heard in reality. Here at least is physical evidence of a sort. These huge stones could only have been lifted by huge men, and the men who lifted them came from the same generations as India's great wrestlers. Indirectly, the stones speak for those wrestlers and argue that they were capable of doing the amazing things that people claim. Since Rajan first brought me here, I've made a special effort to find out exactly how the stones were lifted. They are called *naals*, and I was right to doubt they were balanced on the back of the neck. They were actually held behind the head, then lifted above the head. As I consider the enormity of the larger stones, a feeling of uncertainty takes hold. They are so large that it is almost unimaginable that anyone could lift them in this way. What if no one ever actually did? What if these huge stones are only ornamental? I decide there and then that I have to find out if they have ever been lifted. It feels as if there's a lot at stake.

Pinku asks around and discovers that a man called Shiv Nath Sardar used to be well known for exercising with the stones. He is now dead, but his family have a *chai* shop in the area. Pinku and I visit the place one afternoon. It is small, cavernous and dingy. A man sits on the floor and kneads a hunk of dough. This, Pinku establishes, is Shiv Nath Sardar's son. He stops what he is doing and sits with us at an empty table.

'My father died 23 years ago aged about 66,' he says. 'He competed as a weight-lifter. Every day he went to the park at two o'clock to lift the stones. He also did between 3,000 and 4,000 *dands* and the same number of *bethaks* a day.'

'How big was he?'

'He had a huge body and was as tall as you,' says the son, pointing to Pinku.

'Do you know how heavy the heaviest stone is in Kali Bari that your father lifted?'

'He lifted heavier ones than those. There is a larger one in the Durga Temple in Durgakund that he lifted. He lifted heavier stones in competition too. We threw some of them down the well beside Kali Bari *akhara* because no one could lift them any more, and people were sitting on them or urinating on them. It was a dishonour for the stones, so we threw them down the well.'

The ones remaining at Kali Bari set an open challenge. Anyone at any time has the opportunity to go to the park, accept the challenge, and prove their strength by lifting them. But it's doubtful anyone ever will, and for now they remain dusty and cobwebbed with disuse – goading the younger generation with the certainty that they are not as strong as their grandfathers used to be. Perhaps these stones, too, will soon end up in the well and the public shaming will come to an end.

Much of life at the Pandey household centres on the roof. Mamaji and Poonam go there to dry chillies or sift lentils. Pinku goes there to chat to neighbours. Rene goes there to practise *boneti*. Recently I came home, went out onto the roof and saw that Pinku had just washed the stray cat that the family has adopted. The Pandeys are trying to indoctrinate her into the Brahmin way of life. They want her to wash regularly like a good Hindu. The cat was shivering and sulked near a wall. An empty bucket stood nearby. It had taken four people to wash her, said Pinku. As he spoke, he picked out dirt from her ears. After she was left alone, the cat licked herself clean. The night before, the Pandeys had been on the verge of getting rid of her.

'It is very bad,' Pinku had said. 'She has changed from eating what my mother gives her to non-vegetarian. It is a problem. She brings in the dead mouse. We are thinking of giving her away or throwing her out on the street.'

To highlight her shameful digression from vegetarianism, Pinku's father used a stick to hockey out a tail from under the dining table. Pinku kicked it towards the front door and into the alleyway.

Last night I ate dinner at the same time as Pinku's father. While I sat at the table, he sat on his bed. Mr Pandey held a dish in his left hand, and used his right to make balls of rice and *dhal*. The cat jumped on my lap, so I tipped her off. She went over to Mr Pandey and jumped on his knees. Without putting down his dish, he used his elbow to get her off. She then returned to my lap. It went on and on like this. Every time Mr Pandey got rid of the cat she jumped back on my lap; every time I got rid of her she went back to Mr Pandey. You didn't have to be a pet psychologist to realise she was hungry.

'Maybe she is hungry,' I said, with a lot of understatement.

'She has food in her bowl which she hasn't eaten,' said Mr Pandey.

I looked over at the bowl. A half-moon of chapatti flopped over the side. The cat had been fed rice and *dhal* too, but hadn't touched any of it. I searched for the right language with which to make it clear to a Hindu that perhaps she would prefer to be fed meat.

'Maybe she is non-veg.'

'She is vegetarian and non-vegetarian both,' countered Mr Pandey.

The cat was not the only pet struggling with the Hindu diet. An uneaten chapatti poked through the bars of the parakeet's cage too.

Pinku relays a phone message from Goverdhan Das. He has noted my interest in the spiritual dimension of wrestling and saw how I struggled to comprehend Mahendra's exposition, so he has arranged for us to go together to meet a man, Neel Kanth Shastri, whom he says will be able to clarify everything. Mr Shastri used to be director of the Uttar Pradesh State Museum in Lucknow and is an authority on physical training in India. Whenever Pinku refers to him in the days preceding our meeting, he frowns and adopts a particularly stern voice in order to underline Neel Kanth Shastri's intellectual gravity. He describes him as a 'very luminary guy' – luminosity being a particularly venerated quality in Varanasi, as it is often proudly described as the 'luminous city'.

Mr Shastri's home overlooks the *ghats* near the railway bridge. He is a small, accomplished-looking man. On his shelves are art pieces and knick-knacks – among them a bust of Buddha and an art deco figure – that suggest he is well travelled for a Banarsi and has taken an interest in ideas and cultures beyond the Hindu mainstream. He explains that back in the 1950s he took classes in the history of physical culture in India. He found, though, that there were no books devoted to the subject, only a few stray articles, so he collected material from the Epics, Puranas, Vedas and certain books – such as *Manosollasa*, written by King Someswara, who ruled Vijayanagar in the twelfth century, which devotes a chapter to wrestling – as well as accounts written by travellers, and with this information he compiled a book that remains unpublished. He sifts through the yellowing manuscript and gives a précis of each passage he thinks will be of interest, speaking in a refined, quirky English. After he has spoken for some time, I judge the moment right to ask whether he found any reference to wrestling as a spiritual path.

'Er, no. As a matter of fact, you see, practice of wrestling exercises and practice of spiritual exercises are two different things. Wrestling is as a matter of fact the material aspect of our life, while spiritualism is actually a post-material aspect. A spiritualist can be a wrestler, but a wrestler cannot necessarily be a spiritualist. In one way wrestling is useful, because you see for practising of spiritual exercise and all that you must have your body hale and hearty. It is said that body is the root cause of religious practices, and therefore if body is sound and hale and hearty, only then can you follow the religious practices to the full. And therefore for keeping your body hale and hearty you must practise different exercises, specially yogic exercises, *asanas*, and all that. Now yogic exercises are useful for the wrestling purposes also, but they are not meant for wrestling.'

'So wrestling would give you a healthy body, which is the foundation for spiritual development, but that's it.'

'Ah yes, that's only. . . But it would be too far to say that wrestler would be a saint. Wrestler would not necessarily be a saint.' He uses the word 'saint' for my benefit but means *sadhu*. 'There are some common practices – celibacy, that is a common practice to the saint and the wrestler; control over your food, a common practice to the saint as to the wrestler – but so far as the different passions are concerned, a wrestler may not be required to control all the passions as such, but a spiritual person must control his passions.'

'And you said that wrestling is part of the material world. How do you mean?'

'Yes, it is part in this way: for example, just say affairs of war, battlefields, earning riches, earning name and fame, getting yourself married and getting yourself children – all these form part of worldly activities. They do not have any direct relations with spiritualism. Similarly, wrestling is an activity mostly confined to worldly activities. Even the gods are worshipped not for spiritual welfare, but for physical victory and all that.'

'And you're saying that wrestling is a worldly pursuit in the sense that it is undertaken to increase your name, to give you a reputation.'

'Name, fame, *et cetera*, which are worldly things.'

The conversation moves on to other topics, but I find it difficult to concentrate on the subject in hand, and keep returning in my thoughts to what Mr Shastri has just said. Wrestling can help create a platform for a spiritual life, but nothing more than that. I hoped that wrestling would have spiritual significance in India – value beyond the ordinary – but now, after listening to Mr Shastri, wrestling somehow seems diminished and small.

His exposition is authoritative and apparently conclusive: no direct connection exists between wrestling and the spiritual life. Yet I know for a fact that Goverdhan Das, who is sitting silently out of deference to Mr Shastri, strongly disagrees. Goverdhan Das believes wrestling and the spiritual life can coincide and that proof lies in the story of a wrestler who died over 50 years ago: Bishember Chobe.

It was Bishember Chobe to whom Goverdhan Das was referring during our first meeting when he spoke of a wrestler so celibate that he emitted semen. I've clarified the details of the story since. According to Goverdhan Das, Bishember Chobe was born in 1899 and died in 1942. He lived in Maturah, which is near Delhi and the birthplace of Krishna – to whom the Chobes, a Brahmin caste, are devoted. Goverdhan Das maintains that Bishember Chobe's body proved too weak a vessel to contain the immense pressure that built up inside him due to his celibacy. Semen burst out of his skin as a result.

Up till now I've discounted the tale as too bizarre for words and have been filing it away in my mind as the 'Sperm Stigmata Story' – a story to be shared with other foreigners and travellers when we try to outdo each other with anecdotes about the strangeness of Indian culture. But I'm now beginning to wonder whether that may be a mistake and whether the tale may be worth investigating. I don't for a second believe semen literally erupted from Bishember Chobe's body, but the more I understand wrestling in India and the more I see how, in an oral culture such as *pehalwani*, tales are often tidied into visual and dramatic narratives, the more I realise that this graphic image serves the purpose of communicating a devotion to celibacy that is remarkable in its intensity and fascinating in itself.

I've become more and more interested in the subject of celibacy after reading a book that made it clear it's to do with more than just avoiding sex. In fact the concept Indians talk about, *brahmacharya*, doesn't really translate as 'celibacy' but is a term with wider meaning. To understand this expanded definition, I spoke to two *sadhus* who live in ashrams nearby. *Sadhus* are supposed to retain their semen and sublimate it into spiritual energy, while wrestlers are supposed to retain their semen in order to be strong. Whatever the aim, the principles of *brahmacharya* are the same. According to the Indian health system of Ayurveda, semen is a source of vitality, and wrestlers and *sadhus* should protect their store of the fluid. It can be lost if you so much as think about sex or stare at a woman with lust in mind. Every sexual thought, act or feeling, from flirting to winking, is supposed to have the same effect. You can also lose semen if you express emotions such as anger and greed. Followers of *brahmacharya* should eat *sattvic* foods, which don't inflame desire, go to bed and rise early, and perform *pranayama* (yogic breathing exercises). According to the belief, semen is lost in sweat, urine and stool if these rules are not followed. It is maintained that those who do stick to the rules develop *ooja*, a type of vitality apparent in the lustre and shine of skin, eyes and hair.

These are not ideas that will stand you in good stead if you plan to pass physiology exams in the West, but this is what is believed in India. In effect, a wrestler who follows *brahmacharya* is required to live a monkish life away from worldly passions, which sounds like a fundamentally spiritual existence to me. As far as I can tell, wrestlers no longer actually do follow the full tenets of *brahmacharya* – but if, as the Sperm Stigmata Story suggests, Bishember Chobe kept the tightest of tight loincloths, maybe he did.

I call on Goverdhan Das and tell him I'm thinking about visiting Maturah to find out more about Bishember Chobe.

'You don't have to go to Maturah,' he says. 'There is a place in Varanasi you can visit, the *akhara* of the Chobe people of Maturah, where a man called Thakure Chobe stays whom you can speak with. He knows about Bishember Chobe. I will take you over there to meet him now.'

We leave his house. Goverdhan Das stops at a shop on the way to buy a box of sweets as a gift for Thakure.

'Otherwise he will think we have only come for our purpose,' he says.

Thakure is resting on a bed under some covers in a gallery at one end of the *akhara*. He is a small man in his seventies. His few teeth reflect the faint evening light. After we have been introduced, he gets up to put a light on then sits down again. I ask him about Bishember Chobe.

'The Maharajah of Khadipur kept a hundred wrestlers at his estate. Bishember Chobe was one of them. He was *brahmacharya* from childhood and his semen started to come out of his body.'

'Did you see this?'

'When he died, I was a child, but I know about him. There are 4,000 Chobes in Maturah, all connected with one another. I did not see it myself, but I heard about it from my elders. When Bishember Chobe became sick – he died at an early age – semen came from his foot.'

'Where exactly did it come from?'

Thakure lifts his foot and points to the centre of the sole. 'From here. A doctor advised him to have sex. The doctor said he needed a woman right away, otherwise. . . The rajah sent a prostitute to him, but was not successful.'

'Did the semen emerge when he exercised or when he lay down?' asks Goverdhan Das.

'When he exercised,' says Thakure. 'It has also happened to others, including myself. In winter the soles of our feet stick to our shoes. That means that the semen has come out the body.'

'That is a different thing,' says Goverdhan Das, fiercely. He discusses the subject at length with Thakure. Though the conversation is in Hindi, I can tell Goverdhan Das is wriggling like a barrister who has confidently set out to cross-examine a star witness only for the witness's evidence to undermine his own case. And now that the Sperm Stigmata Story has begun to disown Goverdhan Das and the simplistic ethical universe in which he operates, it becomes more interesting to me – as well as a mystery I can magnanimously step in to solve.

Pinku has to study for exams, so Bablu agrees to come in his place to Maturah to interpret. Bablu is more mature and laid-back than his younger brother, and has a greater personal empathy with the masculine subject matter of wrestling: he boxed as an amateur at university and his gloves and focus mitts hang disintegrating in the place where the Pandeys keep discarded bits and pieces upstairs. Their disintegration mirrors a change within him. He used to have a tough-guy reputation, but now he is married and older, and the young man's bravado has gone.

A note chalked on a board at Varanasi station says the train will only be an hour late. We stand, waiting, on the platform, which is patrolled by beggars. A beaming derelict stalks around, too out of it even to beg. He has a tooth earring and odd shoes – a dirty, dusty, grey canvas lace-up on one foot, a flip-flop on the other – and wears old, dry garlands around his neck, and plastic bags stuffed under his clothes. The train arrives. We quickly find our designated seats. A middle-aged Indian, with a deep, thin U-shape Krishna *puja* mark on his forehead, sits next to me. He too is headed for Maturah. A French backpacker rushes to stow his sitar case in the compartment before the limited luggage space is taken. Afterwards, he sits and relaxes with a roll-up. His hands are pinky-red and shake.

That night I sleep in fits and starts on the top bunk, which is ironing-board thin, and use my laptop bag as a lumpy pillow. In the morning, I sit looking out the window. Villagers squat in the fields either side of the track to go to the toilet. In the towns they squat near the line – near grey pigs and piles of rubbish. A fellow passenger wearing an orange sari covers her nose with her shawl every time we pass the railway-side stench. Bablu and I get off at Maturah with a crippled boy who earlier dragged himself along the floor of the carriage to beg. One of his legs is wasted from the knee downward and folded back along the length of his thigh like the leg of a stuck deckchair; the other is bent from the knee at a right angle, like an insect's. He moves along the platform by pulling himself forwards with his hands, in which he holds a pair of flip-flops.

We find our contact, Ova Guru, the son of Thakure, in the winding alleys behind the *ghats*. He is in his late twenties and unshaven, and has a coarse face, a growly voice and curly black oiled hair. His forehead has a yellow sweaty sheen and there are dark patches around his eyes. He could be stoned: the Chobes of Maturah like to take *bhang*, a derivative of cannabis. For the next couple of days, Ova shows us around. He takes us to Chobe *akharas*, introduces us to Chobe wrestlers and gurus, and reflexively takes us to pilgrimage sites that relate to Krishna – his job is to act as a guide to Krishna-related sites and temples in the city.

On the afternoon of the second day, Ova takes us to the home of Galu Chobe, Bishember's 70-year-old nephew. The four of us sit on sacking in a small and simple room. From behind the building comes an electronic noise that sounds like a pinball machine, a sound that is one of the few modern things in the house. Galu has great flaps for ears and wears a traditional *dhoti-kurta*. He sits back and leans an elbow on a low bed, and speaks about his uncle with a profound love and sincerity that is touching. As he speaks about Bishember, he is filled with a meditative, peaceful force, as though he only has to talk about him to become more holy himself.

'Due to his blessing I get up and he takes care of us and the whole day goes well,' he says. By us, he means he and his wife.

A small, framed photo of Bishember captioned 'Champion of India' hangs from a row of pegs. Every morning Galu smears Bishember's forehead with a sandalwood-paste *tikka* and offers him flowers.

Galu's father died when he was three years old. Bishember took care of him until he too died when Galu was twelve. As the champion wrestler of the Maharajah of Khadipur, Bishember divided most of his time between the *akhara* at the maharajah's estate and an *akhara* in Maturah.

Galu says: 'My father was Falgu Pehalwan, the elder brother of Bishember. My father made Bishember as a wrestler. Five hundred wrestlers would come and go from the Maharajah's estate and at any one time there would be a hundred wrestlers living there. My father was in charge of them all. Bishember began wrestling when he was six. My father took him to Khadipur when he was twenty. He stayed for fourteen months on one loincloth and during that time he became stronger than everybody. Every day he did 5,000 *dands* and 5,000 *bethaks*, and wrestled sixty wrestlers. The maharajah had a rule that the person who could beat everyone would wrestle first in the *akhara*, which Bishember did. It was his daily duty and he was paid one rupiah a day extra for this. The maharajah provided all his food.

'Puran Singh became a disciple of Bishember's.' I assume Puran Singh must be another well-known Pehalwan. 'Bishember was sick when Puran Singh visited the estate. He had diarrhoea and went to the toilet a hundred times, day and night. Puran Singh said, "I have heard about Bishember Chobe's reputation and have come all this way to wrestle him but he won't show."

'The maharajah said to someone, "Puran Singh is here, but where is Pehalwan? What is this?" Bishember said, "All right." He came and drank some water and took some medicine to stop the diarrhoea, and tightened his loincloth. The pair wrestled. Soon Puran said he felt like he was about to die. Bishember replied, "I haven't even warmed my hands up yet and you are telling me you are dying?" But Puran complained that his strength was ineffectual.

'They wrestled in the *akhara* for seven days. Afterwards Puran said, "No one told me he was sick, and while he was sick he did this to me. What would have happened if he were well?" Puran became Bishember's disciple and offered him a loincloth.'

This is part of a wrestler's initiation ritual. The student gives his guru a loincloth, and the guru blesses him and gives it back.

'There was a Pehalwan called Chandra Sane,' continues Galu. 'He used to say that he was prepared to fight Bishember Chobe, so the maharajah called him to Khadipur. Chandra Sane asked for 5,000 rupees. When Bishember Chobe came, they went to the police station, because at that time all bouts had to be registered there. Bishember never wore fancy clothes. He just covered himself with simple cloth and went to the police station. So Chandra Sane said, "I want to see his body. Without seeing his physique, how can I fight?" This was his ruse to see Bishember's body and get an idea of his strength.

'When Bishember uncovered himself, Chandra Sane said there would be wrestling but not right then. And he told his *ustadh* [*teacher*], "Why do you want my prestige to drain away into the soil? If I fight him he will beat me. I will only fight if he plays a fixed match." Bishember never told a lie – he never reneged on his *brahmacharya* or lied. "I don't want to play tricks," he said. "You can give him the full 10,000 rupees rather than 5,000, because I don't need any money. I cannot involve myself in any deception."

'Bishember was never frightened of anyone or anything. People used to say that hundreds of cobras resided in Khadipur. Everyone used to sleep indoors except Bishember. He slept under a tree. People would say, "Why do you sleep outside when there are so many snakes?" He would reply, "But what's the worst thing that can happen to me? Only that I will die." But nothing ever did happen to him.

'He was never afraid. He told us that once he was with a group of people and it was a little late in the day and they had to cross the Ganga at a point where it was very wide. Bishember told the others that it was not the right time to cross. But they replied, "What are you saying? Let's go." They started wading through the river, which was low, and Bishember followed suit. A snake that was drifting in the current coiled itself around his thigh. Anyone else would have died of fear, but Bishember thought that the snake was also a living being and that it had come to him for protection. He crossed the half-mile to the far bank with the snake coiled around his thigh, and when he reached the other side the snake uncoiled itself from his leg and slithered off into a thicket.'

The meaning of these stories is not that Bishember was fearless in the macho sense but that he was spiritually at peace. He was more concerned about the eternal life of the soul, or *atma*, and less about the body. Galu tells some other anecdotes that make this plain – stories in which I sense the still centre from which Bishember lived.

'Bishember followed *brahmacharya* from birth,' says Galu. 'He always stayed away from four things: sexual feelings, anger, greed and worldly attachments. Once the maharajah told him to get married and said he would pay all the expenses. Bishember told him, "I have made a vow that I will follow *brahmacharya*."

'The maharajah said, "But if you stick to *brahmacharya* too closely you will become diseased and your body will be destroyed."

'Bishember replied, "Everyone has to leave their body; nobody can run away from death. I have to keep my vows."

'Then the maharajah said, "If you marry I will give you so much land and money that seven generations of your family will be able to eat without getting up from their seats. You can have whatever you want."

'Bishember told the maharajah, "Never say that again or I will leave. I cannot break my vows."

'The maharajah persisted. He tried using a prostitute. She was the most beautiful prostitute in his kingdom. People were tormented by her beauty. She used to come and sing at court. Bishember used to do *dands* by himself. The maharajah sent her to see him there, alone, but he didn't look at her and she was unable to do a thing.

'She went back to the maharajah and told him, "Maharajah, never bring the subject of Bishember Chobe up again. He is like a god. He doesn't even have the desire to look at me. I cannot do a thing. I realised that if he looked at me I would have been burnt to ashes. He is that intense."'

This focus, this one-pointedness, is said to follow from *brahmacharya*.

'Did the rajah send a prostitute after the semen started to come from his body?'

'No, she went there before it happened. He was fine at the time. The rajah sent the prostitute after Gama came to Khadipur with sixty disciples. Gama visited, but the rajah told him he would not be able to fight Bishember straight away. "Stay here a few days and eat," he said. "After a bit I will arrange a bout."

'Gama told his sixty disciples to fight with Bishember, which they did. He wanted to test Bishember's strength. Bishember fought them all, and the next day Gama told the rajah that he had some work to do and left. Before leaving, he told the maharajah that Bishember's *brahmacharya* was too much. He said, "If you can lighten his *brahmacharya* he can stay young, but otherwise he will be destroyed." That was the reason that the maharajah sent the prostitute.'

'Tell me the story of how semen emerged from your uncle's body.'

'Bishember left this house one night at ten o'clock to sleep on Bengali Ghat.' This is in Maturah. 'That night one of my uncles became sick with fever and left his body at four in the morning. Somebody went to tell Bishember. He awoke suddenly, put his feet on the ground and his left foot burst open. He went to a surgeon for treatment. The surgeon told him he would have to have his little toe amputated, otherwise there would be a serious infection. He told him to smell an anaesthetic. But Bishember said he didn't want to take anaesthetic. "You can make me smell it if I interrupt your surgery," he said. "I will sit here while you do your surgery – do whatever you want. If I stop your hands going about their business, then you can use anaesthetic."

'He sat there while the surgeon worked. I saw this with my own eyes. He just chanted "*Rama, Rama*" and said nothing else. The surgeon said, "I have given thousands of treatments but I have never seen a human being like this. If you cut someone just a little bit they will start to scream. I have given him major surgery and he didn't say a word. He must be a god."

'I held his foot and saw everything. The surgeon drained the liquid, including the semen, from his toe with a needle.'

'How did you know that the liquid was semen?' I ask.

'There was blood and pus, and what we call pus also contains semen. The white-coloured stuff, that is semen.'

I splutter and repeat what he had said, 'Pus is semen?' But there is no point in arguing the point. This is what he believes.

'What age was he when this happened?'

'He was forty-five. After my uncle died he used to stay at this house. He went to the *akhara* very infrequently. He stayed here for six months and after that he died. He died very simply – he was not very sick. He didn't catch any diseases.'

'When Bishember was in Maturah, he lived and slept at Ghiradher Walli *akhara* and only came to the family house to eat,' says Galu. 'He would wake up at three in the morning and start to exercise and do wrestling practice. After that he would let his sweat dry and make *puja*. His disciples would go to cook food, and whatever time they took to cook – one or two hours – during that he used to do *puja*. After that he had lunch. He was very particular and strict about food.'

While we've been speaking, Galu's wife has gone to a metal locker and taken out three packages of papers, notes, documents and letters wrapped in yellow cloth. When our conversation comes to a natural end, Galu unties the knots that bind the bundles and takes out a postcard. It is addressed to Bishember Chobe and dated July 1942, the year of his death. It was sent to his *akhara* in Maturah by wrestlers living in Khadipur and begins: 'To my respected guru, Bishember Nathji, we are saying to you that we are touching your feet. The news is this: we are OK and fine. Every day we pray for your well-being.'

When Bablu and I leave Galu's home it's like leaving a cinema after a film has moved you. We leave in silence by a staircase at the back of the house that leads down to the street. It takes a while to adjust to the lights and noise. In Galu's small room, a new destination was reached: a definition of a wrestler as a spiritual figure. When Goverdhan Das spoke about Bishember Chobe, I imagined him as a bland role model for young wrestlers, but the real Bishember Chobe was far more profound than that. He followed an inner authority. He was in command of his destiny and there was autonomy in his life. He was a devout Hindu who chose a lifestyle of intense self-discipline for religious reasons, but also as a form of economy to remove the worldly attachments and emotions that he believed – that Indians believe – drain you of your masculine energies and undermine wrestling ability. He cut away all wasteful expenditure in his life – sex, sexual thoughts, anger, material wealth – and devoted all his energies towards worship and wrestling. His concentration, his intensity, drill out of his life story and into me. I can feel the surge of his stare from a distance of 70 years.

Bishember Chobe was the living embodiment of the ideal Indian wrestler. He was not only great in a technical sense, but also humble, fiercely self-disciplined and a devotee of *brahmacharya*. He lived a cloistered life behind *akhara* walls that kept him sealed in the correct microclimatic conditions to grow and thrive as a Pehalwan. There he followed a regime of hard exercise, religious devotion and wrestling.

The *akhara* where Bishember Chobe stayed in Maturah is near a bus station. Bablu and I go and find it. We enter a yellow-walled room with blue shutters. A large photo of Bishember Chobe hangs beneath a clock. He stands in the generic Pehalwan pose: chest puffed out, arms thrown back, squinting. He looks heavy in the gangster sense of the word. India thinks in different categories: a holy man can resemble a gangster; a tough guy can build a reputation for never having sex; a wrestler can be worshipped 60 years after his death. India thinks in different categories – and I've been thinking in the wrong ones.

The answer to the question of whether wrestling has spiritual significance has been under my nose all along. I came to India with my own idea of how wrestling could have a spiritual dimension. I saw spiritual value in the process of developing a meditative state of mind to navigate the chaos of sparring and competition, but soon learnt that Indian wrestlers do not think in those terms. The importance of winning is not outweighed by any conceivable spiritual benefits gained from developing a meditative mind-set: Indians wrestle to increase their name, to enhance their status, gain respect, recognition, fame – which are, as Mr Shastri said, worldly aims. This fact remains firm and immovable.

But what I've been missing is that Indians see spiritual significance in the process of preparation as distinct from the moment of competition. The emphasis is different. Wrestling does have a spiritual dimension in India. It exists in the way a wrestler such as Bishember Chobe divorced himself from the rest of the community to live a monkish life. It exists in the discipline of following the full tenets of *brahmacharya* – no flirting, anger or greed. It is present when you ask aching muscles to deliver thousands of *dands* and *bethaks* a day. Indians believe that to become a good wrestler takes monumental devotion: a wrestler's whole life – from emotions to diet, to sexual proclivity, to the time he wakes up and the time he goes to bed – have to be part of this effort, and it is through total alignment of a wrestler's life towards the needs of wrestling that he enters profound spiritual territory. This is why, in India, they compare wrestlers such as Bishember Chobe to *sadhus*. This is what the man in the white *kurta-pyjamas* was alluding to at Kali Bari during that first *akhara* visit when he said wrestlers are holy men. The ideal Indian wrestler lives the life of an ascetic. He leads a life of intense discipline and hard daily training.

The act of wrestling itself is not understood to be a spiritual

act, but in order to win worldly rewards you are supposed to
enter into a contract to lead a life of huge self-sacrifice. I think
back to my own years of peak training as a wrestler and how I
entered into a similar contract. Unlike in India, there was no
wrestlers' code in England, yet I, too, had to be self-disciplined.
My life, too, had to revolve around a heavy schedule of
wrestling, exercise, eating and rest. I, too, retreated from
normal everyday life and became something of a monk.
Wrestling is a hard taskmistress who will ask you to lead a
clean, monkish existence irrespective of whether you live in
India, London or Kyrgyzstan. She, herself, pulls you into
spiritual territory.

★

Bablu and some neighbours are playing cricket along the
corridor of an alley near the Pandey family home. The game is
on pause. Bablu is in to bat, but he has to wait for an ice-cream
seller to move his cart from the middle of the *ad hoc* wicket,
and after that for a man riding a scooter to pass through. The
bowler waits patiently too. He stands at the beginning of his
approach down the alley, with a tennis ball in hand.
Everywhere in Varanasi an enthusiasm for cricket triumphs
over space, equipment and traffic. Careful games are played on
the flat roofs of houses; deliveries are bowled in the alleys with
a sister for a wicketkeeper, without a wicket to keep, with
stumps made from imagination and two brick pieces, and a bat
that needs imagination too, sometimes a stick; or if there is a
real bat it is often missing a handle or made from plastic.

I enjoy seeing the enthusiasm with which cricket is played,
but I can't help but also feel sad. Fifty years ago, a hundred
years ago, the passion channelled into cricket would have been
channelled into wrestling. The local youth would have reported
to local *akharas* every morning, oiled their bodies, performed
dands and *bethaks*, and wrestled. But today, while cricket
prospers, many of the *akharas* in Varanasi are being knocked
down to make way for housing and shopping complexes, or are
derelict, or idle. Cricket, of course, is a recent importation. It
came to India with the British Empire, and Indians have
adopted it as their own. *Kushti* is not like cricket. It is part of
what makes India India and not somewhere else. Cricket is a

modern international sport with uniform rules; *kushti* is a traditional art with its own particular identity. Comparing cricket with *kushti* is like comparing a generic global product with an indigenous local craft.

I gave up trying to establish a history of *kushti* a while ago. Whenever I asked anyone about its origins, they would typically refer to Krishna and Balarama as the first wrestlers in India and then fast-forward to the era of Gama, moving from myth to 1910 within a few sentences. I have my own ideas about the antiquity of India's wrestling culture. Though the rules will have changed and there will have been different styles of wrestling in different parts of India at different times, the idiom in which it is practised that gives it its essential character – oiling the body, wrestling on earth, *brahmacharya*, worship of a god at the *akhara* – could quite conceivably be thousands of years old.

But now *kushti* is dying. India is packing it away in the basement as it makes room for new imports: cricket, Western fashion, love marriages. There it will remain, like an unfashionable piece of furniture. Perhaps one day it will be thrown out onto the street. Yet maybe India will come to regret that. Perhaps a later generation will decide that the modern things it thought would make it happy actually don't, and search within its own culture, look towards its own heritage, for real soul and value, which can be found in *kushti*. In a way, I have journeyed from India's future – I'm an emissary from the modern developed world it aspires to join, from London, a city with no wrestling places – and I, for one, am full of regret.

The ice-cream seller and scooter-rider move out of the way, and the cricket match recommences. The bowler makes a good delivery.

'What was that?' I ask a neighbour, who is sitting watching from the seat of a parked scooter.

'A Yorker,' he replies. 'Super line and length!'

Glossary

Akhara: term for a wrestling gym.

Asana: yoga position.

Atma: soul.

Banarsi: inhabitant of Banaras, which is another name for Varanasi.

Bhagavad Gita: a Hindu scripture.

Bhang: cannabis derivative.

Bethak: traditional physical exercise; a squat without weight performed rapidly on the balls of the feet.

Boneti: weapon art.

Brahmacharya: system of ascetic practices followed by *sadhus*, wrestlers and others. Celibacy is a central tenet.

Chai: type of sweet, spicy, milky tea drunk all over India.

Dahk: a hip throw.

Dahl: typically a lentil stew.

Dand: traditional physical exercise not dissimilar to a press-up (see p. 34 for a description).

Dangal: wrestling competition.

Dharma: ideology of caste duty and obligation that encompasses ritual and moral behaviour.

Dhoti-kurta: traditional Indian clothes combination. A *dhoti* is a loin wrap and is tied intricately, while a *kurta* is a long, collarless shirt.

Gada: either a piece of weight-training equipment, or an ornamental mace typically given to a wrestler as a prize. An exercise *gada* consists of a long wooden handle with a bulb-shaped stone weight at one end, while prize *gadas* are silver or gold and smaller. Hanuman is often depicted carrying the latter.

Ganga: River Ganges.

Ghat: large flight of stone steps descending to a river.

Ghee: clarified butter.

Gunda: mafia figure.

Hanuman: monkey god. His exploits are described in the *Ramayana*.

Jori: traditional Indian exercise performed with two wooden clubs that can weigh as much as 45kg each. The clubs, called *mugdars*, are held behind the back. Each is lifted and powered onto a shoulder in turn. Lifting both counts as one hand of *jori*. There are *akharas* in Varanasi devoted solely to *jori*, and *jori* competitions are also held. *Mugdars* are often beautifully painted with flowers and deities, and so on. Also practised in Iran.

Kurta: a type of long shirt with a collarless neck.

Kurta-pyjamas: traditional men's clothes combination. A long collarless shirt worn with a particular type of trouser.

Kushti: the traditional wrestling style practised in India.

Langota: loincloth.

Lathi: bamboo stick.

Lota: wide-rimmed pot.

Lunghi: a wrap. Like a sarong and worn in the same uncomplicated way.

Malai: thick cream.

Man: unit of weight – just under 40kg.

Mirdung: a type of drum.

Moksha: liberation from the cycle of rebirths.

Naal: stone exercise weight shaped like a ring doughnut. Can be of two types: one kind has a diametrical handle in the centre and is lifted above the head; the other does not have such a handle and is worn around the neck. The person will then either squat, walk or jog.

Neem: sacred tree believed to have medicinal properties. *Neem* twigs are commonly used to brush teeth.

Ooja: vitality and lustre that come from following the tenents of *brahmacharya*.

Paan: mixture of betel nut, lime and other ingredients that is chewed. *Paan* has a stimulant effect and is mildly intoxicating; comes wrapped in a betel leaf.

Pehalwan: title given to a wrestler of standing.

Pehalwani: the training regimen of the serious wrestler.

Pipal: sacred tree associated with shrines and often found at *akharas*.

Pranayama: breathing exercises.

Puja: Hindu act of worship.

Quintel: unit of weight – 100kg.

Sadhu: world-renouncer.

Sattvic: one of three Ayurvedic classifications of food. *Sattvic* food does not inflame passions and is suitable for those on a spiritual path.

Tikka: a dot of colour that is ritually pasted on the middle of the forehead.

Ustadh: teacher or guru.

PART II

Mongolia

May to September 1999

Chapter 6

Giant

The caretaker of the wrestling school says Bayanmunkh has just left though he may still be in the carpark. I find him there, sitting in the driver's seat of his Mitsubishi Land-Cruiser with the door half open, rifling through papers. He is in his fifties and wears a grey suit and tie like a businessman, but his flattened ear betrays the fact that he is a wrestler. A ten-time champion of Mongolia, he holds the title of Giant, the highest attainable in traditional Mongolian wrestling, and has also won an Olympic silver medal in Freestyle. Emkhee, my interpreter, approaches Bayanmunkh, smiles, and affects an incredibly polite and submissive, girly voice to ask him whether he will agree to an interview. Without looking at me, without acknowledging my existence in any way, he speaks firmly to Emkhee in Mongolian, shuts the car door and drives off. Clearly there isn't going to be an interview.

'What did he say exactly?' I ask Emkhee.

'He said he is too busy to talk either now or at any other time. You should find someone else to speak to, he said.'

'Was he polite about it?'

'Yes.'

Taken aback by the speed of the brush-off, I stare in a trance at the Land-Cruiser as it manoeuvres onto the road.

'Don't stare at his car,' hisses Emkhee, as though by staring at Bayanmunkh's car I am staring at him. 'The wrestlers sitting on the bench over there might *see* you.'

During the walk home she says: 'The wrestlers are too rich. They have lost the human touch, I think.'

I part with Emkhee near her apartment block and go to a caff near mine for a consolatory snack of *khuushuur*, bland fried pancakes with minced mutton that don't offer much in the way of consolation. Numbed by the turn-down, I sit at a table and stare into space. A waitress sets down two mugs and pours Sprite into both. The man sitting opposite slides one of the mugs over. A gift. My dejection obviously shows. This is not the first time I've been snubbed. On another occasion, a well-known wrestler agreed to an interview, but when Emkhee phoned to say we were about to come up to his apartment in the lift, his wife answered and said her husband had suddenly gone to the countryside. Of course it was a lie – just something people say here to fob you off.

A photo article in a Sunday magazine back home claimed Mongolia has a big culture of wrestling. It said that all Mongolian boys wrestle, and champions are treated like stars. On the strength of that piece, I flew from Calcutta to Bangkok, Bangkok to Beijing, then took the train to Ulan Baatar, Mongolia's capital. Coming all the way here on the basis of a few sentences in a photo story was always going to be a gamble, but I've since confirmed that the article was absolutely correct: wrestling is huge in Mongolia. Wrestlers feature on TV and in the papers. People routinely hang pictures and posters of wrestlers in their homes. Everyone knows who the current champions are, everyone knows their records, and everyone tells you that mothers want their sons to become wrestlers, not doctors or lawyers, when they grow up.

Wrestling is woven into the fabric of life here to an extent that it is unlikely to be anywhere else in the world. It just didn't occur to me that because wrestling is so big, because wrestlers are celebrities, they would act like celebrities too. They're media savvy, their time is precious, they don't just talk to anyone, but they may be able to slot you in for twenty minutes, but then they may just never get back to you. Turning up in Ulan Baatar out of the blue and trying to interview top wrestlers has been like a Mongolian journalist turning up in London out of the blue and trying to interview famous actors. Why would they want to speak to me?

I lift the mug of Sprite, force a smile to acknowledge the gift, and take a sip. It's come as a bittersweet realisation that for once I'm a victim of wrestling's success.

There is only one way to win a national wrestling title in Mongolia, amounting to one narrow, crowded passageway you have to fight your way through to enter the hall of celebrity and status. During the Naadam festival, which is held from 11–13 July every year, 512 men compete in the traditional wrestling style of *Mongol Bokh* at an open-air stadium in Ulan Baatar for the titles of Falcon, Elephant, Lion and Giant. The rules of *Mongol Bokh* are straightforward: you lose a bout if you touch the ground with any part of your body other than your feet or the flats of your hands – and if you are down on your hands and feet you are in a precarious position, so essentially you are either standing or losing. There are no time limits or weight categories, and there is no points system.

Naadam is a knockout tournament. Every wrestler is paired off in each round. The winners go through to the next, the losers are eliminated and that way the number of wrestlers halves each time – from 512 to 256 to 128 to 64, and so on. By the fifth round, only 32 wrestlers remain. From then onwards, whoever wins their bout wins a title. To become a Falcon, you have to win the fifth round and become one of the last sixteen wrestlers left in the tournament – effectively be one of the sixteen best in Mongolia. To become an Elephant, you have to win the next two rounds and be left in the last four (which is how wrestlers frequently talk about their performance: they say, 'I was in the last sixteen', or 'I was in the last four'). To become a Lion, you have to go onto win Naadam, and to become a Giant like Bayanmunkh, you have to win Naadam twice. If you win the same title more than once, it is given adornments. As winners are pitted against winners in each successive round, there's a greater danger of being thrown in one sense and falling from a ladder of aspiration and status in another. But once you do win a title, it is yours for life.

Simultaneous Naadams are held across Mongolia. Each has the same rules but a smaller entry – such as 128, 64 or 32 – and lesser titles are at stake. During Naadam, horse races and archery contests are held alongside the wrestling. Taken together, these three sports are known as *Eriin Gurvan Naadam*, the 'three manly games', though only wrestling is exclusive to grown men, as children jockey the horses, and women and children enter the archery contests. Of the three, wrestling and horse-racing excite the most passion and interest.

I arrived in Ulan Baatar a few weeks ago, mid-May, well in time for the festival, which I intend to see in the countryside. I'm sharing a seventh-floor apartment with Brandon, an American student of anthropology and medicine who's researching *yadargaa*, a condition that may be like chronic fatigue – no one in the West is sure how to categorise it yet – and Bob, who is making a documentary about Brandon's research journey. We first met on the train from Beijing. Brandon is tall, slim, wears glasses and has a dyed blond tuft of a goatee, while Bob is well built, bearded, funny and has a voice with a feminine softness. They are both in their early twenties, and have a relationship-like intimacy that at first made me wonder whether they might be a gay couple, but it turns out they are not and their easy familiarity flows from the fact that they are old school friends.

Even while staying in the relatively developed capital, you sense that Mongolia is a harsh place in which to live. Mongolians grow up tough, get their hands dirty, work hard and live in spartan homes. Theirs is a raw country with an extreme climate – up to 35°C in summer, as much as 50 below in winter – where life is only made possible by keeping sheep, goats, cows and yaks for their meat and milk. Livestock occupies a crucial role in national life, and reminders are everywhere. Cows graze the capital's grass verges. Cars cruise the boulevards with decapitated goats strapped to the roof racks. Serving women casually chew gum behind horror movies of every conceivable cut of meat at the indoor markets.

Considering Mongolia is such a stark country, it is ironic that I have an interpreter with a metropolitan sensibility that seems perversely out of place. Emkhee is an ex-model and ex-Russian teacher of about 40 who lives in fear of being mistaken for someone from the countryside. Other concerns include moisturising properly to counter the wrinkling effects of the hot summer sun, and avoiding the clouds of dust that blow off the barren land in the fierce winds. In fact Emkhee is generally anxious and concerned. While I step out to cross the road between cars in tame traffic, Emkhee remains on the pavement and shrieks that the cars will *crush us*. It is ironic, too, that Emkhee does not particularly like wrestling. She prefers gymnastics.

In the run-up to Naadam, regular wrestling tournaments are being held at the Palace of *Mongol Bokh*, a large circular building designed to look like a giant *ger*, or felt tent. Often there is an unseemly scrum to get in at the entrance, but once inside you are transported to an ordered and stately world akin to a medieval tournament in its decorum, colour and costume. The wrestlers wear hats, boots, trunks and small jackets cut to leave the chest exposed. The jackets and trunks are usually red or blue and chequered with squares of heavy white stitching; the boots have fairytale toes that curl up, a legacy of Tibetan Buddhism (they are supposed to avoid killing living creatures by digging the ground); and the hats are traditional dome-shaped hats with a spike at the crown that are known as 'heroes' hats'.

The wrestlers may look like they are wearing a strange variation of national costume for ornamental reasons but their clothing is functional. Boots protect feet from scything foot-sweeps, and the strong material of the jackets and trunks facilitates a large number of techniques, many of which are impossible when you wrestle bareskin. An unclothed body can be likened to a large box: it is hard to grip a box until you tie something around it, such as a cord. Clothing the body has the same effect of creating handles. Mongolian wrestlers grip their opponents' trunks and jackets and the heavy drawstring that ties the jackets at the front. Once they have a firm grip they have excellent leverage with which to move their opponent, to jerk him in one direction or another, to rattle and unbalance him, or lift him off the ground – as he does them.

Each tournament follows the same structure and that structure has the reassuring feel of something old that endures because it works so well. The wrestlers follow precise rituals. Each round begins when they slap their thighs and jog into the arena, then slow into a choreographed display. They beat their arms like huge wings and lift their heels behind them in deliberate movements, evoking a sense of lumbering mass and power. Depending on whom you speak to, they are either imitating an eagle or a powerful mythical bird known as a *hangard* in Mongolia and a garuda elsewhere. Whatever the case, the display is usually referred to as the 'eagle dance'. The wrestlers then execute a static variation of the eagle dance near the national flag and separate into two facing wings arranged by rank. Each has a *zasuul*, who acts as his second. *Zasuuls* wear beautiful silk greatcoats called *deels*, and boots and hats. They not only act as seconds but also impartially referee their wrestler's bout – which, ingeniously, means each bout is judged by two referees.

At the beginning of certain rounds, *zasuuls* sing the accomplishments and titles of the highest-ranked wrestlers in a haunting, spoken style. The wrestlers simultaneously eagle-dance with one hand on their *zasuul*'s shoulder, and turn one way, then the other, acknowledging the crowd. A further ritual blunts the sharp moment that can occur when a loser is separated from a winner. The losing wrestler undoes the knot that ties the drawstring of his jacket, and the wrestler with the highest title raises his right arm for the other to duck under. The winner then repeats the eagle dance and awaits the next round. There is no shouting, no fist-pumping, no scrum of friends and trainers around him. Jubilant self-expression is contained within the unchanging form of the eagle dance.

If you created a scale on which to measure wrestling styles in terms of raw intensity and aggression, at one end of the scale you would place sumo, with its characteristic thunderclap collisions, while *Mongol Bokh* would be close to the other end. Proceedings at the palace have the sedate dignity of a chess tournament. Often wrestlers engage slowly. They crouch with hands on thighs and scrutinise each other before carefully coming to grips. Sometimes they break and honourably allow one other to refocus before they recommence. To an outsider unschooled in the technical intricacies of *Mongol Bokh* it can be almost boring to watch. Much of the action is hard to see – in shifts of balance, changes of grip, probing for a way in. A long period in which a wrestler works to get a precise hold and patiently waits for the right moment is followed by a short burst of tussling as he attempts his technique. The rules create a need for caution. Because the definition of what constitutes a fall and therefore elimination from a competition is so liberal – you need only touch the ground with a knee or elbow – wrestlers proceed with care.

One evening, Emkhee and I watch a tournament at the palace. The wrestlers contest their bouts simultaneously, and it's difficult to know who to watch. It's like a muscular tea dance in that each wrestling couple has to find and hold their own space in which to express themselves. I concentrate on the current champion of Mongolia, Bat-erdene Giant. A squat 145kg, Bat-erdene has a head like a large block of statuary, shoulders that eddy with muscle forever and huge thighs. His butter-colour body is enormous without looking anything like the physique of, say, a conventional body-builder. He is intensely grounded and resolutely unthrowable – facts confirmed by a record of eleven Naadam wins in a row. In between rounds he sits on a bench outside the wrestling area. When he is about to wrestle, he stands, calmly takes off his coat, folds it, places it on the bench, ties the cord of his wrestling trunks at the hip, and then takes his place at the front of the column of wrestlers on the left wing, from where he leads the rituals. He appears relaxed, contemplative and humble.

Onkh, a middle-aged friend of Emkhee's husband, watches the action with us. He has a champagne cork of a nose and blotchy red cheeks, and holds the title of Falcon.

'What is it about Bat-erdene that makes him so good?' I ask him through Emkhee.

'He has the right build – it comes from your parents and ancestors,' replies Onkh. 'He has a large chest and a thick neck and wrists.'

Bat-erdene easily deals with a small opponent by pulling his head down with both hands as if trying to drown him in a swimming pool. His opponent eventually resurfaces, shoulders polished with sweat, but Bat-erdene jerks him down again, this time onto his hands and knees, and he is sunk for good.

Onkh now has a question of his own: 'The strong men in your country pull cars with their teeth?'

It's a bizarre question, but then Mongolians know little about England. I imagine he's seen a British strong man contest on TV.

'Yes, it happens,' I tell Onkh.

'What is the difference between the body shape of strong men in your country and Mongolia?'

'In England, they tend to develop muscle by body-building and therefore have more of a body-builder's physique. We don't have many wrestlers.'

'How do you think your strong men would fare against our wrestlers?'

'Your wrestlers would obviously beat our strong men at wrestling because they are more skilful.' I pause for a moment to let this compliment sink in, then add a qualification: 'But our strong men would beat your wrestlers at pulling cars with their teeth.'

'I will *not* translate that,' hisses Emkhee.

Bat-erdene wins the tournament. Spectators surge to the front of the seating area to try to touch his sweat. Mongolians believe you will have a year's good luck if you touch the winner's sweat. The same belief applies to the sweat of successful horses.

A sudden gust of wind swirls up.

'Dust shower!' cries Emkhee.

Specks of debris from a trench are deposited on her black heels. She rests each foot on a ledge in turn and wipes the shoes clean with an emergency napkin taken from her handbag. We go inside the Palace of *Mongol Bokh* and enter the office of Danzan, vice-president of the *Mongol Bokh* Association. He sits behind a plastic desk with invoices laid out on the surface in front of him. He tidies them to one side to prepare a channel between us. An oil painting of Naadam crouches on the floor, waiting to be hung. The phone rings. Danzan answers. He presses buttons on a calculator while he talks. Office, desk, calculator, invoices: it adds up to a setting for a conversation about wrestling that couldn't be more different from what I became accustomed to in India. Danzan puts the phone down and switches his attention to Emkhee and me. He makes a slurping noise as he speaks, like the noise you might make while eating soup. Mongolians speak during inhalations, creating a soft whispery slurping sound that can appear conspiratorial.

I thought we were going to interview Damdin now, but he says we should arrange a meeting for another day because he needs time to prepare. Some words and terms are difficult for a foreigner to understand, he warns. Also, he says, a bad precedent has been set by a foreigner who wrote about the traditional way to hunt marmots, which are a type of ground squirrel and a big part of the summer diet. This foreign journalist, an Australian, wrote that Mongolians simply make a noise to lure marmots from their burrows, which is not the whole truth, says Danzan. In fact hunters also wear hats with pretend ears and perform a special dance that mesmerises the marmots, who are curious by nature. They consequently fail to take cover in their burrows and are easy to shoot in the head. There is a lot of art to marmot-hunting, explains Danzan. He doesn't want me to become another foreigner misrepresenting another Mongolian tradition so the interview better wait. He writes down a list of ten topics I should know about – the history of *Mongol Bokh*, the rules, the wrestling costume and so on – and says we will cover perhaps three or four in our next meeting.

In my negativism, I suspect Danzan is fobbing me off, like the others, but he keeps his word and we meet in his office again a few days later. He gives a brief, fragmentary history of *Mongol Bokh* and Naadam. He says an ancient belt buckle with a wrestler motif indicates that the Huns, who inhabited the Mongolian steppes over 1,500 years ago, wrestled. According to *The Secret History of the Mongols*, written some time after Chinggis Khan's death in 1227, Naadam was held during the period of the great leader's rule. It was also held in summer during the Tibetan Buddhist era, which began in the late sixteenth century. Since the communist revolution of 1921,

Naadam has been anchored to the date 11 July to commemorate the declaration of the People's Republic.

We move on to the subject of the wrestling costume. The jackets used to be made from silk but are now manufactured from parachute material, says Danzan. The hats have a new and innovative design, of which he is obviously proud. Titled wrestlers now wear a badge of a falcon, elephant, lion or *hangard* on the front of their hat, and two red ribbons now hang from the back. One of these ribbons has stripes, like military stripes, which show which rounds the wrestler has reached in Naadam. In effect a wrestler's status and career are recorded by his hat.

These are interesting details, but what I want to know more than anything else is about the life, beliefs and practices of Mongolian wrestlers, and whether there is any resonance between the culture of wrestling in Mongolia and the culture of wrestling in India. Once Danzan has finished telling me his facts, I ask him whether *Mongol Bokh* is considered to develop the mind and spirit of a wrestler. He answers the question in a way that implies there is no such systematic belief in Mongolia. I ask whether Mongolian wrestlers have a particular diet. They eat whatever they want when they are not competing, replies Danzan, but a month before Naadam they congregate at camps to prepare for the tournament, and eat a special diet of mostly milk products and good meat, while avoiding alcohol. Then Danzan says something that makes my ears prick up: wrestlers are not supposed to meet women while at these camps, which are called 'fires'.

'It's the same in India,' I say. 'Indian wrestlers are not allowed to meet women at all.'

'For their whole life?' asks Danzan.

'Some of the most famous wrestlers were celibate all their lives, yes.'

'So they would never have children. In Mongolia we want to have children to continue our lineage.'

Danzan also says there is a belief in Mongolia that women should not touch a wrestler's head and shoulders during a fire and during Naadam – which means that the avoidance of women and sex is in some way integral to a wrestler's preparation in Mongolia, as in India.

Fires are very secretive, states Danzan, but he will be able to arrange a visit for me. I wait and wait but no visit materialises.

Each day I witness the energy and dynamism of Brandon's project, which is going well, in stark contrast with mine, which is going badly. Brandon's team has now swelled to five members. His brother Brook and friend Nova, who are both medical students, are here to help him, while Bob has fellow film-maker Naoko to act as his assistant. Each morning Brandon and Bob follow the same ritual. They gather in Brandon's room, suck on their asthma inhalers, play Fat Boy Slim, which Brandon calls 'auditory Ritalin', to motivate themselves to do sets of sit-ups and press-ups, eat breakfast, hold a team meeting, then go out and attack their work. The results of their labours, piles of filled-in research questionnaires, are already deposited on surfaces around the apartment, laughing at me. Laughing at me because they know that while Brandon and his team are out, I skulk around the apartment doing very little. I might lie on the sofa watching the Fashion Channel on TV or stare out the window trying to think of ways to start making progress with my work. I don't yet know exactly what it is I want to find out anyway, though I'll know it when I see it. I'm waiting for inspiration, a lead, a connection, something. In the meantime, I consider it best to talk to as many informed people as possible about wrestling, but the problem is they don't necessarily want to talk to me.

I feel shut out from the inner circle of Mongolian wrestling and the rejection I'm feeling is merging with the hostility occasionally directed towards me elsewhere to foster a sense of victimisation. It started with a boy begging from passers-by in the street who grabbed my fleece with both hands, squealing. As I peeled one hand away he regripped my fleece with the other and hung on tight. I thought for a moment about what to do and decided to throw his baseball cap on the pavement so that he would have to release his grip to go and pick it up. He did release his grip, but instead of picking up his cap he picked up a half-brick and threw it at me. A passer-by censured him in Mongolian and he stopped. Then there was an incident at the Khan Brau pub in which a drunk guy sitting in the next booth gave me the finger and kept telling me to go home. There have been other flashes of animosity directed towards me too. I don't know how personally to take them. I presume the hostility has something to do with what Mongolians think I represent rather than who I am, and wonder whether they think I'm Russian. Russians are deeply unpopular in Mongolia. Or maybe people can see I am a Westerner and resent me on ideological grounds. Democracy arrived in Mongolia only nine years ago, in 1990, and there is still a lot of support for communism. People often say life was better during the totalitarian years. Mongolians were weaned on anti-Western propaganda and its effects will take a while to wear off.

I feel uncomfortable on the streets and uncomfortable at home. Now that Brandon's full team has arrived, I'm relegated to sleeping on a mattress on the floor of a tiny covered verandah next to the kitchen. It's like sleeping on the edge of an overhanging cliff. Lying lengthways, I barely fit into the room. The window doesn't shut properly and bangs in the wind. Yet I'd rather rough it here and be with friends than stay at a hotel on my own. I intended to spend a lot of time in the countryside anyway, and thought I'd only need a base in the city, but the trips I plan keep on coming to nothing because the interpreters I hire always drop out at the last minute – or some time after the last minute. They proffer excuses such as they have to attend their grandmother's funeral, or their mother and sister have had their passports and money stolen in Beijing and need to be rescued – which is deeply irritating yet also slightly reassuring in that it is nice to know that cultures as distant from one another as those of England and Mongolia have a lot in common when it comes to made-up excuses.

One morning I dream that the Palace of *Mongol Bokh* is a huge drum turning slowly. Lines attached to the drum radiate in every direction over the horizon and into the far corners of Mongolia. As the drum spins, the lines are reeled in. What's on the end of each is revealed as it comes into view: a wrestler. When I wake up, I lie on my front, head propped up on my hands, going over the dream. I know what it's about. Virtually all Mongolia's Giants, Lions, Elephants and Falcons grew up

in the countryside. Titled wrestlers live and compete in Ulan
Baatar – they are reeled in to the capital by a desire to compete
against the best wrestlers for the biggest prizes – yet they spend
their formative years out on the steppes. Something about life
in the countryside makes good wrestlers.

I get up, go into the kitchen, make a cup of coffee and sit at
the table, thinking. Every step I have taken towards wrestling
has been a step towards the country and a step away from the
modern, industrial world. This is true on both a global and a
national level. First I left post-industrial England for India,
essentially an agrarian culture, where I lived in Varanasi, the
most ancient city on the subcontinent. Then I either went into
the villages to speak to Pehalwans or spoke to ageing wrestlers
in Varanasi about their youth. In the first case, I physically took
a step away from India's emerging modern culture by leaving
the city, while in the second case I also left the city in the sense
that I listened to reminiscences about a period in Varanasi's
recent past when it was far less developed and the city and
country were far more intertwined. Now, on a global scale, I
have taken another step against the grain of development by
journeying to a nation still referred to as Outer Mongolia, a
name synonymous with isolation and lack of development, and
the heartland of wrestling is yet another step away against the
grain of development in the stark grassland beyond Ulan
Baatar.

Perhaps it isn't much of a revelation to discover that
traditional wrestling is a country boy and endures in parts of
the world where old country ways survive, but it is a revelation
to discover that wrestling is part of a clearly defined fraternity
within rural cultures. In India it was the Yadav caste, cattle
herders by tradition, who had a particular affinity with
wrestling, and the same association between herding and
wrestling operates in Mongolia, a nation of herders that also
happens to have what has to be the greatest living culture of
wrestling in the world.

The connection between herding and wrestling runs deep
and can be seen in the lives and roles of Indian and Greek
gods. Hermes was sometimes credited with the invention of
wrestling, and shrines devoted to him were common at Ancient
Greek wrestling schools. He was also a god of shepherds and

herders. Krishna, one of the two gods commonly worshipped by wrestlers in India, spent his youth living among herders. Herakles was worshipped by Greek athletes in general and by wrestlers in particular, and during his youth he too lived among herders. It is expressly stated in the story of Herakles that he develops strength, courage and physical stature while living on a cattle farm. Similarly, Mongolians often talk about how strength and other attributes developed during the physical work of herding help them to wrestle.

I need to visit the countryside to see this relationship between herding and wrestling first-hand. That is what the dream is about. I have to go to the places over the horizon where wrestlers are made. But first I need to find an interpreter willing to come along. When I suggested the idea to Emkhee, she shrieked that it was out of the question because there are no showers in the countryside.

With Onkh's help I finally land an interview with a high-titled wrestler, Sosorbaram Elephant. We schedule to meet at the Ulan Baatar Hotel for lunch on a Monday. Emkhee is nervous about meeting a celebrity wrestler and fusses over the preparations, particularly the alcohol arrangements, which play a central role in social interactions between men. She asks her husband for guidance, then gives a briefing over the phone.

'You will have to give him 100 grams of vodka and a bottle of beer with the meal, then a bottle of vodka at the end which must be screw-top.' Bottled beer had more cachet because it is a foreign import, and screw-top vodka is relatively expensive.

On the day of the interview, I ring the buzzer of Emkhee's apartment. Her Doberman scudders and scrapes over the tiles behind the metal security door, and barks loudly. Emkhee lets me in, looks at the bottle of White Horse vodka I've bought following her instructions, and winces a cartoon-like wince – a combination of a sharp intake of breath and a hand held in front of the mouth. Dust from inside the plastic bag in which I am carrying the bottle has stuck to its sides.

'You will give like *this*? Dirty? He will not accept!'

She hurries into the kitchen and wipes the bottle clean with a cloth. We leave the apartment block and take a cut-through to the centre of the city. Sosorbaram is waiting at the hotel. Dressed in a silver-buttoned grey coat tied round the middle by a flame-colour sash, he's a large man of about sixty with an aura of exceptional dignity. The restaurant is grand and ostentatious, with high ceilings, chandeliers like large crystal squid and wood-panelled walls. We are ushered to a table, and order food, vodka and beer.

'Mongolians respect three sports, and *Bokh* is one of them,' says Sosorbaram. 'It has thousands of years of history, and people respect wrestlers with titles. In our country, if people have a newborn stallion they expect him to become a fast race horse, and if people have a newborn son they expect him to become a wrestler.'

Sosorbaram became an Elephant at the end of the 1950s, and says he wrestled well throughout the 1960s and early 1970s. Many times he was left in the last eight at Naadam, but he explains that it was his misfortune to compete during an era when Bayanmunkh and Bayanmunkh's arch rival, Munkhbat Giant, were at their peak, so it was difficult to get a look-in at the higher titles. While he talks, Sosorbaram leaves his vodka, which worries Emkhee. In an aside, she tells me to tell Sosorbaram to drink. I tell her to tell him from me, but she insists I have to tell him directly with a gesture.

'Take your glass and raise it,' she says.

I raise my glass. Sosorbaram follows suit. He dips a finger in the vodka and flicks three drops into the air, the traditional Mongolian libation. He explains the meaning: one drop is for the sky, another for the earth and another for the people.

I blab: 'In England we just say "Cheers", we have a different tradition,' and instantly feel like a complete idiot.

The waitress deposits our starters – mounds of glunky potato salad, a depressing culinary legacy of the communist era. I eat mine while Sosorbaram leaves his and talks. Emkhee hisses at me.

'You have eaten your potato salad! He will have to eat his potato salad alone. It is not polite!'

I start to tire of Emkhee's asides. It's difficult enough to conduct an interview through an interpreter let alone navigate an etiquette assault course at the same time. Our mains arrive. We adjourn the conversation while we eat. Afterwards I ask Sosorbaram what made him such a good wrestler.

'There are many factors. One is genetics, another is that I worked hard. Another factor was that my family had many horses and I had to continually draw water from a well for them, which develops a lot of strength.'

Emkhee begins to panic again: 'Tell him to drink, he is not drinking!'

Sosorbaram still hasn't touched his vodka. I raise my vodka glass in compliance with Emkhee's wish, and wonder whether I also have to raise my glass of Heineken to encourage him to drink his beer, or whether vodka is the only raise-the-glass drink.

'Working with animals gives you a lot of strength,' continues Sosorbaram. He still isn't drinking his vodka. 'Till the age of twenty I lived in the countryside. Even after moving to Ulan Baatar I would return for holidays. Only hard work could bring me my dream and give me the strength I needed to become a titled wrestler.'

'From what age did you wrestle?'

'From an early age. When I was in junior class at secondary school. I tore my *deel* wrestling, and would forget to go home in the evening because I was so absorbed in wrestling. Usually I lost, but by the age of seventeen or eighteen, I wrestled better.'

Water starts to drip onto our table from a crack in the ceiling. A waiter helps us move to the next alcove where we sit in the same pattern as before. Sosorbaram takes a snuff bottle from an inside pocket and passes it over. The rules for handling a snuff bottle are precise and labyrinthine. It's like being handed a live hand grenade: I fear an explosion of bad manners if I handle it incorrectly.

'If you don't smoke, smell it,' advises Emkhee.

I ignore her advice, which amounts to taking the easy option, and attempt to go through the full snuff bottle procedure. Accepting the bottle with my right hand, I pass it to my left, remove the lid, which has a scoop attached, with my right hand and try to dig out and deposit a little snuff on the ridge of the forefinger of my left. The problem is I'm left-handed yet asking my right to do the finesse work. I fail to scoop out any snuff but sniff my finger anyway in the hope that no one will notice its snufflessness. Emkhee takes the easy way out and simply sniffs the bottle lid admiringly.

'I'm learning a lot today about Mongolian customs,' I say.

'The snuff bottle is a Mongolian tradition, especially in the countryside, where our livestock herders like to follow tradition,' replies Sosorbaram.

His beer glass is empty.

Emkhee says: 'Could you call the waitress to order for him and for you one more bottle of beer? Otherwise, just empty one. People can recognise him. He is a *respected* man.'

Sosorbaram still hasn't touched his vodka, which Emkhee tries to top up to encourage him to drink.

'I don't drink vodka,' explains Sosorbaram, finally, as he declines. 'Usually, wrestlers don't drink much vodka.'

I've been drinking too fast and feel drunk. I need to go to the toilet, but Emkhee says it will be impolite to leave Sosorbaram at the table on his own, so I will have to wait.

I ask: 'What are the most important attributes that make a good wrestler? Balance, strength, skill, talent?'

'It depends on a lot of things, including everything you've mentioned.'

Emkhee to me: 'Don't drink so fast!'

'Having a large physique doesn't necessarily make you a good wrestler,' continues Sosorbaram. 'Other things are important too. The first thing I would say is important is genes. Unless you have the right genes, you can't become a good wrestler. The next important thing is your training. You must be motivated and eager to try. Also, you must have some skills, and be able to learn quickly. You need courage and patience too, and need to work hard.'

We talk some more. In another aside Emkhee criticises me for not asking questions that are interesting enough, as though I am placing a burden of boredom on Sosorbaram. The end of our conversation comes as a relief. I stand and pass the gift of a bottle of screw-top vodka to Sosorbaram, as Emkhee has instructed.

'You must hold it in *both* hands!' she cries.

Etiquette dictates I will have to pay for a taxi to take Sosorbaram home, says Emkhee, and I will have to accompany him in the car. Fortunately Sosorbaram decides to walk and says it won't be necessary to accompany him by foot to his front door, which Emkhee insists I offer to do. We part on the steps outside the hotel. Afterwards, I rush back inside to use the toilet.

That afternoon I lie on the sofa back at the apartment, and rewind and replay the meal in my head. To make sense of it, I imagine Emkhee as a piece of social status measuring equipment with an oversensitive needle. Yet though her fussing over etiquette was irritating in the extreme, it did demonstrate the great respect accorded to titled wrestlers by Mongolians. Nevertheless, I decide that it would be better to use a less star-struck interpreter in future.

Chapter 7

The Manly Game

I t's an incredible statistic: of the thirteen wrestlers who have become Giants in the last seventy years, three come from the same tiny part of Khovsgol *aimag* in northern Mongolia. All three grew up near the River Uyalgan, which is situated in a remote area east of Khovsgol Nuur, a huge lake, and close to the border with Siberia. Mongolia is vast – over six times the size of the United Kingdom – yet three Giants were born within a few miles of each other. In which case the River Uyalgan is a good place to visit for Naadam. There, I can try to answer the two related questions of what it is about life in the country in general that makes good wrestlers, and what it is about life near the River Uyalgan in particular. Maybe the circumstances that are generally responsible for creating good wrestlers are present in a more concentrated form in the River Uyalgan region.

Serdaram, the university lecturer who relates the statistic, says that shamanism used to be strong in the area. People there love their mountains, rivers and streams, and believe their landscape is responsible for forging good wrestlers. Serdaram also says that well-known wrestlers who went to the area to compete in the past would always be beaten by low-ranked locals. The way he tells the story – or perhaps it is the way I hear it – something like a force field operated around the River Uyalgan and that force field was somehow connected with shamanism and nature-worship. Damdin, one of the three Giants from the area, is still alive and recuperating at a health spa just outside Ulan Baatar. He is said to be friendly and approachable.

I meet my new interpreter, Ari, who is about thirty and speaks in an American-accented drawl, at a central square as a prelude to taking a car to the spa to meet Damdin.

'What should I buy him as a gift?' I ask Ari.

'Get him a bottle of vodka.'

'But his health is bound to be poor if he's recuperating at a health spa. Surely it's not a good idea to give him vodka?'

'It doesn't matter. You always give men vodka. Even if he doesn't drink it himself straight away, he can save it for later or give it to someone else.'

Reluctantly, I buy a bottle of vodka in a store – along with some apples as a concession to Damdin's probable poor health. Both the apples and a shrink-wrapped pack of shrivelled oranges are displayed in a glass case like the rare, prestigious and expensive items they are here. Ari stops and hires a car, and we head east out of Ulan Baatar. We pass through a suburban shanty town of small bungalows and *gers* in fenced-off plots, and are accompanied in our escape from the city by electricity pylons and telephone lines hurrying ahead. The driver treats the cows that stand in the middle of the road like a chicane, hardly slowing to pass. Eventually we turn off the road, ford a stream, and round a hillside until a gate and group of buildings come into view: the health resort.

Damdin meets us in the hall of the main building. Seventy years old, he looks in good shape. He has strong, tanned hands, a big neck and a compact physique. Together we go and sit on a blue bench outside. I ask Damdin about a medal he's wearing on the lapel of his double-breasted jacket. He says it was given to honour him as a performer. He used to work in the circus. Mongolians know him as both a champion wrestler and a circus strong man. He joined the circus in the early 1950s and became famous for supporting an 850kg load with his legs during the act. He journeyed all over the communist world with the circus, and he tells anecdotes about the leaders he met along the way and laughs at his own irreverence in their presence. In 1957 he was in Moscow for the fortieth anniversary of the October Revolution, he says. A big party had been organised for communist leaders. Both Tsedenbal, the then communist party leader of Mongolia, and Brezhnev, future leader of the Soviet Union, were at the function.

'I approached Brezhnev and talked to him, and occasionally I touched this part of his body with my hand.' Damdin touches his own hip. 'I was just talking with my hands and thought I was being friendly, but the Mongolians accompanying Tsedenbal and the bodyguards and everyone else criticised me: "Why did you touch Brezhnev?" they said. Everyone was criticising me: "Why did you touch Brezhnev's hip?"'

The three of us laugh at the story. It's an anecdote he probably would not have been able to share so freely fifteen years ago during communism. We turn to the subject of wrestling. Damdin says he won Naadam five times in a row and was well known for winning bouts quickly. People said of him: 'He went, he won.' I ask him to describe the River Uyalgan area where he grew up.

'My homeland is beautiful but also vulnerable. There are a lot of floods. When I was a child, I saw some disasters. It's also one of the coldest areas in Mongolia. During winter the temperature drops down to minus 50°C. There's a lot of snow. Growing up there was tough. When the land was flooded, we had to move everything. Sometimes we had to live on flooded land for a few days. And there were also strong winds that would bring down trees.'

'Do you feel that this harsh childhood made you a good wrestler?'

'I don't know exactly how it influenced my career, but of course the cold temperature and weather make people strong. But my training was probably the most important thing.'

'Why do you think the River Uyalgan area has produced a disproportionate number of champions?'

'When I was growing up, people used to say that wrestling

was popular in the area because of a Tibetan Buddhist monastery. This monastery was by a river nearby, and the monks of the monastery were very active during the religious era, up until the 1930s. At that time, the young monks would wrestle. Probably their enthusiasm for wrestling in some way helped the area generate good wrestlers. That's what I was told, anyway.'

For a moment I am dumbstruck. I can't quite believe what Damdin is saying. Never before have I come across a reference to wrestling Tibetan Buddhist monks. I discovered in India that wrestlers lived a monkish life and now I am being told that monks in Mongolia actually wrestled. Familiar questions push themselves to the front of my mind. Did wrestling have spiritual value and significance for the monks? Did they see the discipline of wrestling as a vehicle through which to develop spirituality? Of course there may have been prosaic reasons why the monks wrestled, such as for recreation, but whatever the case, I feel a strong compulsion to find out.

The period of monasticism that Damdin is referring to ended with the Great Purge of the late 1930s during which the communists destroyed the monasteries. A hundred years ago life in Mongolia centred around 700 monastic communities that were like churches, schools and universities rolled into one. Within the monasteries were schools of Buddhist learning, medicine, astrology and tantra, and every family sent at least one son to be initiated as a monk. In 1921, the year of the communist revolution, there were perhaps 110,000 monks in total, representing about a third of the male population, yet two decades later the monasteries had been scrubbed from the landscape. Stalin gave an order to Choibalsan, his puppet ruler in Mongolia, for them to be destroyed, and the Soviet NKVD led death squads that annihilated the settlements and liquidated lamas. Young monks were sent home, but senior monks were either executed on the spot, or imprisoned, or tortured and murdered later, or sent to labour camps in Siberia. Thousands of monks were killed – the exact number is uncertain.

★

Damdin supplies the name of a brother who lives in the River Uyalgan area. With two weeks to go before Naadam, I set about organising a visit. I buy plane tickets for Ari and me to fly to Moron, the administrative capital of Khovsgol, from where we will hire a jeep to take us the 70 or 80 miles or so to Tsaagan Uur *sum*, the county in which the River Uyalgan is located. But the day before we're scheduled to leave, Ari lets me down badly, claiming he can't come because he has a court case to deal with. Despondent, I cancel the tickets.

A few nights later I am propping up the bar at The Carlsberg nightclub, wondering how I'm going to get out into the countryside in time for Naadam, which is only a week away, and find myself casually chatting to a law lecturer called Agaa. We bond over complaining about the glass collectors who are keeping half the bar to themselves. Agaa's English is excellent. He is in his early twenties, wears glasses and has a slight build belied by a deep voice and crushing handshake that feels like an expression of academic tension.

'Look, I'm trying to organise a trip to visit Khovsgol to see Naadam and do some research into wrestling. Would you like to come along as an interpreter?' I ask him.

'When do you want to leave?'

'As soon as possible.'

'Actually, I've always wanted to visit Khovsgol. It's considered to be one of the most beautiful parts of Mongolia. Sure, why not. I'm on holiday at the moment. It would be a pleasure.'

During the next couple of days we shop for a tent, camping equipment, food, riding boots and sunhats, and buy vodka, brick tea, sweets and biscuits to give as gifts. I half expect Agaa to drop out at the last moment too, like all the other interpreters, but he is true to his word. On the morning of departure we go to a bus terminal, load our gear onto a four-wheel-drive Russian minibus bound for Moron, which is 400 miles away, wait for it to fill with passengers and leave. The road comes to an end just outside Ulan Baatar. From then on the minibus follows parallel ruts, like a train travelling on rails, which carve a route through the steppes, and rocks, tips and shakes every inch of the way. Without thinking about the practicalities, Agaa and I have annexed the back seats, which are directly over the wheels – which means even bigger jolts.

The transformation is immediate and total. The Mongolia beyond the capital is friendly and relaxed. We stop off at homes along the way to drink milk tea, and walk straight in without knocking since hospitality is so strong and universal in the countryside that this is the etiquette. Agaa transforms too. He is drily scientific and has strong communist leanings, but he begins to reveal a lighter and more mischievous side, and boasts to the other passengers that we are going to enter Naadam, and will slaughter and eat a sheep to develop strength. He is getting in character for the countryside, intent on having a relaxing break away from the city and clearly intent on using the large hunting knife he has bought especially for the trip. He sits trying to slice salami between the bumps.

'What's the biggest animal you've ever killed?' he asks.

I wonder how best to answer. This is a country in which killing animals is part of normal everyday life. Agaa probably won't be impressed when I tell him I've never slaughtered an animal of any size or understand that this is normal for someone who lives in London.

'I've never really killed any animals of note to be honest. What about you?'

'As a child, I used to kill mice by stuffing up their hole then kicking them as they came out another hole.' Agaa thinks for a moment. 'Once I killed a sheep. I was given a sheep as a gift in the countryside but had to fly back to Ulan Baatar the next day, so I killed it. The Mongolian way to kill a sheep is to kneel on its body, make an incision with a knife in its belly, then put your hand into the body, reach up and either squeeze the heart or pinch a vein till it dies. That way not even a drop of blood is spilled and wasted.'

The minibus hammers along the rail-like ruts through treeless steppe after treeless steppe after treeless steppe. We pass trucks laden with fleeces heading in the opposite direction. Clusters of *gers* act as compasses – their doors face south to shelter from the prevailing northerly winds. Most of the time we are headed west or north-west. The Mongolian passengers sing songs together. The jerking and shaking take their toll on the children. A boy leans his head out the sliding window to throw up. A yellow arc of sick flies from a baby girl's mouth as if in slow motion.

As the sun sets, the minibus heads towards pink-streaked clouds and purple hills. I lean my head against the window and snatch moments of sleep through the night, between being jerked awake by the tipping and shaking. Whenever I wake up and look around, I see a jigsaw of sleeping Mongolians using each other as pillows. In the morning we stop next to a stream for a toilet break. The driver wipes sick from the coachwork. Back on the road, we pass flocks of sheep and goats.

'The best way to kill a goat is to clamp its head between your knees and hit its forehead with a hammer,' commentates Agaa.

Perhaps, I think to myself, scratch any Mongolian townie and there's a slaughter-happy herder waiting to get out.

We overtake families moving their *gers* on the backs of pack-camels. By midday we have arrived at a reindeer statue that marks the head of a pass that leads to Moron. Down below, regular blocks of bungalows sit at the centre of fenced-off plots. Agaa and I are dropped off at the home of an American friend of his, with whom we stay the night, and at six the following morning we begin the second leg of the journey, and head off in a Russian jeep with a driver hired for the week. We pass through valley after valley, each more beautiful than the last, each a little moister and each a deeper green. Wood smoke curls from the chimneys of minty-white *gers*. Pine trees surge down the spurs of the mountains. Herds of yaks, cows, sheep and horses graze the pasture. Sunlight floods under the bottom of a cloudbank, as though into a room under a drawn blind. We pass and ford countless clear-water brooks, streams and rivers. Each tree looks as though it has been placed precisely where it stands and could never be anywhere else. The grassland looks tended and landscaped, like the greens of a golf course. I have never seen anywhere so beautiful, unpolluted and pristine, and sit in the passenger's seat shocked into quiet awe.

In a damp forest of black-trunk trees, we stop at a conical *ovoo* made from branches. An *ovoo* is usually a pile of stones, like a cairn, dedicated to a nature spirit, but in the wooded areas of Mongolia they are often made from branches. Anything at hand has been used to build the *ovoo*, including a roadsign on its pole. After the driver has circumambulated the shrine, we drive on until confronted by a broken-down jeep. A tassled Tibetan Buddhist charm swings impotently from the rearview mirror. Two youths are hanging around. The younger one swings from the car doorframe like a monkey. A pair of empty vodka bottles stand on the grass. Our driver asks the youths what happened. They explain that after their jeep broke down, their driver drank the vodka and wandered off leaving them stranded. While our driver checks under their bonnet, Agaa practises throwing his knife at a tree. I wonder whether there is anything living he doesn't want to harm or kill. The knife bounces off the treetrunk in my direction in a burst of splintering bark. I stand back to keep out of the way. Ever the scientist, Agaa calculates how many more paces he needs to stand away from the tree so that the knife will somersault to the horizontal, and throws again. This time the knife sticks in the tree.

Our driver concludes the jeep's gearbox is broken and tells the youths there's nothing he can do to help. I give them some food, we get back in the jeep and move on. When we near the small administrative centre of Tsaagan Uur *sum*, the driver feels we're close enough to our destination to deserve a break. He points to a cabin.

'Let's go there,' he says. 'They have cows outside so they should give us good milk tea.'

Inside, a watery-eyed old man in a burgundy *deel* sits cross-legged on the floor by a table. His head describes drunken doodles in the air. His wife serves us milk tea and milk vodka. She supports her right arm with her left at the elbow as she passes the bowl, counterpointing her husband's drunkenness with immaculate etiquette. The old man is old enough to have known Damdin when he was young. I ask him whether he ever saw him.

'Yes,' he replies, 'I remember seeing him wrestle when he was eighteen and won the *sum* Naadam. He used to work at the school chopping the wood for the heating. Other people would transport the firewood by ox, but Damdin used to carry it himself.'

Agaa and the driver are embarrassed by the old man's drunkenness and the image it portrays of Mongolians. They cut the visit short. We get back on the road, cross two further rivers, then follow a sandy track through a forest of silver birch and pine. The River Uyalgan, our destination, snakes across beautiful flower-specked grassland beyond the forest. We stop next to a cabin near the riverbank and go inside. Pieces of meat hang drying from the ceiling like party decorations. A pet kid with a shaved face chews washing in an adjoining room. A woman stops putting wood on the stove fire and offers us curd and butter. Her husband enters the room. The driver asks him whether we will be able to ford the river in the jeep.

'It's rained for five days and the river was impossible to ford for some time, but you should be in luck,' he says. 'The water should be low enough now.'

'Where's the best place to cross?' asks the driver.

'I'll get my son to show you.'

Outside, the husband indicates which of the cabins on the far side of the river is Damdin's brother's. His son rides into the current on horseback to look for the shallowest place to cross. Our driver sits studying how far the water reaches up the horse's flank. When he sees that the boy has found the shallowest line, he puts the jeep into four-wheel drive and accelerates into the river. The jeep sticks on the gravel bottom. The driver reverses out, then revs the engine and powers into the sticking area again. This time we surge through to the other side. The boy waves and canters off.

Damdin's brother Jamsran comes in from outside where he has been riding in circles to power a large wooden contraption that crushes hides for leather. He has a white goatee beard like a wisp of smoke, and wears a red *deel* and felt hat. His wife, Maruysa, a stout woman with cropped grey hair, serves milk tea. Her *deel* is grubby and she has blood on the backs of her hands – we've caught her in the middle of something. Having seen us arrive, various sons and daughters enter the cabin and sit quietly. There's an awkward silence. The family sit around looking at their hands. I don't know what to say.

'Ask them about the weather,' advises Agaa. 'Country people like to talk about the weather.'

'I hear that it has rained for five days.'

Yes, it has, the family murmur. They keep looking at their hands.

A daughter serves milk vodka in a silver bowl while holding a

100 togrog note underneath it. The silver bowl and money announce that this is a significant etiquette moment that requires precise handling. Agaa offers guidance.

'Take the money and put your hat on,' he says.

'Wear a hat indoors? You're joking, aren't you?'

'No. It is the custom at important moments in Mongolia to wear a hat if you have one.'

I take the note and put on my sunhat before sipping from the bowl. Agaa tells the family why we are here. When he has finished speaking, there's another awkward silence. A daughter serves *airag*, which is fermented mare's milk. Maruysa makes conversation.

'The children drink *airag* like you would drink water,' she says. 'They drink around four litres each a day. Some people drink as much as seventy litres a day. Wrestlers in particular like to drink *airag*.'

I take a sip.

'Maybe this will make me a better wrestler. In fact I can feel my technique improving already.'

It's a weak joke, but it breaks the ice. Some of the family laugh. I go outside to the jeep and bring back gifts of vodka, brick tea and sweets, which I give to Jamsran. His daughter hands me a bowl of mutton. I try to carve slivers of meat off the bone with a blunt knife, and feel Jamsran's eyes on me, following every artless move.

'Do you eat mutton in England?' he asks.

'Yes.'

'Does it taste different?'

'It doesn't have as strong a taste in England as it does here. It tastes stronger and better here.'

'Tell them about your time in India,' says Agaa. 'They will find it interesting.'

I talk at length about India in general and Indian wrestling in particular. Judging by the family's reaction, they are not particularly captivated. Jamsran sniffs snuff from his forefinger and listens with the look of someone only feigning interest. When I have finished speaking he asks a question.

'What does elephant taste like?'

'I never tried it. India is predominantly a vegetarian country and Indians don't eat elephant as a rule.'

Agaa and I pitch our tent within the family's perimeter fence. Afterwards we stand outside and take in our new environment. To the south is a pine forest and to the east a slope of silver birch, while to the north and west are low mountains covered in pine. There are animals all around – sheep, goats, cows, bulls, yaks and horses. The family have wooden pens for the cows and sheep, and the mares are tied to large stakes. Riding horses are tied to logs set like goalposts with verticals supporting horizontals. A cute colt found abandoned by a river runs in energetic rings around the cabin. A fierce-looking dog is tied up near the pit toilet. Agaa and I go and sit behind the cabin next to a fence. Jamsran's son Gangaa joins us. Red-cheeked, he is in his early thirties and has a life-affirming, giggly laugh.

A yak and bull fight over cows in front of us. The pair butt heads, disengage, then headbutt each other again. The bull is clearly winning, but the yak is determined and won't give up even though he is disadvantaged by a carpet of reddish-brown shaggy fur that leaves him overdressed for summer combat.

'I don't understand why the yak is interested in the cows,' I say to Gangaa. 'Wouldn't that be like me trying to have sex with a gorilla?'

'No, they are of the same origin and the calves they produce are very strong.'

I ask Gangaa where the three local Giants were born. Damdin was born a short distance to the north-east, he says; Beijing was born behind a hill to the south-west; and Tseveenravadan was born near some trees a couple of kilometres north-west. All were born within a short distance of each other.

'Why have so many good wrestlers come from this area, Gangaa?'

'They say that great champions were bound to come from this place because the surrounding mountains look like an elephant, lion, eagle and *hangard*.'

In the morning I awake to the percussion of rain on the tent. Horses' whinnies and a blurting, shouting noise come from outside. Agaa and I go and investigate. The blurting shouts are

being made by one of Jamsran's sons, who is milking a mare
with his sister. Periodically he makes the noise in the ear of the
mare, and the daughter makes a higher-pitched softer sound, a
little like a coo-ey noise you might make to entertain a baby.
They explain that these noises calm the mare.

Milking mares is one of the countryside jobs that is said to
be good training for wrestlers. The son is in charge of the
wrestling-like task of moving and controlling the foals, and his
sister does the milking. The mares are tied up just beyond the
cabin fence, while a short distance away the foals are harnessed
by their necks to a taut rope running between two stakes. The
mare being milked has its left foreleg lifted off the ground and
tied so that it can't move or kick, and its foals are untied and
taken to her teat in turn. Some of the foals are docile, but
others are stubborn and struggle – and they are muscular and
strong enough to make the son slip and slide around in the
mud and have to work hard to keep his balance. Each foal is
allowed to drink from its mother's teat for a moment, then
pulled back to stand with its muzzle at her shoulder while the
daughter steps in to do the milking, but some of the foals don't
want to stop suckling and have to be dragged. After the mare
has been milked with its foal by its side, that foal is walked or
dragged back and refastened to its tether. Then the next foal is
marched over and the process begins again. All the mares are
milked every two hours, so the foals have to be repeatedly
grappled with. As part of a bid to collect country experiences,
Agaa has a go at frogmarching a foal and does well until it
forces him to thrash about in the mud and he falls over.

The plain is covered in a grey mist. Wispy white clouds
slowly drag through the treetops on a mountainside. I consider
the mountain Gangaa has said is shaped like an eagle. It just
looks like a hump to me.

'Agaa, why don't we go and take a walk in the direction of
that mountain and have a closer look? Perhaps we can find
someone to talk to about wrestling as well.'

We follow a cowpath. A rider and a herd of horses gallop by
in a burst of energy. At the base of the mountain are a few
cabins. We choose one to enter, but notice two dogs lying on a
heap of earth outside. One is curled up asleep, but the other is
alert and watches us. We choose another cabin and duck

through the door. An old woman in a torn red dress ushers us into a room and serves milk tea. A girl looks at me from under a bedcover in the corner of the room. She sits up, gets her boots out from under another bed, puts them on while standing, half falls over, drunk with sleep, and marches out the room.

'She was embarrassed,' says Agaa.

I notice an eagle-dancing wrestler ornament on the mantelpiece, and ask the woman whether she has any wrestling sons.

'None of my sons are wrestlers, but I hope a grandson will become one,' she says.

Her husband enters the room. Like Jamsran, he has a wispy white beard. He sits on a bed with his legs crossed and smokes a long-necked pipe. His wife places a stool near the stove and he moves there to be closer to us. I ask him why the River Uyalgan area has produced great wrestlers.

'It could be the environment, the grass and the water,' he says. 'The River Uyalgan is unusual. There used to be precious crystals in the river, though now they have been taken by geologists. It could have something to do with those crystals. It could also be because of the spirits of the mountains and the springs. People don't worship the spirits much any more. Also, the surrounding mountains are shaped like an elephant, lion, eagle and *hangard*, so people say great wrestlers were bound to come from here.'

'Which direction does the eagle face?'

'South-east. Eagles used to nest at the top of that mountain.'

On the way back I stand looking at the mountain again – and this time I can see what the others see. It does look like an eagle: a pyramid-shaped hump is its hood, and the slopes either side are its spreading wings.

Jamsran sits on his bed and places chess pieces on the middle of their opening squares. He seems distant and introverted. He suggests we go and visit Khadaa, the most serious wrestler among his sons, who is currently at a training camp on the other side of the river. The family lends me one of their best horses, an *argamag*. It gives a smooth ride because it puts one

foot down at a time, they say. Because it's a rare and precious
horse and because I've never ridden before, I'm anxious not to
do something wrong. I share my concerns with Agaa.

'I've only got experience of driving cars. If I borrowed a car
at home but had never driven before I'd be frightened of
crashing it. Is there any way you can crash a horse?'

'Cars are machines while horses are living things, so probably
there isn't a way to crash a horse,' says Agaa matter-of-factly.

While holding onto the reins, I board the horse from the left-
hand side – otherwise it will kick.

'Say "Chew, chew, chew" to get the horse to move,' says
Agaa.

It starts forward slowly. Within a few minutes, I'm beginning
to enjoy being in the saddle and want to ride faster, but I can't
get the horse to trot. Then, suddenly, it trots off by its own
accord. I let it go for a while, then use the reins to steer it back,
laughing.

'This is a lot of fun,' I tell Agaa, 'but the saddle is hard and
chafes a lot and I'm not sure whether I'll be able to have
children now.'

It's a weak quip, a sighter to establish whether Mongolians
share the English sense of humour.

'No,' says Agaa, dryly. 'You will still be able to have children.'

Thunder crashes violently nearby. It sounds like a sea
container falling onto a wharf from a great height. Heavy rain
begins to fall as lead-grey clouds blow in from the north. Agaa
and I decide to postpone our visit to the wrestling camp until
the rain has subsided, and go back inside the cabin. The
downpour doesn't stop. Khadaa comes back home in the early
evening anyway. He is tall and friendly and has a soft
handshake. He holds a local wrestling title: *Sum* Falcon. We sit
next to the wood-burning stove and talk. A bleary-eyed drunk
sits with us and drinks milk vodka. He's in the area to look for
a lost horse and has a hobble tucked into the back of his sash.
His head keeps falling towards me as though he's falling asleep,
until he catches himself and jerks upright. Agaa tells me to tell
Khadaa about India. As I speak, the drunk mimics my English
and, disconcertingly, puts his hand on my knee. After he's left,
everyone in the cabin laughs about him.

'Do you have drunks in England?' asks Khadaa.

'Of course, but perhaps our drunks are not as drunk as yours so early in the day.'

'Here they get drunk for three days at a time,' pipes in Maruysa.

I ask Khadaa about the wrestling camp.

'Six other wrestlers and I have been staying by the River Uyalgan for six days,' he says. 'It was like a holiday for us. We wrestled, ran and pushed logs against the current of the river to develop strength.'

I ask him who taught him to wrestle. Agaa doesn't even bother to translate the question.

'Mongolians naturally know the techniques of wrestling from childhood,' says Agaa. 'No one actually teaches them. They just work on improving them.'

This seems impossible to me. There is a lot of technical complexity in Mongolian wrestling. Surely you can't just pick it up.

'So do you know how to wrestle?' I ask Agaa, pointedly, assuming that as a slightly built law lecturer he probably does not.

'Of course,' he replies.

'I started wrestling when I was three years old and just improved through practice,' says Khadaa. 'Wrestling with animals year-round is good practice too. In summer we wrestle with the foals when we milk the mares, and in winter we grapple with the cows. You have to move the cows and lift them – not fully off the ground, of course – and keep them in grass and feed them. Feeding them is hard work. We own over a hundred cows. In autumn, we cut grass, and in spring we have to deal with the sheep.'

I go outside and sit looking at the eagle-shaped mountain. Though I have been around the family for only a couple of days, there is already a lot to reflect upon. I think about what Agaa has just said about how Mongolians don't formally learn to wrestle. I'd been told the same thing back in Ulan Baatar, but I couldn't see how you could casually learn the techniques of *Mongol Bokh*, however I've been watching two of Jamsran's scampish young grandchildren wrestle throughout the day. They play and wrestle and play and wrestle and have good technique even though they can only be about seven years old.

I loved to play football as a child as much as these children like to wrestle, and learnt to play in an unorganised way just by doing and watching others. I didn't go to football school – skill was developed informally. Mongolians probably learn to wrestle in the same unorganised and playful way.

It's twilight now yet no light is coming from inside the cabin – not even candlelight. The family don't have electricity, though they have a satellite dish and a TV indoors, which suggest they have access to a generator some of the year. They live simply, have minimal technology and are self-reliant. Before communism ended, Mongolian herders were state-supported and their livestock was the property of the state; now their animals are theirs and they have to look after themselves. As far as I can tell, the family produce almost all their own food. They drink the milk of their own cattle and mares, make their own cream and butter, slaughter and eat their own sheep, and hunt. Three or four times a year they move to a new location to live.

Clearly, life is predicated on hard physical work, a daily round of gripping, lifting, carrying, shouldering and moving as wood is chopped, fences are built, grass is cut for hay, water is fetched from the spring and untold other jobs are done. This is exactly the type of manual work that develops strength and endurance and has a lot of value to a wrestler, yet there is a world of difference between lifting or moving an inert object, where you know what you are going to do with it, and wrestling a living being, where you don't know what it is going to do to you. There is a common misconception that wrestling is solely about strength and that the type of strength it is about is no different from that which comes from lifting a weight, but when you grapple a living being you are in a world where anything can happen. You don't know how they will react, how they will move, what they will do next, what's on their mind. You have to be present, your reflexes must be sharp and you have to act with spontaneity.

It's time spent grappling with animals that has most value to a Mongolian wrestler. I'm taken by how milking mares is incredibly similar to wrestling. Manhandling a recalcitrant foal is a lot like wrestling another human being. Each side wants to impose their will on the other and not fall over or be forced to move where they don't want to go, which is about as simmered down a definition of the principles of wrestling as you can have. There must be many other jobs that involve grappling with animals – dealing with cattle, as Khadaa said, but also tasks like yoking oxen and breaking in horses – and the aggregate effect of every moment spent tussling with livestock is that Mongolians develop a reservoir of raw grappling ability that can be piped and shaped into the precise techniques of wrestling. Working with animals develops balance and grounding, in particular, because animals are more powerful than humans and obviously have the superior stability that comes with four legs. This means, in turn, that anyone consistently grappling with animals will naturally develop balance and grounding to counter theirs. An emphasis on balance and grounding is also codified by the rules of *Mongol Bokh*. Remaining on your feet is everything.

There is a remarkable convergence here between working life and wrestling. Back home we tend to see sport as the antithesis of work. If you work in an office and play football afterwards, you carry little from one world to the other. In physical terms you sit at a desk, hold a phone and tap a keyboard, make short walks to the water dispenser, then afterwards go to a park where you run and sprint, kick, head, chest and throw a ball. Perhaps the same strategic thinking that helps you market a product will help you unlock the opposition defence, but by and large you play football as a release from work, not an expression of it. You see it as a way to keep fit, to get rid of tension and leave work behind. Mongolian wrestling can also be a recreation but it is one that uses skills developed in everyday work: tussles with foals, horses and cows help a Mongolian wrestle, and wrestling helps him work.

You could say that Mongolians are brought down to their animals' level by working without modern farming technology, yet they have an incline of respect and admiration that runs in favour of animals and the virtues of the body. Exceptional wrestlers are named after powerful animals and birds, such as elephants, lions and falcons, and the outer limits of strength and bravery are recorded in stories of contests with animals. Here, they tell tales of wrestlers who wrestled bears, becalmed crazy yaks and lifted recumbent camels back onto their feet.

★

The first day of Naadam. I enter the cabin to find Khadaa carefully wrapping his wrestling costume in a white cloth and tying it around his waist under an acid-green sash. One of Jamsran's grandsons is standing with his arms out like a scarecrow while an aunt ties a sash around his *deel*. He is going to be a jockey. A group of us get in the jeep and drive to the venue. We pass riders bound for Naadam. The women wear headkerchiefs and beautiful silk *deels*, and their horses shine with polished tack. We stop at a forest *ovoo* on the way and get out. Horses' hair and blue votive scarves called *khadags* are tied to the *ovoo*'s branches. Hoof-shaped puddles of musky-smelling urine circumambulate the shrine to betray the routes of riders who have already passed this way.

After Khadaa and Maruysa have made offerings to the spirit, we get back in the jeep and continue through the forest until we reach a valley on the other side. The wrestling arena is at the far end of the valley and consists of a small flat area up a hillside. The horse-race finish line is nearby – and just beyond that is a collection of stones marking an ancient burial site. Pine trees crowd the surrounding slopes. Herds of sheep and cattle busy themselves grazing. A herb-like smell perfumes the breeze. This is where I'd always imagined wrestling rightfully belonged: out in the open, under the sky, in clear view, at the centre of a community's life, in front of the ancestors. It's a vindication to see wrestling given real status – to see it promoted from dingy London basements and taking centre stage in an idyllic pastoral scene.

'This is beautiful,' I say to Agaa, high on the moment and the idea.

'Yes,' he says. With mock cynicism, he adds: 'I will have to have a cigarette.'

The Naadam is for the River Uyalgan and a neighbouring small community. In everything but scale, it is the same as the national event: the competition follows the same structure and the wrestlers adhere to the same rituals. Appeals to the crowd swell the entry to 32, the minimum requirement. Latecomers wrestle in whatever they are wearing – jeans, riding boots, *deels*, it doesn't matter. There is no real barrier between audience and participants.

Two small wooden stands face each other across the

wrestling arena. One is for wrestlers, while the other is reserved for spectators and honoured guests. An elderly man with a smudge of snuff above his top lip and a kind, blotchy face sits at the centre of the front bench of the spectators' stand. After each bout he takes a handful of cheese cubes from a bowl in front of him and awards them to the winning wrestler, who usually throws the cheese in a shower behind him as he jogs back. The horse-racing and wrestling are contested simultaneously, and the spectators either sit to watch the wrestling or spectate from horseback. Whenever they see the child jockeys come whooping up the hill, slapping their horses' flanks, they run or ride over to the horse-race finish line, then trickle back afterwards.

'This is basically a cattle market,' says Agaa.

'Cattle market?'

I look around.

'I can't see anyone buying and selling cows,' I say.

'No, actually, I mean cattle market in the sense that this is where Mongolian men and women get a chance to meet each other and for romances to develop. During winter, when there's snow and it's cold, people only have the opportunity to visit relatives, but in summer they can travel more easily – and there's also less work to do – so actually they can meet all the people in the community who they don't get an opportunity to see during the rest of the year.'

Somehow I miss Khadaa's first bout, but I pick out the drunk who came by yesterday to look for his lost horse. He crouches over and rests his head on his opponent's shoulder, and grips the jacket tie-cord. His opponent tries to throw him with a sweeping leg movement, but he is sober and alert enough today to quickly disentangle his leg and counter with a trip. I catch Khadaa's second bout. He strokes his hair back, crouches and stamps his foot as a feint. He and his opponent fight for holds while bent over at right-angles. They straighten. Khadaa tries to duck his head under his opponent's arm and get behind him but fails. Soon after Khadaa grabs his opponent's leg, and successfully lifts and topples him. He goes to collect his cheese, which he donates to Agaa and me. Khadaa wrestles cautiously at the outset of his next bout. Eventually he makes a decisive attempt to throw, but both he and his opponent fall at the same time and the decision is given against Khadaa. As he leaves the arena, he looks over, smiles and taps his elbow to explain: he lost because his elbow touched the ground first.

As the tournament nears a climax, the crowd shout instructions. To encourage them to get a move on, the *zasuuls* slap the buttocks of a pair of wrestlers who have been fighting for about half an hour without a result. A stocky friend of Khadaa's goes on to win the competition. On the way home, we find him sitting at the forest *ovoo*.

'I hear it's good luck to touch the sweat of the winning wrestler,' I say.

He laughs. 'You can't. There's none left.'

The monastery ruin is on the banks of the ale-coloured River Url. Two tall wooden struts that once supported the roof stand forlornly with blue *khadags* tied to them. Beams organised like a ground plan lie in the grass. The branches of a small prayer tree struggle to accommodate slithers of brocade, lengths of horses' hair and *khadags* – all of which have been tied as devotional offerings. Clearly the ruin is treated as sacred. Gangaa recounts what he knows about the monastery.

'It was called Dayan Deerkh and built in 1860 around a stone man,' he says. 'There is a legend that the man stole one of Chinggis Khan's queens and was chased here. He turned to stone just as his pursuers were about to catch him. The figure had magical properties. People say that a man used to tie his horse to it before he went hunting but whenever he returned the horse would always be untethered. Scholars who researched the stone figure believe it was actually an ancient Turkic monument.'

Stone men dating from about the seventh century are to be found at burial sites in other parts of Mongolia and beyond. Whatever its origin, the stone figure that used to stand here probably became the centre of a local shamanist cult and the lamas later absorbed it into their religion.

Two large cube-shaped stones are piled one on top of the other next to a silver birch tree, with a sun-bleached horse's skull lodged in its boughs. The top stone has obviously been placed on the bottom one by human hands. I try to budge it but can't and guess it weighs about 100kg.

'What are these stones for?' I ask Gangaa.

'When the monks held Naadam here, there was a ceremony in which the wrestlers left in the last four had to pass these stones to each other while on horseback. Wrestlers who came here from outside the area to compete were intimidated by the stone-passing ceremony because they were worried that they wouldn't be able to perform it properly. Part of my brother Khadaa's training before Naadam was to come here and lift these stones.'

By lifting the stones, Khadaa made a connection with the wrestling monks, which I find deeply poignant. Though the monastery itself has been trashed, it is still possible to connect with its dead monks through the simple act of lifting stones they too used for exercise. These stones must have passed through many hands and are consecrated by a long accumulation of honest efforts to lift them.

'Do you know anything about the wrestling monks, Gangaa?'

'There was a monk called Jaminchoijil Elephant who had a very strong horse. While he wrestled he would ask people to hold his horse and give them the leash, but because the horse was so strong they would always lose it. After wrestling Jaminchoijil would say, "But where's the leash I gave you?" They would reply, "The horse took it," and he would say, "But I can't understand how that could happen. How did the horse escape without the leash breaking?" If the horse ran away while Jaminchoijil held it, he would always be left with a broken length of strap in his hand.'

A man arrives on horseback in a cloud of flies. Gangaa holds the back of his sash to help him down. His horse relaxes, stretches out its back legs and hoses urine into the grass. The man is old and frail. The bridge of his glasses is stuck with tape. He introduces himself, says his name is Senge and sits beside me on a log.

'We used to worship here,' he says. 'Many strong wrestlers came out of this monastery. All of them were great wrestlers.'

He gets up to make an offering at the prayer tree, then sits down again.

'Did you yourself see the monks wrestling here?'

'Sure, I was a child back then, but I saw the monks wrestle.'

He points to a spot near the riverbank.

'Naadam used to be held on the bankside and the lamas used to sit in the back of a tent to watch.'

Senge says he is in a hurry to visit his son and cannot speak at length, but to call on him at his son's home to talk further. Gangaa helps him back onto his horse and he leaves.

We break from scrutinising the ruins and wander towards the river. Grasshoppers and locusts rattle away whenever we step near. Some fall into the water and are carried along by the current. They float downriver to an overhanging bush where swirls meet each one as fish rise to take them.

'What fish are they, Gangaa?'

'Lennok.'

'I have some fishing tackle back in the jeep. I'll go and get it.'

I return with a telescopic rod, reel and a box of small spinners and lures, and lend Gangaa some line and a hook. He catches a grasshopper, baits the hook and lets it float downriver. I try spinning. Gangaa soon pulls a lennok out the water, at which he giggles and laughs. I decide to copy his tactics. Agaa and I attempt to catch a locust or grasshopper to use as bait. We dive at them, and stumble and fall and laugh like children at our own uselessness until we manage to catch a few. I bait a hook with a locust, cast it a short distance and let it float downriver. There's a boil as a fish takes the bait. The rod tip bends and jigs as I haul in a lean lennok weighing a few pounds.

Agaa steps in to kill it with the butt of his hunting knife. He whacks the fish hard on the head. There's a sickening, hollow sound. He whacks it again and again, far harder – and far more times – than necessary, as though channelling all his pent-up urge to kill into this one act of slaughter. A froth of blood forms at the fish's gills, and blood splatters from its head. Its eyes glaze. It's dead.

'Stop, Agaa,' I say.

But Agaa keeps punching its head with the butt of his knife.

'Agaa, it's dead, you can stop now. Agaa, stop! Stop! It's dead!'

Eventually he stops.

*

The pictures on the walls of Vanchinkhorloo's home amount to a raging ideological clash. Photos of communist leaders – Brezhnev, Andropov, Chernenko, Gorbachev, Lenin – hang alongside posters of the Dalai Lama and a golden Tibetan Buddhist statue. Then there's a newspaper photo of Dolly the cloned sheep – always likely to become a celebrity in a country that runs on mutton. Vanchinkhorloo is said to be the local expert on the wrestling monks of Dayan Deerkh. A large man of about sixty with cropped white hair, he used to be Mongolia's deputy chief of police and holds a national wrestling title, Falcon. It seems odd that he is at home, while everyone else is either watching or taking part in the Naadam for the whole of Tsaagan Uur *sum* that is currently being held in a stadium a short walk away. His radio is tuned to the commentary for the national tournament.

Vanchinkhorloo's wife serves milk vodka, while Agaa makes small talk. The atmosphere is strained. While Agaa tries to humour him, Vanchinkhorloo sits and runs a finger over the table in front of him, and sometimes speaks and sometimes falls silent. I sit quietly, and wait for a cue to join in the conversation, but sense the unwelcome intrusion of the same sort of unfathomable hostility towards me experienced before. Eventually Vanchinkhorloo asks me directly why I have paid him a visit.

'I would like to find out about the wrestling monks of Dayan Deerkh.'

He goes outside and returns with an exercise book in which he has written notes. He sits and reads.

'There were 40 or 41 monastery Naadams,' he says.

He gives a list of winners. Jaminchoijil, the wrestler Gangaa mentioned, is among them. Jaminchoijil won the monastery Naadam seven times, says Vanchinkhorloo. Chogdov and Dashbalgar were also monk-wrestlers of note. Chogdov and Jaminchoijil were repressed, he says – in other words murdered by the communists – while Dashbalgar survived the purge and died in old age after falling from a horse.

'How did you find out this information?'

'I spoke to old folk. Jaminchoijil was the best out of the champions. He was born in 1878.'

Vanchinkhorloo lists names of other wrestlers and relates

short anecdotes about a few of them, but there is not much more he can tell other than these bare facts, he says.

'I asked many old folk about the wrestlers of the monastery, but often they couldn't even remember their names. If they couldn't remember their names, what could they tell me?'

He closes his book: 'So that is it – about the monastery.'

Just the basic facts and statistics: a policeman making enquiries. I don't believe Vanchinkhorloo knows so little about the wrestling monks and wonder why he isn't prepared to talk. Perhaps he thinks he'll be giving away hard-earned research too cheaply, or perhaps the old communist in him is suspicious of Westerners. Then again, maybe I'm reading too much into the situation and he simply wants to get me out the way so that he can listen to the radio in peace. I don't want to just leave the conversation there, and try a different tack. I ask Vanchinkhorloo about his own wrestling career with the intention of returning to the subject of the wrestling monks once I've got him to talk more freely, but he is just as unforthcoming, so I reluctantly decide it would be best to leave.

Agaa and I wander over to the stadium. Neat piles of firewood are stacked up outside the local homes.

'Didn't you think it was strange that he had both pictures of communist leaders and Tibetan Buddhist posters on the walls?' I say.

'I wondered about that too,' says Agaa. 'Maybe as he's got older his mind has naturally turned to religious questions.'

'Or maybe the pictures of communist leaders are his and the Tibetan Buddhist stuff is his wife's.'

The stadium is full of spectators. A dog wanders onto the wrestling arena and laps up prize cheese thrown on the grass. A *zasuul* aims a cheese cube at the dog and hits it flush on the back. It runs off through a hole in a fence, the *zasuul* grins and the crowd cheer. The wrestling has progressed to the fourth round. One hundred and twenty-eight wrestlers entered the tournament but only sixteen remain. I look around to see whether Khadaa is among them, and notice him standing on the right wing. Khadaa wins his next two bouts, which means he is down to the last four. At the beginning of the semi-final, he and his opponent rest their hands on their knees and carefully scrutinise one other. Khadaa attacks and lifts his opponent's leg, but his opponent defends by grapevining his leg around Khadaa's, which locks them together in an apparent stalemate. Yet Khadaa has an ingenious counter. He quickly switches grips, grabs his opponent's legs and takes him down.

In the final, Khadaa faces an army Elephant who looks exhausted by his semi-final bout. I will Khadaa to attack quickly to take advantage of his tiredness. He does, but can't make any headway. Then he attempts another attack. He feints a sweep of the Elephant's right foot then quickly sweeps his other foot for real. The Elephant goes down. Khadaa has won. Khadaa's *zasuul* congratulates him with a kiss on each cheek, and the local governor presents him with a brick of tea and a yearling. A crowd spins around him in a vortex of congratulatory excitement. People pluck cubes of lucky cheese from the bowlful he has also been given as a prize.

That evening Jamsran's two grandsons are so pumped with excitement that they hold their own mini Naadam behind the family cabin. They act as *zasuuls* for each other and eagle-dance away. Khadaa does not return home till the following morning.

'People wouldn't let me get away,' he says. 'Everyone was giving me *airag* and shaking my hand.'

He is now a *Sum* Elephant and has a new nickname, 'English Khadaa', which is my unwitting legacy. Apparently Khadaa's victory is being attributed to my presence.

'People say that I must have won because I was trained by the Englishman,' says Khadaa.

It feels good to have entered the local folklore.

'They will still be using that nickname in ten years' time,' predicts Agaa.

Senge's daughter-in-law puts down a suitcase to use as a table, and deposits a bowl of dried cheese, and bread and cream. She then starts rolling out dough to make *khuushuur*. I give Senge a bottle of vodka; he passes his snuff bottle. We sit on mattresses on the floor. I ask Senge to talk about Dayan Deerkh, which he saw first-hand as a child. He says the monastery was large and beautiful, and had a gilded roof. He remembers the statues of

Buddha inside the temple, and he remembers the stone figure. It was shaped like a person, and the rock was white and crumbly. More than 500 monks lived at the monastery, he says.

'Tell me about its Naadams.'

'As I remember it, there were many Naadams there before the purge. The biggest event of the year was Naadam – it was bigger than the *sum* Naadam is today – and many wrestlers from other areas, from Ulan Baatar and maybe even foreign countries, used to go to the monastery to compete. The monks were better wrestlers than today's and a lot of good wrestlers lived in this area besides the monks.'

Senge's son, who is sitting with us, elaborates on this point. The Chinese ruled Mongolia before the communist revolution and moved families into the area to enforce the borders with Russia, he says. There were many strong men among these families such as a wrestler known as Black *Deel* of the Border Patrol who lived in the area over a hundred years ago. He is said to have been able to lift a rock that weighs over 800kg that you can still see on a roadside about 40km away. Someone once tried to move it with a tractor but couldn't.

I ask Senge whether he remembers any of the wrestling monks.

'I remember Jaminchoijil. He was tall, thin and fair-skinned and used to wrestle very well. There was also a monk called Chogdov who wrestled quite well. He was quite tall and well built and a good singer. Dashbalgar was also a good wrestler. Different wrestlers won Dayan Deerkh Naadam in turn. Wrestlers who won five rounds were awarded a red scarf. The monks wrestled at other monasteries too and competed in Danshig Naadam.' This was the name for national Naadam before the communist era.

Senge speaks slowly and soon begins to tire. His son takes over and relates a story he says his father might not remember, now that he is getting old, about a wrestler from Bulgan *aimag* called Luvsandash who was attacked by a bear. Luvsandash wrestled the bear and threw it to the ground, at which point others stepped in and killed it. He boasted before he wrestled at Dayan Deerkh that he was going to win the competition, yet he only made it to the last four. The point of the story is that competition at Dayan Deerkh was so strong that even a man who outwrestled a bear could not win. Senge says that wrestlers from outside the area never won the Naadam at Dayan Deerkh. It dawns on me that these stories and the story Gangaa told about the intimidating rock-passing ceremony are variations of the same tale Serdaram related back in Ulan Baatar about how good wrestlers from outside the area were always beaten by low-ranked locals. The force field I imagined operating in the River Uyalgan area related to the monastery. It was the reputation of the monk wrestlers and the reputation of their Naadam that generated a collection of tales about the River Uyalgan – tales that brought me all the way here to the epicentre of the force field: the monastery.

It is getting dark and late. I ask Senge what happened to the monastery during the purge and instantly regret it because he becomes sad as he answers. He says he isn't sure about the exact details – he didn't see the destruction with his own eyes – but the death squads came four times in late 1937 and spring 1938. Senior lamas were taken away and either shot in Moron or sent to work in Siberia. Nobody knows the precise details. At the time, people just didn't understand why this was happening, says Senge. They couldn't see what the monks were supposed to have done wrong. Anything of value kept at the monastery was stolen, while prayer wheels, thangka paintings and all the rest of the monastery's religious effects were thrown on a pyre and incinerated.

★

Leaving the family is hard to do. Part of me wants to stay here – for ever. I fantasise about marrying a pretty pale local girl, us sleeping together in a *ger* while wrapped in furs, raising wrestlers, and riding side by side with Gangaa on hunting trips in the snow. Of course, in reality, I would be useless here. I'm not conditioned for this type of hands-on physical life, and the winters are unbelievably harsh. I'd probably freeze to death.

We all assemble outside the cabin to say our goodbyes and exchange gifts. I give the family vodka, brick tea and money – gifts that appear unimaginative and mundane now that we have got to know and like one another; touchingly, Agaa gives Khadaa his jacket, which it transpires was given to him by an American wrestler who visited Mongolia; and Khadaa gives me a container of dried curd made from a single piece of silver birch bark. Gangaa judges this is the right moment to bring out and show a woolly mammoth bone he found in the river.

The family tell me to come back next year. They will have a horse ready and waiting, they say.

'And if you're ever in England. . .' I reply.

They laugh and promise to drop by if ever they're out riding that way.

Chapter 8

Namkhai

Norov Falcon lives in a poor, outlying district of Ulan Baatar where roads are rutted tracks and homes have no numbers. Each neighbourhood house or *ger* sits at the centre of a rectangular plot surrounded by a wooden fence taller than a man to guard against the fierce winds. In the still and heat of July the high fences appear overprotective, so that from outside the homes have the mean-spirited air of old codgers wearing greatcoats with turned-up collars in the middle of summer. The neighbourhood blocks are divided by gulleys into which rubbish has been thrown. Electric cables straggle from one pylon to another.

Norov is hammering nails into a section of fence laid out in front of him in his yard. He leads me inside his small home, which he built himself, through the kitchen, where a girl is preparing noodles, into a small back room in the north of the house, the most honoured place. On an altar-neat dressing table are boxes, necklaces, a china horse and white china rabbits, and above the table is the painting Norov wants to

show me of Namkhai Giant, the greatest wrestler in Mongolia's
remembered history. He won Naadam many times and died in
1911 aged only 41. Mongolians believe that hanging pictures
of great wrestlers in your home brings good luck, but Norov
has another reason for having the painting: Namkhai was his
great-uncle.

It's a crude painting – more a caricature than anything else –
but the veneration that surrounds it is palpable and touching.
Namkhai is depicted in a crouch, ready to wrestle. His
abdominals are regular and defined, like roof tiles; his neck, a
thick curve of ridged muscle like a horse's; and his large chest
narrows into a tiny waist – people say his lower back was so
hollow you could pass a bowl of sweets underneath him while
he lay on a bed. He looks like a familiar figure – a hod-carrier
perhaps, or a body-builder on steroids who works nights as a
doorman – but the truth is very different: Namkhai was a
Tibetan Buddhist monk. I have been told a number of stories
about Namkhai, so I know for certain that unlike the wrestling
monks of Dayan Deerkh he is well remembered. Maybe if I can
uncover further details about Namkhai's life, a background
story that explains the place of wrestling at the monasteries will
come attached.

We go and sit in Norov's homely living room, which is
stuffy and hot. Carpets hang from the walls. The plastic ceiling
tiles shine and appear to perspire in the heat. The way
Mongolians live makes no sense until you take into account the
harshness of the winters, and the fact that the hot summers are
all too brief. I give Norov presents of a bottle of vodka and
twisty, doughy snacks bought from an expensive department
store.

'This food and vodka does not know who its owner is,' he
says, which is an ornate way of saying we will share them.

Less decorum is evident in the way Norov tries to open the
bottle. He uses his teeth but fails. He gets up, goes to the
kitchen, opens the bottle there, returns, pours a little vodka
into the bottle lid and flicks it into the air as an offering to the
sky. His wife brings wooden tumblers, thinks about it, then
replaces them with better blue china ones. Norov fills my
tumbler and vigilantly gives refills every time he judges my liver
is in danger of surviving the afternoon.

I ask Norov to talk about his own wrestling career first, which seems only right considering he is a national Falcon. By the end of his account he is quiet and emotional, and clearly still aggrieved by the fact that his job robbed him of the time he'd have needed were he to progress further as a wrestler. I switch subjects and ask him to talk about his great-uncle. Namkhai became a monk when he was about eight or nine years old, says Norov. Each lama had one or two pupils whom they taught. Many children would congregate together at the monasteries because of this, and they were like today's schoolchildren in that they would play together, fight and wrestle.

'When Namkhai was seventeen he followed some wrestlers who were going to a local Naadam. They didn't want him to come and had left without telling him. One night the wrestlers were sleeping outside with their horses. Namkhai was sleeping nearby, and the wrestlers saw him and asked why he wasn't at home. They told him to go back and look after his animals, but Namkhai replied that he wanted to wrestle. The next morning he followed the wrestlers again and arrived at the Naadam with them. He went on to win the tournament. From that point on he almost never lost. People say he was defeated only once or twice.'

Namkhai's brother Luvsanjamba was also a great wrestler, says Norov. Luvsanjamba was physically bigger than Namkhai, but he was not as good. Namkhai became the champion wrestler of the eighth Jebsundamba, the highest-ranked lama in Mongolia and its spiritual head, while Luvsanjamba became the champion of the eighth Jebsundamba's wife, Dondogulam.

'Once Dondogulam organised a wrestling competition and Luvsanjamba and Namkhai had to wrestle each other – they were the last two. Dondogulam called Luvsanjamba and showed him a big brown sweet, almost the size of a head, with a yellow *khadag* and told him, "I will give this to the winner." Luvsanjamba didn't tell his brother about it and perhaps thought he could beat him. But when they wrestled, Namkhai easily beat Luvsanjamba, who became angry. Namkhai asked another wrestler why his brother was angry with him. He said that Mother – they called Dondogulam "Mother" – had promised Luvsanjamba a big sweet and yellow *khadag* if he won but he'd been beaten. Namkhai said, "He's such a fool. Before we wrestled he was behaving differently and was very aggressive, so I got annoyed with him." It was silly of Luvsanjamba. They shared the same *ger*, so if one of them won a sweet they would have shared it. At that time sweets were very rare.'

Norov relates that Namkhai once wrestled an up-and-coming wrestler called Buyantogtokh at a tournament in the east of Mongolia. Namkhai and Buyantogtokh were left in the last two, and Namkhai easily lifted and pulled Buyantogtokh across his arm to throw him. Before Buyantogtokh died, people asked him how strong Namkhai had been. He said that he was just happy to have survived his wrestling match with Namkhai. If he had tried to beat him he reckoned he would have been torn limb from limb. He said that yaks and horses could not compare with Namkhai in strength, though he had not fought a bear so he could not say whether Namkhai was as strong as a bear.

I ask Norov to repeat something he told me when we first met that may cut to the heart of the question of whether the monks believed wrestling had a spiritual dimension. Norov said that when Namkhai wrestled at Danshig Naadam, he painted hair on his head so that God – by which he meant Buddha – did not recognise he was a monk. Monks shaved their heads at the time while ordinary Mongolians grew a tuft of hair at the back. Norov said that Namkhai painted hair on his head to avoid bad karma, as you have to be aggressive to wrestle.

'It was a contradiction for Namkhai to be a monk and wrestler,' explains Norov. 'He was a very spiritual person and those who adopt the Buddhist path are not allowed to look at people or even animals with staring eyes. When you wrestle you have to call on hate to increase your strength. Monks were not supposed to look at others with evil eyes – and if he beat other wrestlers they would also think ill of him.'

The story sounds a little fanciful – predicated, as it is, on the idea that God looks down on the world from a great height, a distance from which he cannot make out whether hair is real or not. Also, I don't accept that you have to channel hate to wrestle. Aggression, perhaps, but not hate.

Norov gets up and says he is going to look at the horses – another ornate expression. He means he's going to take a pee outside. When he returns I ask him whether he has anything that belonged to Namkhai.

'I have his wrestling costume.'

'Can I see it?'

'I don't really show it to people. It's very precious. I keep it in a very holy place. The museum say they will pay as much as I want for it, but I won't sell it to them.'

I plead with Norov to let me see the costume, and perhaps because we have now finished the bottle of vodka between us and warmed to one other, he relents and grandly calls his wife in from the kitchen to fetch it. She takes a brown holdall from under a pile of materials. Inside, the jacket and trunks are neatly rolled and tied into a baton. Norov touches his forehead with the jacket and passes it over.

'It's a sacred relic,' he says.

I handle it with care. The jacket is made from red silk and has been torn and patched. It was one of Namkhai's first costumes, says Norov, which is why it is small. Between the shoulderblades is a small capsule made from material.

'Namkhai would place protective mantras there.'

I have one more question, a question saved till now, the end of our conversation, because Mongolians consider it impolite to talk about death. There are various stories about what happened to Namkhai's corpse. The disposal of his body was a delicate issue. People used to believe that in whichever direction a wrestler's head pointed when his body was left to be eaten by animals and birds, the Tibetan Buddhist way of dealing with the dead, the region that lay in that direction would subsequently produce great wrestlers. It was believed, too, that if you could take the bones of a great wrestler back to your homeland, your area would produce great wrestlers as a consequence. The story goes that Namkhai's bones were stolen for that reason. I ask Norov whether this is true. He is not offended by the question, and becomes animated and impassioned.

'That's right!' he says. 'Namkhai's bones were lost. People say they were taken to Arkhangai *aimag*, that a wrestler from there stole them.'

He re-rolls and ties the costume, and puts it back in the holdall.

The story of Namkhai's stolen bones, with its implication that wrestlers used shamanic practices to gain an advantage over rivals, is symptomatic of a magical rather than a spiritual dimension to wrestling. Nevertheless it is still intriguing and I consider going to Arkhangai *aimag* to search for the bones and the descendants of the person who stole them, and fantasise about finding a *ger* where an old man lives, who eventually admits that yes, his father took Namkhai's bones, before going to fetch them from a chest of drawers. Even if I don't find the robber's family, or it becomes clear that the story is probably a folk legend, by making the journey and asking relevant questions I might learn about the magical beliefs that used to couch wrestling. But, on further reflection, I see that it is whimsical to think you can investigate a theft nearly 90 years after it occurred – and Agaa points out that Namkhai's bones would have been offered to a spirit at an *ovoo*, so there appears to be zero point in making the trip. However, it would make sense to visit Bulgan *aimag*: Norov has a half-brother, an Elephant nicknamed Red Boots, who lives there in Saikhan *sum*, which is where Namkhai was born, and it is likely that he and others in the area will know more about Namkhai's life as a wrestler and monk.

Agaa is too busy to come with me to Saikhan *sum*, so I find another interpreter, a 21-year-old English student called Ouyuntsetseg who is girly and innocent, and afraid of dogs and slamming doors, yet dependable and has excellent English. Brandon and Brook decide to come along as well to continue their research into *yadargaa* in the countryside, and they arrange for their young female interpreter, Shuree, to accompany us. We hire a sour-faced driver who always wears the same suit jacket and trousers, and takes over a day and a half to reach Saikhan *sum*, which is about 300 miles north-east of Ulan Baatar, in his new Russian four-wheel-drive minibus.

The *sum* centre is a typical Mongolian settlement of small wooden homes, *ger*s and dilapidated brick buildings surrounded by low mountains. We go and introduce ourselves to the local governor, whose home is at the top of a hill. He is a middle-aged man with cropped white hair and big cheekbones, and he moves slowly. Brandon and I hand him gifts – cigarettes, a box of chocolates and a bottle of vodka wrapped in a spread from one of the *Observer* newspaper's magazine supplements. The governor gives the gifts a quizzical look, hesitates for a moment then accepts them. I notice that a painting of Namkhai, similar to the one in Norov's home, takes pride of place in the room above a mirror and has a fresh *khadag* draped on the frame.

'I see you have a painting of Namkhai,' I say. 'By coincidence, I'm visiting the area to find out all I can about him. Do you know much about him?'

'You're very lucky,' says the governor. 'I am a local historian and an expert on Namkhai Giant. In fact my name is Namkhai. My parents named me after him. We are distantly related.'

Brandon and Brook groan with envy at my good fortune.

'The painting was given to me by a well-known Lion called Jamayndorj who is famous throughout Mongolia for having lifted a camel. Last year, we, the people of this *sum*, decided to honour Jamayndorj by presenting him with a hundred sheep. He is from this *sum* though he now lives in the town of Bulgan. He thanked me for the sheep by presenting me with the painting of Namkhai.'

The governor says he has to go and milk the mares before he can talk further. While he is gone there is a spontaneous outbreak of wrestling as his two young grandchildren play-grapple on the carpet. The younger one tries to totter out the door, but the other grabs him round the waist and pulls him back inside, at which point they both wrestle and laugh. Brandon and Brook give the boys toy cars to play with and make a ramp with a roll of carpet to run the cars down.

The governor returns. He takes a book of handwritten notes from a briefcase on top of a cupboard and pulls up a chair. Namkhai was born in 1870, he says. He was one of five children – four boys and a girl. His father was a titled wrestler. When his four sons were young, Namkhai's father evaluated their strength. Though he believed Namkhai and Luvsanjamba would be tough wrestlers, he judged that his youngest son, Purevjav, was destined to be the best wrestler among his children. However Purevjav died aged thirteen after falling from a fence. When the birds had eaten his flesh, people saw that his ribs were not connected by flesh but cartilage. The governor moves on to talking about Namkhai.

'My great-grandfather was also born in 1870. Once, he and a friend were with Namkhai who said, "If you are strong, can you separate my two fingers?" And he pinched some snuff between his two fingers.'

The governor gets up and goes to a cabinet to find his snuff bottle, then comes back and pinches snuff between his forefinger and thumb to illustrate. 'My great-grandfather tried to pull one finger and his friend pulled the other, but they couldn't prise Namkhai's fingers apart. Those who were watching who were not wrestlers said that they had to be very weak to be unable to pull apart two fingers, but those who were watching who were wrestlers said that Namkhai's strength ran round his body and he had focused it at his fingertips.

'There was a wrestler called Gombsuren Lion. He was about the same age as Namkhai Giant and very strong. When he was quite old he squeezed a horse's body so tightly that it peed itself. People said to him, "Considering how strong you are, why did you never become a Giant?" He replied, "What do you mean? I was lucky to become a Lion. I won the title when Namkhai didn't challenge me in Naadam. If he had wrestled me, I wouldn't have become a Lion." Gombsuren said that neither a stallion nor a male camel could compare with Namkhai in terms of strength, though he did not know how strong tigers and lions were, and if they were stronger than camels and stallions then you could compare their strength with Namkhai's.

'A local family had a very strong and untamed horse, and each year that family used to give the horse to Namkhai to ride to Naadam. It was not very placid and people couldn't catch it easily, but Namkhai liked to ride it. One year, Namkhai, Luvsanjamba and twenty or thirty other wrestlers left this area to go to Ulan Baatar for Naadam. The wrestlers camped overnight on the way. To make a horse stay in one place, usually people tie their legs together with a hobble.'

The governor gets up and finds a hobble made from rope and leather to illustrate. 'In those days they used cow's leather so the hobble was very strong. When the wrestlers got up the next morning they found that Namkhai's horse was not outside the tent. It had broken its hobble and was running free. The wrestlers discussed the matter, and decided that they better try to catch it. They encircled the horses and Namkhai's was among them. Namkhai and Luvsanjamba told them to grab it as it tried to break out the circle, but the other wrestlers didn't like the idea, and talked among themselves, saying, "Who wants to be injured by a wild horse? The Giants take pride in their strength, so why don't they catch it?" So the wrestlers made the horse run towards the two Giants. Together they made it lie down like a little lamb. Namkhai held the horse's neck and pushed it upwards, lifting its front legs off the ground, while his brother grabbed its tail. That was how strong Namkhai was.'

He was also a good runner, says the governor. The lamas used to organise competitions. Young monks would carry big containers of soup, food or tea, and run with them. The containers were made from wood and had a capacity of about forty or sixty litres.

'Once they organised a running competition and Namkhai and my great-grandfather's older brother, Tudev, carried a container together. You see, they competed in pairs, each holding one of the container's two handles. Namkhai and Tudev were leading but were overtaken, so Namkhai pulled so hard on the handle that he broke Tudev's collarbone. Then he just carried the container by himself and won the race.'

A grandson tries to come into the room through the window. The governor shoos him away.

'There are a lot of stories I can tell you,' says the governor, when he is seated again.

The picture he is painting of Namkhai in words is the same one that hangs from his wall in oils. These are stories about a strong man that reveal nothing about Namkhai the monk. Namkhai remains curiously anonymous in these tales; they could be told about any strong wrestler. It is difficult to tire of hearing folky tales in which strength is expressed in encounters with animals and other ways that appear ingenious and rustic to someone used to hearing achievements expressed in cold measurements and statistics, but nothing is being revealed here about the religious dimension of Namkhai's life. I ask the governor to explain the connection between Tibetan Buddhism and wrestling.

'At that time most men in Mongolia were monks,' he says. 'It was impossible to celebrate Naadam if monks did not take part, because there were few men who were not monks.'

A commonsense answer, but it sounds glib and over-simplistic.

'Before the monks wrestled in Naadam they used to grow a circle of hair the size of a bowl back here.' The governor pats his head at the back to illustrate. 'This was so that it was as though they were not monks.'

'Norov told me that they painted hair on their heads so that God would not recognise them.'

'They tried to show God that they were just simple people. Why, I don't know, but before Danshig Naadam they grew their hair. In smaller Naadams they would wrestle with their heads shaved.'

The governor has nothing more to say about the links between wrestling and Tibetan Buddhism. I wonder whether he has so little to say because there really is no more to tell or whether the monk's tale was dropped from the story of Namkhai's life during the communist era. It is possible that a religious dimension would not have survived the years of religious suppression, and that the monk's tale was censored and lost over time. It had been my hope that the monk's story would have been hidden away while the communists ruled Mongolia and now that communism is over it is safe to give it a new airing. I want to believe that enduring communism was like having to endure a painful house guest and now that the guest has left, you can breathe a sigh of relief and act and speak as you please again. But the fact is that the guest utterly trashed the furniture, carpets, floorboards and everything before leaving, utterly destroying the monastic culture that dominated Mongolia, of which Namkhai was a part. Under the circumstances it would be entirely predictable if his story lost any religious dimension it may have had.

It is getting late. We stop talking. Brandon and Brook slinked out earlier to do some interviews. They return and we sit together at a table and eat stacks of mutton dumplings that the governor's wife cooks. Afterwards, we find the local school. The governor says we can sleep there while the children are away on holiday. Ouyuntsetseg and Shuree take one dormitory room, while Brandon, Brook and I take another. Laughing, we bounce up and down on the metal spring beds, which sag like hammocks. Brandon and Brook leave to find more people to interview. I am tired out by the long journey and want to get to bed early, but the school director comes and sits on a bed in the room and obviously wants to socialise. He is a tall man with a creased, worn face and a thin moustache. His flies and belt are undone and his breath smells of drink. He details an erratic list of facts about the area. He says there is a coal mine nearby and a French professor has just left who studied traditional dairy products – not before giving a few thousand dollars to renovate the school – and there are many stray dogs in the neighbourhood and this *sum* has the most livestock per head of population of any in Bulgan *aimag* and the third most in the whole of Mongolia. He sits and lingers and braves out the embarrassing silences in between his statements. Either he is being genuinely friendly or he is angling for a gift, a bottle of vodka perhaps, in return for letting us sleep at the school.

The caretaker comes and puts a bulb in the ceiling socket. The director gets up to leave, but changes his mind and sits down. Then he stands again. I look out the window to try to disengage from his attention; he looks out the window to see what it is that has caught my eye, then moves slowly to the door. He changes his mind again and sits back down. Then he really does leave, only to return with the lid of a thermos flask to use as an ashtray. We should smoke together, he says. I tell him I don't smoke. He says I should come and see the school heating plant. I follow him along the corridor and dig deep into my repertoire of diplomatic expressions to find something suitable to express admiration for a wood-burning stove. Afterwards the school director leaves.

The governor is not at home the following morning. Before going to look for him, I use the pit toilet in the corner of his yard. As I stand to pee between the slats, I am forced to hunch over and look down by the low ceiling. The face of Teletubby

Po, red as though crimson with embarrassment at her reduced circumstances, stares back from among the yellow excrement below. Obviously, the *Observer* magazine used to wrap the governor's vodka was put to practical use.

I wander over the top of the hill to find the governor milking mares with his wife on the far side, and stand back and enjoy the spectacle. It's not often you see a politician milking a horse. When the governor has finished, he returns home to smarten up in preparation for giving a guided tour of the places where Namkhai lived. He changes out of his jogging pants into a pair of brown slacks, a double-breasted grey jacket and felt hat, and his son fetches him his snuff bottle from a chest of drawers. We get in the minibus and drive through treeless steppes and craggy mountains, and pass scatterings of *gers*. The vehicle scares chubby marmots into their burrows.

'We've had a good summer,' says the governor. 'There's been lots of rain, the grass has grown well and the marmots are fat. In summer, the people around here like to relax, take it easy, drink *airag* and eat marmot meat.'

The place where the governor says Namkhai spent winter is under the brow of a hill that gives shelter from northerly winds. The site is still in use. A circular area has been levelled so that a *ger* can be pitched, and timbers are piled up ready to build fences. Fresh grass grows in a churn of mud where an animal pen was situated last winter. A contorted twist of a cow's skeleton lies on the ground. The governor relates an anecdote about how, one year, Namkhai and Luvsanjamba neglected to peel away the dung that collected on the ground before the temperature dropped and it froze. In treeless areas such as these, dung was a valuable commodity and would be used as both fuel and to build fences. When the brothers did peel away the dung it was frozen into one huge unbreakable sheet – at which point the governor's great-grandfather, an old Falcon, came along and lifted and dropped a large rock onto the dung sheet to break it into pieces. The point of the anecdote is that it flatters the strength of the governor's ancestor.

The area where Namkhai spent summer is a short drive away. A flock of rams grazes on a rocky outcrop nearby. Namkhai's monastery was situated about 50 miles away again, near the town of Bulgan. The governor maintains that when

Namkhai became a champion he remained a monk but left the monastery to live in this area and look after livestock, like a normal Mongolian. I sense that there is going to be little chance of finding out detailed information about Namkhai's life, in which case the broad facts, such as where exactly he lived, take on greater relevance. If Namkhai lived at the monastery that would at least imply that the monks embraced wrestling and a serious wrestler would not have to give up his commitments to the religious path; but if Namkhai left the monastery, it may have been because he could not be both a committed monk and a serious wrestler at the same time. The governor takes the latter view, but he strikes me as someone with little or no religious feeling who is unlikely to give Buddhism a proper place in the story of Namkhai's life. He is a socialist politician and I have noticed that there is no Buddhist paraphernalia in his home, unlike in the homes of many other Mongolians. Perhaps, when the governor speaks about Namkhai, he is acting like a ventriloquist and throwing his voice and beliefs onto the lips of Namkhai's life.

We walk to the top of a gently sloping hill from where there is a panoramic view of the area. Below, the narrow Ugalz River snakes towards the mighty Orkhon. The governor says that Namkhai was born around here. I ask him why Namkhai died early, aged 41, and he responds with a remarkable story. Namkhai was killed by a curse, he says. This region of Mongolia used to have an intense rivalry with Tsetsenkhaan, a large pre-revolutionary province in the west. Namkhai became ill and bedbound and did not wrestle in 1905 or 1906. In 1906 Luvsanjamba lost to Chultem, the champion of Tsetsenkhaan, in two Danshig Naadams. When Luvsanjamba came home he told Namkhai that Chultem had become so good that even he would not be able to beat him.

Namkhai rose to the challenge. He recovered enough to wrestle at Naadam the next year and insulted Chultem by challenging him in the third round. From the third round onwards, titled wrestlers pick their opponent. Usually wrestlers do not challenge strong opponents early on, because that way there is a chance they will be knocked out of the competition by someone else. Chultem was impatient to wrestle but had to wait for Namkhai's *zasuul* to sing both the titles of the eighth Jebsundamba and Namkhai. (Namkhai's went: 'Really powerful, foremost, imposing, immensely capable, unshakeable, heroic, brave, forever majestic, wonderful, the most active, always improving, the most handsome, very interesting, enthusiastic, resourceful, magnificent, peaceful, with unlimited strength, truly reliable, beneficent, incredible, praiseworthy, considerably quick, proud, of great strength, too sharp, calm, impressive Giant'.)

As Namkhai eagle-danced, Chultem is supposed to have told him to get on with it, and Namkhai is supposed to have replied, 'I, who will win, am in no rush, but you, who will be beaten, are.' When they wrestled, Namkhai quickly beat Chultem. The curse was his revenge. However, the governor says that according to the records, Namkhai didn't actually challenge Chultem in the lower rounds. He suggests the story may have been created by Namkhai's admirers to further inflate his reputation.

We return to the van and drive to the area where Red Boots, Namkhai's great-nephew, is likely to have pitched his *ger* for the summer. After asking for directions, we locate the *ger*, go inside and sit down. Red Boots is sitting cross-legged on the floor at the back. He is tall, and has a strong voice and cackly laugh. There is a volatile excitement about him that suggests he is at least half drunk. Red Boots' son lies sleeping next to a bowl of fatty sheep's guts, organs and bones. A baby girl straddles and crawls over his drunk body. Ouyuntsetseg makes introductions, after which I stand to present Red Boots with a bottle of vodka.

'Wait, wait,' he says.

He instructs a boy to fetch something. The boy opens a drawer and brings out a plastic bag from which he takes a hero's hat with an Elephant badge. He gives the hat to Red Boots, who puts it on. Now Red Boots is ready to accept the vodka.

'It is our tradition,' he says.

Red Boots wants us to drink the bottle straight away, but Ouyuntsetseg convinces him that we should talk first. He says he is 76 years old and won the title of Elephant in 1951. A thousand and twenty-four wrestlers participated in Naadam, and Red Boots made it to the last eight. As that year was an anniversary of the communist revolution, titles were awarded a little more generously than usual. Red Boots' real name is Janchivdorj. He got his nickname after he wrestled in Naadam wearing boots made from red cow's leather. The audience noticed he was wrestling well and referred to him as 'Red Boots' because they didn't know his proper name. The nickname stuck.

'I only participated in Naadam three times because I worked on a collective farm during the communist era and had to look after five or six hundred sheep that had to be sheared in summer, when Naadam was held. If I couldn't meet the wool quota I had to pay the difference out of my own pocket. Had I wrestled in Naadam more often I don't know what would have happened. I believe that had I wrestled in Naadam ten times I would have stayed in the upper rounds five times.

'Life is very hard. I have many children. My children were very young and my wife died. You see the photo?'

He points to a picture of his wife on a chest of drawers. He is close to tears. I wait a moment while he composes himself, then ask him to talk about his great-uncles, Namkhai and Luvsanjamba.

'I never saw Namkhai, but I saw Luvsanjamba. I remember that he was a very big man. He had a small face with red skin. My parents had quite a large *ger*. When he sat at the back, his head reached there.' Red Boots points to where the rafters meet the wooden latticework walls – about four feet off the ground. Mongolians sit on low stools, so this indicates that Luvsanjamba was a big man. 'People say that Namkhai was smaller than Luvsanjamba.'

Red Boots clears his throat.

'As I have heard it, Namkhai was a very intelligent, active and strong man. People say he had hide instead of skin. He was good at giving people advice. For example, if people had an argument or something, he would say just a few good words to solve the dispute.'

The son wakes up, yawns and sits on the bed on the east side of the *ger* beside the governor. Then he stands and takes the governor's arm and makes them switch places so that the governor sits towards the back. It's correct etiquette, but the governor is irritated by being manhandled. While I speak to Red Boots, his son chats loudly to the governor, who leans forward, wipes his forehead, looks down or away in embarrassment, and nervously bends back the fingers of one hand with the other. Now and then he forces a smile to acknowledge something the son has said, to humour the drunk.

'Namkhai wasn't so large, but he was well built with unrivalled strength,' says Red Boots. 'If he lived today, he would be the best wrestler in Mongolia and famous internationally in many styles of wrestling.'

He tells the same story the governor related about the time Namkhai was ill and stayed in his *ger* while his brother went to Danshig Naadam and lost to Chultem. He leaves the story half hanging. Red Boots tells other stories that are variations of the same folky tales I have already heard – and now and then the governor corrects him, which suggests he knows these stories better than Red Boots. I feel disappointed. I hoped that Namkhai's oldest living relative would be the guardian of exclusive and valuable information, but that doesn't appear to be the case.

The drunk son vandalises the dignity of the proceedings and it becomes impossible to concentrate on the conversation. He manically picks cigarette butts from the floor and bins them in a cigarette packet. Then he plays with the little girl too energetically. She has a toy fluffy rabbit eating a fluffy carrot, and adds to the interference by biting the label off and crying. The son pours *airag* into a bowl, picks out a horse's hair, passes it to me, then throws his arms back in an exaggerated motion, the international gesture for down in one. Irritated by him, I force a smile, drink a little *airag*, but pointedly put the bowl down quickly, avoiding his gaze. To spare the governor further embarrassment, I decide we should leave not long after.

A *ger* pitched next door to the governor's cabin doubles as his den. In the morning a Russian jeep is parked outside. Someone's arrived. I go inside. The governor is sitting on a stool and leaning against a ceiling prop with his legs extended, smoking. The guest is sitting with him – along with the school director, who already has a drunken beam on his face, and our driver. They are sharing a bottle of Bolor vodka, the best

Mongolian brand, and bowls of *airag*. A newspaper is being passed round too. The governor breaks from talking to his friends to relate more anecdotes about Namkhai. Afterwards he says I should be paying him for the information. It is difficult to tell whether he means it or is joking. I ask Ouyuntsetseg whether she thinks he is serious. She is not sure but thinks he may be. I react as though he is joking.

The governor suggests we go and meet a local man called Lunden who owns Namkhai's snuff bottle. We should be able to find him at a nearby lake with healing waters where people go to holiday, he says. We get in the minibus and find the lake. Tents and *gers* are pitched around it. Children splash about in the shallows, while their parents sit in the water. Bras and underwear lie out to dry on the grass next to sun-bleached bones. We park near the jeep of a family about to leave. A girl brushes her hair, which she holds out to one side; a boy sits waiting on a plastic water container; a man washes a car mat; another boy folds up his clothes.

Lunden is sitting in the water and busy rubbing mud on his body then washing it off. An old woman with bare, pale and saggy breasts, who is probably his wife, sits beside him. The governor goes over to speak to Lunden, then returns and says Lunden will come over to talk in about fifteen minutes, before going off to bathe in the lake himself. While I wait, an ancient man arrives holding a walking stick with one hand and a crutch with the other. I wonder how healing these healing waters are supposed to be. He walks in a semicircle, uses his stick to flick away a dried cowpat and sits down. Then he drags himself into the water and lies on his front. When he is finished bathing, he pulls himself backwards out of the water, puts on his *deel* and smokes a pipe.

Lunden, too, gets out the water, dresses and comes over. He looks in his sixties and has a forceful voice. He says he doesn't have Namkhai's snuff bottle with him – which is disappointing. His son took it to Ulan Baatar to be valued and to confirm that it is made from black jade. Lunden says he bought the snuff bottle in the 1980s and paid an *argamag* for it. The man who sold it to him said that Namkhai was given it for doing a good deed. Someone from western Mongolia was passing through the area in a caravan when one of his camels got stuck in a local river. Namkhai lifted the camel out, and the man gave him the snuff bottle to thank him. It amounts to another folk tale – and Lunden says he can't be certain whether it is true. He has been doing his own research and he is not sure whether the snuff bottle ever really belonged to Namkhai – though he knows for a fact that Luvsanjamba once owned it.

Yesterday's bottle of Bolor vodka lies empty on the floor of the *ger*. I give the governor leaving presents to thank him for his help – cigarettes, vodka and sweets in a plastic bag. He takes the bag and deposits it on a bed without looking inside or acknowledging the gifts in any way. Maybe he is disappointed. Perhaps he really did expect to be given money for his help. His wife takes a cigarette packet and quickly stashes it under a mattress. The governor says he will tell one more story about Namkhai and relates the tale that Norov also told about the time Namkhai wrestled and beat Buyantogtokh, and how Buyantogtokh later told people he considered himself lucky to have survived the encounter. I feign interest, but inside I'm thinking about how I'm going round in circles and hearing the same folky stories again and again. I've been looking for information about Namkhai the monk but have been hearing the tale of Namkhai the strong man, and behind that story has been another story about an era of intense regional rivalry. Competition between provinces used to be so strong that wrestlers might steal human bones, or place a curse, to gain an advantage. Maybe this explains why Namkhai kept a protective mantra in his jacket: perhaps he used it to ward off malicious supernatural forces summoned by rivals.

Brandon, Brook and I load up our stuff on the minibus. We set off. A marmot hunter is coming with us and sits with his son in the passenger seat. He has offered to show us the route to Olziit if we give him and his son a lift to their *ger*, which is on the way. Not long after we've left the town, the hunter spots marmots near the side of the road and the driver stops the vehicle. The hunter takes off his hat and excitedly loads his rifle. He reaches for a costume in his sack. I will him to pull out a hat with pretend ears. Ever since Danzan mentioned that marmot hunters wear hats with pretend ears, I've been eager to see a dancing marmot hunter with pretend ears in action. The hunter takes out a white shirt but no hat with ears. He does have another marmot-hunting prop though: a white, frizzed, cow tail on a stick. By the time he has put on his costume and assembled his equipment, the marmots have taken cover down their burrows. We move on until we sight some more. This time the hunter is prepared. He gets out the minibus and heads up a hillside. I get out too and watch from a distance. The hunter crouches and spins the frizzy white cow tail like a propeller as he inches forward. The cow tail must be a device, like pretend ears, to transfix the curious marmots and leave them vulnerable. The hunter disappears over the brow of the hill. Half a minute later he returns with a fat marmot shot clean through the head.

We get back on the road and head on till we reach someone's winter place. The hunter hangs the marmot on the back of a cabin. Its innards slurp and suck as he cuts it open and removes the inedible organs, which he throws on a metal sheet where they come to rest looking like an anatomical diagram. He turns the marmot inside out like a sock, and tells everyone to start a fire and find stones. He heats the stones in the fire, then stuffs them inside the marmot and turns it outside out again. The marmot smokes and fizzes as he shakes the stones inside it. The hunter then rolls the marmot on the ground like a rolling pin to knead the hot stones into its flesh. It sizzles, stews and steams. When it is cooked, we first share the liver, which is supposed to be the best part and which we eat with a piece of fat, then we share the rest of the animal and drink the juices. Two hunters arrive on horseback and join the picnic. The driver finds a cheap bottle of vodka and uses his plastic car ashtray to serve out measures. By the time the picnic is over, the bottle of vodka is empty and the driver is well on the way to being drunk.

We drop the marmot hunter off at his *ger*. The driver says he wants to follow him inside and drink *airag*. Convinced that he will be too drunk to drive afterwards, Brandon and Brook forcefully tell him he can't. The driver flies into a rage. He says he's not having Americans tell him what to do in his own country and threatens to leave us stranded by the roadside. He is a Mongolian, and it is the birthright of all Mongolians to drink *airag* in summer, he says, emotionally. He storms off and disappears into the *ger*. We sit in the minibus, and wonder whether the driver will ever come back. But he soon returns. We continue down the road in silence. The driver drunkenly veers off the road only the once.

★

There's one last way to try to find out about Namkhai's life as a wrestling monk. A newspaper article says monks initiated before the purge have been trickling back to the new monasteries since the institution of religious freedom. There's a slim chance that someone who lived at Namkhai's monastery before it was destroyed has returned to live at the new one built on its site. If so, he should know how wrestling fitted into monastic life.

Ouyuntsetseg and I take the overnight sleeper train from Ulan Baatar to Erdenet, then a shared jeep to the town of Bulgan. In the morning we follow a pair of claret-robed young monks who are heading out of town across the hills. We pass through herds of munching and snorting black goats and dirty sheep until we reach the side of the valley where Namkhai's monastery used to be. A small, lonely temple stands down below. Five thousand monks lived here before the purge. There were temples and rows of *gers* and cabins and at least twenty stupas, yet nothing remains apart from a single crumbling stupa that horses are using for shade. We walk down the hillside and enter the new temple. Inside, two rows of monks are sitting opposite each other, their bodies curved over oblong sheaves of Tibetan script. They are reading a sutra in a fast murmur at the request of a woman, who is standing with her son. The woman looks as though she's worn her best clothes – but best going-out clothes, not clothes for a religious ritual. At precise moments in the recitation, the monks ring a bell or shake a drum and prompt the mother and her son to make circular motions with plates of apples and sweets they are holding. When the ritual is over, the monks wrap their sheaves in cloth and touch their foreheads with them.

I approach a silver-haired man in a golden robe and ask him whether any of the monks initiated at the original monastery have returned. He says that a few have and that one, Bilegjamts, is giving consultations from a *ger* next door. I can't believe my luck. Ouyuntsetseg and I enter Bilegjamts' *ger* to find him sitting on a rolled-up mattress at the back, with his legs extended under a low table. He is sleuthing a sutra using a magnifying glass held right up to his face, and is very old. He has a white moustache and watery eyes, and is wearing a floppy sunhat.

Bilegjamts puts down the sutra and turns to us. He speaks with a calm and childlike voice, and says he joined the monastery when he was seven. He was 27 years old when the monastery was destroyed in 1938, which means he was mature enough to understand the monastic world that surrounded him before the purge and should be a reliable witness. He was born in 1911, the year Namkhai died, and by a remarkable piece of luck he followed the same path of study as Namkhai and Luvsanjamba. All three studied at the *Choir* temple, which means that Bilegjamts is the closest living link to Namkhai's world that I am ever likely to find and the stories he knows about Namkhai will have been circulating before the Great Purge – before they could be distorted and changed during the era of communist suppression.

I ask Bilegjamts to sketch out a picture of monastic life.

'Each day, after getting up we would make tea and have breakfast. Then we would study and after that see our teachers. Then we would study again. Our teachers lived and taught in their *gers*. First novice monks would study the Tibetan alphabet. We learnt the letters one by one. Then they learnt to read. After that they would study the teachings and sutras. In the *Choir* temple we studied the techniques of how to become like Buddha. If a monk studied the teaching of *Choir*, he would get the title *Gavj*, the second highest title in rank.'

'Did Namkhai live at the monastery?'

'Yes, until the day he died.'

'Was he a good monk?'

'Yes, he was, though he did not rise to a senior rank – but that was only because he died at an early age.'

An old man enters the *ger*. He swaps snuff bottles with Bilegjamts then sits down.

'Was Namkhai cursed?'

'People at the time used to say that people from the province of Tsetsenkhaan cursed him.'

'Were his bones stolen?'

'I have heard that his bones were stolen by someone from the western part of Mongolia. Perhaps whoever stole the bones wanted there to be good, strong wrestlers in their area, but I don't know whether it would have helped.'

'And why did the monks wrestle?'

'There were a lot of good wrestlers at the monastery. The leader of the area ordered that wrestling competitions be held to find strong wrestlers because he wanted to win Naadam. Some monks enjoyed wrestling, while others did not. Those monks who were not particularly good wrestlers could choose whether to enter competitions, but the strong monks were compelled to wrestle. I used to wrestle, but I wasn't very good.

'Danshig Naadam was held as an offering to senior lamas, such as the Dalai Lama if he visited. An auspicious date would be chosen by the lunar calendar. Danshig means 'safe life' in Tibetan. Danshig Naadam would be held to wish a long life to the senior monks. This monastery also used to hold three monks' Naadams a year at Tasag Ovoo. After gathering and reading teachings, the monks used to wrestle. It signified that they had studied successfully. The wrestling meant that they had become good students of Buddha, that they had become part of God. Different temples learnt different teachings, and afterwards they celebrated and showed through wrestling that they had become part of God.'

Bilegjamts has little more to add, but what he has said is enough to reveal the place of wrestling at the monasteries. It was outside the perimeter of religious devotion but inside the perimeter of monastic life. The fact that Namkhai lived his entire life at a monastery and remained a committed monk suggests that by and large nothing within wrestling contradicted the religious path. If Norov is correct, the only time that happened was when Namkhai competed at Danshig Naadam and disguised himself to hide aggressive emotions from God. But wrestling was not in any sense a spiritual path. Essentially the monks wrestled because they were Mongolians, not because wrestling had anything to do with being a monk. Yet it is beguiling to think that Mongolia's greatest wrestler also happened to be a Tibetan Buddhist monk – and I wonder whether, had I been able to meet Namkhai, he would have spoken about how the life of devotion and self-sacrifice necessary to become a great wrestler has a lot in common with the life of a monk.

A young couple have entered the room and are waiting patiently, along with the old man, for an audience with Bilegjamts. I've found out all I need to know. I stand and give Bilegjamts two 500 togrog notes. He places the money in a drawer and turns to the old man.

A final call to make. At an indoor market in Bulgan, Ouyuntsetseg gets directions to the home of Jamayndorj, the wrestler Governor Namkhai said is famous throughout Mongolia for having lifted a camel. We leave the market just as a fight is breaking up outside. Two men have to be held apart. They shout and swear at each other. One has his fist cocked. Their friends steer them away, but they keep turning and trying to wade through their friends' restraints to resume fighting.

Jamayndorj's home is up a nearby hill. He greets Ouyuntsetseg and me enthusiastically and asks us to sit with him. His chubby-armed wife sits smoking in the background and listens. Jamayndorj is in his late sixties but still in excellent shape. He says he became a Lion in 1961. He was a top-flight wrestler, and he rattles off a list of Lions and Giants he wrestled whom he both sometimes beat and was sometimes beaten by. He lifted a camel twice, he says.

'I first did it on the May Day holiday in 1955. I was in the centre of Saikhan *sum* and there was a herder there with a stray camel. At the time you had to report strays. It was spring and during the previous autumn I'd returned from the army, and I looked a lot stronger than before. Old wrestlers such as Red Boots and Elephant Sodnom saw I was in good shape and challenged me to lift the camel. I managed to lift its front legs off the ground so that it was standing on its hind legs, and was then given the nickname "Camel-lifter from Bulgan".

'The second time was in Ulan Baatar. I was taken to a livestock market on a Sunday morning because people wanted confirmation that I could lift a camel. They told me that if I repeated the feat it would be reported throughout the country. At the market, wrestlers held each of a camel's legs by a rope to prevent it kicking, because no one knew whether it was tame or not, and I got under the camel and lifted it on my back.'

He gets up to illustrate how. He squats down under an imaginary camel then stands. He simply squatted a camel.

'And did all four legs come off the ground this time?'

'Yes, all the legs.' He shows how far – from his elbow to fingertips, about a foot and a half.

'How much did the camel weigh?'

'I think it weighed about 300 or 400 kilos. Usually camels don't weigh more than 300 or 400 in spring. In autumn, maybe a big, fat camel would weigh 700, 800 or even 900 kilos. After I lifted it, the people in the market lifted me like I was the winner of Naadam, and gave me money and clapped.'

'And after that you became famous as the Camel-lifter?'

'Yes, I did. My parents gave me the name Jamayndorj, but now, when I go to Ulan Baatar, wrestlers and others of my generation simply call me "Camel".'

Jamayndorj outlines how he developed his great strength.

'You have to live the right way,' he says. 'Don't drink vodka, avoid women, practise all the time and be modest. Regular training, cold water, getting up early in the morning and eating dairy products all make a person strong.'

It's a description that could have been given by a wrestler in India.

Glossary

Aimag: large administrative district – a province.
Airag: fermented mare's milk.
Argamag: ambler horse. Gives a smooth ride.
Deel: traditional greatcoat.
Eriin Gurvan Naadam: the 'three manly games' of wrestling, horse-racing and archery.
Ger: circular felt tent in which Mongolians traditionally live on the steppes.
Gutuls: a type of boot with a characteristic turned-up toe. They are worn by Mongolians and Tibetans alike.
Hangard: mythical bird. Known as garuda elsewhere.

Khadag: votive scarf.

Khuushuur: fried pancake made with minced mutton.

Mongol Bokh: traditional Mongolian style of wrestling. *Mongol Bokh* is a standing style – in other words the aim is to throw your opponent to the ground. Touching the ground with any part of your body other than your feet or the flats of your hands constitutes defeat.

Ovoo: a spirit shrine. An *ovoo* typically consists of a pile of stones.

Sum: administrative district. A number of *sums* make up an *aimag*.

Yadargaa: health condition characterised by severe fatigue.

Zasuul: acts as a second for wrestlers and also referees bouts.

PART III

Australia and England

1999–2002

Chapter 9

Testosterone's Fingerprints

Tickets to watch Greco-Roman wrestling at the forthcoming Sydney 2000 Olympic Games have not been selling well. In Australia, wrestling is an obscure minority sport about which people generally know very little. The little that they do know – that it entails man-to-man contact – can cause smirks. People think there is something gay about two men rolling around together on a mat.

Eleven months before the Games, which begin in September, a TV crew arrives at Larry Papadopoulos's gym in Castlereagh Street, in central Sydney, to film a piece to publicise the Greco-Roman event, correct misapprehensions and encourage Australians to book seats. The crew talk to Alex Cook, who wants to qualify for the Greco-Roman division and represent Australia. Alex has been apprehensive about what they will ask him to do. He doesn't want to be asked to do anything embarrassing, or that portrays Greco-Roman as a bit of a joke. The crew decide to film outside first and leave with Alex. While they are gone, Justin Turtle sits and waits in the lounge area. He is in two minds whether or not to act as Alex's workout partner when he returns. Justin competes in Freestyle, the other Olympic style, and has a playful prejudice against those he calls 'Greco monkeys'. He decides it would be best not to partner Alex partly because Alex has a tendency to injure training partners. Discussion about the subject breaks out among those gathered round the table. Larry ends a phone call, comes over and joins in. He currently has a shoulder injury that he says Alex caused. He puts Alex's overaggressive attitude down to his prior rugby training.

'Football mentality, mate,' he says. 'He wants to rip your head off.'

The TV crew return. They've been having a bit of fun with the item, says Sonia, the tall reporter. They unfurled a banner publicising Greco-Roman wrestling on a bridge in north Sydney, and shot footage in a shopping centre of Alex giving out leaflets and using a megaphone to drum up interest. They did nothing to embarrass him.

Nick turns up and agrees to partner Alex. Alex gives him a blue wrestler's leotard, which he changes into. It's a couple of sizes too small and far too tight.

'These things are killing me,' says Nick. 'My legs are going numb – I'm serious.'

He keeps pulling and lifting the material to counter the discomfort. Alex demonstrates throws on Nick to give the TV crew an idea of what Greco-Roman is like. Contrary to popular belief, Greco-Roman is neither Greek nor Roman but hails from France. Its main distinguishing characteristics are that you cannot hold your opponent below the waist, which means you can't shoot for his legs, or use your legs and feet to trip and throw. Alex runs through some of the most visually arresting throws in wrestling. He executes a flying mare, illustrations of which can be found decorating the sides of Ancient Greek pots. He performs an underarm spin, which involves a fast back-arch and spinning motion on the part of the thrower and is beautiful to watch. He demonstrates a *souplesse*, the most spectacular throw of all. He holds Nick round the waist, lifts him off the ground, arches backwards right the way till his head is just about to hit the mat, then rapidly spins and slams Nick into the mat instead.

Sonia watches from beside a carpeted pillar and appears unmoved by these polished examples of Greco-Roman wrestling's display-cabinet techniques. This is a language she doesn't understand – a language few Australians do. After the demonstration there is a moment of awkward silence. Alex breaks the silence to ask Sonia what it is she wants exactly.

'This is for TV, so what's visual,' says Sonia.

Alex decides that he and Nick should just spar this time. He executes the same throws as before: flying mare, underarm spin, *souplesse*. Nick lands on his elbow. He stands and shakes his arm and grimaces. The fall has aggravated an old injury. He goes downstairs to the lounge area to look for a replacement sparring partner. The soundman kills time by punching a punch bag; he tells his colleagues he used to do kung fu. Trent comes upstairs to partner Alex. Alex throws him, rolls him, pins him. The cameraman holds his camera next to the mat to help make what is already visual more so. Rolls, throws, pins. Alex misjudges distance from the camera and smacks his head into the lens. Blood seeps from his forehead. Everyone stops.

Behind the counter downstairs, Larry is folding used towels while wearing hygienic gloves. Alex comes down holding a tissue blotted with blood to his forehead. He and Larry go a long way back. As they're good mates, Larry has the right to mock him.

'Camera one, Alex nil,' he says.

All wrestlers in Australia suffer from a lack of decent training partners. As in England, few people wrestle. As in England, too, many of those that do are first- or second-generation immigrants from countries with a stronger wrestling culture. Justin flies to Canada in November to solve his partner problem by training at a college. Larry and Alex stay in Sydney but also have a trip to Greece planned. All three see this as a once in a lifetime opportunity not only to compete in an Olympic Games but also an Olympic Games in their home city and are determined to give themselves the best chance of qualification.

I spend mornings, afternoons and evenings watching Alex and Larry's sessions at Larry's gym, which is called Boxing

Works. My aim is to record their experiences as they attempt to qualify – and then, all going well, shadow them as they compete in the Games themselves – but every time I witness a training session I feel a deep sense of frustration. I have reached the limits of my capacity to watch others wrestle while not being able to join in myself. It seems perverse to spend so much time around wrestling without taking part. Occasionally I go for a short run to gauge whether there has been any change in my health. I jog up a hill near my Bondi home to a small park where people exercise their dogs, run around it a few times and do a few wrestling exercises: back-bridges, cartwheels, back-arches. Familiar symptoms return an hour later. Everything around me appears somehow brighter. I can't think straight. It takes a lot of effort to hold a conversation or read a book, and not long after I've spoken to someone or put the book down I can hardly remember what was said or what I just read. The following morning I feel incapacitated by a fatigue that cannot be slept off. Alongside the fatigue comes a depression that appears to have a physical cause – it feels as though it springs from a process of physical depletion – rather than psychological. It takes at least another day and a half to get back to feeling normal again.

The frustration I feel at not being healthy enough to wrestle is compounded by frustration at not having any real idea what my health problem is. I have consultations with orthodox doctors, but they are no help whatsoever. They do the standard blood tests, the results come back showing no irregularities and the doctors either have no idea how to proceed from there or think there is nothing wrong with me – though they never actually come out and say so. Australia is a sports-oriented culture and my health problem centres on the effect of exercise, so I thought before coming here that I would be able to find a sports doctor who would either be familiar with my symptoms and know how to treat them, or have a good idea how to go about reaching a diagnosis. Unfortunately, the sports doctor I am referred to has never come across anyone with my symptoms. She has wild and speculative theories about what could be wrong, and sends me to be checked out by a neurologist and to be tested for a rare form of epilepsy.

Demoralised by my health condition and by the inability of

doctors to get to its root cause, I decide to leave Australia a few months before the Olympics. Unfortunately Larry, Alex and Justin all go out during the national championships in April and fail to qualify to represent Australia, so there would be little point in staying anyway. Back in England, my health slumps even further. Whereas before, I felt OK most of the time as long as I didn't exercise, now I feel lethargic and low all the time. I stay at my dad's house in Surrey for a few months because I don't have the energy to do regular work and pay rent in London.

Despairing with conventional medicine, I visit a charismatic psychic healer and a geezerish kinesiologist who has photos of a pet Doberman on the walls along with his chakra chart, but neither can get to the root of my condition. Eventually I reluctantly return to orthodox medicine and have a consultation with an endocrinologist who is supposed to be an expert on chronic fatigue. I prepare a synopsis of my case history and a list of symptoms – some of which are so peculiar that I hope they will act like the idiosyncratic squiggles and flourishes in a signature and reveal what it is that is the author of my health condition (for example, my body doesn't cope with changes in temperature: a hot or warm bath or shower leaves me feeling fatigued, and the same thing happens after a cold shower or after sitting in the sun). The endocrinologist ignores these peculiar symptoms and instead ticks a box in his head every time I mention a symptom characteristic of Chronic Fatigue Syndrome (CFS). After a while he has ticked enough boxes to diagnose CFS, which he does in a self-congratulatory tone. It's a diagnosis I have resisted partly because of the air of hopelessness surrounding CFS (joke on a CFS website – a doctor diagnoses a patient with CFS: 'The good news is you're not going to die; the bad news is you're not going to die') and partly because it is just another way to label symptoms and offers no insight into their cause. The endocrinologist says there is no known cure for CFS though some people spontaneously get better and patients who undergo cognitive behavioural therapy and do a little exercise respond quite well. I tell him I have a physical problem, not a psychological one, with underlying physical causes that it should be possible to diagnose, and repeat that I feel total physical and emotional annihilation after even a little exercise, so exercise is out of the question. The doctor grins smugly and says nothing, as if to imply that I should just try harder. I feel like punching him in the face. I have had to give up wrestling, the sport I love, for three years now because of this health condition. I can't just think my way to recovery, or learn to live with a health problem I'm convinced can be resolved.

The endocrinologist does have one constructive suggestion. He recommends a hormone test, though he says it is unlikely that anything will come up. Yet something does: low testosterone. I feel euphoric and vindicated: the test result suggests there are underlying physical causes for my health problem that can be diagnosed, as I thought all along – and if they can be diagnosed they should be treatable. I see another doctor, who also diagnoses adrenal insufficiency from a further blood test. I follow a course of treatment to raise my testosterone level and strengthen my adrenal glands, and within a couple of weeks I feel a lot more energy and get-up-and-go, and more emotionally capable and resilient than ever before. The depression lifts completely. My body feels as though it has come back into sharp definition. I feel as though I have edges and corners again, and a more defined presence when I walk down the street. Yet though my general health is a lot better, I still don't recover properly after exercise and still can't wrestle seriously. Something happens when I exercise that not even this doctor can properly identify.

Before treatment for low testosterone, I only had vague ideas about the hormone. The word 'testosterone' triggered unflattering associations with Arnold Schwarzenegger films, aggression on stock exchange trading-floors and rage. Following the discovery that my poor health has been partly based on a lack of it, testosterone takes on new meaning and value. I read as much as I can about the hormone to help understand why my health has been transformed and realise that it suffers from an undeservedly bad image. The more I read about testosterone, the more I also realise that it has huge relevance to wrestling – and the more I see that it suggests a radically different way to understand the sport.

I need a new approach. My search for wrestling's spiritual dimension was rewarded in India but ran aground in Mongolia amid stories of intense regional rivalry, exemplified by the tale of how a wrestler placed a curse on Namkhai. By the time I left Mongolia I had a gut feeling that I was missing something important, something absolutely fundamental, about the essence of wrestling and that whatever that something was, I was missing it because of the way I approached the subject rather than for any other reason. My spiritual perspective no longer worked. It began to dawn on me that the need to win, which remained such a resolute and central presence in the cultures of wrestling of both India and Mongolia, was an important common trait that might provide a clue to what it was I'd been missing. Even in India, a culture shaped by powerful spiritual forces for many centuries, wrestling's worldly core had not been neutralised and transformed. Though wrestling training can have a profound spiritual dimension, as Neel Kanth Shastri said in Varanasi, the act of competition itself is essentially worldly, because it centres upon winning matches, and the respect and status that come with victory.

Testosterone can be described as a worldly hormone, and it provides a vantage point from which to plausibly explain the enduring importance of winning – as well as suggesting an explanation for the origins and purpose of wrestling that is simple yet revelatory.

Testosterone is of fundamental importance to life. It is a cornerstone of masculinity and produces characteristics that differentiate men from women, who have far less of the hormone. During puberty, testosterone matures males' bodies into muscular forms instantly distinguishable from the physiques of females. Boys' testosterone levels rise exponentially, which facilitates the growth of muscle. By adulthood, males have larger frames than females and twice as much muscle. They also have more red blood cells with which to carry oxygen to their muscle than females. Testosterone gives males their pronounced upper body development – strong arms, chests and shoulders – as well as bigger legs. The importance of large and strong muscles, particularly of the upper body, to sports reliant on strength and power such as wrestling is self-evident.

Testosterone not only gives men their characteristic muscular equipment but also their virility. The hormone maintains sperm production in the testes, which are its main production points. The welcome appearance of libido in adolescence is predicated on a huge rise in testosterone level, and the hormone modulates sex drive throughout a man's life. It has effects on other behaviours as well, though there is much discussion and argument over the precise nature of these. You can inject male lizards with testosterone and track how they travel longer distances and fight more, or castrate rats and watch them become more placid, but isolating the effects of changes in the hormone's level in humans is complicated. Evidence that testosterone can increase aggression is not accepted by everyone, though it is a clear effect demonstrated by experiments with animals and something often reported anecdotally. A consensual position concerning testosterone's influence on human behaviour is that it helps men gain dominance. When testosterone researchers talk about dominance, they tend to talk about how studies suggest the hormone gives men confidence and assertiveness in, say, social and work environments. The fact that testosterone is also a governing factor in physical contests between men for dominance, currently categorised as sports, tends to be regarded as a separate issue.

In humans, testosterone has effects that may on the face of it appear to be random and unconnected – it builds the body, plays a role in helping men gain dominance, possibly increases aggression and governs virility. However, when you look at the role of testosterone in the lives of certain animals, a clear picture emerges in which its effects are intimately connected and parts of a larger whole: the hormone triggers and facilitates physical growth and aggression to help males fight one another for dominance *specifically to win mates and thereby reproduce.* Fighting is the route to sex, and testosterone is the sex-and-fighting hormone.

Perhaps testosterone once enabled men to fight for females too and the descendants of these physical contests endure today in the guise of sports such as wrestling – yet so far no one has noticed.

*

A summery day at the beginning of autumn. Signs are up in Richmond Park warning people to keep their distance from the deer. Stags compete for hinds during the rutting season and can be dangerous. A noise like a loud, aggressive yawn registers above the hiss of the wind in the trees and bracken. The stag responsible stands at the edge of a wooded area. His coat is muddy brown, his antlers grey with white tines. He groans again. If you didn't know what was making the noise, you could almost mistake the sound for something mechanical – a distant chainsaw perhaps or trail bike.

Roaring is a characteristic of the rut, which lasts roughly six weeks and occurs in September and October. For the rest of the year, red deer are relatively placid and roam in single sex groups, but during the rut they congregate, and the stags roar and fight for control of females. Red deer are polygynous. Dominant males corral hinds together and guard them fiercely. A single stag can gather and mate with as many as forty. This dramatic change in behaviour is facilitated by a huge seasonal rise in the stags' testosterone level, which triggers the shedding of sensitive velvet from antlers to reveal hard calcified bone underneath, as well as the development of the neck muscles and mane, and an increase in the size of the testes.

Though the stag that has just roared does not have a harem of hinds, he is big enough to challenge others that do. He looks directly at me and walks in my direction. His antlers are impressive and look lethal. I turn and walk away slowly but keep glancing over my shoulder to check he isn't about to charge. Thankfully I'm ignored as he goes to lie in a muddy pool. He rolls about and shakes his head from side to side so that his antlers scoop and fling mud over his body, and uses the underside of an antler to rub his back. Afterwards he stands, stretches out and releases a belchy roar.

Groans and roars resonate within a small wood nearby. The sounds are primeval and fill you with foreboding – they would be perfect sound effects for a fireside reading of a cruel European folk story. The sound is intimidating to a human, and perhaps for stags too. The rate at which stags roar indicates their condition and fighting ability. Listening to a rival's roar is probably one way in which males assess each other's strength.

There is also evidence that hinds are attracted to stags that lead bouts of roaring and have a high roaring rate.

I walk to the edge of the wood, sit on a treestump and watch. Towards the centre of the wood are two dominant males about 75 metres apart. They pace about and periodically lift their heads to roar. One is surrounded by a harem of about ten hinds, the other by about thirty. Potential challengers orbit the two groups. Some don't have the physiques and antlers to seriously threaten either of the two dominant stags, but a few do. The serious challengers also roar.

Behind the back of one of the dominant males, a stag crashes into his harem. The hinds split and bolt. The dominant stag turns and chases the would-be thief away, but while his back is turned another challenger seizes his chance to steal hinds. The hinds riot nervously and scatter until the dominant male chases the second interloper off too and restores order. He then mounts one of his becalmed hinds for a couple of seconds. He will wait for each to come into oestrus and mate with them all.

I'm hoping to see two males fight, as they compete in a ritualised way resonant with wrestling. When we think about animals fighting, we tend to think in terms of violent life-or-death struggles. Rutting competitions between stags are a matter of life and death in the sense that winners reproduce and thereby transmit their genes to the next generation, but actual bouts are ritualised contests in which the opponents test each other's strength rather than primarily aim to wound or kill. Stags do not creep up on one another like alleyway muggers and viciously use their antlers to stab; instead they compete in a way that can be described as honourable. They typically trot alongside each other, apparently assessing each other's strength, before deciding whether to fight or not. If both stags are willing to fight, they will turn their heads to engage one another. Their antlers then interlock and become a connecting device to allow each stag to transmit his power into the body of the other. Though injuries can and do occur, the principal aim is to enter into a shoving contest to see who is strongest, not to eviscerate. This is why the stags' neck muscles strengthen for the rut, and perhaps the mane grows to give them a larger profile so that they appear more intimidating when they assess each other's strength.

Kedar Nath Yadav shows a photo of himself as a young wrestler in which he lifts a piece of exercise equipment

The simple wrestling arena at Sadho Pehalwan's village. The mound of earth on the left crowned with a garland is a shrine to Hanuman, the monkey god

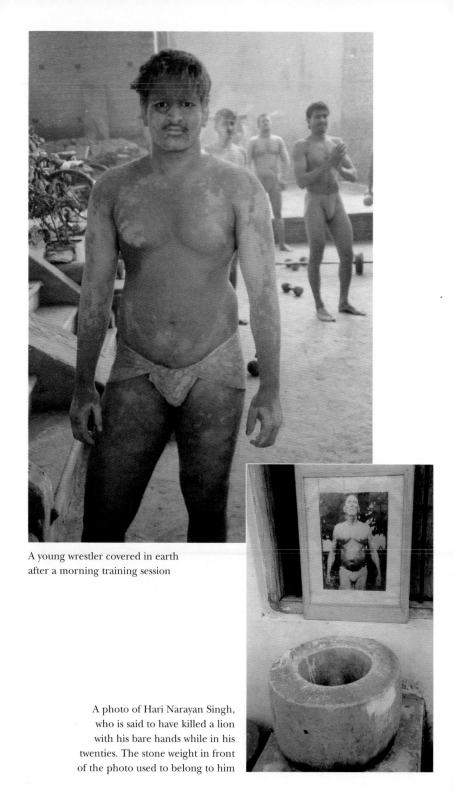

A young wrestler covered in earth
after a morning training session

A photo of Hari Narayan Singh,
who is said to have killed a lion
with his bare hands while in his
twenties. The stone weight in front
of the photo used to belong to him

In the countryside, Mongolians typically live in circular felt tents such as this

Jamsran's family. Jamsran sits at the front with his wife, Maruysa. Gangaa is squatting on the left, while Khadaa stands at the back on the right

In summer, Mongolians often have to grapple with their foals during the process of milking mares. It's an activity that develops wrestling ability

Wrestlers compete at the local Naadam festival for the
River Uyalgan area and a small neighbouring community

Bat-erdene Giant (far right) eagle-dances at the Palace of *Mongol Bokh* while his second sings

Two Dukawa men
demonstrate their
tribe's traditional
style of wrestling

A drummer accompanies girls from the Dukawa tribe as they give a demonstration
of the dancing and singing that characterise wrestling competitions

Linus Okere, professor of anthropology

Ejam Ihejirika, the 'really cat wrestler'

Rocinha, the largest *favela* in Rio de Janeiro

Baby poses near his Rocinha home with his bull terrier – a breed of dog favoured by Jiu-Jitsu fighters in Brazil

Sparring at
Tata's Jiu-Jitsu
club in Rocinha

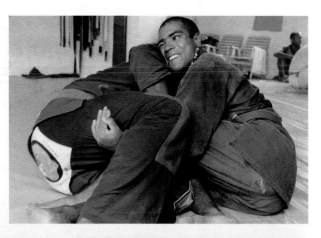

Wrestling training at
the Brazilian Top
Team gym in Rio.
Minotauro, one of
the most famous
MMA fighters in the
world, is on the right

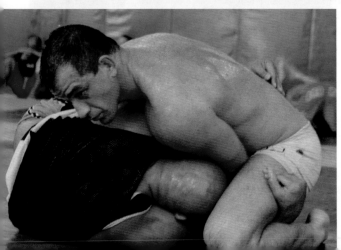

Ze Mario Sperry,
one of the
founders of
Brazilian Top
Team, works his
ground game

After a couple of hours of waiting, I hear a noise like hockey sticks being smacked together from a far edge of the wood. I quickly walk towards the sound and come across two powerful stags in the middle of a fight. The moment is infused with incredible energy. The clattering noise is made by the clash of their entangling antlers. Each stag arches its back powerfully as it strains every muscle to try to shunt the other backwards. Soon their heads turn as one of them gives in and disengages. He runs off, slows into a jog and then into a defiant walk. He comes to a halt about 50 metres beyond the wood, where he stands and roars, all mouth and no trousers. The winner rubs his antlers against a tree and lies down.

Jubilant at having witnessed the contest, I leave the wood and find the path that leads back towards the park gate. I have just seen something exhilarating that will stay with me for a long time. The road that bisects Richmond Park comes as a rude reminder of a civilisation that follows a different order. The drivers who drone by doing a steady 20mph appear moronic in comparison with those potent stags.

A sumo match. Two wrestlers face each other across a circular arena. They crouch with their knuckles on the ground so that they momentarily resemble four-legged animals, and stare deep into each other's eyes. Suddenly they explode into one another simultaneously. The heavier wrestler fires off a succession of rapid thrusts at his opponent's chest. Within moments the thrusts have off-balanced the lighter man. The heavier wrestler presses his advantage by lifting his opponent by the belt and shunting him out of the ring. He is the winner.

The resonance between this description of a sumo match and the contests of red deer is unmistakeable and needs no further elucidation. Of all the many styles of wrestling, sumo is capable of coming closest in form to the contests of stags. The rule that shoving an opponent from a territory counts as victory is not common in wrestling, yet schematically both contests between stags and between wrestlers of all styles fall into the same category: in both cases the aim is to decide who is the most dominant male on a stark physical level without using techniques that cause permanent harm. Deer prove their dominance by shunting each other backwards; wrestlers prove their dominance typically by throwing their opponent to the ground or pinning him on his shoulders or back. Whether this contest ritualisation is instinctive, as it appears to be in red deer, or learned and mediated by rules and referees, as it appears to be in wrestling, the result is that both protagonists connive to compete in a way that is a test of one another's strength, power and endurance – and in the case of wrestlers who, of course, unlike deer have the use of dextrous hands, also skill and technique.

There are other parallels between wrestling and the contests of stags. An obvious yet significant similarity is that wrestling comes down to us in the history of all cultures that embrace it as an overwhelmingly male activity rather than female. Also obvious but also significant is the fact that wrestling, like contests between stags, is a one-to-one struggle – and a one-to-one struggle in which the protagonists solely use their bodies (with the qualification that some styles feature clothing that can be gripped). These last two characteristics distinguish wrestling from the many modern sports that involve teams and use props like rackets and balls. A stag's rutting success has been found to correlate with body size – the bigger the stag, the better it fares. Similarly, it is widely acknowledged that a big wrestler will generally beat a smaller man. Modern wrestling styles such as Freestyle and Greco-Roman feature weight categories in recognition of the fact that larger size gives a huge advantage, yet indigenous wrestling styles generally have not traditionally featured formal weight categories – or time limits or points systems for that matter. Like stags, wrestlers in these styles have traditionally competed without such artificial constraints.

The timing of the peak period in fighting ability for both stags and wrestlers relates to testosterone levels. Stags' testosterone levels rise exponentially before the rut and drop exponentially afterwards, and their aggressive behaviour and capacity to fight are governed by this huge hormonal change. Men are also at their most competitive when their testosterone levels are at their highest – though in men the significant variations in the hormone's level occur over the life cycle, not across any one year. The developments in physique and muscle mass that occur during puberty, initiated by a huge rise in testosterone, mark a moment when youths, like stags shedding velvet, upgrade soft and vulnerable physical equipment for something harder and more robust to spar with. It is self-evident that puberty brings a huge increase in a man's wrestling ability, which reaches a peak between the ages of roughly eighteen and thirty. Similarly, testosterone levels peak at about twenty, remain near their highest level till a man's late twenties, then begin to decline at more of a pace. Obviously testosterone is not solely responsible for a peak in wrestling ability – factors such as skill, dedication, opportunity and experience have their part to play – but you would anticipate that, given its muscle-building role and effect on behaviour, the hormone's high level is a crucial factor, even if its precise significance may be difficult to establish through research.

When the clear resonances between stags' rutting contests and wrestling are taken into account – and the way in which testosterone facilitates competition in both cases is acknowledged – the suggestion hangs heavily in the air that these two activities are not simply analogous to one another but may actually be examples of the same behaviour practised by two different species. Except, of course, in human culture males do not on the face of it win females by winning a wrestling bout. But imagine if, in our evolutionary past, men did literally fight for women during testosterone-underpinned contests reminiscent of the ruts of stags. Imagine if there used to be clashes between males in which they fought one another exclusively with the equipment of their bodies to decide who would mate. If that were the case, you might anticipate that the behaviour would have evolved and changed over the millennia, and the culture surrounding the behaviour might have also evolved and changed, perhaps to the extent that it doesn't use the behaviour for its original purpose any more and has forgotten that it ever did, yet the stark evolutionary imperative to win might remain encapsulated within the behaviour even though females are no longer the prize. Today, the activity might have evolved into a heavily ritualised form of fighting and be categorised as a sport.

It may be that wrestling either is, or is descended from, a type of human rutting behaviour and is built on an ancient

testosterone-driven urge to win females in the same way that
a modern house might be built on the strong, ancient
foundations of an old one without the present occupiers
realising. Those occupiers would go about their everyday lives
without thinking about what their home was originally built
on, yet their daily existence would rely on those foundations.
Perhaps the same is true of other sports too.

Alternatively, if wrestling is descended from a form of
human rutting, maybe there actually are outposts still left in
the world where men win wives through wrestling – remote
pockets insulated from the forces of modernisation where
wrestling's original purpose more or less remains the same.
With little expectation of success, I go online and scour the
Web for any references to a practice of competing to win
women in a living culture anywhere in the world.
Astonishingly, there are descriptions of just such present-day
marriage customs among tribes in West Africa. In parts of
Africa today, suggest the posts, men are winning women by
virtue of their skill as wrestlers.

*

White blood cells are beautiful: lone transparent creatures busy
at work in the deep seas of your blood. Red blood cells, on the
other hand, are like flocks of balloons. Dr Han van de Braak
looks at my blood under a microscope while I see what he sees
on a TV monitor. He points out that some of my red blood cells
are misshapen and clumping together, as well as lines like
scratch marks, *fibrin spiculae*, which indicate issues to do with
blood coagulation and liver function. He then scrutinises a
dried spot of blood under the microscope. It looks like
magnified dried paint speckled with white dandruff. Han
identifies evidence on the edge of the dried blood spot of heavy
metal poisoning, probably from mercury, while the dandruff-
like specks point to adrenal insufficiency. It's an epiphany. After
having been convinced for years now that I have underlying
physical problems yet having had to suffer the frustration of
not being able to have those problems diagnosed – aside from
low testosterone and adrenal insufficiency, diagnoses that in
the end did not lead to full recovery – not only can Han
confirm that I was right all along but he can also actually show

me some of my physical problems on TV. I feel vindicated, and want to lock all the doctors I've seen who failed to diagnose my health problems, or thought I didn't have any, or didn't really care either way, into a room and force them to watch this TV footage in a loop for hours on end with their eyes sewn open.

By running tests on urine, saliva and blood samples, Han also discovers I suffer from a high level of oxidative stress and also have overacidic body fluids. He draws up a course of vitamins, minerals, enzymes, antioxidants, detoxifiers and an alkalinising compound, and suggests I take up juicing fruit and veg. In the coming weeks, I follow the course of supplements to the letter and take his advice about juicing. The transformation is fast and dramatic. By the time I leave for Africa my health is better than it's been for years.

PART IV

Nigeria

August and September 2002

Chapter 10

Nigeria Welcomes You

'How long do you plan to stay in Nigeria?' asks an official at Lagos airport. He flicks through my passport.

'I'm not sure. It depends how nice the people are.'

The official laughs and hands back my passport. I make my way to the luggage carousel, wait for my backpack to emerge, place it on a trolley, clear customs and scan the name cards held by people waiting to meet passengers off the planes. My name is not among them, which is not surprising. Brother Stephen was supposed to pick me up and take me to stay the night at a church in nearby Mafoluku, but I am seven hours late. At Paris, where we changed planes, Nigerian passengers argued with cabin crew over a delay. The arguments became so heated that the pilot ordered everyone off the plane. Police arrived with dogs and arrested some passengers. We had to wait while Air France found another crew willing to take us on to Lagos. Just after the plane landed, passengers booed when a member of the cabin crew gave the standard speech about how they hoped to see us fly with Air France again.

I was warned that Murtala Muhammad Airport is dangerous after dark. For that reason I booked a flight scheduled to arrive in the afternoon, but because of the delay it's now midnight, the worst time to be here. I search among the waiting taxi drivers for someone who appears trustworthy. I've heard stories about bogus taxi drivers who pick up foreigners at the airport and stop to let in an accomplice who shoots, kills and robs them. A driver approaches me who I instinctively feel I'll be safe with. He's small and middle-aged and has an uncle-ish air about him. To prove that he's a genuine taxi driver, he proffers an official ID card that hangs around his neck. I change some money and get in his car.

'I want to go to St Jude's Church in Mafoluku,' I say. Only about a mile away. 'How much will that be?'

'The minimum rate is 2,000 naira,' replies the driver. About ten pounds.

This is it: the first attempt to rip me off. I have to start in Nigeria as I mean to go on. I have to make sure people don't think I'm easy to con, a soft target.

I force a laugh. 'I come from London, one of the most expensive cities in the world, where we have very expensive taxis, yet it would only cost me something like 600 naira to go a mile there – and even that's too much.'

The driver brandishes his ID card again.

'I am the vice president of the taxi drivers' association, so I would not overcharge. There is a set minimum fare. It is not possible to go below the minimum price of 2,000 naira.'

'I'll give you a thousand.'

'That's not possible.'

I stand my ground. The driver backs down and says he will accept 1,500 naira.

'You will have to keep it a secret that you are paying so little. Don't tell anyone. Otherwise I will be in trouble with the other drivers in the taxi drivers' association. I may lose my job.'

'One thousand two hundred naira.'

Now he stands firm. I surprise myself with how my dislike of being ripped off can override concerns about personal safety and half open the door to indicate I will get out and find another cab if he doesn't drop his price. I would have to be insane to actually get out and loiter around outside the airport at this time of night. Fortunately the taxi driver gives in.

'Close the door,' he says. 'Maybe you are a Father. Maybe I will receive a blessing by taking you.'

The airport road is eerily devoid of cars and people. There is no herd of taxis ferrying other foreigners to hide in – there are no other vehicles at all – and I feel vulnerable and exposed. Ours is the only car on the road and because it is the only car, we are the only potential targets for armed robbers. Though it feels like ages, it can only be a matter of minutes before we have crossed a flyover, doubled back and taken the turn-off for Mafoluku. The taxi halts outside a security gate at the end of a road. A tall guard stands in the light of the headlamps, tense and frowning, with a long stick raised in his right hand as though about to whack the bonnet. The driver converses with him in Yoruba. They speak for a long time. I worry that the guard isn't going to let us through.

'What is he saying?' I ask the driver.

'He is addressing me,' he replies, brusquely.

The guard relaxes. He opens the gate and lets us in. St Jude's is on the right a little further down the road but its gate is locked. The driver and guard call into the compound. No response. They shake and rattle the heavy chain against the metal gate. Still nothing. The taxi driver returns to his car. I assume he feels he's done enough to help and is about to drive off and leave me stranded. He opens the car door, but instead of getting in the driver's seat, he picks something up from off the car mat and shuts the door again. He returns with a metal rod in his hand – a weapon. All the time I was in the car with him he had a weapon ready and waiting by his feet. The taxi driver hammers the gate with the rod. After ten minutes' hammering, chain-rattling and hailing, a man emerges from the building. He opens the gate and introduces himself as Brother Stephen.

'I was too frightened to meet you at the airport after dark,' he says.

Brother Stephen shows me to my room, where I take a shower. After I've washed and dried, I sit on the bed, wearing a towel, trying to calm down. I'm spooked. Nigeria is a notoriously dangerous country, and I was inducted into its tension and volatility before even arriving – I think back to the passengers' booming voices as they argued on the plane, the police arrests, the dogs – as though this is such a fractious place that its tension and volatility rush out to meet you before you're even here. The fact that the taxi driver had a weapon has unsettled me no end. Perhaps the metal rod was for self-defence, but perhaps not. I thought I had the driver sized up at the airport, but maybe I didn't. Perhaps instincts that have served me well elsewhere are of no use here. Maybe the rules are totally different.

I consider my luggage. The taxi driver thought I might be a Father and I feel like one: Father Christmas. My backpack is stuffed with gifts – cheap watches, T-shirts, pens and Frisbees – along with clothes and supplies. I'm also carrying a laptop computer in a discreet laptop bag, a camera in a camera bag, a telescopic fishing rod, a bottle of Jim Beam in a plastic bag and a small cool bag containing bars of chocolate to give as gifts to Father Peter, my main contact in Nigeria, who asked me to bring chocolate as a special request. Carrying all this stuff makes me feel sluggish and vulnerable. I empty the backpack and get rid of unnecessary packaging for pills and medicines, excess plastic bags, surfeit bottles – anything and everything that can be thrown away. It amounts to only a small pile, yet afterwards I somehow feel more in control.

We drive down grey dual carriageways with broken crash barriers. Women with dustpans and brooms bend over to sweep up rubbish in the gutter while cars doing 50mph speed by within feet. Brother Stephen at the wheel, giving a lift to a market from where I will take a shared taxi to Ibadan, a city a few hours' drive away, to meet Father Peter at the Dominican seminary. Father Peter has promised to help me reach the Dukawa, a small tribe in the north among whom he used to work and who are of huge interest. According to information posted on the Net, wrestling is an integral part of Dukawa culture, and girls from the tribe choose husbands at wrestling matches.

Suddenly I'm aware of people running at our car. They look aggressive and full of intent. Any moment now, I imagine, one of them is going to try to open the door to get in and rob me. But then I realise they are not running at the car, but running behind the car – they are running past the car. They are timing their runs so they just miss us. I look along the length of the road. There are no pedestrian bridges, no traffic lights, no places to cross safely. To cross the road, people have to sprint or jog through traffic doing between 40 and 60mph. They are the ones with the right to be scared. In my paranoia, I mistook their expressions of fear and concentration for aggression. A man bounds sideways across the road ahead. He faces the traffic, proud and defiant, arms flying up by his sides every time he skips so that his limbs form an 'X'.

'What is your programme?' asks Brother Stephen.

'I'm in Nigeria to discover whether men still win wives through wrestling.'

'Still happening, still happening,' says Brother Stephen. 'In the north, where I grew up, among the Hausa people. But as areas become more' – he pauses to search for the appropriate word – '*civilised,* the practice is going into decline.'

We reach the market. Brother Stephen speaks at length to a taxi driver headed for Ibadan. He impresses upon him that he must take me to the very door of the Dominican seminary. The driver waits for his beat-up Peugeot 505 estate to fill, then we depart. I look out the window for clues, tentative evidence. I want to be prepared, to know what to expect. I want to know what type of people the Nigerians are; whether they share the same kind of values. Above all I want to feel safe, reassured – or at least know how unsafe to feel. We pass rusting skeletons of trucks. Men cross the road to pee on the central reservation. An oil tanker has 'Holy Mary' written on the back, a minibus says 'More blessing'. We pass a place called Prayer City that bears the slogan: 'Where fervent prayer goes on 24 hours a day'. It is reassuring to see expressions of a familiar faith with familiar values, but the evangelical tone is off-putting in that it hints at intoxication and extremism.

The driver drops me off last, at the door of the Dominican seminary as Brother Stephen requested. Father Peter greets me in reception. He is in his early seventies, a charismatic and warm American with podgy pale legs that squint in the sun, and a big shorn head and neck. He gives a tour of the seminary

and church, and introduces me to various Brothers and
Fathers. Drained and jet-lagged, I soon retire to a bedroom for
a nap but can't get to sleep. In the evening I find Peter in his
room and give him the gifts of chocolate and the bottle of Jim
Beam. He is pleased with the chocolate, but less enamoured by
the whiskey. He says he has given up drinking for health
reasons. We talk about my journey so far. I tell Father Peter
about the plane delay and how I ended up arriving late at night.

'How much did you pay for your taxi from the airport?' he asks.

'1,200 naira, which I'm sure was far too much.'

'Oh, you did better than a lot of people.'

'The taxi driver said he was vice-president of the taxi drivers'
association so he wouldn't rip me off.'

'Oh, a lot of them say that. Did you have to bang the chain
against the gate to rouse them at the church in Mafoluku?'

'Yes, we did. It took about ten minutes.'

'But Brother Stephen eventually came out to let you in. And
the taxi to Ibadan dropped you here at the seminary?'

'Yes, it did.'

'They don't normally do that. Are you a religious man,
Marcus?'

'Not in a formal way.'

'Well, you've been very fortunate to make it to St Jude's and
then have a taxi come all the way to the compound here and
drop you.'

'I feel very fortunate.'

The suggestion that I've been divinely assisted hangs in the
air without further elaboration.

At dinner Father Peter speaks with affection about his time
among the Dukawa tribe. He was based at a church in Yelwa,
which is situated on the east bank of the River Niger in Kebbi
state, and which is where he has arranged for me to stay. He
spent 22 years at Yelwa. Worryingly, however, Father Peter can't
recall ever having seen the Dukawa wrestle in all the time he
was there.

We talk into the night. When we finish talking there is no one
else left in the dining hall. Father Peter walks me back to my
room. As we part, he presses a comradely finger into my back.

'By the way,' he says. 'You made a hero out of me with the
Sisters with that chocolate.'

★

Father Peter makes a special point of meeting me before I leave for Yelwa early the following morning. He has important advice. Never get into conversations or arguments with the police at roadblocks, he says. Let the driver sort out any problems with the police and don't get involved. He has also written a letter of introduction for me to give the Emir of Yelwa, the traditional Muslim ruler, whom he says he has known since he was a child. Hopefully, the emir will be able to help.

A Brother drops me off at a local terminal for shared taxis, and I get in a beat-up Peugeot 505 estate, with scarified windscreen, bound for Sokoto – Yelwa is on the way. The driver leaves once the car is full. The scenes that confront us on the roads as we head north are truly shocking. We pass between fifteen and twenty trucks that have been involved in accidents. During an incident involving three lorries, two travelling in the opposite direction swerved off the road to avoid one another and crashed, while a third smashed into one of them from behind. It has a huge dent in its cabin. A truck with a crushed cabin lies flipped over. In the trailer of another are corpses of cattle cut to pieces during a smash-up. No doubt people have also been killed and seriously injured in the accidents. Some of the lorries are missing windscreens, or the windscreen remains but has a sickening spiderweb of cracks centring on the point where the driver's head hit the glass. Goods are strewn over the road as though the trucks threw up in fear the moment they realised they were about to be involved in a collision. Every time we pass an accident aftermath we are forced to slow down and slalom round the trucks and their sicked-up contents.

The passengers go quiet as they survey each scene and try to work out what happened. It feels appropriate that we slow down and fall silent, as though paying our respects to those who died. A fellow passenger explains that the trucks would have been travelling last night. The drivers are frightened of armed robbers, so they go as fast as they can. There is no lighting and the roads are maliciously pot-holed in sections. These accidents are the consequence.

Unchastened by the carnage, our driver does 60 or 70mph and recklessly overtakes whenever possible. At one point he swings out to overtake a lorry only to confront another coming the other way. There is no time to accelerate and finish the manoeuvre, so instead he swings out further and passes both trucks on the track on the inside of the other side of the road. He grins when the passengers heckle him. The taxi's cracked windscreen squeaks and rattles and perpetually sounds on the verge of shattering and falling onto the front seats. I sit on additional seats behind the rear ones with my knees crunched up and head bowed. There is no seatbelt, so I brace my head against the roof whenever the driver breaks sharply. I do the same whenever we slow down or stop at the many police and army checkpoints. If I brace my head against the roof I can't see the men in uniform and hope they can't see me. I'm worried that if they do see me, the only white person around, they will ask for a bribe.

The driver follows a clear protocol at roadblocks. If the police or army who flag us down have automatic weapons, he slows or stops to *dash* them a ten naira note; if they don't have automatic weapons, he doesn't slow down or stop. But at one checkpoint where the police are armed the driver doesn't automatically give money. The police tell him to get out the car and open up the back. An officer taps my backpack with a stick.

'What's in it?' he asks me.

'Clothes, medical supplies, that sort of thing.'

'*Medical* supplies?' he says. As though a euphemism for drugs. 'Open.'

I nervously get out of the car, lift up the backpack, stand it on-end on the road, undo the zip and step back. I force a smile and try to appear relaxed, but inside I am full of dread, and intimidated by the black uniforms and machine guns. At best I expect to have to give a bribe. At worst the police will detain me here, in which case the driver is likely to leave without me. Everyone is in a rush. No one wants to be out on the roads after dark.

The officer rummages through my backpack. He stops after only a few seconds.

'Close,' he says. 'You can go.'

Stunned by his lack of bribe-acquiring ambition, I return to my seat. We set off again. The other passengers castigate the driver for failing to automatically give *dash*.

The driver drops me off at a junction and leaves before I've had a chance to confirm that it's the right turn-off for Yelwa church. Fortunately the church compound turns out to be close by. Father Daniel meets me in the reception area. Eager to confirm that, despite what Peter said, the Dukawa wrestle, I ask him whether they do.

'Yes, the Dukawa wrestle, but there is no wrestling at the moment,' he says. 'They are famine.'

'They're starving?'

'No. They are *famine*.'

It takes a moment to understand his accent.

'You mean the Dukawa are *farming*?'

'Yes.'

'You're saying that they are too preoccupied with farming to hold wrestling festivals?'

'Yes, they are busy on their farms. This is the rainy season.'

'But I don't understand. Before I came to Nigeria, I spoke to an anthropologist who told me that this is the right time of year for wrestling.'

'Then he was wrong. He doesn't know what he is talking about. Did he come here?'

'Yes, he did. At least a few times, I think.'

'Well, he is wrong. The Dukawa are farming. This is the rainy season. They only wrestle in the dry season. There is no wrestling at the moment.'

Dejected, I go for a lie-down.

An early morning phone call. Father Peter. Faint. Wants to confirm I made it to Yelwa safely. Asks how the journey went.

'Fine. We passed a lot of crashed trucks, but fortunately we didn't have any problems ourselves.'

'What about the roads? A bit holed in sections?'

'They were smooth for long sections but holed in others.'

'Where are the Fathers putting you?'

'I'm in one of the rooms near the compound wall. It's got mosquito screens, a double bed, desk, bathroom and shower.'

'Oh, you have the de luxe accommodation. How's the weather?'

'Cool and pleasant right now, and it rained earlier.'

'That's good. Well, Marcus, you've been very lucky. You said you had no formal religion, but you've been very lucky.'

'I know. Perhaps I should have a rethink about where I stand vis-a-vis religion.' I am only half joking.

'I don't know,' says Peter. 'You've been so lucky, maybe I should come over to your side.'

There are two Fathers at the church but there should be three. The missing third, Father Charles, is recuperating after a serious car accident. His smashed vehicle sulks under a tarpaulin next to a tree in the compound. The two Fathers present, Raj and Daniel, are both in their thirties. Father Raj comes from India. He is short and stocky, with a receding hairline and back-combed hair, and wears a polo shirt and slacks when he is not in a vestment. He is new to the parish. Father Daniel comes from Kaduna, the capital of nearby Kaduna state, and has been at Yelwa for some time. He is slim, wears glasses and has a shaved head and small diagonal tribal scar next to his nose. There is an intelligent and thoughtful air about him.

Within the compound wall are a church, classrooms, accommodation for Sisters, dusty football pitch, volleyball net and fish pond. Normally, says Daniel, the place would be full of people and activity, but because the local tribespeople are busy farming, this is something of a holiday for the church. In the dry season, which, roughly speaking, starts in December, Daniel and Raj will go into the bush to minister from Catholic stations, but that is not possible right now, not only because the tribespeople are farming, but also because the terrain is difficult to cover because of the rains.

The Dukawa are staying on their farmland, which is often far away from their home villages, which means they are even more difficult to reach at this time of year – which means in turn that I am going to have a hard time getting to talk to them about wrestling. But Daniel says he will help as much as he can and asks a seminarian, Moses, to go into the bush to see if he can set up a meeting with Dukawa elders and wrestlers. I decide to visit the Emir of Yelwa in the meantime and deliver the letter of introduction from Father Peter. Despite my innate reluctance to have anything to do with officialdom in a remote part of a country like Nigeria that is notorious for its corruption, I feel honour-bound to give him the letter – and besides, it will give me something to do while I wait. Raj says he will come too, as he hasn't met the emir yet.

We drive over to the emir's palace. Everything outside it is painted green and white – the pillars, the compound wall, even a tree. Men in robes and headscarves stand around near their cars and chat while they wait their turn for an audience. A young girl moves from vehicle to vehicle and sells groundnuts. A policeman carrying a sub-machine gun stands sentry near the entrance. When it's our time to go in, Raj and I take off our shoes and walk down a passageway. Servants sit on the floor along its length. Beyond the hallway is a chamber. At the opposite end, the emir sits on a swinging chair that looks like a piece of 1970s suburban garden furniture. He has a kind, intelligent and dark face, and is wearing blue robes and a white scarf tied around his head. Councillors sit on armchairs and settees near him. A man prostrates himself in front of the emir, who indicates that chairs should be brought for Raj and me. I sit forward, nervously, while Raj sits back, relaxed.

'I have a letter of introduction to give you from Father Peter Otillio,' I tell the emir.

I hand the letter to a councillor who hands it to him. He sits, reading. He takes his time over it. The letter is longer than I anticipated.

'So, you are interested in traditional wrestling?' he says, eventually.

'That's right, Your Highness.'

'Are you interested in the physicality of wrestling?'

'Yes, I am, Your Highness.'

'It is not the right season. At the moment the people are farming.'

It hurts to be reminded of the fact. I grin to hide the pain.

'I know, but it would still help if I could speak to tribes-people about their tradition of wrestling. I am particularly interested in whether they wrestle for brides.'

The emir calls for the chairman of local government, who goes down on one knee in front of him. The emir instructs the chairman to help as much as he can. I approach the emir and shake his hand, then Raj introduces himself. Afterwards we leave the palace together and make our way to the chairman of local government's office. He is a large man with a big, dark face and he speaks with a booming voice. The chairman, too, explains that it's the wrong time of year for wrestling. About ten men sit in claret-red armchairs and on settees in his office. The room is a hubbub of Hausa as the chairman confers with the others about what to do to help. He decides to call for the cultural director, who enters wearing a golden hat and robe. The cultural director escorts me to his office. He says I should return the following day, when he will have arranged for a wrestler to be present whom I can interview.

My head is spinning by the time I return to the church compound. I feel like the parcel in a game of pass the parcel – which may yet turn out to be a more accurate analogy than I would wish. As I'm handed from government department to government department, from politician to politician, the moment will near when the music stops and the person holding the parcel – ie, me – will want to unwrap the gift and extract a bribe.

Father Daniel talks about the emir over dinner. He is not an elected representative, but he has the real power in the area, he says. Theoretically the emir has no role in electing local government officials, but the men he suggests get the jobs. Whatever he says is done.

'If the emir said, "Go and capture Marcus," they would come here straight away without question and take you away. If the emir said, "Burn down that church," he gestures towards the church, 'they would come here and burn down that church.'

Daniel despises the submissive etiquette that defines the emir's authority – the fact that you have to take off your shoes before you see him, and that people prostrate themselves in front of him. However, he says, the emir does not adhere to tradition in every respect. He is criticised within the Muslim community for not following the custom of taking more than one wife. He studied in the West, at Edinburgh University, and has been influenced by Western ways picked up during a Western education.

*

The cultural director's office is a dingy green cell that lacks the aura of a place of genuine bureaucratic work. Under the desk is a pile of papers covered in dirt and dust. Yellowing papers in folders on the desk flutter in the current of air created by a wall-mounted fan. On the wall is a calendar with a photo of the emir and underneath that is a calendar with pictures of the wives of Nigerian military leaders – not girly shots, just pictures of wives. Raj and I sit in front of the director's desk, while the director sits behind it. Two men, Muhammad and Ibrahim, sit to our side. We have been waiting for over an hour for the wrestler to arrive. Raj gestures towards the calendar with the photo of the emir.

'He's a very simple man, a very simple man,' he says. 'I was very impressed with him when I met him. He is an educated man. He only has taken the one wife. That is very good in the eyes of God. I am a Reverend Father of the church, and I know that God will be happy.'

I sit there in disbelief. Here we are, in a citadel of Islamic power, and Raj is racking up the emir's monogamy, which is something that rankles with the local Muslims, as a points-scorer in the eyes of the one true Christian God. An intense theological debate ensues. Ibrahim and Muhammad stress that it's written in the Koran that a man should have more than one wife. I try to look neutral, but imagine the Muslims will have me down as a Christian by association and therefore a supporter of Raj and his views.

A man who looks like a slimmed-down version of Idi Amin enters the room. He wears a light brown uniform with shiny silver buttons, a beret, polished patent leather black shoes and sunglasses, and has a moustache and toothy grin. He starts talking about immigration, and the need to enter the country by an authorised route. Clearly he is an immigration officer – and clearly he is here for me – but he too becomes drawn into the theological argument. He quotes chapter and verse of the Koran and emphasises his points with a downward-jabbing finger, and says that it is proper for a Muslim to have two, three or four wives. Raj repeats that in the eyes of God one wife is sufficient. I move my chair so that it faces away from Raj, as if the furniture arrangements are a sign language I can use to uncouple myself ideologically from him. Ibrahim says that the

Koran, unlike the Bible, has never been altered, and that it is incontrovertible, therefore a superior text. I get up and leave the room for a moment to breathe in air uncontaminated by dogmatic theological argument. I see Daniel arrive.

'Raj is getting into a big theological debate with them,' I hiss to him.

'Oh no,' he says, horrified.

Daniel joins those assembled in the room. Soon the wrestler arrives too. He is from the Gungawa tribe, not the Dukawa, and is pensive and nervous. The director of culture says the actual interview will be conducted in the chairman's office. We go downstairs, cross a yard and enter the office. The chairman motions for me to sit across the desk from him.

'I'm very interested in learning about local wrestling, so I will interpret for you,' he says.

I don't believe him. Either he wants to censor the wrestler's responses in some way, or obligate me into giving him *dash* for his help, or both. I place my tape-recorder on his desk and press 'Record'.

'I'd like to start by asking the wrestler his name and where he comes from.'

'You do not need to know his name or where he comes from,' says the chairman, abruptly. 'He is just a wrestler.'

Probably because he's uncomfortable with the fact that the interview will be recorded, the chairman decides we should return to the director of culture's office, which we do. The director takes a clean page of A4, and writes 'Local Wrestling Interview' at the top and the date. He says that everyone in the room should write their name, address and the organisation they work for – beginning with me. Obviously he's hoping I will absentmindedly confess to working for a company or organisation, then point out I don't have the correct visa. A bribe will then smooth things over.

While I write my name and address I say: 'Actually, I'm here independently – I don't work for an organisation. I used to wrestle myself, which is where my interest comes from.'

The director looks surprised. We wait till everyone has filled in the form.

'This interview will only be about local wrestling and no other subject,' announces the director.

The immigration officer begins to say something: 'Mr Marcus—'

The director of culture cuts him off: 'No, let us finish, then later on.'

Daniel says: 'Mr Marcus is particularly interested in how wrestling relates to marriage.'

'We cannot talk about marriage, only local wrestling,' snaps the director.

Just as the interview is about to start, Muhammad cuts in, and makes a long, ornate speech. How nice it is, he says, that Raj and I respect the emir, for whom he himself would do anything. He points out that there are good relations between the Christian Fathers and the local government. I don't know where he is headed with this, but there's a 'but' coming. The 'but' eventually arrives: but he wants to know whether I have the right travel documents and how I entered the country. Raj begins to answer on my behalf. Irritated, I cut him off.

'All my documents are in order. In London, I went to the Nigerian High Commission and told them why I wanted to come to Nigeria – that I wanted to learn about traditional wrestling – and they gave me a visa. When I arrived at Lagos airport that visa was stamped by immigration control.'

Muhammad smiles.

'Can I see your passport?' he says.

I open my passport on the page of the visa and give it to him. He takes an inordinate amount of time to scrutinise it, then passes it to the immigration officer.

'But you don't have a resident's visa,' says the immigration officer.

'That's right. I'm not a resident – I'm here as a visitor.'

'But this is not stamped.'

I stand, go over to him, and use my forefinger to point out the outlines of two rubber stamps.

'That's a stamp and that's a stamp and *there's* some writing. They are in faint ink, but that's not my problem.'

I sit down again, angry. The interview begins. By now I have no interest in the actual interview, but just want to talk long enough to satisfy the politicians that they are satisfying me so that I can get my passport back and leave. While I speak to the wrestler, the Idi Amin lookalike sits with an arm extended

across the back of the adjoining chair. He has bookmarked a
page of my passport with a finger, apparently smug in the
certainty that he's spotted an irregularity. But when the
interview is over, he doesn't pounce. The director says I have to
visit the chairman again. This time the chairman is sitting
slouched sideways in his chair and watching a music video on a
large-screen TV.

'Did you get what you wanted?' he asks.

'Yes, it was interesting,' I lie.

'Do you need anything else?'

'No.' Not from you.

'You will be leaving Yelwa now?'

'I will stay here for a while longer.'

The chairman looks me straight in the eye.

'Well, thank you for hiring us.'

The music has stopped. I act naive, as though I don't
understand the implication of his use of the verb 'to hire'.

'Thanks for helping me,' I say.

Muhammad holds on to my passport. He converses with the
chairman in Hausa. Judging by their body language,
Muhammad is unwilling to give it back, but the chairman is
telling him to return it. Muhammad reluctantly gives in. I
make a point of remaining seated so that he has to cross the
room to give the passport back.

Raj and I spontaneously shake hands after we leave the
office. That evening we sit on a wall outside the dining room in
the church compound and drink bottled beer together.

'The fuckers, the fuckers,' intones Raj.

He is angry because the Idi Amin lookalike said he will visit
to check Raj's documents, too, in the morning. Thankfully he
never does.

Father Daniel suspected the visit to the emir would be a waste
of time. He doesn't know why I approached him anyway, he
says, as there is no need to get his permission or anyone else's
before talking to tribal groups.

Moses has made the arrangements for me to talk to Dukawa
elders and witness a demonstration of wrestling. Daniel and I
set off in a utility vehicle and head north along a road without

traffic. Boys carrying catapults wave from the roadside. We turn off onto a dirt track and pass through a landscape of bushes, small trees and ant or termite hills. Daniel parks the vehicle and we walk to a small church with a corrugated roof, mud and straw walls, wooden benches and a blackboard. Dukawa huts are nearby – mud walls and stone bases. Chickens shelter underneath. Three Dukawa elders sit waiting on a bench in the shade of a tree. Their clothes are grubby, their lower legs are caked in mud and their front teeth cut into points. Daniel and I sit with them.

The elders are friendly and only too happy to talk about wrestling. Daniel translates. The elders say that the Dukawa tradition of wrestling is as old as the tribe itself, and is something they very much want to preserve. They wrestle in the dry season, from harvest time till the beginning of the farming season – roughly December till April – and during this period they hold competitions between communities. Wrestling contests are first held to select who will represent a community, then an inter-village competition is held. Competitions also feature singing and dancing. Girls from both communities attend.

I move on to the subject of whether Dukawa men win brides through wrestling – or, as the post I read on the Web implied, girls choose their husbands on the basis of wrestling ability. The elders say that Dukawa girls crave good wrestlers as husbands. They like strong and brave men, and want to marry champion wrestlers. The men wrestle to show how brave, strong and powerful they are, and the presence of the girls gives them the motivation to compete hard. Good wrestlers are loved by the girls, while poor wrestlers are teased mercilessly. The girls sing songs about poor wrestlers that say they are weak and not real men. This, of course, motivates them to try harder next time. The winner of a wrestling bout has ground guinea corn wiped on his head by a girl, and is carried around on people's shoulders.

The Dukawa follow a custom of arranging marriages at a very early age, so I ask the elders how it is that marriages are engineered between a wrestling champion and a female admirer, because surely by the time a youth proves himself as a wrestler he will already be committed to marry a particular girl. The elders explain that champion wrestlers make their own rules. If a youth proves himself as a wrestler, he can leave the girl he has arranged to marry and instead marry a girl of his choice from among his group of female admirers. The special marriage rules that apply to wrestlers also apply to chiefs and the best farmers, say the elders. Dukawa males are supposed to be living with their wife by the age of 25, at which point they stop wrestling, otherwise they risk feeling great shame if they are ever beaten in front of her.

Champion wrestlers are given special treatment after they die. Wrestling is held during their funeral celebrations, and sometimes cement will be used to beautify a champion's grave and make it more visible. The cementing of the grave signifies that the deceased was an important person, and the same is done for chiefs, who also have wrestling at their funeral ceremonies. Marriage ceremonies, too, include wrestling. I ask the elders whether they know any folklore or stories about well-known Dukawa wrestlers. They say they do not, which is surprising. They say, too, that wrestling is not as popular as it used to be among their tribe.

Two brothers are going to give a demonstration of Dukawa wrestling. First they wait for a group of girls to turn up. They explain that otherwise they cannot summon up the necessary passion. The girls arrive. They are beautifully dressed in colourful printed wraps for skirts, headkerchiefs, necklaces and black bras, or go bare-breasted. Their faces are heavily made up with simple dark lines and some have similarly tattooed bodies. Their front teeth are cut to points, which the Dukawa consider attractive. A drummer leads the girls, who dance together in a circle like a happy, shuffling queue. Coins hanging from the girls' belts and skirts tinkle and jangle. One girl leads the singing, while the others join in. I can understand why the wrestlers said they had to wait: the girls' dancing and singing inject a celebratory energy into the day and totally transform the mood. You can sense the excitement and passion that must characterise a full-blown wrestling competition.

The two wrestlers grip the cloth each has tied around his waist. Normally they would wear a goatskin, they explain. You are not allowed to grip anywhere else. Though this is only a demonstration and the brothers are not going to wrestle for real, the elder brother doesn't want to be seen to be the loser. He trips his younger brother back, who touches the ground with his back, which constitutes a fall. A girl with a powdering of guinea corn flour on her hand instantly steps in and rubs the powder on the winner's head. He stands, grinning. The girls tease the loser and laugh.

As I watch, I have a feeling that I'm witnessing something unlike anything I have ever seen before, but can't quite put my finger on why. Then I realise it's because I have never seen girls take such a direct and active interest in wrestling. It's as though the girls' dancing and singing and the men's wrestling are a single entity, a single organism, and you can't have the one without the other. The girls are in control and pull the strings and push the buttons of the men. They are both cheerleaders and boo-leaders who both encourage and goad.

Later that day I sit at the desk in my room and listen to the tape of the interview with the elders. They did not talk at any great length about wrestling, yet it is still possible to winnow a lot of meaning from what they said and from the demonstration. First, the Web post I came across back in England was either incorrect or did not apply to this particular group of Dukawa. Girls don't choose husbands from among the wrestlers; instead a wrestler has the opportunity to choose a wife from among his admirers. Those admirers, of course, have chosen him too, so the marriage is made by mutual consent.

Secondly, the chorus of girls is a powerful motor that drives the wrestlers to prove themselves – and this dynamic operates beyond the dry season tournaments and throughout Dukawa culture as a whole. The women encourage the men to be good wrestlers because they like and want to marry such men, and inadequate wrestlers are teased. There can be few greater motivating forces for young men than the approval of women. Wrestling is a way for men to demonstrate manliness, and Dukawa women like manly men.

Thirdly, the timing of inter-community wrestling competitions appears to be dictated by farming. Farming takes precedence. The Dukawa convene tournaments after the harvest, when all major farm work is done. This is reminiscent of Mongolia, where, as I discovered for myself, Naadam is held during a period when herders have less work to do and like to relax. In both cases, this also happens to be the hottest time of the year: the dry season in Nigeria, and summer in Mongolia.

Fourthly, it is significant that Dukawa wrestling tournaments are held between different communities. While the Dukawa are busy living and working on their farms, their lives must be insular. But during the dry season, when they have harvested crops and there is more food and less work, their attention can turn outwards again, and this is the time to wrestle and meet others from the same tribe but different communities. The dry season is a time of social extroversion. Because tournaments are held between different communities, wrestlers have a larger platform on which to display their skills. If there are more girls watching, they have an opportunity to develop a larger fan base and choose from among more admirers – and conversely they will lose more face if they are beaten. Also, the intermarrying between wrestlers and girls from different communities that results must play a role in strengthening the bonds that bind the tribal group together as a whole.

Obviously, the way in which Dukawa men win women is not as stark as the winner-takes-females clashes of the animal kingdom. Young Dukawa women do not loiter passively at wrestling matches and wait to be carried off by whoever it is who succeeds in throwing an opponent onto his back. Human culture is complex and sophisticated and you would not expect things to be as crude as that. But embedded in the marriage customs of the Dukawa is the simple principle that a man can win over a woman and marry her on the basis of his skill as a wrestler, and maybe this convention represents the survival of an ancient form of human rutting behaviour into the modern era – the endurance of a practice that has evolved and changed over thousands of years yet retained its essential characteristics.

The custom of wrestling at funerals that the elders mentioned is fascinating, too, and something I have only read about before in sources from Ancient Greece, such as Homer's *Iliad*, which describes how contests including wrestling are held at the funeral of the dead warrior Patroklos. It is troubling, however, that the elders had no stories about well-known wrestlers. The lack of stories would seem to indicate that their wrestling culture does not survive well – that the natural process of transmitting tales from one generation to another has stuttered for some reason. I broach the subject with Father Daniel over breakfast the following morning and ask him whether, had I visited the Dukawa 50 years ago, he thinks they would have had folk tales and stories to tell.

'Yes,' he says. 'Their culture has been eroded. It is because of the influence of the Hausas. The Dukawa are losing their culture fast.'

Daniel explains that the British rulers gave power to the Hausas. He moves a thermos flask lid and slaps it down on the table, as though it represents that power being handed over. The British ruled Nigeria indirectly through the Hausas, and they were given political dominance. Cultural dominance has followed. Today, says Daniel, the Hausas are forcing tribal groups to convert to Islam.

'All the people follow their chief, so the Hausas threaten the chiefs. They tell them that they will take away their land if they do not convert. When the chief converts, all his people do too.'

'This is happening now?'

'It is still happening,' replies Daniel. 'I can introduce you to a man who is physically a Muslim but spiritually a Christian. He has had to convert.'

Daniel says the Catholic Church wants to help local ethnic groups to retain their culture and language. I suddenly see how I fit into the big picture. The Church wants to protect indigenous cultures from aggressive attempts by Muslims to convert them, and it welcomes people like me who are interested in the Dukawa's traditions and could conceivably play a role in their preservation.

It feels like flu: sore throat, cough, aching body, foggy-mindedness, headache. I've been bitten a few times by mosquitoes while standing outside to enjoy the cool evening air. Eager to rule out malaria, I describe my symptoms to Raj.

'You have malaria and typhoid both,' he says in a matter-of-fact way. 'Recently I had same.'

Raj drives me over to a local clinic. In reception, women sit on benches with babies strapped to their backs. One baby makes an unhealthy coughing sound like an espresso machine.

Raj and I enter a cluttered lab, and sit next to a young and pretty nurse. She takes blood from the back of my hand, and places it in a vibrating machine on the floor. Then she places blobs on a white tile that looks suspiciously like it was designed for a bathroom wall. She adds a blue liquid to each blob, then a reddish liquid, takes the tile in her hand and tilts and turns it so that the liquids mix.

'What are you looking for?' I ask.

'A reaction,' says the nurse.

After a few minutes she concludes I have both malaria and the early signs of typhoid. I go to another room for a consultation with a man deputising for the doctor, who is away.

'But I don't understand how I can have come down with malaria,' I say. 'I've been taking Doxycycline.'

'Doxycycline is an antibiotic,' he says. 'You have to combine it with an antimalarial.'

'I was told in England that Doxycycline *is* an antimalarial. It cost me *sixty quid.*'

The man laughs.

'No. Perhaps Doxycycline alone would work against malaria in temperate countries like England, but not here in our tropical Nigeria.'

He writes down the strain of malaria that I have: *P Falciparum,* the serious kind.

'Do you like injections?' he asks.

'I'd prefer tablets.'

'Injections will work faster.'

'OK, I'll take the injections.'

He prescribes chloroquine injections, along with Fansidar, vitamin B tablets and paracetamol. I take my prescription to the receptionist, pay her and go to a treatment room. A nurse breaks a phial of chloroquine with wire cutters. Brown glass explodes all over the floor. Other patients enter the room while the nurse fills a syringe. She booms at them.

'Did I say you could come in here? Get out, all of you, get out!'

I stand, trousers down, with my back to the nurse, and brace myself against the treatment couch, like a criminal about to be searched by a cop in an American TV show. It feels as though the nurse's hostility towards the other patients is directed into my body; as the needle enters my buttock, I have to neutralise the intense pain by growling. I return to the church compound, and lie on the bed in my room. Delirious, I fall asleep and have a vivid dream in which I think I am reading a book line by line. When I wake up, it takes me a while to realise that I was actually asleep. I go back to the clinic the next day for another injection – this time given by a male nurse who administers it without hostility. Another patient is sitting on a bench in the treatment room.

'What have you got?' he asks.

'Malaria.'

'Malaria? How long have you been in Nigeria?'

'Less than a week.'

'Less than a week?' He chuckles. 'You've been in Nigeria less than a week and you already have malaria?'

When he puts it like that, it's funny. We both laugh. He searches for another way to sum up my misfortune to further fuel our laughter.

'Welcome to Nigeria,' he says. 'Nigeria welcomes you with malaria.'

Chapter 11

Mr Capable of Killing a Cow

Malaria is not as bad as I expected it to be. Probably because it is diagnosed and treated immediately, it never takes a proper hold and I recover within a couple of days. When I feel strong again, I begin the second leg of the trip and head south to investigate the place of wrestling in the marriage customs of the Igbo, a large ethnic group who predominate in south-east Nigeria. According to posts on the Web, the Igbo used to wrestle for the hand in marriage of beautiful women – and perhaps they still do. I've also been encouraged to visit the Igbo by a book set in Igboland towards the end of the nineteenth century: *Things Fall Apart* by Chinua Achebe. The book's protagonist, Okonkwo, wins over one of his four wives through his skill as a wrestler. Though fiction, *Things Fall Apart* is widely regarded as an accurate evocation of Igbo life both before and during culturally fatal encounters with Christian missionaries and British colonialists – and is also considered one of the great books of world literature. It's feasible that it was once commonplace for Igbo men to win over women through wrestling in the way described in *Things Fall Apart* – and I'm hoping that if that's the case, the practice endures to this day.

From Yelwa I travel to Zuru, where I stay for a few nights at the Catholic church; from Zuru, I get a lift to Kontagora and from Kontagora I take a shared taxi to Minna, where I stay in church accommodation next to the cathedral. I don't know what I would do without the welcoming network of churches and Fathers and places to stay. At Minna I meet Father Jerome, a tall priest from Awka in Anambra state, which is in Igboland. He says he can give me a lift there and that I'll be able to stay at the retreat centre where he is based. He has a driver with a new 4x4, and we bomb down the roads at 70 to 80mph. The landscape changes as we head south. The earth, which is almost pink in the north, becomes browner; the vegetation is more lush and a deeper green. There are more cars and trucks on the roads, and the area is more densely populated and developed. The balance of religions reverses: an area with a large Muslim majority and a small Christian minority gives way to an area with a large Christian majority and a small Muslim minority.

The Catholic Retreat Centre at Awka is built around a central garden with lifesize statues re-enacting the stations of the Cross. I take a simple room facing the garden. Father Jerome has an apartment in the block next door. His hospitality is overwhelming. He invites me over for coffee, which he calls 'tea', coconut, Hobnobs, cashew nuts, malt drinks, corn on the cob ('In England you just throw this to the cows?') and fruits he calls 'Nigerian pears', which taste disgusting. He is continually joking. Whenever he cracks up at a thought or idea, there is happy percussion as he stands, stamps a foot and claps his hands.

I have no contacts in Igboland and no idea where to look for wrestling, but the experiences of being in India and Mongolia have taught that it is best to go against the grain of development and investigate the rural backwaters. Yet the Igbo of Nigeria number perhaps 25 million, and the area in the south-east where they predominate is vast. It's difficult to know where to begin to look. Father Jerome suggests asking Power Mike, who he says is a well-known wrestler and has a sports

centre in the nearby city of Onitsha. Marcel, the bishop's
volatile driver, agrees to take me there in Jerome's rusting
Peugeot. A seminarian called Charles says he can come along
to translate.

On the morning of the trip, the car breaks down soon after
we join the expressway to Onitsha. Marcel parks on the inside
lane and finds a roadside mechanic. I try to get out the car, but
the rear inside door handle is broken. Charles has to let me out
from outside, which makes me feel unnecessarily regal. We
stand around while the mechanic gives the engine a look-over.
An argument erupts between Marcel and the mechanic
because he wants to charge 250 naira for simply tightening
something. The pitch at which they shout and argue would be
a prelude to a fist fight back home. I anxiously think about
what I should do if they do start to fight, yet they never come to
blows.

Once the engine is fixed, we drive on to Onitsha, which turns
out to be an ugly city of boxy concrete homes and shops. An
anarchy of cars and motorbikes crowds its streets. Squeegee
merchants and hawkers flit between vehicles stalled in heavy
traffic. The dirt roads are so rutted that they look as though
they have been shelled – like the no-man's land of the First
World War. The feeling of being in a battle zone is heightened
by the drivers who fight for every inch of space. There are no
traffic lights to discipline road-users, and everyone uses their
horn all the time. No one lets anyone else in. When Marcel uses
the wrong side of the road, a driver snarls at him. I ask Charles
what was said. Charles smiles awkwardly, clearly embarrassed
by the acidity of the abuse, then explains that the driver called
Marcel a goat.

Power Mike's sports centre is down a wide avenue transformed by the rains into a series of lakes. Marcel tries to
navigate a course through the first but the car gets stuck. A boy
interrupts pushing his wheelbarrow to help push us out.
Charles and I continue by foot until we see a large, crude
statue of Power Mike standing sentry outside his sports
complex. His name used to be spelt out, but only a single letter
remains – the 'M', 'K' and 'E' have dropped off. In reception, a
tall and powerful-looking man introduces himself as Power
Mike's son. Unfortunately, he says, his father is away in Abuja

on business. He looks up his father's phone numbers on a mobile and passes them on. I ask him if he knows whether traditional Igbo wrestling survives in the rural villages.

'My father will be able to tell you,' he says.

'But you must know something about it.'

'Ask my father. But I've heard that there is still wrestling in Arondizuogu and the villages around Owerri.'

He fetches a biography of his father, which he gives me as a gift. Charles and I trek back to the car. We pick a path through the filth, squalor, spilled oil and heaps of rubbish that lie along the edges of the lakes of water.

'This is terrible,' Charles keeps saying in genuine shock. 'This is *terrible*.'

The backcover blurb of Power Mike's biography describes it as a 'masterpiece that will turn budding sportsmen and women into champions'. Entitled *The African Strongest Man: Power Mike Who Ruled the World*, it is written by 'internationally recognised scholar' Prof Chidi Maduka.

In his introduction, the professor writes:

> Power Mike is a household word in Nigeria, Africa and even beyond. To most people he is a colossus, a titan, a mythical figure. How can a person use his sheer physical strength to stop two cars from moving? Win a tug of war against 20 hefty and able-bodied men? Carry with ease several bags of cement placed on his belly? Become a heavy-weight wrestling champion in a matter of months?

Judging by photos of a grimacing Power Mike applying the comic-book techniques of professional wrestling, the answer to the last question is straightforward: because he was a faker, a show wrestler.

The book's first photo portrait of Power Mike is captioned 'but Power Mike looks a lot different when rigged out in his leather and python-skin strongman outfit'. He certainly does. As he flexes his impressive V of a physique, Power Mike looks like either a member of a 1980s glam metal band or of a self-consciously camp dance troupe. 'It is important to have a peep into the galaxy of his displays,' writes the professor. He lists Power Mike's feats, such as how he hammered a six-inch nail into wood then removed it with his teeth, and how he stopped two cars from being driven in opposite directions.

Father Jerome cold-calls Power Mike on my behalf to set up a meeting. Power Mike is initially suspicious, probably because he is worried that the call may be part of a scam, a 419, the number of the government statute passed to fight fraud that is universally used to label scam-mongers, who are dubbed '419ers'. To allay Power Mike's fears, Father Jerome establishes his credentials again and again and stresses that he is a clergyman. A few days later Power Mike calls Father Jerome back and gives a message that he will be at the Cordial Hotel in Enugu at midday the following Sunday.

On the day, Charles and I take the bus to Enugu, then ride pillion on motorbike taxis across town in the rain. The rear wheels slick up mud. By the time I have reached the hotel, my arms and clothes are spattered with earth. I go to the men's room to clean up, but there is no soap and there are no paper towels. Neither is there toilet paper in the cubicles, and the innards of the toilets, their grotty cisterns, are exposed because the toilet lids are missing. Back in reception, the receptionist hands me some tissues. A head pokes out from the top of the stairwell.

'Are you the people who've come to see me?' asks Power Mike.

He is smaller and older than I anticipated. Time has eroded the chiselled physique pictured in his biography – it's as though the 'M', 'K' and 'E' have been lost from his physical presence as well as his statue. Power Mike ushers us upstairs to his room, where he sits on the edge of the bed, legs apart, elbow on knee, with one eye in darkness, the other in light. He wears a Nike polo shirt, and a gold chain and watch – gaudy baubles of success. In the corner of the room, Southampton play Liverpool on a TV that has the name of the hotel scratched into the screen as a security measure. Wherever you look in Nigeria you are confronted by hostility and spiritual antagonism staring back at you – by reminders of the prevalence of theft and crime, or evidence of decay and lack.

'Wrestling has just died away,' says Power Mike. 'It has died out. Just like scarification.' He points to his cheeks: 'I do not have.'

'Before wrestling died out, was there a tradition of wrestlers wrestling for a bride?'

'That is true. Women would marry a winner. Even a footballer, they can just. . . ' He leaves the sentence unfinished, but he means footballers can just have their pick of women. 'That's how they get married.'

Even if wrestling has declined, it's unlikely to have died out completely – and even if it has died out completely, there must be old men around who can remember the era when wrestling was alive. I ask Power Mike to recommend an area where I can talk to old men who wrestled when they were young, in order to form a picture of how things used to be. He doesn't seem to comprehend the question. Instead he bulldozes over it and talks grandly about how he is reviving traditional wrestling. He is scheduling a traditional wrestling tournament for October, he says, and claims to have pumped half a million naira into the project. He wants me to help him secure government funding. I recognise this as a textbook case of the Westerner-equals-prime-mover misunderstanding. Obviously Power Mike believes that because I'm white, from England, I have the status and power to act as a business ambassador, a facilitator, in negotiations. Perhaps he also thinks I can help fund the venture out of my own pocket.

I try to let Power Mike down gently. I tell him that though I would like to help, I will be leaving Nigeria before October, so can't. Once again I bring the conversation back to the question of where he would advise me to go to meet old men who remember the Igbo tradition of wrestling, but Power Mike again ignores the question and instead talks about his forthcoming tournament. I feel frustrated and angry, and try to get through to him a couple more times, yet he still won't answer the question. It is difficult to avoid the conclusion that Power Mike is either dense or self-obsessed or both. I give in and find another subject to talk about to at least stop him banging on about his tournament.

'So, I read in your book that you visited England.'

'Yes, I was with David Frost. I stopped two cars on the David Frost programme. I went to Bedford.'

He turns to Charles.

'All the vehicles we drive in Nigeria with "Bedford" on them – it is the name of a town.'

At the end of the meeting Power Mike gives me his phone numbers – the same numbers I used to contact him in the first place.

I'm left with no leads except the casual tip-off Power Mike's son gave that he'd heard that traditional wrestling can still be found in Arondizuogu and the villages around Owerri. Father Jerome suggests I accompany Father Ethel, a flamboyant and chubby-faced columnist for *Fides*, a Catholic newspaper based at the retreat centre, on a visit to the *eze*, or traditional ruler, of Arondizuogu, and suggests we should also visit the Eze of Awka while we are at it. Father Ethel can ask about kidnapping cases for an article he plans to write, and I can ask about traditional wrestling.

Marcel drives us in the dilapidated Peugeot. Ethel is upset because he cannot sit in the front passenger seat, which he says is the best place from which to deal with the police. Marcel has put the graphic equaliser and speakers on the floor of the front seat, where they rest in a tangle of wires, and says they cannot be moved. Ethel reluctantly sits on the back seat beside me. Whenever we stop for more than a few seconds at checkpoints, he winds down the window and shouts impatiently.

'Cop! Police! What is the delay?'

Remembering the advice Father Peter gave about avoiding talking to the police at checkpoints, I cringe every time – yet the authority of Ethel's white vestment seems to count for something and we are never detained.

Deep in the jungle the roads are so rutted that they are like advanced archaeological excavations. Marcel edges forwards through pits up to six-foot deep and ponds of rainwater. The Eze of Arondizuogu's so-called palace turns out to be a detached, suburban-style home within a compound wall. We go inside. A large woman sits on a sofa watching motocross on TV, with the curtains drawn.

'This is Her Royal Highness,' says Father Ethel.

Ethel sits in an armchair and yawns while we wait for the *eze*.

The *eze* enters the room and sends for kola nut, which he blesses elaborately.

'This is native kola nut and it only understands native language, so excuse me while I speak to it in our language,' he says.

When the *eze* has finished, a piece of kola nut is passed to me. I chew and swallow small bits. It tastes bitter and disgusting. I have to concentrate for a moment to stop myself throwing up.

'Eze, you are close to the ancestors, so I brought Marcus here,' says Ethel.

He explains the purpose of my visit.

'You will have to see wrestling before you can understand it and talk to elders,' says the *eze*. 'I am going to have wrestling and drumming here at the palace on 3rd September, when I am going to hold a New Yam Festival. It is part of our culture. You should come to the festival. I will introduce you to some old wrestlers.'

I thank the *eze* profusely for the invite. This is an exceptional piece of luck. Not only will I be able to see traditional Igbo wrestling but also the drumming that is an important aspect of Igbo wrestling culture – and both will occur at a New Yam Festival like one that plays a central part in the narrative of *Things Fall Apart*.

'Good,' says Ethel. 'Now it is my time. I am journalist.'

He holds a microcassette recorder and plays a snatch of an interview he did with a senior policeman in which they discuss kidnapping. He asks the *eze* whether he knows of any cases of kidnapping in the area. The *eze* says he does not.

We drive back to Awka to see the Eze of Awka. He receives visitors in a long room with red and gold floral-patterned sofas along the walls, and chairs set out at one end for an audience. Near the entrance door is a statue of Jesus. Steps lead to an ornately carved throne chair at the other end. We stand when the *eze* enters the room. He carries a carved tusk in one hand and wears a red pillar-box hat, like a fez, which is a mark of status. He takes his seat on the throne. The *eze* first deals with three federal government men who have come to discuss a radio mast project. While they converse, Ethel sits back on a sofa, waggling his legs impatiently, nonchalant and imperious –

as if to demonstrate that he, a Father, a man of God, is submissive only in front of a higher authority than the local traditional ruler. When it is our turn for an audience, Ethel introduces me as 'Marcel'.

'He is an English, a British,' he continues.

I tell the *eze* about my interest in traditional Igbo wrestling.

'It is almost extinct,' says the *eze*. 'In my time it was an activity conducted during the full moon. Wrestling was also an act of competition between villages and a serious affair.'

Without my having to broach the subject, he recounts how it used to be the case that a beautiful girl with many suitors would be wrestled for.

'You should have given me time to find out where there's wrestling,' he says. 'Do you have time?'

'I do, yes.'

'Then come back on Sunday at 5pm. I will send my secretary out to ask old men about wrestling.'

Ethel now takes his turn to speak to the *eze*. He introduces himself and plays another spurt of the interview he taped with the senior policeman. But this *eze*, too, says he knows of no local cases of kidnapping.

The car breaks down on the expressway during the return journey to the retreat centre. We all get out. Ethel stands near the boot and looks back towards the approaching vehicles. Any moment now he expects to see someone he knows who can give us a lift.

'I am sensational!' he says. 'Everyone recognises me!'

He is full of himself because he was only recently initiated as a Father. A truck belching fumes drives by and forces Ethel to jump out of the way, as though a cosmic instrument sent to dampen his pride. Soon a priest stops to give us a lift. We all get in his car. It quickly becomes apparent that the priest can't drive. Within moments he crashes the car into another and we have to get out and wait for yet another Father to stop.

Malaria symptoms make an unwelcome return. A Sister drops me at a local hospital near the cathedral. I sit on a bench on the verandah and wait to be seen by a doctor. Apprehensive about the hospital's standards of hygiene and healthcare, I look around for signs of reassurance. As if on cue a body is wheeled out on a trolley. Its wheels shudder on the uneven surface. The corpse's fat wobbles, sending ripples through the green plastic sheeting in which it is wrapped.

The doctor is young and shaven-headed. He sits bent over his desk, pen poised to write. I tell him that I am pretty certain I have malaria, as the symptoms are the same as before. He wipes a hand over his head and writes a long list of medicines to take, then asks whether I am rich. Fearing he may be angling for a bribe, I ask why he wants to know.

'It will affect the drugs you can take,' he says.

'Oh, I see. How rich do I need to be?'

'It will cost about 3,000 naira.'

'I can definitely afford that.'

The doctor explains that the medication I took during the first bout of malaria probably did not kill it off completely. He prescribes a powerful drug, Paluther, which should be able to deal with it once and for all.

Charles meets me at the hospital. He takes the prescription and leaves on his scooter to search for a pharmacy that stocks Paluther. While he is gone, I go for a blood test in one room, then to another for an injection. The nurse in the treatment room is huge and wears her hair in cute, girly bunches. I don't ask her what the injection is for but just stand, as she asks, braced against the treatment couch with my trousers down a little.

'This will pain you,' she says.

I presume her English is muddled and what she really means is 'This will not hurt', or 'You will only feel a scratch' – the things nurses usually say before giving an injection. The needle enters my buttock. A clenched fist of pain shoots down my leg. I cry out involuntarily.

'Sorry, sorry, sorry,' soothes the nurse.

The pain is more acute than any I have ever experienced. It is so intense that I sob and laugh hysterically at the same time. The nurse massages my shoulders and back.

'Sorry, sorry, sorry,' she says. 'Jesus loves you. Sorry, sorry, sorry. I love you. Sorry, sorry, sorry.'

I put my arm around her, rest my head on her bosom and surrender to her motherly tenderness. After a few minutes the pain starts to subside.

'Where are you staying?' asks the nurse. 'I'll come and visit you.'

I'm touched by her compassion. How nice of her to want to visit later to monitor my recovery.

'I'm staying at the Catholic Retreat Centre.'

'You will give me small present,' she demands.

The compassionate mood dies instantly.

Charles returns with a packet of Paluther vials. Before the nurse will give the injection, she asks for money.

'Give me naira for snacks,' she says.

Unwilling to risk alienating someone about to stab me with a needle, I reluctantly hand her 60 naira. After the treatment, I return to the bench on the verandah and sit there, depressed. Malaria has laid me low, but what is more demoralising is the fiscal dimension that sours so many encounters in Nigeria. A female patient comes and sits down next to me. Her leg is in a cast and she has crutches.

'I need your help,' she says.

'I'm sorry but I'm not a doctor.'

'No, I need money.'

Everyone thinks I'm Father Christmas.

The second audience with the Eze of Awka proves fruitless. He says his secretary went out to look for old men with whom to talk about wrestling, but the information they had to impart was only slight. The era of wrestling is over, he says. I return to my room and ponder what to do next. The only lead I have left is that Power Mike's son said there is wrestling in the villages around Owerri. He was right about Arondizuogu, so hopefully he will be right again.

The morning I finish the course of antimalarial injections, I leave for Owerri. The journey is supposed to take two or three hours but lasts more than six. At one point the minibus sits in almost stationary bumper-to-bumper traffic, a 'go-slow', for a couple of hours. Eventually we pass the reason for the delay: a Peugeot has been so violently twisted and contorted during an accident that it is folded in on itself, like complex origami. The car is covered in an avalanche of scrap metal that tipped out of a dumper truck that itself slid down a steep road.

I'm dropped off at Owerri Cathedral from where a Father gives me a lift to Assumpta Pastoral Centre, which has accommodation. I take an upstairs room with a desk, chair and luminous green figure of Christ on the cross above the bed, and mentally tick off the now familiar signs of poor building skills and zero maintenance – dictated either by a lack of spare parts, or money, or both: the door to the small bathroom has no handle; the keyhole to the wardrobe is upside down; the fan settings are back to front – '1' gives the strongest breeze, '5' is the weakest; and the cracked, plastic toilet seat is both unattached and incapable of being attached to the toilet.

The pastoral centre is teeming with Fathers, who are here for a course. They have lectures in the mornings and afternoons, and crowd the dining hall at breakfast, lunch and dinner. They are good-humoured and full of bonhomie, and give each other finger-click handshakes and spontaneously sing. Many of the Fathers assume that I, too, must be a Father, so I get in the habit of reflexively saying 'I'm not a Father' at the outset of a conversation to avoid any misunderstanding. One of the clergy, Father Peter, says he will help with my research when the course is over. He tells me to relax, be patient and wait a few days, after which he will take me to some of the towns and villages in the surrounding jungle where we should be able to find old wrestlers to talk with. Instinctively, I don't quite trust him but play along anyway. For a few days I just sit in my room, listen to music, handwash clothes, play computer Solitaire, and kill more time by eating too much at lunchtime so that I need to nap afterwards. Occasionally I leave the compound, but there is nowhere to go and little to do.

While I wait for him to finish the course and start giving help, Father Peter suggests I visit Umuapu, which is half an hour's drive away and, he says, well known for its wrestling. John, a young cook at the centre, drives me there in a borrowed car. Close to Umuapu, we stop at a junction to ask for directions. Instantly a hostile gang surrounds the car.

'Obstruction! Obstruction!' shout the youths and men.

They bang on the bonnet. John gets out to talk to them. I sit in the passenger seat, looking forward, trying to remain calm, with little idea what this is about, or whether we are in physical danger. John smiles and grins, and tries to talk his way out of the situation by saying that he is a seminarian and I am a Father. A man asks me whether this is true.

'No,' I reply, unable to shake off the reflex of denial. Fortunately he doesn't appear to understand my accent.

'Is he your driver, is he your driver?' asks a youth.

'Er, yes.'

To John I say: 'If we're causing an obstruction, why don't we drive off? Why can't we just drive off?'

He ignores me and keeps talking to the youths and men. One of them points at a tiny insect on my arm and picks if off, as though grooming me like a fellow primate. Eventually the heat leaves the situation. Someone in the gang repeats, 'Next time, next time.' John gets back in the car. A youth removes a block of wood that was placed in front of the front wheel so that we couldn't drive off. We leave.

'Hungry young lions, hungry young lions!' says John.

'What did they want?'

'They wanted to take the car to the local government office and fine us 3,000 naira for illegal parking.'

It was a scam obviously. There were no parking signs or road markings. The gang just wanted to intimidate us into giving money.

Father Calistus, the priest at Umuapu church, isn't at home. I write a note asking him to contact me at the retreat centre and leave it with the caretaker. We get back in the car and head home. A car coming the other way overtakes another on a blind bend and heads straight at us on our side of the road. It swerves back into its lane.

'This is how Nigerians are killing themselves,' says John.

Moments later he does exactly the same thing, as he switches to the other side of the road to avoid potholes and into the path of an oncoming car. The motorist wags his finger at John. John grins.

Father Calistus gets the note and introduces himself. He wears glasses and has a face constantly on the verge of laughter. He invites me to stay in accommodation next to his church, and together we call on Chief Ogbuehi, who used to be a wrestler, at his nearby home.

'Let's do our traditional ceremony,' says the chief.

He leaves the room and returns carrying an old-fashioned, carved, wooden kola nut tray with a handle shaped like a lion. Father Calistus holds a hand above the kola nut while he gives it a Christian blessing. Pieces are served afterwards. I chew but don't swallow this time. You're not supposed to swallow, which I wish I'd known before. A young girl enters the room holding a toddler by her upper arms and plonks her down. The toddler has never seen a white man before. She turns, crying, and runs out the room. Her sister laughs. A group of children stand outside, craning to look through the window.

Chief Ogbuehi is well built, and has bright eyes and a large head. Physically, he looks about 40 years old but he is actually 67. When he talks, he speaks with his hands, and as he talks about wrestling, he finds it difficult to sit still on the settee. Just speaking about wrestling energises him to the point that he has to stand up and act out. Father Calistus told the chief that I would visit, so he has prepared notes, which he reads in English. He uses formal language and says things like 'the *modus operandi*, otherwise known as mode of operation' and 'a winner, otherwise known as a victor'. He gives a list of wrestling techniques with inventive names, such as 'Confrontational Headlong Carriage', 'Foot Jack' and 'Irresistible Foot Encounter', and outlines the rules of Igbo wrestling, which is called *mgba*: you win when you throw your opponent on his back, get behind him, lift your foot over his head, or lift him off the ground.

'Tell me about your own experiences as a wrestler, Chief.'

'I wrestled when I was a young man. I was a very good wrestler. If you give me the opportunity now I can still wrestle. My father taught me to wrestle, because he was an advocate of wrestling when he was alive. If anybody is born in the family and is unable to wrestle, that person is a scallywag. He cannot be regarded in society as someone good, because that thing, wrestling, makes you physically fit and mentally alert. Physically fit and mentally alert. So our fathers, our ancestors, delighted in wrestling. So any child of theirs that refuses to wrestle – then that person will not be loved by its parents.'

'Was wrestling still a big part of Igbo life and culture when you were young?'

'Yes. It is a part of us. The Igbo man cannot do without wrestling.'

The chief says that wrestling took place during festivals, including *Iwaji*, the New Yam Festival. Though *Iwaji* falls towards the end of the rainy season, wrestling was predominantly an activity for later on, in the dry season – which, in Igboland, runs from about October till early March. If this holds true for the whole of Igboland, it means that the dry season is the main season for wrestling here just as in the north. Which also means I am here at the wrong time of year to witness wrestling, just as in the north. The chief says that during the dry season each village would hold competitions to decide who should represent them with honour, then inter-village tournaments were held. Champions of the inter-village competitions were given the title *dingba*.

'The champion is greatly compensated. In those days, a beautiful girl – the most beautiful girl in the city – would be given to him to marry.'

'By whom?' asks Calistus.

'By society. You marry my daughter because you are a champion and you know how to wrestle. You may not even pay anything for her. In those days, if I see that you are a champion, I say this: my daughter will be for you. Because you're a champion. Because we believe that a champion in wrestling is physically fit and mentally alert, and anyone that worries him will measure their length on the ground. Every time. In a twinkling of an eye you will be on the ground. So the elders like such people. People who cannot wrestle are relegated to the background.'

I ask the chief whether he personally knows any wrestlers who won wives through wrestling.

'Here? Yes, of course. We have so many of them.'

He gives a list, but unfortunately they have all passed away so I won't be able to meet any of them. He says his father, too, married many women because he was a wrestling champion.

'How many wives did your father have?'

'Fifteen, because my father was a wonderful farmer – a farmer of repute – and he was also a nice wrestler, so little wonder he married these wives. I saw the fifteen wives myself, and my mum was one of them. My mum was a beautiful woman.'

'Did your father marry your mother because of wrestling?'

'No, he didn't. My mother saw him as a handsome man. And she heard that he was a very strong man. And because of his handsomeness and his steadfastness, he could feed himself confidently, so my mother succumbed to the marriage.'

Calistus asks the chief whether wrestlers used to use magic charms – a good question. The use of charms is common throughout Nigeria and West Africa.

'Yes, of course. In those days, in my childhood, they used charms to wrestle. They used charms so that when you touched their body it would be slippy. At times you come in and their eyes will be dark – you will not even see them. You look more and you see less. You will be confused. You wouldn't know when they grip your two legs – and you'll be on the ground.'

I fish around by asking questions suggested by a knowledge of other wrestling cultures. I score a direct hit when I ask whether Igbo wrestlers believed you should avoid sex to maintain strength.

'Yes, of course. For you to go for a serious wrestling match, you must have nothing to do with women, because it lowers your physical ability. In those days, when they were using charms, if you go in contact with any woman sexually, then it means your charm wouldn't work.'

So there were two reasons to avoid sex: it weakened you and cancelled out the power of your charm.

'Were good wrestlers compared with animals?'

Calistus answers first: 'Yes, I know a wrestler whose name is Lion. I know another one called the Killer of Tigers, and another who beat a wrestler called Lion, so he became Defeater of the Lion.'

'My father got this name, Ogbuehi, through wrestling,' says the chief. 'It means the "Killer of Cow", or "Cow-killer".'

The chief explains that his father didn't actually kill a cow. The name translates more precisely as 'Capable of Killing a Cow', which is considered a powerful animal by the Igbo. Both Calistus and the chief explain that the Igbo language does not differentiate between a cow and a bull.

'And did you have wrestling at funeral ceremonies?'

'Yes,' says the chief. 'When an old man dies, the wrestlers will be invited to come. When they start beating the drums, if you are a good wrestler you wouldn't be here now – you go out and see what is happening. So when the elderly man is dead, the most important thing that will be done first and foremost for the old man is to stage a wrestling match. We have a belief that the dead person is around watching what is happening. Here it is our common belief that when a man is dead, he is not completely dead – he's around. The wrestling is for him to see we are doing what he said would be done after his lifetime, and if you don't do that you'll be in trouble. That's the belief. We treasure our custom so much here. Our custom is very important.'

Payment for a bride used to be standard practice in Igbo culture. There is a scene in Chinua Achebe's *Things Fall Apart* where two families conduct marriage negotiations using short broomsticks to represent how many bags of cowries the groom's family will give for a wife-to-be. The fact that champion wrestlers acquired wives without having to pay such bride prices indicates the high esteem in which they were held. Like in Dukawa culture, it appears that champion Igbo wrestlers could override normal marriage customs.

Chief Ogbuehi said his father was a good farmer as well as a strong wrestler and that this combination made him attractive to women. Skill as a yam farmer used to be central to an Igbo man's status. Yams were the staple food and considered a man's crop. Men took charge of their cultivation and nurture, and a man's status and wealth was measured by how many yams he kept in his barn. Okonkwo in *Things Fall Apart* is also a good farmer as well as a wrestling champion. Women must have considered men like Okonkwo and the chief's father to be an attractive package. Not only did they demonstrate their strength through success as a wrestler, but they were also good providers. Judging by the interview with the chief, winning wives through wrestling was a routine occurrence, and whether wrestling has largely declined among the Igbo or not, it won't be necessary to dig too far down into people's memories to expose the seams of recollections in which it's embedded.

When the Fathers' conference comes to an end, I meet Father Peter in the canteen, eager to get out and interview more old wrestlers with his help, as promised. He grins and explains he can't help after all because he has too many other things to do back at the school where he teaches. It sounds like he is telling me something he knew he was going to tell me all along. Too angry to sit and chat, I return to my room and brood. I kick myself for relying on him and not having trusted my instincts. Now that the conference is over, most of the Fathers have either left or are about to return to their churches in the countryside. It would have been the easiest thing in the world to befriend some of them and make arrangements to stay in their villages, but now it's too late, and I'm back to square one with no car, driver, interpreter, or guide. It's even likely that I won't be able to arrange to go to the New Yam Festival, which is in only a few days' time.

At breakfast the following day I sit at a table with Monsignor Theophilus Okere, who is in his fifties and balding, and lives at the hostel while his new house is being built. We talk about this and that. He says he has visited Britain to do research at archives and libraries because he intends to set up a cultural institute. We discuss politics, Iraq, the US, and talk about journalism too. Theophilus says he called a press conference in July to publicise the fact that 30 priests have been attacked by armed robbers since the previous November.

'In the whole of Nigeria or just Igboland?'

'No, in this diocese alone. Some of the priests at the conference would have been attacked.'

The robbers are after church donations, says Theophilus. One priest was beaten to a pulp and put in a coma. He recovered but needed reconstructive surgery and can hardly make the sign of the cross any more. In another incident, armed men entered a seminary through an air-conditioning vent. A priest shot one of them dead and wounded another, who later died – the police were in no hurry to take him to a hospital. The priest was in shock afterwards and has had psychological problems ever since. Some of the robbers are obviously students, says Theophilus. They demand specific things: watches, mobile phones and, strangely, clean underwear.

'We now have a policy of not keeping any money on church premises. Everything has to be banked. But we expect that a couple of Fathers will make the ultimate sacrifice before the message gets across that it is not worth robbing our churches.'

After breakfast I go and sit alone in my room and hit a low. I knew Nigeria was an insane country, but Theophilus's account of attacks on the clergy has left me feeling more unsettled than ever. I've been operating under the assumption that the Fathers have a special immunity from attack – a special dispensation to do their work, like the Red Cross in a war zone – and that by associating with the clergy I was safe too, but the reality is that robbers actively target the Fathers because they are relatively wealthy and collect church donations. I've had enough of everything: the fact that my preconceptions are so consistently wrong, the threat of robbery and violence, intimidation, the Igbo propensity to argue, recurrent malaria, the dangerous roads, the broken plastic toilet seat, the corruption, and particularly the fact that Peter isn't going to help like he said he would, a situation that demonstrates that I haven't mastered how to operate in this culture – how to read between the lines, to understand the hiddens in dealings, the things not explicitly stated yet implicitly meant. I know what people are saying, but I have no idea what they are leaving unsaid, which is often more important. Perhaps there is a culture of saying 'yes' when you really mean 'no'. Maybe I should have offered to pay Peter for his help, though maybe he would have found the offer offensive.

Part of me wants to abandon the trip, though I know I would come to regret it. To have come all this way and not continue would be crazy. I force myself to think positively, and make a list of the things I can do to move forwards. The best option is to appeal to Theophilus for help. After all, he has visited England, so he knows that people operate differently back home, and maybe, as someone who has also done research abroad, he will be sympathetic and understand my difficulties. I call on Theophilus in his room and tell him that I've been left high and dry by Father Peter, and desperately need a guide and interpreter. He considers this and replies that he can arrange a meeting with his brother, Linus, a professor of anthropology, who may be able to help.

The following evening Theophilus's nephew, Edwin, knocks on my door and politely ushers me to Theophilus's room, where Linus is waiting. Linus is small, perhaps no more than five feet tall, and has an air of effervescing enthusiasm that bubbles up to fill the room. He wears round-framed glasses and talks in a rapid, breathless way. He rattles off information about Igbo wrestling, and says his father used to be one of the men who would keep the spectators back at village competitions with a whip. I get my notebook out and start to take notes.

'I am not giving an interview!' shouts Linus.

'Sorry. I was just writing down a few words so that I could remember the subjects you've mentioned.'

I put the notebook away. By the end of the meeting we have arranged to go to the New Yam Festival together in a few days' time – and I have found a saviour.

Chapter 12

If You Win, People Will Clap

Two young brothers appear on the walkway outside my room. Curious, they want to meet me, the white man. They come in and sit down. The younger one, who is perhaps ten, is more forward than his brother. He is wearing a Nike clone T-shirt with 'Just Do Me' written in large type, and other slang terms for sex current in Australia in smaller print, such as 'Just bone me' and 'Just shag me'. Presumably someone in Australia cleared out their wardrobe, gave their cast-offs to a charity that works in Africa, and the result is a ten-year-old walking around Nigeria wearing a T-shirt asking for sex in colloquial English. The boy looks around the room at my things and asks about the fishing tackle. I pick up the rod and a lure and talk him through fishing.

'A big fish thinks this lure is a little fish swimming through the water, bites it and gets hooked, and then I turn the handle of this reel to wind it in.'

The boy looks puzzled, and I feel slightly ridiculous. Though he understands English, I can tell he hasn't a clue what I'm talking about. Nigeria doesn't do leisure. Fishing tackle must appear bizarre and senseless to Nigerians. Why go to all that effort to catch one fish when you can use a net and catch many? Nigerians do survival, not pastimes.

We sit in silence for a moment. Then the boy says he wants to 'follow me' to England – in other words accompany me when I return home.

'No, you can't follow me. What would your parents think? You've got to go to school. What would you do in England, anyway?'

'I'd be a doctor,' he says. He thinks for a moment. 'Or a manservant.'

He is prepared to go and tell his mother, who is in the market, right this minute that he is going to leave for England with me, he says. His father is dead and he doesn't go to school, he explains. I try to distract him from thinking about imminent economic migration by letting him listen to music on a tape player.

'So,' I say after a while. 'What hobbies do you have?'

He speaks to his brother in Igbo to clarify the meaning of the word 'hobby'.

'My hobby is that I'll follow you to England and be your manservant.'

I repeat that I can't take him back to England and tell him that he should stay here, with his mother, who loves him, and try to get an education. I take out some money, 40 naira, and go to give it to him. He looks pained. He doesn't want to accept the money. He knows that it is being given as a consolation for not bringing him back to England and employing him as a manservant. As we part, he stares at me with eyes on the verge of tears.

'I will never see you again,' he says.

But we do see each other again. There's a soft knock on the door the next day: same boy, this time alone.

'I will go and tell my mother now that I am going to follow you to England,' he says.

'You can't. You have to stay here with your mother and get an education if you can. Then, when you're older, maybe you can travel to England.'

At his age, he should be playing, not considering leaving the country behind his mother's back. I find one of the Frisbees I've been meaning to give away as gifts. We go out onto the walkway, where I show the boy how to throw and catch a Frisbee as a prelude to giving it to him as another consolation for not employing him as a manservant. He quickly gets the idea, but I can tell that he is only interested in playing Frisbee in as much as he believes it makes me happy. He doesn't get any particular enjoyment out of playing Frisbee himself. He wants to please me to demonstrate he has the right credentials. Playing Frisbee, he probably believes, is the kind of thing that being a manservant in England will entail.

It counts as a real coup to have been invited to the New Yam Festival in Arondizuogu. The gathering marks the beginning of a rolling yam harvest, which begins towards the end of August, when ripe yam tubers are carefully disengaged from the rest of the roots or stem. By the end of October, the final harvesting gets into full swing. In the past, sacrifices would be made to Ifejioku, the god of yams, at the festival. Yams were eaten only after these sacrifices, first by people of high status. Chinua Achebe vividly describes a New Yam Festival in *Things Fall Apart*, and says it was also held to honour the earth goddess and ancestral spirits of the clan. Everyone looked forward to it because it marked the beginning of the season of plenty.

The event Achebe describes commences with feasting and drinking, and wrestling is held on the second day. He writes: 'It was difficult to say which the people enjoyed more – the feasting and fellowship of the first day or the wrestling contest of the second.' Achebe's protagonist Okonkwo beats the famous wrestler Amalinze at a New Yam Festival. Ekwefi, the village beauty, is so impressed that she later marries him. Today, the festival has been Christianised. Pagan gods and ancestral spirits are no longer honoured, yet there will be wrestling and drumming at the event in Arondizuogu – and hopefully these will be authentic.

The walls of Linus's department building at Imo State University are wallpapered with tables of exam results. Embarrassed students have used pens to cross out their name or marks. I find Linus's office and go in. There are bookshelves in the room but few books. Linus sits behind his desk. He has a cane, which he calls his 'deterrent mechanism'. He says proudly that he is the only lecturer to use a cane on students. The New Yam Festival is tomorrow. The Eze of Arondizuogu has said on the phone that he will introduce me to a few old wrestlers at the festival, but he stressed that I will have to give them presents. Small gifts are OK, he said, but there have to be presents. I tell Linus this. He considers what would be suitable for old men. As he ponders, he periodically takes off his hat, rubs his head, then quickly replaces the hat, lost in thought. He writes down suggestions on a piece of paper. The first is to bring 25kg containers of rice, which cost 5,000 naira each, or about £25.

'I can't really afford that, Linus. I was thinking of spending something more in the region of 400 to 600 naira on each present to be honest.'

Linus refers to the suggestions lower down the list.

'In that case, containers of mineral water. Or perhaps tobacco or snuff.'

In the event I buy bottles of brandy for 600 naira each the following morning. They are both easy to come by and easy to carry. I load the bottles in the boot of a red Nissan Cherry owned by Michi, a student hired to drive us to the festival, and we head out of Owerri. Deep in the surrounding villages, Linus enthusiastically points out anything illustrative of traditional Igbo culture. We pass a man wearing a bobble hat and sunglasses who is sitting under a shack and passing a cup to a friend.

'Look!' says Linus, excited. 'They're sharing palm wine! They're sharing the same cup-oh!'

When we are near Arondizuogu, Linus gives a tutorial in what to say to the *eze* when we are introduced. He recommends 'May the power be with you, Eze,' or 'May you have a long life, Eze.' I toy with the idea of subverting the pomposity of the moment by saying 'Live long and prosper, Eze' while giving the Vulcan salute, but quickly drop the idea as it is possible that Nigerians watch *Star Trek* and would recognise the conceit.

The *eze* presides over the festival from a throne chair in a shack within the grounds of his compound. An air of nonchalant authority surrounds him and the policemen in black uniforms who slouch on sofas around him. Women wearing white shirts, red headscarves and red tartan wraps round their waists sit in rows of seats. The new yams are lined up on the fringe of the celebrations like a row of nervous singletons trying to summon up the courage to join in. They are ugly and primal, with protrusions and wart-like growths. These are not the sweet-potato-like root vegetables I expected to see but entire tubers. The largest is about the size of a car engine. Prizes for winners of the new yam competition – among them a fridge, wall clock, spade, fan and wheelbarrow – are laid out as a centrepiece.

Linus and I approach the *eze*. The compere introduces me as 'special guest Marcus Trailer'.

'May you have a long life, Eze,' I say.

He looks through me. Today he is not the approachable man he was the first time we met, but the proud and stern leader of a community's celebrations. We go and sit down on the palace porch, next to a clergyman. Kola nut, sweets, peanuts and palm wine are passed to us. A student Linus used to teach comes over. He explains the importance of the kola nut and its route.

'Kola nut is a symbol of friendship,' he says. 'It has come from the *eze* to me and must go to the prof, then to me, and then you must pass it back to the prof, who will pass it back to me. If you have any problems, you must follow the same route. Talk to the prof first, then he will tell me and I will tell the *eze*.'

'I have brandy to give to the *eze* to give to some old wrestlers he's going to introduce me to. What should I do with it?'

'You must go back up to the *eze* and give the bottles to him.'

This time the compere introduces me as 'Marcus Travers'. I hand the *eze* a bag of three brandy bottles, then return to my seat, glad that the etiquette is out the way and I can relax properly. I tell the student that I would like to take photos.

'Then you should give the *eze* money, fifty pounds sterling, then video the event or whatever you want,' he says.

Linus erupts at the student and says that this is a ridiculous amount of money for someone to pay who is doing independent research. The student defers to him and concedes the point.

'You will have to go back to see the *eze*,' says the student. 'He will honour you by sending the band over. You will dance.'

'Dance?'

'Yes, it is an honour. The *eze* will send the band over and you must dance behind the musicians.'

I have never danced before while sober in front of strangers in broad daylight. As the only white man present, I cynically conclude that I'm being singled out for ritual humiliation rather than being honoured. The compere announces over the PA that Linus and I are both going to make a donation to the *eze*. A train of musicians comes over – drummers, a flute player and band leader who carries a staff. I nervously drop in behind the musicians and shuffle towards the chief, sticking my bum out to mimic the style of dance common in Nigeria. Linus dances in a similar way. A man jumps out the audience to join in. For a moment I think he is parodying me, but when I look in his eyes I see only encouragement. Women rise from their seats, and smile and sing. Our dancing makes them happy. It takes Linus and I perhaps a minute to dance in a big looping circle and arrive at the *eze*'s shack. We both give him money, then go and sit down again.

Linus is adamant that Igbo wrestling cannot be understood without first understanding the drums. The drummers are sitting under an awning to one side. Each log drum, or *ekwe*, has wide slits and is played with fat, stubby sticks. The drummers beat out a fast, intoxicating rhythm that rattles inside your body and makes you want to get up and move. The drums talk, says Linus. They use the same tones of spoken Igbo to call out a wrestler by name or to tell proverbs. Linus asks a drummer what these drums are saying.

'Come and wrestle,' he replies. 'If you win, people will clap.'

The drumming fires up the celebrations. A stiff elderly wrestler answers their call. He enters the wrestling arena to issue a challenge, but no one accepts, probably because he is so old and his challenge is more symbolic than real. He does a shuffle dance, while the women sing a song that says he's the unchallenged champion. He returns to his seat. A young man in T-shirt and jeans, weighing about 16 stone or more, goes to the arena, picks up a stick planted in a small mound of earth and throws it, which must amount to a way of issuing a challenge. Another big young guy steps up to meet him. The two prepare to wrestle. They spin and dance while avoiding

each other's gaze. Periodically they shake hands. Then they
crouch over, still without looking each other in the eye,
apparently on the verge of wrestling, yet break off to spin and
dance again. At last they fight for holds. The bigger man shunts
his opponent backwards. He gains a quick advantage and tries
to lock his hands round his opponent's back. He nearly has the
grip, and will soon be set to throw. But the action suddenly
halts and a finger-wagging maelstrom ensues. About twenty
men crowd around the wrestlers, shout, point at each other,
wave sticks, remonstrate, and have to be pulled apart from one
another.

'What's happening?' I ask Linus.

'There is a rule that this is just wrestling for entertainment
only. The *eze* has given the instruction that no one should be
thrown.'

Upset that the wrestling lacks authenticity, the drummers
stop drumming. Two shots ring out. A man wearing a red hat
and carrying a shotgun in one hand and a carved tusk in the
other stands imperiously in the gateway. He sweeps into the
compound with his wife and two boys, who hold chickens by
their wings. After he has greeted the *eze* and given him the
chickens, he comes over to talk to me. He is a professor, he
says. I notice a hole in his carved tusk and ask about it.

'In the past, chiefs used to send musical messages with this,'
says the prof.

He holds the tusk to his mouth, blows across the hole but
fails to get a note.

The *eze* rises from his throne with a microphone in his hand
to give a speech. Then the auspicious moment comes when he
cuts a new yam, which is a cue for plates to be handed out with
pieces of baked yam in a hot palm-oil sauce. It is decreed that
the wrestling will be competitive after all. A wrestler strides
out, dances, kicks the stick away, and spins and dances. A
challenger joins him, and also dances and whirls. There is a
cheer when the first wrestler lifts his opponent off the ground
and throws him. Men slap banknotes on his forehead. Women
stand from their seats, cheer and dance. Two more wrestlers
fight manically for grips, but one retires from the bout because
his T-shirt is ripped. Men slap banknotes on the winner's
forehead. He donates his winnings to the drummers. A fourth

wrestling bout ends in another big argument. One wrestler is about to throw the other when he stops. He realises that if he continues he will throw his opponent into the collection of prizes. For a split-second he is vulnerable to counter-attack, and his opponent cynically takes advantage and throws him. That bout is the last till the evening.

The festival erupts into intense dancing and singing. The *eze* lets off rounds from a rifle and does a little dance outside the palatial shack. Men slap banknotes on his forehead. The policemen join in, casually holding their automatic weapons in one hand and letting loose rounds, which crack and pop. Linus goes over to the *eze* and slaps banknotes on his forehead, then just manically throws money at him. The prof loads his shotgun, goes over to the *eze* and – in contradiction to the general rule that states the more you like or respect someone, the less you want to fire a weapon towards or at them – holds the gun so that it points as close to the chief's head as possible, without actually aiming at him, before firing twice. This must somehow be more honorific than simply shooting skyward, but I nevertheless make a mental note to consider setting up a business importing party-poppers to Nigeria.

The partying reaches a crescendo of euphoria the like of which I have never experienced. Unfortunately, Michi says we have to leave before the afternoon slides into dusk because the headlights on his car don't work and there are no streetlights. Reluctantly, we head back to Owerri early. That evening I sit alone in the refectory, eating spaghetti. It's only now that I remember that I was supposed to interview some old wrestlers. Somehow it doesn't seem to matter any more. Under the table, my feet move with a life of their own. Infected by the rhythm of the talking drums, they move like that for days afterwards.

The students' loss is my gain. Staff at Imo State University have not been paid for months. Most of the tutors are on strike and the university is not functioning properly. Consequently, though Linus still sees students, he has plenty of time to spare to help me with my research. Together we visit villages outside Owerri to talk to old wrestlers. Michi drives and Linus acts as interpreter. His enthusiasm is overwhelming. He has an unselfconscious ability to turn each moment, each new fact recounted, into a reason for celebration. He meets each revelation with a 'You see that?' or a breathless 'Aaaah!', and slaps me on the leg, or punches me lightly on the shoulder.

A tentative picture of the Igbo culture of wrestling develops from information we gather: the rules of *mgba* are as Chief Ogbuehi described and do not vary from place to place; charms were widely used in the past; wrestlers routinely believed that celibacy was important before a match to preserve strength; wrestling was part of funeral ceremonies for men of high status and wrestling champions; and wrestling was predominantly an activity for the dry season – which means that, as Chief Ogbuehi indicated, this really is the wrong time of year for wrestling in Igboland, as in the north. Nought out of two. Igbo inter-village wrestling matches fit the same pattern as those of the Dukawa in that they are predominantly held during the dry season and come after the major work is done on the farms and the staple crop – yams in this case – has been harvested. Again, this mirrors Mongolia, where Naadam is held in summer, the equivalent of the dry season, during a break in the work cycle.

Linus himself is a great source of information about wrestling. He clarifies its function at funerals. The Igbo traditionally believe the dead reincarnate within the same family, he says. They therefore used to perform rituals and act out certain rites at funerals to encourage the deceased to come back as a better and more effective human being. Say the deceased was not particularly agile and brave, they might have killed a dog and dripped its blood on his eye to ensure that next time he would be brave and agile like a dog. Say the man was poor, they might have wished for riches and thrown money in his coffin. Similarly, the aim of holding wrestling matches and playing wrestling music at a funeral ceremony was to ensure that the person buried would reincarnate as a strong wrestler. We interview an old wrestler who adds that in the past a cat or kite might also be killed during the funeral ceremony so that the man would reincarnate with the qualities of a cat, which never lands on its back, or a kite, which is considered a powerful, aggressive and wily bird of prey. As Chief Ogbuehi said, people also feared they would be haunted by a wrestler's spirit if wrestling did not feature at his funeral.

Linus recounts that inter-village wrestling contests used to serve the function of providing an opportunity for young men to come from outside and look for girls to marry, and vice versa. In the 1930s and 1940s, wrestlers were worshipped and found it easy to woo women, he says. A man in his nineties whom we interview says that, in his day, a girl who saw a wrestler she liked at a competition might immediately go home, collect all her worldly possessions and go to his compound to wait for him to return, then marry him. There would be no bride price negotiations or anything. Other old Igbo men confirm that women would commonly throw themselves at champion wrestlers.

Michi says it would be productive for us to visit his home area and talk to old men there as well. One morning he picks me up from the pastoral centre the standard two hours late. Linus is marking papers when we finally meet him at his home at about eleven. Yellowy images from CNN flicker on the television in a corner of the room. High on a wall is a graduation photo of a young Linus wearing a mortarboard and grinning like a benevolent gargoyle. Bundles of students' papers sit next to a cabinet.

'You're late,' says Linus.

'I know, I'm sorry. It's because Michi operates on Nigerian time.'

Michi grins and doesn't say anything.

'It's cold,' says Linus.

He goes to a cabinet and returns with glasses and a bottle of brandy, which he says we should drink to warm us up. By my reckoning the temperature must be approaching 20°C.

'It's too early to drink,' I say to Linus.

'Just a little, then we'll go.'

We get going soon after downing the brandy. It's a relief to swap the antagonism of the city streets for the laid-back village roads and circumvent the police checkpoints, which are predominantly set up on the main roads, where more passing traffic means more money to collect. We drive along tracks lined with palm trees, coconut and orange. Boys play football in wide avenues. Women wearing bright, happy clothes cycle by on rattling gearless bikes, carrying bunches of bananas on their heads. A roadside sign advertises 'Dog pepper soup'.

'I didn't realise you ate dog here, Linus. Have you ever tried it?'

'No, but Chi Chi, my housekeeper, has and she likes it.'

We pass a small boarded-up town hall in Michi's home area. Michi is running for the post of councillor in a forthcoming election. He points excitedly at one of his campaign posters pasted to a telegraph pole. While he has his eyes off the road, the car smacks into a boulder.

'You see,' says Linus, narrating events as if Michi is not there. 'In the excitement he forgot himself.'

We all get out the car to assess the damage. The front fender has come apart. Michi shrugs it off and we drive on. In a village nearby Michi takes us to meet a middle-aged woman called Josephine, who lives in a stone house with a large front entrance gate. Her late husband, Prince Whobas, was well known in the area. He revived and promoted traditional Igbo wrestling.

'You are a white man,' she says, in surprise, as we are introduced.

Josephine leads the way through a side door and into a pink room with bags of cement in a corner. We all sit down. Linus takes a while to explain the purpose of our visit and set Josephine's mind at rest so that she doesn't think we are 419ers. She fetches photos and passes them around – wrestlers, girls dancing at wrestling competitions, her late husband. I ask her whether there used to be a custom of wrestling for a bride. She replies in English and says that yes, it used to be a common occurrence in the area.

'If you happen to see a lady that you love and you want to marry her, but she insists that you will not marry her, then you will go to her village and you will tell the people of that village, or the brother of that very girl, that you are now bringing traditional wrestling to their village. You will say, since you refused to give your sister to marry me, then I heard that you are a *dingba*, a wrestling champion, so if I am able to throw you down I will marry the lady. Then he, knowing fully what you are, will accept that challenge. Then a date will be fixed when they come to the market square for that very wrestling.'

Josephine acts out how, on the day of the wrestling for the girl's hand in marriage, the suitor would touch the talking drums, place his hands on his chest, then beckon his opponent to come and wrestle.

'Then if he happens to throw him down, he takes the girl as his wife – no auction, no argument. We had such wives in this village.'

Josephine speaks to Linus at length in Igbo. Periodically Linus reacts with an enthusiastic 'Chai' or 'Yes?' or 'Is that so?' Afterwards he translates. There was a woman called Theresa Nwanyi-Nkwo who lived in a nearby town and was very beautiful, he says. She turned down all suitors. A wrestler from this village wanted to marry Theresa, who had a brother who was a wrestling champion. Her brother said to him, 'If you want to marry my sister we will have to wrestle first.' So the talking drums were carried from this village to Theresa's village and after all the dancing and posing and preparation the two men wrestled. The suitor from this village threw Theresa's brother and won Theresa for his wife. This happened in the 1930s.

'This is another dimension,' annotates Linus, excited. 'Superb! I have not heard this before.'

Josephine fetches wrestling drums still kept in the house – a small *ekwe*, and a couple of tall, upright ones with leather skins. She asks a girl to go and fetch drumsticks, then taps the *ekwe*. An old woman sitting in the corner of the room starts to cry. She hides her face and tears behind her hand.

'The sound of the drums and all this talk remind her of Prince Whobas,' explains Josephine.

After the interview, we give Josephine a lift to a nearby junction. Linus raves about her when she's gone, like a critic raving about a good film.

'Very intelligent! A beautiful exposition! This is top notch! A gold mine. Intelligent, beautiful analysis!'

I'm eager to try to corroborate the story of how a suitor won Theresa through a wrestling match. Umuman, the village where she came from, is close. We drive over and locate the home of a living relative. He comes out to meet us, doing up the buttons of his black and white shirt as he approaches. He says his name is Ahamufule Uperete and the elder son of Theresa's brother, the wrestling champion whom the suitor had to beat. We go and sit in his small home to talk. A Christian poster hangs on the wall, and a wig lies on the table. Ahamufule says his father was nicknamed 'Akwaja', which means 'wall'.

'They called him that because if you push the "wall" you're in trouble,' expounds Linus.

Ahamufule says his father took top billing at wrestling contests. Once he wrestled the competition was over. I ask Ahamufule to tell his version of the story of how his father wrestled Theresa's suitor. He says that it used to be understood that a woman from a family of good wrestlers would be strong in both farming and domestic chores, as well as healthy.

'Healthy!' repeats Linus, creasing up, as he translates.

You had to prove yourself if you wanted to marry a girl from such a background. This means there were two reasons that Theresa's suitor had to wrestle for her: first, because she didn't want to marry him; secondly, because they were a family of strong wrestlers who ruled that you had to wrestle for their daughters if you wanted to marry them anyway – so even if Theresa had wanted to marry a suitor he would have had to wrestle for her. Ahamufule confirms that the other details of the story are as Josephine described. Theresa died only two or three years ago, he adds.

'We would have met her alive,' says Linus. 'Almost!'

Linus reaches a crescendo of excitement after we have heard Ahamufule's account and left.

'On-the-spot verification! Verification on the spot! We found balance straight away. Very rarely does this happen in research. Very rarely. I never heard anything like this!'

'I had to come all the way from England to teach you something about your own culture.'

'Yes!'

The story represents something greater than I ever really expected to find in Nigeria: it is an account of a practice, apparently common, characterised by the same kind of decisiveness found in animal ruts. An Igbo wrestler could win a woman by winning a wrestling match, then take her as his wife whether she wanted to marry him or not. She was not won over by the wrestler, as Ekwefi is by Okonkwo in *Things Fall Apart*, but simply the prize he was given, like a cup. The custom followed a stark evolutionary logic, yet perhaps there was something transformative about the act of wrestling for a woman's hand in marriage. Maybe once a suitor proved himself by beating an opponent she would consider him a worthy husband, even if she didn't before.

Euphoric, I go to take a quick pee in the jungle among yam or cassava mounds. I notice a woman weeding and turn my back to her to be discreet. When I return to the car, Michi is telling Linus that he wants me to pay him more. Whenever you're on a high, someone has to bring you back down to earth.

Theophilus knows an old lady whose father kept a wrestling chimp. The Igbo admire chimpanzees for their wrestling ability, and would sometimes wrestle them. They are known as *Ozu, Dingba*, which translates as 'Chimpanzee, the champion wrestler'.

Edwin drives Theophilus and me across town to meet the woman, who lives in a large house with a statue of her late husband in the garden. She is bedbound and perhaps in her eighties. A couple of pink waterbottles rest on her bed, and a bucket stands on a chair covered by a towel nearby. Theophilus clears a walking frame out of the way so that I can shake her hand, then we do the kola nut ceremony. He and the woman's son, who is also present, joke about whether the kola nut can understand English, concluding that it must be multilingual because it is not native kola. I recognise, in their easy conviviality, a good-natured attempt to try to eke some humour out of the proceedings to entertain the poorly old lady.

Theophilus blesses the kola nut and we say a prayer for the lady, whom Theophilus affectionately calls 'Mama'. Mama says that her father, who died in about 1948 and was made a Warrant Chief by the British colonialists, owned a pet chimp. It was trained so that her father only had to clap his hands – she claps hers to illustrate – and the chimp would answer a wrestling challenge. It was only a small chimp, but like a cat it could never be thrown onto its back.

'The chimp always won,' she says. 'The thing was that it understood that it was wrestling, not fighting, and never bit or scratched its opponent. My father only had to clap and he wrestled anyone in front of him.'

'Did your father have just one wrestling chimp or a succession of wrestling chimps?'

'Let me explain that I was baptised when I was very young, which was against the normal practice of the time, so immediately afterwards there was a furore. At the time the children of chiefs were not supposed to be baptised. My uncle took me away to live in Calabar, which is where I actually spent my childhood, so I didn't have any more experience of this chimp wrestling tradition. But I know that my father only had to clap his hands for the chimp to accept a challenge.'

We politely talk a little more but don't want to detain Mama for too long because of her age and poor health. Before we leave, Theophilus blesses Mama again. Afterwards she looks me in the eye and wishes me a long life with piercing sincerity. Then she asks me to relay a message to an old friend in England.

'I met Queen Elizabeth when she visited Nigeria after her coronation,' says Mama. 'Do please give her my regards.'

'I will when I next see her.'

Michi and I reach Linus's office the standard two hours late.

'Why so late?' asks Linus.

I don't say anything, but instead gesture towards Michi, who grins and laughs in embarrassment. He explains he had to take a phone call from one of his political supporters this morning and had to phone the supporter back, which took a while, and they spoke for half an hour. There's a pride in the way he relates what happened. He spells everything out so he can hear the details again himself and recognise in them a description of the day-to-day life of a would-be big-shot politician. At first I thought the post he's running for, councillor, was only a minor one, but I've since learnt that councillors are paid a huge amount by Nigerian standards and even have their own staff, including a cook – and manservant.

Linus wants me to meet a man he describes as a 'really cat wrestler' who used to be well known in the area where he grew up, and we head off in the car. Before leaving the outskirts of Owerri, we have to queue at a petrol station. Nigeria is one of the largest oil producers in the world yet there are frequent shortages. The petrol station has six pumps, but only one works. Three queues converge on the one pump – a line of vehicles either side, and a line of scooters and motorbikes between the pump and one of the queues of cars. Everyone is standing around, waiting and becoming frustrated. Children sell bottles of mineral water, peanuts and guinea-fowl eggs to the captive market. After we've been queuing for about 40 minutes, we finally inch onto the forecourt. A huge quarrel erupts when an *eze* arrives, jumps the queue and is served straight away.

'You know, Linus, you Igbo are always arguing. There is a culture of argument in Igboland. I have never been anywhere in the world where people argue as much as they do here.'

Linus decides to resolve the dispute. He gets out the car and walks to the epicentre of the enraged men. Too far away to hear exactly what Linus is saying, I watch him throw his arms in the air and shout. Everyone scatters. There's a chorus of clunking car doors as all the drivers get back in their vehicles. I'm deeply impressed. Linus returns to the car.

'What did you say to them?'

'I said, "You Igbos should be ashamed of yourselves – you are always arguing. Why do you need to shout at him? You are standing right next to him, and he is standing next to you. All you Igbos ever do is argue. We need action. The *eze* has been served – he's gone. What's the point in arguing? Just get a move on."'

We swap the city streets for relaxed back roads and drive to the village of Umuota, where we locate the compound of the 'really cat wrestler'. His name is Ejam Ihejirika. A small man, he is in his early seventies but has the energy of an eighteen-year-old. He greets me by holding up my hand, then using a baseball-like swing to smack it with his. He slaps it so hard that it smarts and reddens. We sit together on a porch. Ejam pours shots of brandy. A group of young children who I assume are Ejam's grandchildren stand near us. The young girls roughly pick up puppies lying on the porch and remove them. One of them kicks the puppies' mother away. Next to the porch is a room in which a young woman is sitting forwards on a bench, leaning on her fist. I presume she must be Ejam's daughter.

Linus acts as interpreter, but judging by the exclamations in English that Ejam gives to reinforce Linus's translations, Ejam has a good understanding of English too. He says his father was a wrestling champion, a *dingba*. He used to be hired to go and wrestle, often some way away.

'He was a mercenary – a wrestling mercenary,' underlines Linus.

When a community wanted to hire him to represent them in a competition, they would pay him a big he-goat and one pound and four shillings in British money.

'Chum!' says Ejam, looking directly at me. 'Yah!'

'So your father was a great wrestler. Did he have many wives partly because he was a wrestler?'

Linus puts the question to Ejam, then relays the answer.

'He said yes. He said himself also – he married by wrestling.'

'Yes!' says Ejam.

This is amazing. Ejam is an actual living example of a wrestler who won over women by wrestling and also a follower of the custom of polygyny, which has largely died out since the advent of Christianity. I ask Linus to ask Ejam first about his father's marriages through wrestling. He says that after his father wrestled successfully ('Yes!'), women would follow him immediately, and he would marry them ('Yes!').

'And how many wives did his father have?' I ask Linus.

An answer comes back: 'Nineteen.'

'Yes!' says Ejam.

'And how many wives does he himself have?'

'He himself has four wives, with seven sons and fourteen females,' says Linus. He gives a croaky laugh and giggles at the thought.

It begins to rain heavily. Ejam talks about the two wives he won through wrestling. He points to an old woman leaning on the wall of the porch outside her small concrete home nearby and says that she is one of them. The old lady goes inside to take shelter. Ejam recounts how he attracted the other wife. He was wrestling in Linus's town, Nnorie. By virtue of his skill and strength, he even defeated wrestlers who used charms, he says. This other wife wanted to marry Ejam after seeing him compete, so later he paid a bride price and they wed in the normal way. Ejam points to the young woman I presume is his daughter. She is also one of his wives, he says.

'This young woman here – she's your wife?' I say, incredulously. 'She looks about *eighteen* years old.'

'She's so small, so young,' echoes Linus. 'She's the mother of all these four ones,' he says, pointing to the children I assumed were Ejam's grandchildren.

I am shocked: 'She's the *mother*?'

But now that I look at her more closely, I can see that she could be any age between eighteen and thirty-two. She has one of those faces.

'So at what age was Ejam actively wrestling?' I ask Linus.

'When he was about twenty-four years old he was in his prime,' translates Linus. 'He was very sexy and making love to women.'

Linus and the children break out into laughter at the idea.

'It cracked them up,' says Linus, in hysterics.

Ejam says he is a *dibia*, an intermediary between this world and the spirit world. His father, too, was a *dibia* and would summon up the spirit of an opponent the night before a wrestling match and throw him. By beating a wrestler's spirit he ensured he won the actual bout. Ejam says his father used charms and would kill a goat or cat to give them power. Cats were frequently used in charms for the same reason that they were sacrificed at funeral ceremonies – because they always land on their feet when they fall. When a cat was killed, its belly was opened and its blood rubbed on the wrestler's body, then its heart was rubbed on something wrestlers wore round their waist. Linus asks about which roots were mixed with the charm, but Ejam says he cannot reveal any more information.

'Ahh, some secrets,' says Linus.

Ejam also used to use charms when he wrestled. Whatever kind of charm an opponent had would not affect him, because he had his own protective one ('Yes!').

I ask him whether he was well respected because of his skill as a wrestler. He says he was and still is, and has a special seat at gatherings.

'Yes!' says Ejam, slapping his chest.

'You look like you could wrestle today.'

In response, Ejam rolls up his sleeves to show his lean but muscly forearms, slaps his body, smacks the bottle lid down on the table and pours out more measures. When we part he holds my hand up again and delivers another smarting baseball swing of a hand slap.

'Chum!'

★

Edwin drives me over to see Linus at home for the last time to say goodbye.

'Do you want a drink?' says Linus. 'It's quite cold.'

He fixes a brandy. The TV is on: first rollerblading in a half-pipe, then stunt motorcycling. We discuss the news that another priest has been shot dead during an armed robbery – this time in Aba. Linus says it is bound to happen, because priests display too much pride and not enough humility. They show off their wealth and status and act like gods around people – and conspicuous wealth attracts robbers. He leaves the room and returns with a plate of rice and dried fish, which he puts down on the table in front of me, then sits on the settee and hugs a cushion. We reminisce about all the things we have done and experienced together – our dance adventure at the New Yam Festival, the talking drums, the interviews we did and the excellence of some of the information gathered. I have gifts for Linus – brandy and bottles of sparkling grape juice, plus some money in an envelope. I have agonised over whether to give him cash as a token of my gratitude and decided that I should. Linus opens the envelope, takes out the notes, then puts them back in the envelope.

'You didn't have to do that,' he says.

He gets up to put the money away, then sits down. We carry on as though nothing happened. The programme on TV changes to a dog competition. The dogs run through a slalom and a plastic tunnel, and jump fences.

'You see that?' says Linus. 'You see that, Eddie?' Jai! Amazing-oh!'

Not for the first time, I marvel at Linus's capacity to reach crescendos of excitement at the mundane. In a country of constant argument, go-slows, routine serious road accidents, chronic violence, bribery, corruption, 419ers, broken toilet seats and general malaise, Linus remains buoyant and defiant and capable of finding reasons for ecstatic laughter from moment to moment, surfing the insanity with good humour and a sense of the absurd. I know I will miss him deeply.

'Look!' he says, pointing to the screen. 'Kiyaa, yaaah! Chai! Chai! Chai!'

The animals have to locate and bring back plastic ducks as though they are gundogs with vegetarian owners.

'It knows!' exclaims Linus, as a woman directs her dog with blows from a whistle.

'You see, Linus,' I say. 'This is the type of thing dogs in Nigeria could achieve if only you stopped eating them.'

★

I fly from Owerri to Lagos then back to England where I stay at my mother's house in Surrey. After a couple of days, the symptoms of fever and aches and pains make a return. Convinced that it's yet another bout of malaria, I see a local GP and ask him for antimalarials. He pleads with me to go to the local hospital to be checked out properly. Reluctantly I go to Crawley Hospital and am admitted to a ward. My condition quickly deteriorates. I have bouts where my temperature rockets and I sweat so much that the nurses have to keep changing my sheets, followed by bouts of intense cold during which the bed rattles and chatters as I involuntarily shake. My skin breaks out into a rash of red spots. The doctors take blood test after blood test, but can't diagnose my condition. I keep insisting that it must be malaria, but the malaria test results come back negative. I have an undiagnosable tropical disease. All the doctors and nurses can do is prescribe Ibuprofen and paracetamol, and monitor my condition.

I'm admitted to an isolation ward. The doctors keep doing blood tests, and one reports that my blood has even been sent for analysis at the military biochemical research facility at Porton Down, but not even they can make a diagnosis. Whatever I've brought back from Nigeria is off the medical radar screen. I'm transferred by ambulance to a specialist unit at St George's Hospital, Tooting. Some of the country's best doctors in the field of tropical medicine come and stand at the foot of my bed, but they are all mystified. After about ten days of serious illness my condition rapidly deteriorates. I feel incredibly weak and in constant pain, and have intense migraines as well as the rash and constant bouts of cold shakes followed by high fever.

Then, just as suddenly, the symptoms start to lift. A few days later the bouts of fever and cold come to an end. I'm discharged but return later for a follow-up consultation. Only now am I told that there was a point at which the doctors seriously wondered whether I would pull through. Some of my test result readings were completely off the recognised scale.

I feel like my soul has been scraped out with a penknife. It takes a further three months to recover fully. Nigeria may have welcomed me with malaria but its leaving present was far worse.

Glossary

Dash: bribe. The term is used as a verb ('to *dash*') and noun.
Dibia: an Igbo shaman.
Dingba: title given to champion wrestler (Igbo).
Ekwe: musical instrument; a log drum (Igbo).
Eze: title given to a traditional Igbo ruler.
Iwaji: New Yam Festival (Igbo).
Mgba: traditional Igbo wrestling style.
Ozu, Dingba: Chimpanzee, the champion wrestler (Igbo).
419er: a scam artist.

PART V

England and Ancient Greece

Chapter 13

The Primal Underworld

Summer was once a time when men in London also demonstrated their manliness through wrestling. In *A Survey of London*, first printed in 1598, John Stow includes a transcript of a description of London life written by William Fitzstephen towards the end of the twelfth century:

> In the holy dayes all the Sommer the youths are exercised in leaping, dancing, shooting, wrastling, casting the stone, and practizing their shields: the Maidens trip in their Timbrels, and daunce as long as they can well see.

London's youths displayed their manliness through contests against one another, while unmarried women displayed their sensuous beauty through dance and music (a timbrel is like a tambourine and produces a jangly sound). The image evoked of dancing young women and young men competing in manly arts such as wrestling resonates unmistakably with the festivals of the Dukawa and Igbo – though it is not specifically stated that the women danced at the same time and place as the men competed, or that the youths' games were organised into a formal festival – but perhaps in medieval London, as in Africa today, young men displayed their masculinity at summer contests while watched by admiring girls.

Stow goes on to write:

> Ye may reade in mine Annales, how that in the yeare 1222 the Citizens kept games of defence, and wrestlings neare vnto the Hospitall of Saint Giles in the field where they chalenged, and had the mastrie of the men in the Suburbs, and other commoners, &c. . . Which is sufficient to proue that of olde time the exercising of wrestling, and such like hath beene much more vsed then of later yeares.

Already, four hundred years ago, a writer was moaning about the decline of wrestling in London. Stow's *Annales* relate that the contests near St Giles' Hospital took place on Saint James' Day (25 July). After his faction was beaten, the Bailiff of Westminster, a neighbourhood outside the walls of London, proclaimed that a return match would be held at Westminster on Lammas Day (1 August). At that event, serious fighting broke out between the Westminster faction and the London faction. The Londoners ran for their lives back to the city, but later returned to Westminster mob-handed. They exacted revenge by pulling down houses and running riot. Later a Chief Justice arrived in London with an army to restore order. He hanged three of the retributive Londoners' ringleaders, and cut the hands and feet off others who were apprehended and found to be culpable for the violence. Londoners fled to avoid the cruel justice.

Clearly Stow writes about the first tournament because it forms the back story to the violence and rioting that characterised the second, not for any reason to do with the tournament itself – the reference to wrestling hitches a ride on a larger story – but the passage is nevertheless revealing. In 1222 wrestlers in England were taking part in inter-community summer wrestling contests, just like the Dukawa do today and the Igbo once did.

I take the Tube to Leicester Square, and walk up Charing

Cross Road past the big chain book stores and the few remaining secondhand bookshops. St Giles' Hospital used to be around here somewhere. It was established in 1101 by Queen Matilda, the wife of Henry I, as a hospital for lepers. Its chapel was turned into a parish church in 1547, by which time the hospital itself had closed. I head down St Giles High Street and find the current church. It is probably the third architectural incarnation on the site and opened its doors in 1734. A sign outside says a lunchtime communion service is in progress. Inside there are only three people taking part in the act of worship. They sit right at the front, like swots in class. St Giles used to be a place for lepers and still is – the few remaining Christians who actively worship during weekday daytime hours.

I leave the church and turn right down St Giles High Street, then right again along Shaftesbury Avenue. The triangle of Charing Cross Road, St Giles High Street and Shaftesbury Avenue delineates what used to be the hospital's compound wall. I try to imagine the area outside that triangle as the fields where the first tournament Stow mentions took place. What with the noise of the traffic, pneumatic drills and aggressive walking of fellow pedestrians, it is impossible to find a quiet place within myself where I can conjure a picture of green fields and wrestlers taking hold. I have often worked in offices around here, particularly from one in nearby Leicester Square, and find it difficult to impose an imaginative framework on the area other than one predicated on work. I feel disorientated, almost seasick, as I attempt to compute the fact that two worlds I thought were completely distinct from one another actually intersect at this place: the world of summer wrestling and office life. I went all the way to Africa and Mongolia to witness a type of wrestling tournament that was under my feet in London all along.

Stow says that the practice of summer wrestling endured in his time and refers to a declining tradition of regular tournaments between Londoners and suburbanites held in Clerkenwell on St Bartholomew's Day (24 August), so it is safe to assume that the tradition extended from the late twelfth century to the end of the sixteenth – and maybe contests were held from a far earlier date yet went unrecorded, as the

tournament near St Giles would have been had it not been the
prelude to a serious riot. Perhaps regular inter-community
summer wrestling contests were also held in other parts of the
country. Maybe they were common.

It is impossible to know for sure. Wrestling in England has
been routinely ignored by chroniclers and historians. In fact
more is known about wrestling in Ancient Greece than about
wrestling in London during the Middle Ages.

A flash flood of schoolchildren bursts into one of the Greek
and Roman rooms at the British Museum. Clutching
clipboards and questionnaires, they talk and hubbub and
ignore their teachers who weakly shush them. After the rabble
has passed into the next room, I share a wry smile with a
member of the museum's staff.

'Do you think the kids enjoy it here?' I ask him.

'It's just a day out for them,' he says, acidly. 'They don't have
any interest at all.'

'Do you know where the vases depicting athletic scenes are?
I know they're upstairs somewhere.'

'Yeah, in room sixty-eight, I think.'

I find a staircase and pause on the landing to consider a
Roman copy of the famous statue of a discus thrower by
Myron. It's an attitude of latent power reminiscent of the
prelude to a certain judo throw. For a brief moment, the athlete
is turned inward and appears to almost curl up as he searches
within for the focus to direct all his power into the coming
throw. In a second he will explosively unfurl and fling the
discus. Hopefully it will hit one of the noisy schoolkids in the
solar plexus.

I locate room 68, which is devoted to money. The athlete
vases are actually in the adjoining room. Each cabinet contains
items that relate to specific aspects of Greek and Roman life.
One is devoted to boxing and wrestling. Inside the case are a
few pots and artefacts. A small Greek amphora is painted with
two fighting boxers, one of whom is bleeding from the nose,
while two wrestlers square up on the amphora's neck.
Something labelled an 'Athlete's bronze toilet set' is also on
display. It consists of a Roman example of an aryballos linked

to two strigils. Such equipment was adopted by the Romans from Greek athletic culture. Like Pehalwans in India, Greek athletes and wrestlers oiled their bodies – but with olive oil, not mustard – and Greek wrestlers wrestled on earth. An aryballos was a bottle for carrying the oil, and strigils were scrapers used to wipe off earth and oil after training. The label says this equipment was found in a stone coffin near Dusseldorf and dates from the 1st or 2nd century AD. Perhaps whoever was buried with it wanted to keep to their exercise schedule in the afterlife. I know the feeling: when I was wrestling seriously, I wouldn't let anything stand in the way of training, either.

The Greek and Roman rooms are good places to visit to get your confidence back and remind yourself that you hold in high esteem something that other cultures have also held in high esteem – which is important when you're in London, where wrestling has no place or status. But wrestling had a respectable place in the life of Ancient Greece. The Greeks wrestled, decorated pots with wrestling scenes, wrote about wrestling and used wrestling analogies to discuss other aspects of life. Fortunately, their love of wrestling can still be savoured from a distance of 2,000 years.

Artefacts in display cases at the British Museum and others housed in museums around the world are part of the largest sustained body of evidence relating to sport in an ancient culture. Evidence has been found for athletics predating the historic Greek era – such as a fresco of boy boxers discovered on the Greek island of Thera that dates from about 1500 BC – but it remains enigmatic due to a lack of further contexualising information. In the absence of good information concerning sport anywhere else in the ancient world, evidence that relates to the athletes of Ancient Greece has enhanced importance and value.

Greek athletics mark the moment when sports emerge from a murky tunnel of obscurity into the glare of history. It's plausible to assume that Greek sports culture inherited traits from its ancestors in the same way that human beings inherit traits from theirs, and that by scrutinising the descendant we can learn about the ancestor. If the theory is correct that wrestling, and perhaps other sports as well, are descended from a form of human rutting, you would therefore hope to find supporting evidence in the picture of Ancient Greek athletics that has been produced by a study of artefacts such as these at the British Museum, as well as archaeological sites and written sources.

The most important athletic contests in Ancient Greece were held at festival gatherings, of which there were many – but none was more important than the Olympic Games and there is no other about which more is known. Eventually there would be three further primary festivals at which Greeks competed – the Nemean, Pythian and Isthmian Games – but the Olympics, which ancient sources say began in 776 BC, were the first and most prestigious. The ancient version of the event was very different from the modern one. Then, as now, the festival was held every four years, but always at the same place. There was no flame-carrying procession of runners to precede events, no marathon, no linked hoop symbol and definitely no synchronised swimming.

The Games consisted of athletic contests for Greek men and youths, chariot races and horse races, and contests for heralds and trumpeteers were also added in 396 BC. Nike had a presence in her original capacity as the goddess of victory, not a brand of sports wear. Zeus held a statue of Nike in his right hand as he sat enthroned inside his temple in the Altis, the sacred precinct at Olympia, the venue for the Games. The Olympics were held to honour Zeus and featured a lot of religious ritual that culminated in the sacrifice of a hundred oxen at his altar.

Much of our knowledge of the ancient festival comes from Pausanias, who visited Olympia in the 2nd century AD and recorded what he saw in the book, *Guide to Greece*. He was not to know that his visit came towards what was probably the end of the ancient Olympic era: it's uncertain when the Games ended exactly, but one theory is that they came to a halt at the end of the 4th century AD after a run of over a thousand years. According to Pausanias, sports were added to the Olympics in stages. By 520 BC, when the roster of athletic contests had reached its fullest expression, there were only eight athletic events and four out of these either were, or involved, a combat sport: wrestling, pankration, boxing and pentathlon, which included wrestling. The other four were running events. The prevalence of combat sports at the Games demonstrates that the Greeks liked man-to-man ritualised fighting contests.

The rules of boxing, wrestling and pankration shaped these disciplines into severe tests. There were no weight categories, rounds, time limits or points systems. Boxers did not hit each other with padded gloves but instead punched with a minimum of wrapping to protect their hands, not opponents' ribs and faces. Wrestlers were allowed to strangle each other into submission. Pankration allowed the techniques of boxing and wrestling, along with kicks. There were only two rules – no biting or eye-gouging – and it appears that by and large pankratiasts did not bind their fists like boxers. To win the combat events, you either had to score three falls (wrestling), knock your opponent out (boxing and pankration), force him to submit (wrestling, boxing and pankration), or possibly shunt him from the arena like a stag (wrestling).

Welcome to the primal underworld showcased in the greatest arena of the overworld. Welcome to a culture that admires fighting for pure physical dominance so much that it allows athletes to come to grips under liberal and unconstrained rules. Welcome to a festival overlaid with religious ceremony, custom and tradition that preserves, celebrates and gives biggest billing to the primal and animalistic. The central importance to the Greeks of their combat sports is demonstrated by the fact that they formed the climax of the athletic schedule. Out of the three combat disciplines, pankration came last. Boxers and wrestlers could enter the pankration, as well as athletes solely devoted to the discipline, which means that the Games climaxed with a contest to find the most dominant male from among all fighters, effectively the most dominant athlete in the Greek world.

The idiom in which Greek athletes competed resonates strongly with that in which animals rut. Just how strongly becomes clearer if you compare the ancient Games with, say, the modern version. First, only men competed in the ancient Games, yet women are allowed to compete in the modern event. Secondly, both rutting animals and Ancient Greek athletes compete and competed as individuals, while the modern Games has team events, such as hockey, football and basketball. Thirdly, Greek athletes competed naked, like wild animals – something you don't see at the modern event. Fourthly, the ancient Games emphasised man-to-man physical combat sports – something that the modern Games do not. Fifthly, the unarmed combat sports in the modern event (wrestling, judo, boxing, Tae Kwon Do) have time limits, points systems, weight categories and protective equipment, none of which are a feature of the natural world, and none of which, with the exception of binding for boxers and pankratiasts, was a feature of the Ancient Greek combat events. Sixthly, there were no prizes for second or third at the ancient event, just as only winners prosper in the ruts of the animal kingdom; whereas losers are given prizes at the modern Olympics – silver and bronze medals.

The athletic events at the ancient Games betray a particular emphasis on the combative application of physical equipment produced by testosterone, just like the ruts of animal species such as red deer. Boxing, wrestling and pankration self-evidently stressed upper body power and strength, which is governed by testosterone, and an emphasis on testing testosterone-governed attributes also extended to the non-combat disciplines. The Greeks liked a particular type of running event: sprints. Three out of the four races at the Olympics were sprints – the *stadion* (192.27 metres), *diaulos* (twice the length of the *stadion*, or about 385 metres) and race in armour (same distance again). This is significant, because testosterone is central to sprinting but not so important to long-distance running. Modern track-and-field competition demonstrates that sprinters benefit from good muscular development, including of the upper body, underscored by testosterone, while endurance running favours athletes with slight physiques. Consequently, the illegal use of testosterone and other anabolic steroids that mimic the effects of testosterone has been an enduring issue in modern sprinting. Two out of the three events unique to the pentathlon, the javelin and discus, stressed the upper body development necessary to throw with explosive power, so their reliance on the effects of testosterone is also clear.

Considered together, the disciplines at the ancient Games betray a remarkably strong testosterone profile. The three combat sports displayed an overwhelming similarity with the ruts of animals in terms of both reliance on testosterone-governed attributes and the form the contests took. The running events and disciplines peculiar to the pentathlon were a step removed from the idiom in which other species rut – sprinters ran alongside each other rather than clashed head-on; pentathletes used equipment other than their bodies, such as a discus and javelin – yet they too were predicated on the expression of testosterone-governed attributes. The javelin and race in armour were the disciplines furthest removed from the idiom in which animals rut, as the first transparently related to warfare and hunting, while the second transparently related to warfare, yet they too were testosterone-underpinned events.

The ancient Olympics had the fingerprints of testosterone all over them. The athletic events were celebrations of masculine attributes governed by the hormone and were of exactly the form you would expect were they to have represented a stage – closer to its original ancestor than to modern sports – in the descent of sport from a kind of testosterone-mediated human rutting behaviour.

The festival strictly encoded the same sexual dynamic seen in the festivals of the Igbo and Dukawa. Pausanias writes that, with one notable exception, married women were barred from watching the athletes compete – apparently on pain of death – yet unmarried women were not. These young women, known as *parthenoi*, would have been aged between about eleven and fourteen years old, and physically mature but not yet married. Greek girls married early – from the age of about fourteen onwards – so these were eligible young women. It's remarkable that the distinction between which women could watch the Games and which could not was made on the basis of marital status. It is impossible to know the reason for sure – Pausanias is silent on this score – but it may have been that the Greeks allowed unmarried girls to watch for the same reasons that the Dukawa have unmarried young women at their wrestling festivals: so that athletes could demonstrate their manliness in front of women who would both admire them and be in a position to marry. In his *Ode to Telesikrates of Kyrene*, a winner of

the race in armour at the Pythian Games, Pindar eludes to this
dimension when he writes that Telesikrates competed, 'While
maidens watched, and in silence each one wished/You,
Telesikrates/Were her dearest husband, or her son.'

However the Olympics were held once every four years, a
frequency that had limited practical value if finding mates was
its primary purpose, and the Games were contested by only a
relatively small band of elite athletes, some of whom would
presumably be married, which means there would not be many
men to go around. Yet if it were the case that the custom of
allowing *parthenoi* to watch athletes compete was routinely
followed at other Greek festivals, concerning which there is far
less surviving evidence – and Pindar's *Ode to Telesikrates*
indicates that this was true of the Pythian Games for one – it's
easy to imagine that these events, particularly the local events,
would have played a more significant role in introducing
eligible men to eligible women, just as inter-community
wrestling contests provide that function among the Dukawa
and once did for the Igbo.

Similarities between the ancient Olympics and modern athletic
gatherings in both Nigeria and Mongolia hint that they may all
represent branches of the same tree and have grown from the
same root. The ancient Olympics took place during the same
slot in the farming calendar as inter-community tournaments
among the Dukawa and Igbo. They were held in July or August
after the grain harvest, which ran from May to June, and before
the next round of sowing, which took place in November.
Wheat and barley were the staple Greek crops, so the Games
effectively took place soon after their most important harvest.
Likewise, Dukawa wrestling tournaments take place after the
all-important guinea corn harvest, and the Igbo traditionally
wrestled during and after the period in which yams, their staple
crop, were harvested. Similarly, Naadam is held at a time when
Mongolians are less burdened by the work involved in herding.
In all cases the period in which these athletic gatherings are
convened is the hottest time of year – summer in Mongolia and
Greece, and the dry season in Nigeria.

All these gatherings represent social extroversion after a

period of introversion. They occur during a period in the annual cycle when communities that normally focus on their own life and farming now look outward to interact with their extended ethnic group – and they personify this extroversion. In all instances these gatherings are a time to refresh social bonds, and to renew and re-establish connections with other members of the same extended community. The gatherings both create and are held during a context of tribal bonding, which is the right context for forging marriage arrangements. This dimension is particularly apparent in the ancient Games, which were held during the famous Olympic truce that allowed Greeks who were even at war with one another to put aside their differences for a while and compete in athletics. That same dimension, on a small scale, is also apparent in the description of a New Yam Festival that Chinua Achebe gives in *Things Fall Apart*, where he talks about the feasting and the fellowship of the first day of the festival.

Hyper-masculine sport is at the core of all these gatherings: men compete against one another, particularly in sports predicated upon establishing pure physical dominance, such as wrestling. These hyper-masculine sports are circumscribed by rules that make them tests of masculine virtues, not routinely fatal contests. The general purpose seems to be to give athletes the licence to prove their manliness, but by and large no licence is given to cause one another lasting harm. Men compete in front of a large audience, which means the festival gives the men a large stage on which to display their abilities. In all cases, eligible women are among those watching. It is explicit in Dukawa culture – and used to be in Igbo culture – that some of the women present at the gatherings admire and want to marry a man who proves his virtues as an athlete. That may also be explicit at Naadam in Mongolia – it wasn't in my mind to find out while I was there – and have been at the ancient Olympic Games, as well as other Greek festivals.

All these festivals share essential characteristics with the ruts of the animal kingdom: males compete against one another in ritualised contests for physical dominance; females are present but don't take an active part in these physical contests; and they share a particular slot in the calendar – summer, or the dry season – just as both sexes of many species of animal

congregate at a particular time of year to rut. This timing may
relate to the work cycle but may also have deeper causes.
Naadam betrays further elements reminiscent of rutting
behaviour. Mongolian wrestlers perform the eagle dance and
have their titles sung, which is resonant with the display
behaviour of stags, who wave their antler crowns and roar, a
behaviour that demonstrates power, attracts females and
probably intimidates opponents. Mongolian wrestlers also wear
hats, which give an illusion of greater size, just as stags develop
a mane during rutting that makes them look bigger. Maybe the
eagle dance, title-singing and hat-wearing originated as tactics
to intimidate rivals and impress those watching.

There is enough evidence of a recurring pattern in the deep
structure of these gatherings, and there are enough similarities
between this recurring pattern and the idiom in which other
species rut, to suggest that these summer athletic festivals may
well be the various descendants of the same ancient form of
human rutting behaviour – relatively sophisticated cultural
superstructures erected on a crude primal understructure of a
seasonal breeding behaviour. Far more evidence would have to
be produced to make a really good case. It would be interesting
to see how many other traditional cultures have summer
athletic gatherings that include wrestling or similarly masculine
sports, and to discover how many further cultures there are in
which men explicitly compete for females in some kind of
manly contest. Africa would be the best place to look. While in
Nigeria, I discovered that the Dakikari tribe, living near Zuru
in the north, have a strong tradition of wrestling and hold inter-
village tournaments after the harvest in the dry season.
Exceptional Dakikari wrestlers can have the pick of the girls,
just like exceptional wrestlers among the Dukawa. It is also
documented that Nuba tribes in Sudan hold inter-village
wrestling tournaments during the dry season after the harvest,
but it is not known whether these have any marriage
dimension.

Today's humans are not currently understood to follow a
seasonal rutting behaviour, but some primates, such as
ringtailed lemurs, squirrel monkeys and rhesus macaques, do
have a seasonal breeding season. However, none of the apes,
including chimpanzees and gorillas, our closest evolutionary

relatives, is currently believed to follow any seasonal pattern. If the human rutting theory turns out to be correct, but humans are – and they and their ancestors always were – more like today's chimps and gorillas and less like ringtailed lemurs and rhesus macaques, then perhaps annual tournaments are actually a cultural construct. Maybe summer athletic festivals represent a conscious effort by man to organise an activity, fighting for females, which he would otherwise practise in an unstructured way. Our ancestors may have created such festivals to channel and police a behaviour that could otherwise sporadically erupt into violence. Perhaps they noticed how animals such as stags confine their contests over females to a couple of months a year, then co-exist relatively peacefully for the rest of the time.

If, on the other hand, our remote ancestors were once like seasonal-breeding primates and took part in an annual summer rutting behaviour triggered by biological changes, you might anticipate that biological scaffolding supporting that behaviour would still survive. In particular, you might anticipate a rise in men's testosterone levels during summer, echoing the rise in the testosterone levels of other animals during their rut. Studies have shown the existence of just such a summer rise. Research undertaken by a team in Denmark and published in 2003 found that testosterone levels in male subjects peaked in June and July, and fell in winter and early spring. Similarly, a small Dutch study published in 1976 reported that testosterone levels reached a near-peak in August and reached their maximum level a little later in the year in October. However, a large-scale study of military veterans, undertaken by American testosterone researcher James Dabbs, showed a different picture: levels troughed in late spring and early summer, and peaked in late autumn and early winter.

Until possible mechanisms that seasonally affect men's testosterone levels are isolated and understood, it will be difficult to extricate one possible cause of annual variation from another and impossible to know for certain whether the summer rise identified by some research represents the faint trace of an ancient biological trigger for seasonal breeding or has other causes. But if testosterone does come to a peak, or near-peak, during summer for a reason, or reasons, as yet unknown, this could help explain why Zeus was venerated and worshipped by athletes at the ancient Olympics during July or August: it may mean that summer is the time of year when men are most preoccupied with, and capable of asserting, physical dominance, the ruling quality of Zeus, the most dominant male in the universe, who throws thunderbolts and fights for power.

It would be wrong to assume that one unifying theory can explain the whole of wrestling in all cultures at all times, but it would also be wrong to assume that wrestling has no common origins or themes that explain its place in some cultures, some of the time – or a lot of cultures a lot of the time. If the human rutting theory is correct, the implications are huge: it would mean that wrestling, or a precursor, was once a motor that drove evolution. Men had to prove their dominance over one another in physical contests to win women. Winners reproduced, losers did not. These contests either were, or involved, or evolved into, wrestling. Instead of being on the fringes of human life, wrestling was once at the centre of the struggle for existence.

It is conceivable that the mating system of humans, or their remote ancestors, was once as stark as that of red deer, but that is unlikely to have been the case during the last so many tens of thousands of years. People have lived in complex cultures for a long time, and it is difficult to imagine that the capacity to beat others in physical encounters has been the sole criterion for winning women for quite a while. Even in pre-modern societies where men with wrestling ability are highly prized, such as Igbo villages of 60 or a 100 years ago, other attributes were valued in potential husbands, particularly farming ability. Factors such as social standing and wealth, capacity to provide, personality, attractiveness, lust, love, chemistry and parents' wishes must have also been – and continue to be – significant in determining who marries whom.

It's easy to imagine that the ability to establish dominance in physical contests was originally the most important factor in determining who would mate, but as cultures grew in complexity other factors rose to prominence and jostled alongside it for significance. Today its relative importance varies. In some pre-modern cultures, such as among the Dukawa, wrestling ability has central significance; in other cultures, such as post-industrial England, it has lost all the significance it may once have had.

If someone had told me when I was in my mid-twenties that wrestling might somehow be a route to winning women, I would have laughed at the idea. Wrestling had no standing whatsoever among the women I met. Often they thought it bizarre and odd. The human rutting theory provides an elegant explanatory context for the decline in the fortunes and reputation of wrestling in England and elsewhere: it no longer prospers because it no longer serves its intended biological function. The world has changed. Women in England may possibly have once been attracted to men who could demonstrate physical dominance in wrestling contests, but unfortunately today they tend to favour men who can demonstrate qualities other than an ability to throw members of the same sex onto their backs.

In places where the forces of modernisation have been strong – industrialisation, urbanisation, the move away from an agrarian economy, the rise of mass education, and so on – manly physical virtues have lost much of their significance and attraction. Women want men who can demonstrate qualities that will help them succeed in the modern world. They tend to judge potential partners in terms such as intelligence and education, wealth and economic viability, work status, sense of humour, appearance, sensitivity, ability to listen, personal hygiene, and lack of ear and nasal hair. Consequently, though wrestling may have once been a motor that drove evolution, it is now outmoded. It has been abandoned and left to languish on the cultural scrapheap because it no longer serves its original purpose. No one is interested in it any more. It has associations with a rustic and primitive past, not the urban and sophisticated present and future. The entertainment industry has bought wrestling for its scrap value and continues to set about exploiting its residual power for the purpose of making money. The little status and respect it may have once had has been lost. Wrestling is now a joke, a laughing stock.

Yet though modern cultures have undergone rapid transformations over the last couple of hundred years, human biology has not. Men still live in bodies built and driven by a hormone, testosterone, which propels them towards physical contests with one another. Men's impulses are not going to change overnight. The result is a lag – between instinct and culture, between wanting to beat someone in a physical contest and having to sit for eight hours a day in an office. Caught in the gap between what our instincts and bodies want us to do and what our modern culture expects of us, we feel a deep sense of discomfort and unease. We feel the world is not organised in a way that allows us to be who we really are. We feel like I did in my twenties when I fell for wrestling but discovered that there were few places to train, mats or instructors – that England did not want me to wrestle. We feel frustrated and abandoned and bristle at how our culture curbs our natural masculine exuberance, our urge to express ourselves as males through action, adventure and sport – through the body. Our senses become supersensitive to it, like teeth sensitised to ice cream and sugary tea. We feel pain every time we come into contact with the ice cream and sugary tea of 'no ball games' signs, the ice cream and sugary tea of the lobby who want to ban boxing, the ice cream and sugary tea of another sports field turned into housing.

The human rutting theory finds some support in evolutionary biology. The evolution of traits that help males compete for females, and females attract males, is termed 'sexual selection'. The belief is that these traits evolve because individuals who possess them in a form and to a degree that give them an advantage over rivals will mate more successfully, and thereby win the competition to pass on genes to the next generation. Different species have different sexually selected traits that reflect different mating strategies. These can take the form of horns, antlers and bright colours, as well as song and other types of display, such as the roaring of stags.

Males of most mammal species are bigger than females. The differences can be huge: for example, male northern elephant seals tip the scales at more than three times the weight of their female sweethearts. A widely held view is that sexual selection is an overriding cause of such differences in body size. Size differences are particularly pronounced in polygynous species in which males fight for females, such as elephant seals and red deer, as the bigger the males are, the greater their chance of winning a harem. Men are larger than women, and it is commonly believed that this is a sexually selected characteristic to equip them for contests for females.

Sexual selection theory suggests that men are given larger bodies so that they can compete with one another for women. Women's bodies are designed with the purpose of having children as a principal consideration – ovaries, wide hips, breasts. Men's bodies are chiselled by testosterone into muscular forms that reflect a purpose that also revolves around reproduction. Men's bodies help them compete against one another for the opportunity to have sex with women and thereby have children. Women sometimes talk about how they have a ticking biological clock that imposes its own schedule on their life. Men, too, have ticking biological clocks. Their biological clock tells them to fight and compete against one another in their teens, twenties and early thirties – and, perhaps, to fight and compete during the summers of those summer years in particular.

When I first began to wrestle, I was amazed by the depth of feeling that the sport could engender. I believe that this passion sprang in part from the fact that I was doing what nature intended me to do. Women often say that their life suddenly makes sense when they have a baby. My life suddenly made sense when I wrestled. The human rutting theory suggests that wrestling occupies a comparable role for men as the one that having a baby occupies for women. It is what their bodies are designed for. Men tend to be obsessed with the act of sex, but it is the act of getting into a position to be able to have sex – in other words the act of competing against other men for women – that our biology is geared towards most. When we wrestle, we are instruments of nature's grand purpose. Nature wants us to wrestle. We fight, wrestle or compete against one another in sports with a passion that flows from the fact that physical contests were once a way – perhaps even *the* way – in which it was determined who would have a genetic legacy. The fact that, in many cultures, success in physical contests has become irrelevant to whether we can win females has not been recognised by our biology. We want to carry on fighting regardless.

The human rutting theory gives a strong explanation for the enduring importance of winning in the wrestling cultures of India, Mongolia and everywhere else. An implication of the theory is that losing really used to be the tragedy for males that they often think of it as. Men's genetic existence used to be at stake when they competed. Losers lost the opportunity to reproduce and have children. This may be hardwired into men. Even if, in the modern day, loss in a wrestling match is actually irrelevant to a man's chances of procreating, his primal biological programming continues to tell him the opposite. Loss is experienced with a depth of feeling commensurate with its former status as a step on the road to genetic extinction, and winning is experienced with a depth of feeling commensurate with its former status as a step towards securing genetic immortality. Perhaps sports in general are erected on the same biological bedrock as wrestling and other ritualised fighting contests. Players in a football team thrashed 4–0 therefore feel a deep sense of dejection because loss is still experienced as commensurate with its ancient status as a step on the path towards genetic extinction – even if those players actually go home to have sex with their wives afterwards.

At its core, wrestling is raw and primal, yet when you consider a wrestling culture like India's you also see a different face. Men like Bishember Chobe lived an ascetic life comparable to that of a monk. They followed the Indian wrestler's code of discipline and sacrifice, which they took to extremes. The Varanasi journalist Goverdhan Das Malhotra was a strong advocate of wrestling because he believed that this life of sacrifice and discipline has great social value. Youths who go to wrestling schools are encouraged to follow a clean existence, and lead a structured and ordered life.

Wrestling cultures like India's represent conduits that channel and transform the biological urge to fight. The impulse to pit oneself against others that could explode out on the streets is instead directed into wrestling, a form of fighting without hurting, and the structured and ordered life of the student at the wrestling school. Youths and young men agree to embrace this path because they want the status, recognition and wealth that they have seen is the prize of great athletes.

To the modern mind, wrestling cultures may appear crude and old-fashioned, but maybe our ancestors saw the ritualisation and structuring of fighting as revolutionary steps in social evolution. By directing men who feel the eternal desire to fight towards ritualised combat sports, they could curb and contain violence and hostility that might otherwise occur, and thereby help to foster social cohesion.

The problem of fractious aggression between men is a perennial one – and this must surely have a lot to do with the way that our mating system is configured and the way testosterone is allocated. Nature only equips stags with the physical equipment and inclination to fight for females for about six weeks a year, whereas human males are handed the physical equipment and inclination to fight for females all year, every year from adolescence onwards. A stag is Clark Kent for ten months a year, then Superman for six weeks, while human males are Clark Kents till puberty, then Supermen for their entire adult lives competing for the same Lois Lanes. Mature hinds are only fertile during the rut, while women are fertile all the time from puberty to menopause (at particular moments in their cycles, of course), so this central stimulus for stags to fight is passing, while for men it is constant. Yet this system offers humans a tremendous opportunity. If a way can be found to establish dominance that reduces the physical cost and social divisiveness of fighting, men's continual testosterone-underwritten capacity and inclination to fight might instead be directed towards projects of group benefit.

Among males of the great ape species, only humans and chimpanzees have indeed found a way to collaborate. The male-bonding characteristic of communities of chimps and humans allows them to form hunting parties, raiding parties and defensive units to protect their clan. Both chimps and men within the same group fight in a ritualised way, and perhaps a major factor in the development of their capacity for shared action has been the ritualisation of fighting, which humans have taken to advanced levels through sports such as wrestling, so that contests are resolved relatively harmlessly without causing deep divisions or permanent injury, both of which would impair the ability of males to join together in collaborative action at other times.

As we allow wrestling cultures to decline, it could be that we are reneging on our side of a clever bargain our ancestors made with human nature both to contain and harness the testosterone-driven urge to fight for females. Having long forgotten the importance of the deal, we abandon wrestling at our peril and invite male aggression to manifest itself elsewhere.

PART VI

Brazil

December 2003–March 2004

Chapter 14

A Welcome Outbreak of Masculine Fundamentalism

I jolt awake and take a while to come to. It's the middle of the night. The plane is at Washington airport. By the time I booked a ticket to Rio there were no direct flights left. It's snowing. A member of the cabin crew relays the message that the plane will have to wait its turn to be de-iced. We may be here a couple of hours. Next stop Sao Paulo, then Rio. I went to India, Mongolia and Nigeria to explore traditions of wrestling that have their origins in the distant past; I'm going to Rio to understand forces shaping its future.

I first came into contact with those forces nine years ago when I made another journey to the States. That time an American city was the final destination, not a stop-off. In 1994 I flew to Charlotte in North Carolina to cover the third Ultimate Fighting Championships (UFC) for a men's magazine. The UFC pitted fighters from different martial arts and grappling disciplines against one another – karate, kung fu,

sumo wrestling and judo among them. Its aim was to discover
which man and which style was king. The matches took place
in an octagonal arena with mesh fencing. The rules, or lack of
them, allowed each athlete to express himself fully in his own
combat idiom. Only biting and eye-gouging were disallowed.
There were no rounds, time limits or weight categories, and
fighters did not wear protective equipment, such as gloves or
headguards. Theoretically each fighter was free to kick, punch,
elbow, headbutt or strangle his opponent into defeat or
submission. Because everything went, no one could claim the
rules favoured another fighter's style.

As far as it was known, the UFC was the first no-holds-
barred tournament of its kind ever to be held in the Western
world in the modern era. Weaned on boxing, the press were
hostile towards it. They characterised the UFC as violent and
labelled it 'human cockfighting'. They thought that saying 'no'
to gloves meant saying 'yes' to bloodshed and gore. What they
failed to understand, or were unwilling to acknowledge, was
that one reason the gloves came off was to allow grapplers to
wrestle, and that the best defence against being hit is to close,
clinch and wrestle an opponent to the ground where he can be
contained and subdued. Boxing is theoretically more dangerous than fighting in the UFC because the rules of boxing insist
that protagonists stand and hit each other in the head and stop
them from clinching and wrestling, which are the best defences
against punches. I, of course, was for the UFC on both philosophical and historical grounds. It was a welcome outbreak of
masculine fundamentalism and marked the re-emergence of
ritualised fighting under the same rules as pankration in
Ancient Greece.

I met a member of the fabled Brazilian Gracie family for the
first time at the tournament. Rorion Gracie was tall and
disarmingly charming, and had a light handshake. Alongside
UFC promoter Art Davie, Rorion was the prime mover behind
the event, which was a means to demonstrate the brilliance of
his family's grappling style to the rest of the world. Rorion's
uncle, Carlos Gracie, had been taught techniques from judo
and Jiu-Jitsu while a teenager growing up in Belem, near the
mouth of the Amazon, in the 1910s. Carlos and his brothers,
sons and nephews took those techniques and used them as a

basis for a remarkable invention, Gracie Jiu-Jitsu, which represents a novel and fundamentally different style of grappling from any other in existence. The Gracies' principal concern was to create a method of self-defence that would equip them in real fights. They maintained that most real fights end up on the ground, so they perfected the art of ground-grappling above everything else.

To prove the efficiency of their new invention, the Gracies challenged and beat all-comers. Sometimes the fights were contested under the rules of Vale Tudo (which, roughly translated from the Portuguese, means 'anything goes'). Only if the Gracies triumphed when everything was allowed – punching and kicking as well as grappling – could they claim without fear of contradiction that Gracie Jiu-Jitsu was the best fighting style in existence. Through the UFC, the Gracies now wanted to teach the world the same lesson about the superiority of Gracie Jiu-Jitsu that they had already given in their native Brazil. The octagonal cage would be a new lecture theatre and Rorion's younger brother, 27-year-old Royce Gracie, was the family member chosen to deliver the lesson.

I spoke to many of the fighters before the tournament, but not to Royce. I sensed, though, that upholding the Gracie family honour was something of a burden as well as a duty and pleasure for him – or maybe I was projecting onto him the emotions I would feel in his position. Whatever the case, a lot was riding on Royce. If he succeeded, if he could convince everybody that Gracie Jiu-Jitsu was invincible, his family would never look back. There would be a worldwide clamour for their teaching.

By the third UFC, Royce had already won a total of seven fights to triumph in the two previous tournaments. He followed a simple strategy. He would try to quickly clinch and take his opponent to the ground, instantly neutralising their ability to punch or kick effectively. Then he would typically sit on his opponent's chest and throw a few punches to force him to either give in or protect his face by turning, at which point he would apply a strangle, or if his opponent did not turn, Royce might grab an arm, change position and apply an armlock. The significance of the use of submission holds such as chokes and armlocks was lost on the prejudiced media. The aim of boxing is to hurt and knock out your opponent. In contrast, the aim of Gracie Jiu-Jitsu, as applied by Royce Gracie, was to win by forcing opponents to tap either him, or the mat, at least twice, which is the universal signal that you give in.

The beauty of submission holds is that they remove the need to injure or knock out an opponent in order to win. If your arm is hyper-extended by an armlock or you are being strangled, you have no real option but to tap. Such techniques appear dangerous, but normally they are not. Say a straight armlock is being applied, the convention is that the person using the hold will freeze at the point just before further extension of the arm will cause damage to the elbow joint. As you apply the technique you give your opponent the opportunity to submit, rather than simply apply the technique with malice. So far Royce had won five out of seven fights at the UFC with armlocks and strangles. Neither he nor his opponents had been badly hurt in the course of seven no-holds-barred bouts fought with knuckles bared.

Royce was giving grappling back its dignity by demonstrating its value in raw confrontations, yet as the tournament was about to begin and I considered where my allegiances lay, I knew I was for Ken Shamrock and not Royce. I respected Royce, but was more drawn to Ken, a talented bareskin wrestler who was well known as a fighter in Japan. Ken was a brooding 210lb of pure muscle. A wrestler's wrestler, he was a physical extremist who would do 50 straight reps at 100kg on the bench-press and who said he carried on training after he broke his neck as if nothing had happened. Ken was the individual while Royce was the corporate representative of a mysterious branded product, Gracie Jiu-Jitsu, who wore a white uniform, his Japanese-style kimono, to work. Ken was also the underdog. Royce had beaten Ken in their first UFC encounter and Ken now wanted revenge.

Both grapplers were seeded. If they won their first two fights they would meet in the final. In the second bout of the tournament, Ken beat a judo player, Christophe Leineger, to begin his climb to the final, but Royce faltered two bouts later as he started his ascent. He faced Kimo, a powerful and fierce-looking 250lb fighter with 'Jesus' tattooed in big capital letters across his midriff. Kimo rushed Royce and they went to the ground. Incredibly, at one point Kimo got behind Royce, a position from which, had he known how to ride an opponent and strangle, he might have won. Kimo also threw some heavy punches towards Royce's head that appeared to connect, though it was difficult to tell for sure. Royce appeared to be rattled and hurt, yet he still submitted Kimo from underneath with an armlock. However, he was incapable of continuing and his corner decided he should not contest his second bout.

At the after-show party for journalists, fighters and their factions, the Kimo–Royce match was replayed on a screen. Kimo's entourage cheered every time Kimo punched Royce. They treated the fight like a victory for their man. Rorion turned up with his brother Royce, who was woozy, and looked weak and faint. Rorion tried to explain his brother's condition away by saying he was suffering from low blood sugar. As Gracie Jiu-Jitsu's propagandist-in-chief, Rorion didn't want his family to lose face. He didn't want anyone to think an invincible Gracie had been caught by something as crude as a bludgeony punch. My attitude towards Royce and Gracie Jiu-Jitsu changed when I caught a glimpse of Royce's arm under his kimono. It was like a flash of something that you are not supposed to see – like an overgenerous view of a hostess's cleavage or thigh. His arm was unimpressive and unintimidating. He had the slim, unmuscular physique of a long-distance runner.

Me and some other journalists covering the tournament had earlier discussed why Royce would want to wear his kimono in the arena. Surely, we thought, opponents would be able to grip his clothing to throw him. Surely he was handing them an advantage. Now I suddenly saw a good reason why Royce might want to wear that kimono: it made him look physically bigger. He was like a car salesman wearing a double-breasted suit one size too big, with padded shoulders to give himself more presence. My admiration for both Gracie Jiu-Jitsu and Royce grew in that moment. Weighing only 176lbs, he had entered a fierce no-holds-barred tournament as the smallest man. After apparently taking blows to the head, he still had the determination and presence of mind to submit his opponent. Gracie Jiu-Jitsu had to be an incredibly accomplished art to allow someone who looked like he should be running marathons to overcome someone four stones heavier who looked like he should be organising a prison riot.

Despite the hiccup at UFC III, Royce successfully helped establish Gracie Jiu-Jitsu's credentials as the most effective fighting style in one-to-one unarmed combat. The true sophistication of Gracie Jiu-Jitsu was made transparent in the following years. It became clear that turning up at a no-holds-barred fighting tournament in the States in 1994, with a black belt in Gracie Jiu-Jitsu, had been like turning up at a battle during the Middle Ages brandishing a machine gun – it was that far ahead of everything else. Gracie Jiu-Jitsu appeared magical in that it defied both common sense and gravity. The Gracies actively sought to lie on their back under an opponent – usually with their legs wrapped around his back. Lying on your back constitutes defeat in many wrestling styles, but the Gracies had developed ingenious ways to attack from this position, which they called the guard.

The UFC made the Gracies famous beyond their native Brazil and initiated a boom in no-holds-barred fighting tournaments. Soon there were similar events all over the world – such as in Russia, Australia, France, England, Holland, Ukraine. The UFC kept its status as one of the most prestigious, but Pride, a ring-based tournament held in Japan, also rose to pre-eminence. Suddenly arenas were being made available within which to determine who was the best fighter on the planet. Soon, ultimate fighting was no longer about pitting men from different styles against one another but a style in itself, like the pankration of the Ancient Greeks, with its own name, Mixed Martial Arts (MMA). By and large tournament promoters shrank back from the extremism of pankration rules. Weight categories, rounds and further rules were introduced, along with small gloves to protect the hands but which allowed fighters to grapple. Normally, fighters were no longer asked to compete more than once on the same night.

Denied sympathetic coverage by the mainstream media, MMA nevertheless boomed and found the perfect means of dissemination in the form of the emerging World Wide Web. 'Cross-training' became a buzzword on Internet chat forums. Everyone looked to the same reality-tested disciplines for technical inspiration – principally Gracie Jiu-Jitsu, wrestling, Thai boxing, kickboxing and boxing. Whether a fighter started out as a wrestler, Thai boxer or Gracie Jiu-Jitsu practitioner, they now wanted to either master both grappling and 'stand-up' (punching and kicking), or master how to counter experts in whichever area they were deficient. Above all, everyone wanted to understand Gracie Jiu-Jitsu and the Gracies' ingenious guard position.

From the outset, the toughest opponents that Gracie Jiu-Jitsu fighters faced were wrestlers – in particular Olympic-standard American wrestlers who switched to no-holds-barred fighting and proved that they were worthy challengers. As wrestlers succeeded in MMA competition, people began to realise that wrestling has validity both as a combat sport and a method of self-defence. The result is that many of those who go to wrestling schools in England and around the world today, do so because they were inspired by watching wrestlers succeed in MMA tournaments.

The Gracies are directly responsible for a huge resurgence of interest in grappling and wrestling. (Personally, I consider Gracie Jiu-Jitsu to be a form of wrestling too: if you are rolling around on the floor with an opponent and using your hands to grip and hold, you are wrestling whether or not you wear clothing; however, when people within MMA talk about wrestling they are referring to the bareskin styles of Greco-Roman, Freestyle and American collegiate as distinct from Gracie Jiu-Jitsu – and it's a useful distinction to make in this context.) One day the Gracies may come to be regarded as the saviours of wrestling – the family responsible for a revival of interest in a craft in general decline – yet I'm curious to know what they have to give the world beyond technique. I wonder what they are selling apart from armlocks, the guard and strangles. Do the Gracies teach Jiu-Jitsu in an ethical context, or, if not, does an implicit creed come attached anyway? What exactly is at the heart of the culture of Gracie Jiu-Jitsu, which no doubt will spread right across the world over the next 50 years?

Rio is the place to go to find out. It is the epicentre of the Gracie Jiu-Jitsu earthquake. Carlos Gracie opened his first school in Rio in the 1920s, and Jiu-Jitsu flourishes there. The city is home to some of the best Jiu-Jitsu fighters competing in MMA today, which in itself is a good reason to visit. I want to get to know them, watch them train, find out what motivates them and generally get to understand the emerging fighting subculture of which they are a key part.

I fall asleep again but awake just as our de-iced plane begins to accelerate down the runway. Thankfully there'll be no more cold weather for me for at least three months.

Chapter 15

Pride, UFC. . .

While Felipe makes me a toasted cheese and ham sandwich in the kitchen of his pousada, I sit at the counter and ask him where he lives and whether the attractive woman I've seen around with the cleavage scrunched together by a tight-fitting top is his wife. He points to a room upstairs to answer the first question and answers 'yes' to the second.

'Do you have any children?'

'Yes, but not with her,' says Felipe.

He grins and his eyes brighten.

'In Brazil we have four or five wives.' He pauses, then adds: 'Like the Arabs.' As a further afterthought: 'But one at a time.'

I take the sandwich and go and sit on a recliner next to the pool. Felipe's place is the perfect place to stay – quiet, peaceful, secure. It's on an island in a lagoon in Barra. When people think of Rio they think of Copacabana, Ipanema and the statue of Christ the Redeemer. Barra is a few miles west of those places and a world away from the majority of the tourists and the minority of Cariocas (residents of Rio) who prey on them. It used to be outside the city proper, but now Rio has expanded and marched westwards well beyond the neighbourhood.

This is my second trip to Rio. I spent seven weeks here a year ago and learnt a lot, but found that the Jiu-Jitsu picture was complex and I needed to return. I wanted to return for other reasons too: this is where I feel most at home. Rio has a body-orientated culture. This is a city where the life of the body is acknowledged and cherished. Cariocas are into sport and exercise and being outdoors. They like to surf, hike to waterfalls, play football, tennis, volleyball and *futevolei*, a form of volleyball with football skills. At weekends joggers and power walkers stream by on the tracks behind the beaches. There are gyms and fitness centres everywhere with spinning classes, aqua aerobics, ashtanga yoga, Pilates and aerobics. In the weights areas, the men concentrate on their upper bodies and abs, while the women concentrate on their lower bodies, specifically their buttocks, much to the liking of the men.

Cariocas like to show off their bodies and embellish them with tattoos. Men tend to go for big designs – a Japanese warrior perhaps, or koi carp or calligraphy – while women favour the small and discreet. You sit behind a girl on the bus, enjoying the smell of her wet hair, and while she adjusts her hair to put on a scrunchie you notice she has a butterfly tattooed on the back of her neck.

Everyone goes to the beach at weekends. The men wear narrow trunks to get as much of a tan as possible and display their lean and muscular physiques; the women wear dental floss bikinis to get as much of a tan as possible and display their behinds. As today is Sunday, a beach day, I should really be there too, but I'm too tired out by a 24-hour-plus flight to do anything other than go back to my room and slumber.

I ring the bell on the jetty of the pousada and wait. Red-liveried crabs pick around in the mangrove roots. I ring the bell again. A boatman hears this time and comes over from the far island. He drops me at a jetty next to the carpark and I walk along the main road beside the speeding traffic. Iridescent fish scales scattered like confetti shimmer on the pavement of the bridge across the lagoon. Fishermen in flip-flops and shorts stand looking down into the murky water below for shoals of mullet. Whenever they see the camera-flash of a fish's silver flank, they cast out circular nets.

I cross the pedestrian bridge over the main highway to enter Barra proper, walk down a shopping street and turn left into a leafy avenue of low-rise apartments. Carlinhos Gracie's school, Gracie Barra, is on the top floor of a fitness centre on the left called Fit Express. Carlinhos ('Little Carlos') is a son of Carlos, the founder of Gracie Jiu-Jitsu. Just as I'm about to climb the last flight of steps to the mat room, Marcio Feitosa, Carlinhos's second in command, comes downstairs to take a quick break from teaching. He is wearing a new kimono with 'Professor' written on the back. It means 'teacher' in Portuguese, but the English meaning is just as fitting. Marcio is one of the Jiu-Jitsu greats. I ask Marcio what's been happening since the last time I visited.

'Now we have a Vale Tudo team,' he says. 'They are training now.'

Marcio's class are running through their moves in the middle of the mat, while a group of tattooed and glistening fighters sit and recline by the wall at the far end. They have just finished training. I consider each of the fighters in turn but recognise hardly any of them. One has an intense and dangerous look about him. His dark hair is spiked and scrunched up in the middle, and he has a werewolf-wild sketch of a beard. A large spiky tattoo climbs vine-like beyond the collar line of his neck. His smouldering presence and spiky tattoo add up to a warning to keep out, an invocation to keep away, but there is also something magnetic about him and I can't help but look at him. The whole gym appears to defer to him on an unspoken level. He is its magnetic north, the man whom everyone else aligns themselves towards. Dennis, an American who is training with the team, comes over to say hello.

'Who's the guy with his back turned to us who looks tasty?' I ask him.

'That's Babalu,' says Dennis.

I scrutinise the other fighters. One looks like Cacareco, but it can't be him, as Cacareco trains at another gym: Marco Ruas Vale Tudo. Allegiance to a particular gym is a serious affair here. Like biker gang members, fighters are fiercely tribal and loyal to their team, which they regard as a second family. Team members train together and socialise together. They wear team clothing and paraphernalia and have team tattoos. Cacareco therefore can't be training here, yet this fighter really does look like him. He has the same dome-shaped shaven head and the same distinctive physique as Cacareco, who is relatively short but prodigiously over-muscled. He looks as though he has been inflated by a footpump and the person doing the inflating became distracted – by a passing woman perhaps – and kept pumping by mistake until his body reached bursting point. Or as though he was born in a place with twice the gravitational field of the Earth's, and as he grew upwards he was pushed doubly downwards and adjusted by growing doubly outwards. Everything about his physique looks too big to get a proper hold of. I look for tattoos. Cacareco has a distinctive warrior on the side of his abdomen and a dragon on his upper arm. They are there. It is Cacareco. I'm shocked. Cacareco has switched from Marco Ruas to Gracie Barra, which is like a Liverpool fan switching allegiance to Everton or Manchester United. Marcio breaks from teaching to come over and replace a book that has fallen on the mat from the table behind me.

'That's Cacareco,' I say to him, stating the obvious in disbelief. 'He used to train at Marco Ruas.'

'Yes,' replies Marcio. 'Now he's training with us.'

'And Babalu? Where did he come from?'

'He's also from Marco Ruas.'

Back at the pousada I dig out the tape of an interview I did with Cacareco last time and listen to it again. He wasn't the most talkative person. He said he came from the suburbs – in other words from the North Zone, the poorer area away from the South Zone of affluent neighbourhoods and beachside apartments. His father died when he was five and his mother worked as a housekeeper to support the family. In fighting, he said, he had found a way to survive with dignity.

I press 'Stop' on the tape-recorder and take off the headphones. Since we spoke, Cacareco came second in both the under 98kg division and absolute division of the Abu Dhabi Combat Club Submission Wrestling World Championships, which is the most prestigious submission wrestling tournament in the world. Those placings will have given him an international reputation to trade on if he wants to talk to promoters about fighting Vale Tudo. Cacareco must have switched teams because he thinks he will have better career prospects if he is part of Gracie Barra, but he will also have to pay a price for making the switch. Fighters who swap teams are regarded as traitors in Jiu-Jitsu circles. They have a term for such people, 'Creonte', which was the name of a traitorous character in a TV soap.

Such occurrences are becoming more and more frequent. The emergence of MMA around the world is transforming the scene in Brazil. The lure of fighting abroad for money has affected people's behaviour. Before the current boom, fighters in Rio were inward-looking and insular. There were deep rivalries between both teams and styles, and sometimes those rivalries erupted into feuds and challenge matches. Now everything is changing. Everyone is looking at the big picture beyond Brazil. People from different styles and different teams are forming alliances. The heat is leaving the situation. Fighters would rather compete abroad for money than against each other in Rio for nothing, except perhaps honour. Everyone wants to get on the escalator of aggrandisement that ultimately leads to the big, prestigious events, Pride and the UFC – and some will break a code of loyalty to do it.

Roberto Leitao Snr takes out pages of charts and tables from a folder. They represent information that is going to form part of a book about Luta Livre, the bareskin submission wrestling style to which he has devoted much of his life. The charts catalogue submission holds in terms of qualities such as pain and injury. Applying pain in order to make your opponent tap is good, says Roberto, but threatening to injure him is better, because he will tap out of fear whether he is in any real danger or not. He shows pictures that will be included in the book. Lines revealing the geometry of underlying biomechanical forces overlay the wrestlers. Roberto teaches mechanics and trained as an engineer. He is the only man I know who quotes Archimedes in the context of wrestling.

About 40 years ago Roberto laid the foundations of Luta Livre by combining techniques from judo with real techniques from pro wrestling and his own research and inventions. He is obsessed with wrestling. He keeps a notebook by his bed in which to write down any new ideas that come to him in dreams, and he endures the intense pain of a shoulder injury rather than have an operation to put it right that would also unfortunately end his wrestling career. When Roberto's son, Roberto Jnr, was four, he resolved that he would wrestle at the Olympics one day. He did too – twice – which is a remarkable achievement considering Brazil has no real tradition of Olympic wrestling. As there is clearly no space in Roberto's life for anything but grappling, I ask him what his wife thinks about his obsession. He begins his reply with a word – 'She's. . . ' – and ends it by repeating a staccato, grating noise that could be used on a sci-fi film soundtrack as the alarm that warns the crew of a space station that it is about to explode.

Roberto and I sit together on the mat at the small Marco Ruas Vale Tudo (MRVT) gym, which is above shops on Praia Da Botafogo in Flamengo. Roberto uses a kick pad for a cushion, and a strip of grey duct tape covers a cyst on his knee. He is in his sixties, and has back-combed white hair. I want to talk to him about the defections of Cacareco and Babalu from MRVT to Gracie Barra, but I'd rather we stumble across the subject than for me to have to bring it up directly, as I assume it must be a painful topic for Roberto to discuss. It must be particularly hard because Gracie Jiu-Jitsu and Luta Livre have a lot of previous.

An intense ongoing dispute over which style was best came to a head in 1991, when three leading fighters from each style fought each other under Vale Tudo rules. Unfortunately for Luta Livre, Gracie Jiu-Jitsu fighters won all three bouts. Rickson Gracie, the Gracie family champion, also fought two impromptu challenge matches against Hugo Duarte, a leading Luta Livre fighter, and beat him both times. Last time I visited Rio, I asked Roberto about the feud between Luta Livre and Gracie Jiu-Jitsu, but he didn't want to be drawn on the subject. It was all history, he said, and now the feud was over. The world had moved on. Yet the fact that there used to be deep animosity between Luta Livre and Gracie Jiu-Jitsu must add piquancy to the defections by Cacareco and Babalu from MRVT to Gracie Barra. After we've talked some more about Roberto's book, I judge the moment right to ask him what's happened at MRVT since I last visited.

'In the last month a new academy in Rio de Janeiro, Barra Gracie, picked up many grapplers from other teams,' says Roberto. 'They pick Cacareco and Babalu, and they pick other guys from other teams.'

'I've been to Gracie Barra and seen Cacareco and Babalu there and was very surprised because I thought their loyalty was to this place.'

'That's normal.'

'But is that normal? I thought Brazilians had a very strong sense of loyalty to their gym.'

'Yeah, but sometimes they forget that.'

'How do you feel about it personally?'

Roberto looks down and plays with the corner of a printed sheet. He is obviously not happy about it though he wants to put on a brave face. There are precedents for this kind of behaviour, he says.

'You know it's as old as walking forward.' He gives a little forced laugh. 'It's so old.'

'Obviously Cacareco and Babalu must have thought it would be good for their careers to join Gracie Barra.'

'Yeah, but they will be surprised. It will not help them, because here they have much better training. Punching and grappling Barra Gracie don't have things to teach them. In wrestling I guarantee you that they are teaching them.'

'Were they paid to move to Gracie Barra?'

'Yeah, it was commercial. But it's very easy to make an agreement with you for one year and I will pay you one, two, three months – it's easy. But let's see in twelve months if it will work, that's the problem. If the guys doesn't fight. . . Eeergh, it's complicated. Everybody wants to fly.' Roberto uses his hands to imitate the flapping wings of a bird. 'Sometimes the flight is not so good. They haven't got good wind. You can go down. But they try.'

A training session begins. Wearing 16oz gloves and shin pads, the class spar under Thai boxing rules. They don't hold much back. One fighter doubles up after taking a knee to the midsection. He taps gloves with his sparring partner a moment later and they recommence. At the end of their intense bouts, the fighters slap gloves with one another, take off their pads, and sit around and rest. A sudden stillness and silence descends on the gym. It's like the respite after a storm when the weather coolly contemplates its next move.

Roberto takes off his polo shirt and wrestles with an opponent half his age. I sit on the mat in the corner of the gym and talk to his son, Roberto Jnr, but keep an eye on how Roberto Snr fares. Soon, his opponent stands up smiling, bemused by the fact that he's just been submitted. While Roberto Snr wrestles another bout, he is ambushed from behind. A second fighter wraps his legs around his body and an arm around his neck to strangle him. No one has submitted Roberto in 30 years and there's a good-natured competition to see who will be the first. Roberto tries to dislodge the arm sunk around his neck but can't. He gives up and instead nonchalantly waggles his fingers as if playing a musical instrument, to make it clear that the strangle is having no effect and he is nowhere near either passing out or tapping. The ambusher gives in and laughs.

I ask Roberto Jnr whether no one can really submit his father, or whether the fighters are humouring him out of deference to his age, seniority and status as the founder of Luta Livre. He says no, they really can't make him tap. His father submits everyone, except him and Pedro Rizzo, who are both wise to his tricks. Roberto Jnr uses his finger to draw an imaginary bar chart on the mat to explain why his father is so hard to beat. Though he has only 50 per cent of the strength and conditioning of the younger athletes, he uses his 50 per cent to the full. By comparison, Roberto Jnr says he himself has 100 per cent strength and conditioning, but can only mobilise 40 per cent. So his father has a 10 per cent advantage.

I put the same question to Roberto about the defections of Carareco and Babalu that I put to his father. He, too, puts on a brave face. He is particularly disappointed to see Babalu leave, because he spent many years training him and they are friends, but he is less upset about losing Cacareco.

'Our team is a family team,' says Roberto. 'Barra Gracie is a professional team just created now. It has no history – they just hire fighters. They didn't make the fighter. I understand nowadays this is going to be more usual. Big business guys want to invest in teams and have the money.'

He sums up how things are changing with a one-word concluding sentence: 'Professionalism.'

The following morning I return to Gracie Barra to watch the Vale Tudo team train. Sure enough, just as Roberto Leitao predicted, Babalu is teaching them wrestling. Carlinhos Gracie arrives – he's been away in the States – and stands watching from over in the area where everyone leaves their shoes. I go and greet him. He seems genuinely happy to see me and pats me on the shoulder as we shake hands.

'So, now you've got a combat team,' I say.

'Yes, Vale Tudo,' says Carlinhos. 'The guys train for Pride, UFC.'

My first excursion into the world of Gracie Jiu-Jitsu does not go well. One evening I join the 6pm class at Gracie Barra. A group of Brazilians sit in a circle talking to each other. I feel like a rank outsider. This is their gym, their family, their team, their territory. Fortunately I recently saw a documentary about a male macaque monkey that had been banished from one troop and wanted to join another that lived in a temple, so I understand the social dynamics of the situation perfectly. For a long time the isolated monkey had to hang around on the edge of the troop without entering its territory, otherwise it feared it would be attacked. Like that monkey, I have to hover around on the fringes of the group and wait to be accepted. I almost don't want to take my kimono out of my bag, as that would signal my intention to join in the class and enter their territory, and commit me to playing the role of a lone monkey that wants to be taken in. They won't attack me exactly, but they may give me a cold reception.

I join the warm-up and feel self-conscious as we run round the gym a few times without our jackets on. I'm not in the best of shape, while in contrast there is probably only an ounce of extra body fat for every ten Brazilian Gracie Barra fighters. All of them are well defined and tanned. When it comes to going through technique drills, I have lost the small amount of vision

and awareness I developed when I trained here before. Trying
to find and apply the right technique is like groping around for
the bathroom light switch when you're staying in an unfamiliar
hotel room, you've got up at 3.30 in the morning and you're
still half asleep. We practise some techniques from foot-in-hip
guard then line up against the wall for sparring. I'm partnered
with Rafael, a pale young Brazilian who is large and strong but
clumsy. Like me, he is a white belt. During the one-handed
sparring drill, he clunks me squarely on the chin with his
elbow. We then spar properly and start uncharacteristically
from standing. Rafael quickly drops down to the ground to try
to take up the guard position. I anticipate the move and
instantly drop with him with the intention of trying to pass his
guard before he can organise his leg-defence properly.
Unfortunately, he drops to the ground in an uncoordinated
way and his knee lands on my leg just below my knee with all
his bodyweight behind it. I feel a sharp pain and hear a
succession of sickening cracks in my knee joint. I grimace and
involuntarily shout 'Aaaah!' The whole room goes quiet.
Everyone stops and looks.

'You should stop now,' says Arroz, an instructor, in English.

I'm worried that this could be a serious injury. Knee
injuries are the worst. The class returns to what they were
doing.

'Do you have any ice?' I ask Arroz.

'No.'

Not 'no' though I'll get you some, just plain 'no'.

'You don't have any ice?'

'No.'

'Not even downstairs in the fridge?'

'No.'

'You really don't have any ice?'

'No.'

I let out a deep sigh, shake my head in disbelief and sit down
by the wall. Twenty seconds later I feel the area around my
knee to see how the injury is developing. It doesn't actually feel
that painful or appear to be swelling too much. I start to feel
embarrassed for possibly having overreacted, and crying out. I
wait a while then prod the area around the knee again. There is
still no real pain or swelling. The knee seems to be OK. Now I

really do feel embarrassed. I make sure to affect a slight limp when I cross the mat to go and get changed.

You go up some steps along an L-shaped corridor, through a doorway and then you're there: the Brazilian Top Team gym. If real life followed the type of plot line thankfully only seen in low-budget martial arts films and a cosmic catastrophe had the effect of transforming the world into a single kingdom ruled by whichever band of men prove their dominance in ritual fighting contests, Top Team would command Planet Earth. The twenty or thirty fighters who come to workout in this room most days of the week have more fighting ability between them than an army division. They also have better tattoos and a higher cauliflower-ear count.

Top Team are in the vanguard of professional MMA both in Rio and the world. A number of Top Team members either currently are, or have been, encamped at the pinnacle of the MMA mountain – Ze Mario Sperry, Murilo Bustamante, Minotauro, his identical twin brother Minotouro, Ricardo Arona, Allan Goes, Carlao Barreto. The team has a strong Gracie Jiu-Jitsu pedigree. It was established three years ago by Ricardo Liborio, Ze Mario, Murilo and Bebeo, who were all students of Carlson Gracie, the eldest son of founder Carlos Gracie by his first marriage. Consequently all Top Team fighters are masters of the guard, but today, a Saturday, is a wrestling day. Top Team has a new wrestling coach. Unfortunately the previous instructor, Darrell Gholar, defected to Brasil Dojo, a new team set up by the infamous Wallid Ismail, along with one of the team's most talented young fighters, Paulo Filho.

While Ze Mario waits for the class to start, he sits on the mat near the door. Dark-haired and charismatic, Ze Mario looks like he would be just as at home dressed up in a tuxedo and playing roulette at a swanky casino as he is rolling around with some of the toughest grapplers around. The class begins with an exercise in which the fighters attempt to do a dynamic handstand and flip over to land on their feet. First try, Ze Mario nearly lands on his feet, but not quite.

'That's difficult,' I say.

'I'm 102 kilos and doing that shit?' he replies, rhetorically, in agreement.

The class progresses onto more drills and then into bouts of sparring. During breaks Ze Mario sits on a bench with his head down, elbows on thighs. Frequent drips of sweat fall to the floor from his nose and chin. I move my bag away from the puddle growing at his feet.

'Sorry,' he says, noticing.

'You sweat a lot.'

'I piss it, man. It's good. It cleanses the body.'

Carlao Barreto enters the gym. He gives his fellow Top Team members the standard hand-clasp and fist-shunt greeting, then comes over to sit down on the bench next to me. Carlao is six foot four. He has long limbs and the hard, dark eyes of a born fighter. A large tattoo of Jesus dominates the dark skin of one arm, and the Carlson Gracie symbol of two slavering head-to-head dogs is on the other. He is beaming and obviously excited about something.

'How's it going?' I ask him.

'Good, but after Thursday I'll be better.'

He holds his arms aloft to act out what is going to happen on Thursday: 'Champion!'

He explains that he is going to fight a wrestler from Minnesota called Travis Wiuff in HEAT, a MMA tournament that will be held in Natal, a city on the north-east coast of Brazil. Wiuff is highly experienced in MMA competition, says Carlao. He has fought 29 times and lost only four, but Carlao is still confident he will win.

'I'm very excited for fight. I'm training six hours a day, six days a week. I'm member Top Team with the best fighters in the world. I want good show for promoters. Watch me. Eighteen December, great battle in Natal. This day, my day, you know.'

The fight will be a classic battle between wrestling and Jiu-Jitsu, he says. I ask him whether he intends to do any more training before Thursday. He says that on Monday he will practise grappling on the ground, on Tuesday he will leave for the north, and then on Wednesday he will rest.

'Mental,' he says, tapping his head to get across what type of training he will be doing on the Wednesday. 'Yoga, breath. Thursday: fight, battle.' With a roar, he concludes: 'War!'

This will be his 19th professional fight. He has fought in Pride twice – the first time in 1999, the second time the following year. He lost the first fight but won the second. He wants to use victory in HEAT as a springboard to re-enter top-flight MMA competition – hopefully in Pride again.

'I think I will make a lot of money in next year,' he says. 'I believe in me, I believe in God.'

'How old are you now?'

He hesitates for a moment and searches for an upbeat way to present the fact that he is 34.

'I'm old guy, but my spirit is very young.'

At the end of the wrestling class, Ze Mario successfully executes a flip. Everyone cheers. All the Top Team fighters form a huddle, including those such as Carlao who didn't train. I have watched sessions here many times before but never seen Top Team huddle. Ze Mario makes a speech. I recognise the Portuguese for 'team' and 'family' and surmise that he must be giving a pep talk about loyalty. Clearly, in the current climate of professionalism in which fighters are more ready to switch teams, the huddle is a new emergency bonding measure to help guard against further defections.

The HEAT results are posted on the Internet. Carlao loses by a unanimous decision to Wiuff. The wrestler beat the Jiu-Jitsu fighter. Carlao couldn't prevent Wiuff from taking him down, says a report, and was unable to work any submissions from the guard. I wonder how he will feel about the loss and imagine that as an outgoing, happy-go-lucky type of person he probably won't be brooding unnecessarily over it.

I pay Top Team a visit and sit on a bench watching Ze Mario spar. He has a fight coming up against Yuki Kondo in Pride on New Year's Eve. Today he is sparring with Minowa, a well-known Japanese fighter. The pair twist, slip and spin on the ground. Afterwards Ze Mario stands against the blue matting that covers the far wall. He then sits down, leaving a glistening smear of sweat behind him. It's like the crime scene created by the murder of a waterbed. Carlao arrives wearing sunglasses. He walks with a slight limp. Everyone greets him enthusiastically – more enthusiastically than usual in fact.

Carlao takes off his sunglasses. He has stitching in the eyebrow area above both eyes, and black patches underneath them. He describes his fight in both Portuguese and the universal acting-out language of men describing a recent altercation. He keeps describing Wiuff as 'very strong' and punching the palm of his hand. Ze Mario comes across from the far wall. Carlao enlists me to help act out what happened for his sake. On Carlao's instructions, I clinch with him over-under – each of us has one arm snaked under each other's armpit and the other over the arm on the other side. Carlao switches to a bearhug, then breaks from our clinch completely to mime what happened next. He lifts an imaginary opponent off the ground and puts them down on the mat.

'Is this what you did to him, or he did to you?' I ask.

'He did to me,' replies Carlao.

He goes and sits in the corner on a white plastic chair. I sit on the mat beside him to talk further about the fight.

'All he did was ground and pound, ground and pound,' says Carlao. 'He didn't try to pass my guard.'

This means Wiuff's strategy was to take Carlao to the ground and then attempt to hit him without trying to break free from between Carlao's legs and pin him. Passing the guard is technically difficult, though the reward is huge. Once past the guard, you are no longer in danger of being submitted and can maybe kneel on your opponent's chest, a position called the 'mount', from which it is relatively easy to punch your opponent in the face or change position and submit him with an armlock. The skill of maintaining the guard is at the heart of Gracie Jiu-Jitsu, and it is virtually impossible to pass the guard of someone like Carlao. However, a while back it dawned on MMA fighters that as long as they were vigilant and avoided being submitted or spun onto their backs, they could safely stay within their opponent's guard and try to punch his head and body – ground and pound. Suddenly, passing the guard was no longer considered all-important.

'I tried to go for armlock on the ground but he was very strong,' continues Carlao. He flexes his own arm to illustrate.

Beforehand Carlao characterised the fight as a struggle between Jiu-Jitsu and wrestling. He concludes that he has been neglecting his Jiu-Jitsu and needs to go back to basics and drill submitting opponents from the guard. My conclusion, on the other hand, is that he would have profited from a better grasp of wrestling, because the arts of stopping your opponent from locking his hands around you – or from lifting you off the ground once he has – are basic wrestling skills.

I'm about to go upstairs to Gracie Barra when I notice that Babalu, the Magnetic North of the Gym, is sitting on a stool at the snack bar next to the pool. He's wearing a black singlet with 'Bad Azz Muthafucka' written on it – which, in his case, is an accurate self-assessment – and reading *O Globo*. I pull up a stool next to him, introduce myself, and ask him questions about his life and career as a fighter. I want to see whether I can glean any clues about where his incredible aura comes from.

Babalu speaks more softly than I anticipated, and apologises for his English. He is 28, he says, and got into Bruce Lee and Jean-Claude Van Damme films as a kid, which inspired him to take up martial arts. He started Thai boxing at 12, and Luta Livre and wrestling when he was 16. He was a good swimmer as well, and his parents wanted him to be a professional swimming coach, not a fighter. By the age of 18, he was training a lot. He did a year's national service, which he says toughened him up and made him more mature and responsible. When he was 23, he fought three times in one night at a MMA tournament in Brazil. However, that was not as great an ordeal as being a parachutist, he says.

'You know, I was not very scared, because parachutes much more scary than all the fights. You can fight against a bear, no problem at all. Jungle survival training in Pantanal was the worst part. PoW training is very tough, because people beat you, shock you.' He mimes receiving an electric shock.

'So going in the ring and fighting three times in one night is easy by comparison?'

'Not easy, but easier.'

He won that tournament and fought more, but last year he came close to giving up fighting altogether.

'I didn't know whether it's right or wrong to hit people in the face,' he says.

He explains that he really battered Elvis Sinosic, an Australian fighter, in UFC 38, which was held in London in July 2002. He felt bad about it afterwards and pondered whether he was doing the right thing in life.

'Like, I stop fighting and think about this, because I'm Catholic and I don't know if Jesus Christ think it's right or wrong for me to fight. I stop fighting for six months, but I was unhappy, you know. I thought, I'm a fighter, I'm born to fight, I need to fight again – because it's my life, you know.'

'You decided that Jesus Christ doesn't mind you hitting people in the face?'

'Jesus Christ said also, I think, if you are born to do something, you are born to do something. I don't think it's wrong any more, because I was born to do this. I do it with my heart – I love to do this.'

'Now, when you fight, would you rather beat someone with submissions than hit them or do you feel—'

Babalu stubs out the end of my question with a frank admission.

'I go to kill. If the referee don't stop the fight, I kill the guy.'

'That's how you feel now? But Jesus wouldn't like that.'

'I know, but this is my life. I'm not happy unless I do this. I tried the other way.'

I ask him what the tattoo across his back says. He turns and lifts his singlet to reveal it. Psalm 23.4: 'Yea, though I walk through the valley of the shadow of death, I will fear no evil: for thou art with me.'

I leave Babalu and go to Juice Co, a juice bar and restaurant near Fit Express. A snow-boarding video is on the TV monitor inside. Crates of wheatgrass are stacked on a shelf behind the counter. I order a pineapple and mint juice, and go and sit outside. The air-con unit whirrs loudly. I feel troubled by what Babalu has just said. I don't know how literally to take the idea that his intent is to kill opponents unless the referee stops the fight. I doubt he would really want to kill anybody and reason that this must be his new mantra to ensure maximum commitment in the ring following a period of self-doubt and self-reproach. I hope it's just a visualisation technique to ensure follow-through. I think about the tension between faith and fighting. Babalu's solution to the conundrum is to believe

Jesus wants him to fight, to do what he has to do, to be who he is – which means, on a profound level, everything inside him is aligned, which means in turn that he can enter the ring with real conviction, confidence and strength.

Babalu said he was born to fight – and he certainly looks like he was. Men in general are born to fight, too, though they don't have to necessarily fight in MMA matches to answer that need. Some people, like Babalu, feel a compulsion to fight more acutely than others and some, like him, are also better at it. Though I don't know my New Testament, I doubt even an oblique justification for fighting can really be found there. It is biology that compels us to fight – and fighting can therefore feel like it is our destiny, which in turn can be confused with a religious calling. I don't begrudge Babalu his invocation of Jesus to justify fighting, but instead begrudge Christianity for not offering role models whom we can take inspiration from when we navigate this area of life in our twenties. Were Babalu to have lived in Ancient Greece, he could have found convergence between his natural urge to fight and his spiritual needs through the worship of the gods Herakles or Hermes. By contrast, Jesus has nothing to say to men who want to test themselves against one another in physical contests.

I return to Gracie Barra to watch the Vale Tudo team's stand-up session. The fighters wear large gloves and execute combinations of kicks and punches on hand-held pads. The noise of leathery thwacks and splats is like the sound of twenty basketballs bouncing erratically on a court. A gloved fighter asks me to undo the zip of his bag so he can get a kneepad; another trots over a couple of times to ask me to retie the laces of his gloves. Though these are tough men and one has murder in mind, sometimes they are demoted to the helplessness of toddlers.

Ze Mario loses to Yuki Kondo in Pride on New Year's Eve. The referee stops the fight due to a cut. I give Ze Mario a call a few days after his return from Japan.

'Sorry to hear about the fight.'

'Oh, no problem.'

'Are you going to rest for now or still train?'

'I did already. I train again tomorrow, one o'clock.'

The following day I visit Top Team to see Ze Mario. He comes over to talk and turns his head to show the cut in his left eyebrow. He had the stitches taken out earlier in the day. The eye is bloodshot.

'Ten stitches,' says Ze Mario. 'It was a deep cut, man. I couldn't see. He kneed me from half-guard. The knee went through my hands.'

The doctor looked at the cut and declared that Ze Mario couldn't continue. Ze Mario thought he could – until he heard the audience reaction as they saw the cut, and so began to wonder himself. Murilo Bustamante was in his corner.

'Murilo said, "He can continue, he can continue," but when he saw the cut' – Ze Mario affects an expression of severe concern – 'he said, "Maybe not."'

'It's not a good way for a fight to end,' I say. What I mean is that it would be better to resolve the fight properly by knockout or submission rather than inconclusively with a cut.

'Eeeech, what can we do? Only thing we can do is train more and get better.'

He turns, shouts 'Let's work!' to the others, and starts the training session. Later Ze Mario acts out what happened for everyone's benefit. He plays Yuki Kondo. His sparring partner, playing Ze Mario, lies on his back and adopts half-guard, a position where instead of wrapping your legs around your opponent's back you wrap them around one of their legs. This is still a good position in Jiu-Jitsu, but in MMA competitions such as Pride, which allows the kicking and kneeing of an opponent on the ground, you are vulnerable to being kneed in the head by the free leg – which is exactly what happened to Ze Mario. He demonstrates by bringing his knee up and then down on his sparring partner's face.

'Boom!'

I chat idly to Carlao, who is also training today, and ask whether he ever used to fight in the street when he was growing up.

'Yes, I used to be a *torcedor*,' he says.

I don't know what the word means. We look it up in a dictionary. It means 'supporter' – football supporter in this context.

'This when I was a teenager,' says Carlao. 'I support Flamengo.'

He acts out what he and other Flamengo fans used to do. He punches his hand, stomps on the ground and swings an imaginary plank or bat.

'We fought with wood,' he affirms.

'So you were a football hooligan?'

'No, not a football hooligan, a *torcedor* – a football supporter.'

Carlao gets up to spar. Gracie Jiu-Jitsu is a unique language of grappling. In the overwhelming majority of wrestling styles, a bout starts with both wrestlers standing, but Gracie Jiu-Jitsu fighters usually commence sparring either seated, kneeling or lying on their backs. Carlao's opponent lies on his back with his head up to monitor Carlao's movements. He probes with his feet, uses them to push Carlao away, hooks them behind Carlao's legs and creates barriers with his shins.

The game he is playing is called 'open guard'. Instead of wrapping your legs around an opponent's back, 'closed guard', you actively use your legs and feet like an extra pair of arms and hands to control and frustrate him. Those skilled at open guard can use their feet to help spin an opponent 180 degrees and turn him on his back, a manoeuvre called a 'sweep'. Carlao wants to steal past his opponent's legs – pass the guard – and pin him chest-to-chest or gain the mount position. He either kneels or stands and uses his hands to try to control his opponent's legs and move beyond them. His opponent turns and swivels and always keeps the barriers of either his legs, or arms, or both, in Carlao's way. Even if Carlao does control and pass one leg, while trying to control and pass the other he loses control of the first – which is re-deployed in his way.

Just watching this happen is frustrating and draining. Trying to pass the guard can be like entering a hurdle race that follows a cartoon logic: every time you jump one hurdle and sprint towards the next, someone comes round behind you to pick up the first hurdle and set it down again further along the track. You end up having to hurdle the same hurdles again and again *ad infinitum*. This is what grappling would be like in a Kafka novel.

After fifteen minutes' sparring, Carlao has failed to hurdle his opponent's legs. He comes and sits down on the bench to rest, chest heaving.

'Does it not make you frustrated when you spend so much time trying to pass the guard?'

'I know. But this guy has the best guard, the best submissions, the best everything.'

Chapter 16

Snake Handling

Towering above Barra is a mountain called Pedra Da Gavea. Jungle clings to the slopes and a path through the jungle leads up the mountainside. Jiu-Jitsu fighters often hike up Pedra Da Gavea to develop endurance just before a competition. Carlinhos Gracie does the hike every Saturday morning and considers it a test of endurance and character. The ascent becomes steep and difficult in places. Tangles of roots criss-cross the path. At one point you have to pull yourself up a steep rock face by a cord.

Carlinhos is tall, slim and long-limbed – in other words, designed for hiking. I am of medium height and stocky – in other words, not designed for hiking. I was moved to reflect upon these two facts when I did the climb with Carlinhos and others from Gracie Barra the last time I was in Rio. I remember being directly behind Carlinhos to begin with, then that his ankles were at my eye level as he took deliberate steps through the roots and undergrowth, then seeing snatches of him up ahead between the trees, a ghostly shape in a white T-shirt, then not being able to see him at all. I sweated so much during the hike that afterwards I looked like I'd swum in my clothes.

When I reached Turtle Rock, the finishing point, Carlinhos was sitting with the others. He called over and executed a waggling steerhorn hand gesture to acknowledge that I'd made it. The steerhorn hand gesture is popular in surf culture, which, in the Venn diagram of subcultures in Rio, overlaps with Jiu-Jitsu culture. You clench the middle three fingers of your hand, and extend the thumb and little finger. I took the fact that Carlinhos added a waggle to the steerhorn hand gesture to signify he wanted to make a particular effort to congratulate me for finishing the hike, as earlier I'd said I was only going to come along to watch. Maybe Carlinhos would have injected even more waggle into the waggling steerhorn hand gesture had he known that I finished the climb through willpower alone. I was nowhere near being in good enough shape for the hike and was breathing hard 95 per cent of the way. It took so much out of me that I was ill for two days afterwards.

When I was last in Rio, I felt Carlinhos was a little wary of me to begin with. He was friendly and hospitable, but I also sensed that he was trying to gauge me. One night at the academy, I was sitting and watching the class and taking notes while Carlinhos stretched nearby.

'Why don't you do?' he asked.

I said I would and trained the next time. I intended to train anyway, but hadn't up to that point. Of course, Carlinhos wanted me to experience Gracie Jiu-Jitsu as an aid to understanding, but maybe he also wanted to see how I performed, because he wanted to know who I really was. Carlinhos struck me as a watcher. During classes he would often sit quietly and apparently take a back seat. But I got the feeling that he missed nothing that happened in that room. I sensed he was assessing everyone all the time by their actions and behaviour on the mats. I got the impression that he sees Jiu-Jitsu as a test that reveals who you really are, like the climb up Pedra Da Gavea, and he is only comfortable when he can come to know you by your actions.

After I had been training at Gracie Barra for a while, Carlinhos was willing to talk to me about himself, his family and Gracie Jiu-Jitsu. Beforehand, I considered him to be fairly introverted, but when he spoke about his family he became demonstrative and passionate. What he said was a revelation. Carlos, his father, the founder of Gracie Jiu-Jitsu, was a deeply spiritual man – 'like a monk', he said. Carlos believed in reincarnation. He believed he had come to Earth in his present incarnation to spread Jiu-Jitsu, which he considered to be hugely beneficial because it improved people's health, steered them away from bad habits, gave them confidence, helped them to mature socially, and developed their spirit. For Carlos, Jiu-Jitsu had profound value. Carlinhos said that he, too, believes in reincarnation – and, his mission, too, is to spread Gracie Jiu-Jitsu. He wasn't born into the Gracie family for nothing, he maintained. As Gracies, he said, 'Our goal in this life is to be in the Jiu-Jitsu way no matter what.' Gracies who remain within Jiu-Jitsu make a success of their lives, while those who leave Jiu-Jitsu – Carlinhos didn't mince his words – 'their lives are shit'.

During the initial period of intense interest in the Gracie family that followed the first UFCs, people outside Brazil were led to believe that Carlos's brother Helio, who is Royce and Rorion's father, was largely responsible for Gracie Jiu-Jitsu, but that is not the case. If Gracie Jiu-Jitsu were a religion, Carlos Gracie, not Helio, would be its messiah. He was the man with a vision who had a profound teaching to share. He was the prime mover. Helio played a very significant role in the development and popularisation of Gracie Jiu-Jitsu, but it was Carlos's conception. An understanding of Carlos is key to understanding the Gracie family story and mission.

I walk over to the jungly base of Pedra Da Gavea. Near the start of the mountain track is another path that peels away to a waterfall. I take that trail now. The sweet smell of rotting jackfruit is overwhelming. Each festering fruit supports a community of flies. A troop of capuchin monkeys thrash about in the treetops nearby. Down by the waterfall, I sit on a rock near the pool, and take out and read a brief sketch of Carlos's life largely composed on the basis of interviews with Carlinhos and his brother Rilion, who teaches in Leblon:

The Gracie family are of Scots descent and originally lived in Belem in Para state. Carlos was born in 1902. He was the first of five brothers and three sisters. As a child he was small but brave. He was hyper and had a lot of energy, and was always on the look-out for adventure and challenges. He was mischievous, and would throw stones then run away before anyone could catch him – he was a good sprinter. There were a lot of mango trees in the street where Carlos lived. He told people that the mangoes were his and threw stones at anyone he saw picking them.

I stop reading for a moment and visualise Carlos as a boy – territorial, boisterous, athletic, aggressive, combative – then continue.

In later life Carlos would describe himself as having been a problem child. He wasn't malicious, but he was a handful and he made enemies. If he had continued to behave the same way, he didn't know what would have happened to him. Perhaps he would have even ended up dead. When he was in his teens, Carlos was taught grappling techniques by a Japanese teacher, Mitsuyo Maeda. Jiu-Jitsu saved his life, Carlos would later say.

I pause again. Presumably Carlos told his sons these stories about himself. He cast his life as having followed a classic pattern: he was the archetypal aggressive youth who found a useful and productive way to channel his energies when he took up a challenging physical discipline. Jiu-Jitsu soaked up his energy and aggression like a sponge soaks up water, and gave his life direction and structure.

The story goes on:

During one of the first classes, Maeda wanted to demonstrate the power of strangles by putting a volunteer to sleep. Only Carlos offered to be strangled. Maeda said he would demonstrate on anyone other than him, as he could already tell that Carlos was going to be a champion, and a future champion should not begin his career by being strangled unconscious. Carlos became Maeda's favourite. Maeda taught him as though he were his own son. Carlos would arrive early for class and receive special teaching.

Maeda taught Carlos during a period of four or five years, and Carlos taught Jiu-Jitsu to his brothers Osvaldo, Gastao, Jorge and Helio. Because the brothers were physically small, they concentrated on developing good defensive technique. They invented their own moves and modified techniques Maeda taught them, and in that way created an art with a distinct character of its own, which they called 'Gracie Jiu-Jitsu'.

Carlos taught Jiu-Jitsu for a living, and opened his first academy in the 1920s in Rio. When he arrived at a new place to teach, people would often take one look at him, see how skinny he was and question his ability as a fighter. He would frequently have to prove both himself and the effectiveness of Gracie Jiu-Jitsu in challenge matches. Sometimes these encounters were grappling contests, but sometimes striking was allowed, because people were convinced that they could beat Carlos if they were allowed to hit. Such contests were known as 'Vale Tudo' matches. Carlos's brothers also fought challenge matches. When Carlos and his brothers beat their challengers, the reputation of Gracie Jiu-Jitsu naturally grew.

Carlos's youngest brother, Helio, became his most important protégé. Helio was the instrument through which Carlos continued to spread Gracie Jiu-Jitsu as he got older, and Helio was like a son to Carlos. Carlos would tell him how to train, what to focus upon, how to live, how many hours to sleep at night, and what to eat. Helio was – and is – highly disciplined and used to be utterly devoted to his brother. He became Gracie Jiu-Jitsu's standard-bearer and fought a series of highly publicised matches in the 1930s, 1940s and 1950s that did much to popularise the art in Brazil. He became a focus of national pride, and played a significant role in the technical development of Gracie Jiu-Jitsu, particularly its defensive techniques.

Carlos mellowed as he grew older. He was a seeker and deeply concerned by spiritual matters. He believed in the power of the will and maintained that you must train your mind to control desire. He saw desire as like a horse that needs to be broken in. He developed willpower by doing things like going on a retreat in the mountains for a month and rigidly following a set schedule. For instance, he might wake up at five in the morning no matter what and go and jump in a lake of cold water just to discipline his mind. Carlos also meditated and said that if you learnt how to switch off your conscious mind you could learn everything you needed to know. Sometimes people would ask him questions and he would later provide them with an answer revealed to him during meditation. Carlos was a highly principled man. He was firmly anti-abortion and did not believe in contraception. In total, he had 21 children by seven women.

He was also deeply interested in nutrition. When he was young, he suffered from a lot of health problems, including migraines. No doctor could help. One day he came across a book that quoted Hippocrates: 'Make your food your medicine.' The phrase struck him like a bolt of lightning. He studied nutrition and cured himself by changing his eating habits. He eventually developed a sophisticated diet based in part on the principle of food-combining, which is known as the Gracie Diet. In his later years, he was consulted by people with health problems, which he treated through nutrition and the use of herbs.

Carlos's son Rolls took over the leadership of the Gracie clan from his father. By all accounts he was charismatic, magnetic and fearless. Tragically, however, he died early, aged only 33, in a hang-gliding accident in 1982. The Gracie clan has effectively been without a leader since. Carlos himself died in 1993.

I put the summary down, fold my arms and think. Carlos clearly had a philosophy of how to live. He saw the bigger picture. For him, Jiu-Jitsu was about a lot more than chokes and armlocks. It was at the centre of a way of life. He had an approach to diet and health, a belief in willpower, a method for taming desire. He saw Jiu-Jitsu as a spiritual enterprise as well as a technical one. He was a man of wisdom who did his own research into grappling, nutrition and health, and formulated and transmitted his own ideas. He is just the kind of person a new movement needs to have in charge: charismatic, altruistic, philosophical, profound, practical. Yet when I look around Rio

today, I don't see a Jiu-Jitsu that has much to do with Carlos
Gracie's ideas. Maybe Carlos never found an effective enough
way to transmit his philosophy alongside the techniques of Jiu-
Jitsu. Or perhaps he considered his philosophy to be purely
personal, and did not make any attempt to systematise it and
teach it to others. Maybe, maybe not.

Even if he did try to transmit his philosophy, the Gracie clan
splintered after his death and the death of Rolls, which means
lines of communication down which any central philosophy
could be transmitted were broken. The world has moved on
since Carlos's era anyway. Concepts such as meditation and
controlling desire appear musty and old-fashioned. Today the
Gracies trade on technical sophistication, which in itself is
significant and valuable, but they have no overarching ethical
or spiritual philosophy. Which is not to say Jiu-Jitsu doesn't
play a constructive role in people's lives – Carlinhos often talks
about how it gives people confidence and self-respect, and steers
them away from bad habits like drinking and smoking – yet,
philosophically, everything is loose and unstructured, and the
Gracie movement's social value is diminished as a consequence.

I take out an issue of *Tatame* magazine, which covers Jiu-Jitsu
and MMA. The backcover ad for Rags Fightwear says a lot
about the Jiu-Jitsu scene today. A photo shows a tattooed
fighter standing wearing surf shorts and sunglasses on the
breakwater at Barra. Four good-looking women in bikinis
surround him. Two stand beside him with a hand on his
shoulders, while the other two kneel at his feet. One embraces
his thigh. A fierce-looking Rottweiler sits obediently in front of
the fighter, who controls it with a short leash. The ad's
underlying message is simple. Dogs are admired for being
game fighters and are Jiu-Jitsu's totemic animal, so the
Rottweiler stands for the toughness and aggression of the
fighter himself. The women, of course, are trophies who are
throwing themselves at him. The ad is saying, 'Do this' – ie,
fight – 'and you get this' – women. Women love fighters: the
human rutting principle in operation.

The slopes around where I'm sitting used to be a coffee
plantation. You can see the ruins of a plantation building in the
undergrowth near the road. Today it's jungle. Perhaps what has
happened to Gracie Jiu-Jitsu can be compared with what has

happened on this mountainside. Carlos wanted to cultivate Jiu-Jitsu for higher purposes, yet it has reverted back to a state dictated by nature.

The first time I heard about Joe was when a senior Gracie Barra black belt asked what the words 'wanky' and 'ballocks' meant. He said a crazy guy from Birmingham was staying with him at his apartment who was using the vocabulary. I corrected his English and gave him definitions – as well as teaching him the all-important auxiliary hand signal for use in conjunction with the first word. I met Joe at Gracie Barra that night. It turned out he came from Yorkshire, not Birmingham. As the only Englishmen at the club, we gravitated towards one another and became friends. Over the following days I learnt that Joe's goal was to become the first British black belt, and that he was single-minded about his training and hated anything getting in the way. Carnival, for instance, was a big irritant as it meant the gym was closed for more than a week while everyone flew up to Bahia to party.

'I'm not interested in seeing women shaking their boobies and stood on floats with feathers in their hair,' affirmed Joe – which, when he put it like that, it was difficult to see why not.

Joe flies into Rio again and we meet at Gracie Barra one night. He is annoyed because he can't train for the time being, as he has a bad case of mat burn. I look down at the big toe on his left foot. There are two nasty, weeping wounds from where the mat has scraped away the skin.

'That looks really bad,' I say.

'My doctor asked me whether I'd been bitten by a snake,' recounts Joe, incredulously. 'In Yorkshire!'

He doesn't want to take the antibiotics the doctor prescribed unless it's completely necessary. For now he is trying to heal the wounds with the aid of willpower.

'I lie awake at night staring at them intensely saying, "Die, you bastards, die!"'

I join in the training session, while Joe sits and watches. During sparring I am paired off with a young white belt. He grips the end of my sleeve, twists his hand to make the grip tighter and pulls. At the same time he pushes my bicep away with a foot and places the other on my hip. I pass his guard a few times, but can't submit him. I then make the basic error of trying to pass his guard with only one arm. He instantly puts on a triangle-choke, squeezing my head into a tight package to strangle me (the terms 'choke' and 'strangle' are often used interchangeably though they are really different things). I hear little cracks in my neck and head as he squeezes and squeezes. The hold feels too tight for me to escape. My head pounds.

I click a mental shutter to take a picture of this moment so that I will have it ready in my mind next time. When you haven't trained submissions-style for a while, you need to refamiliarise yourself with what it feels like to be at the point where it's time to give in and tap. You need to submit at the right moment – neither too late nor too soon. Tap too early, and you will reproach yourself for not having fully explored the possibilities of escape; stubbornly wait too long and you end up fighting a lost cause and could be harmed unnecessarily or, in the case of a choke, pass out.

My opponent grasps the back of my head with his hands to squeeze my head further. I'm just about to tap when I feel him relax the hold a little – he's obviously losing heart and can't tell how close I am to giving in. I take advantage by turning side-on, ducking my head out of the pit of his knee and pinning him. Now I'm in control. I move around his head and pin him from the other side, then figure-four lock his far arm and crank it, but he has supple joints and doesn't tap. Time is called without either of us having submitted the other. I take my jacket off – semaphore that I'm done.

After the class, Joe and I go to eat at Guaranamania, a Jiu-Jitsu haunt a couple of minutes' walk away from the gym. We sit at a table outside and order food and coconut water. We talk about Jiu-Jitsu, fighting and just generally catch up. I am only really a tourist at Gracie Barra, but Joe is fully committed to the Gracie Jiu-Jitsu path of training and as much of an insider at Gracie Barra as a gringo can ever be. He is a protagonist in the drama of training at Gracie Barra, while I'm just watching it from the stalls. He says he feels he was only really accepted there after Roger Gracie broke his finger in sparring – as though an informal initiation policy operates that, like initiation policies the world over, involves the disciple having to go through pain or suffer injury before they can join the group.

Joe recounts how he got into Gracie Jiu-Jitsu in the first place. During his early twenties, he just smoked, drank and held parties with the other guys in his house. One day, for fun, he suggested to a friend he used to box with as a kid that they should have a boxing session. They bought gloves and had a go, but within minutes were exhausted and wheezing. Both of them resolved never to smoke again. Joe started doing a bit of boxing training but then saw the first UFC, which introduced him to Royce Gracie and Gracie Jiu-Jitsu and inspired him to go down a different path. That path eventually brought him here, to Rio, to learn Gracie Jiu-Jitsu from the masters.

'I always wanted to be part of something like the army – but not the army – but to be part of something big that is always with you,' says Joe.

He found that something in the shape of Gracie Jiu-Jitsu and Gracie Barra. He's a lone monkey who has been accepted into a troop. Though I don't tell him, I, too, have often felt the same urge to be part of something bigger – a mafia, team, squad or brotherhood that is bonded through physical action. It's just that I've never found the right troop for me.

Wallid Ismail says to call him at 10am tomorrow for directions to the gym of his new team, Brasil Dojo.

'It's a little complicated,' he states.

The following morning, I call as arranged from a public phone near Academia Da Praia, a fitness centre for beautiful people in Barra where a lot of fighters work out.

'If it's difficult to find, why don't we meet beforehand outside Academia Da Praia?' I say.

'OK, I'll pick you up there in half an hour.'

To kill time, I walk round to the Academia and check my emails on the computer in the lobby. Coincidentally, Bebeo, one of the leaders of Top Team, is there. I'm not sure exactly why, but Wallid and Bebeo are currently having a spat. Wallid antagonised Top Team by approaching and, in two cases, poaching personnel – Darrell Gholar, Paulo Filho – for his team, which must be a big contributory factor. Bebeo has challenged Brasil Dojo to a match against Top Team, but so far nothing has been arranged. Wallid knows Bebeo and the rest of the Top Team crew from the days when they trained together with Carlson Gracie. He stayed with Carlson when the others split. Wallid is well known for his talent for antagonising people. He is the shock-jock of Jiu-Jitsu, an opinionated and shameless self-promoter who is always at the centre of some controversy or other.

I wonder whether I should try to engineer an encounter between Wallid and Bebeo when he arrives. Maybe they hate each other enough to fight right here and now. I could then stand back, notebook in hand, and record every nuance of what happens for the sake of gaining a greater understanding of the anthropology of feuding within Jiu-Jitsu. On the other hand, Bebeo doesn't strike me as the impetuous, volatile type who would be provoked easily – or would readily provoke someone else – and, besides, there is something fundamentally wrong about going out of your way to try to engineer a scuffle. It is tempting though.

In the end Wallid forces the situation. He doesn't get out of his big dusty black Citroën but instead parks it right in front of the Academia and waves for me to come over. He has a big oval head, shaved hair, caterpillar eyebrows and sticky-out ears so heroically mangled they make you smile spontaneously every time you look at them. I get in the passenger seat and we drive off. Our destination, The House, is not far. It has a discreet entrance with a large, anonymous security gate. The story goes that the place is owned by a rich businessman who likes to keep his identity a secret. He likes fighters, apparently, and lets them use the facility in his grounds, but doesn't want any publicity for himself.

We pass through the gate, get out the car and enter the workout rooms. I hear the distinctive gruff, booming voice of Darrell Gholar barking wrestling instructions. About fifteen sweaty, tattooed fighters drill technique in the small mat room. Wallid and I continue past the exercise equipment to the back room, which houses a ring. We sit in a bay window next to a stack of pads and gloves. Wallid extends his legs and rests his two mobile phones by his side.

I ask Wallid about his early life. He says he grew up in

Manaus, the capital of Amazon state in the north. As a kid he
was crazy, he says.

'I fight almost every day in the street. The guy shoot me, the
guys. . .' he breaks off and makes a stabbing motion. 'I was very
fat when I was a kid. A crazy fat guy.'

Jiu-Jitsu, says Wallid, had a calming effect on him. He never
fought again in the street after he took it up. He first came to
Rio when he was 14. He relates how it took him three days and
nights to travel here by bus, and that he slept in the gym. You
get the feeling that this is an oft-repeated story and a central
part of his personal mythology. He joined Carlson Gracie's
school in Copacabana and is still loyal to Carlson, the black
sheep of the Gracie family who now lives and teaches in
Chicago. Wallid says he was never the most talented fighter, but
he had a lot of heart and always trained hard. I ask him how he
got the ears.

'I train the whole day. When I have a problem with my ears
Carlson say, "Hey, you stop training for one or two weeks." I
say, "Why? I'm not going to be top model. I gonna be a fighter.
I don't care about my ears."'

Somehow we get onto the subject of Wallid's run-ins with the
Gracies. You get the impression the subject is never far from the
surface. Wallid's victories over Gracies are his biggest claims to
fame. He says he was the first person to take them on and
prove that they are not invincible – though this is not strictly
true: to begin with, Helio Gracie was beaten twice during his
career. Wallid claims four Gracies as scalps. He has beaten
Ralph and Renzo on points in Jiu-Jitsu matches, and logs an
altercation he says he won against Ryan Gracie that took place
during a fashion show in Sao Paulo as a further victory. His
version of events is that Ryan came to punch him from behind,
he sensed the attack, got out the way and choked Ryan
unconscious. A win against Royce represents his most spectacular victory over a Gracie. Trading on the reputation he'd
established in the UFC, Royce returned to Rio from the States
to challenge all-comers to a Jiu-Jitsu match. Wallid accepted,
and the bout was held in a stadium on Copacabana Beach in
1998. It ended in humiliation for Royce. Ten thousand people
watched Wallid strangle him with his own collar after only five
minutes. He passed out rather than tap. Afterwards, Wallid was

scathing towards Royce. You get the impression that he is not the Gracies' favourite person in the world.

'Do you still have differences or a vendetta against the Gracies?'

'No, now is fine. Now is OK.'

'But back then you didn't like the fact that they claimed to be the best in the world?'

'All the time it made me pissed off.'

Wallid says that he is less outspoken on the subject than he used to be. If we had talked three years ago about the Gracies, he would have had a lot more to say on the subject, but now his philosophy is more 'live and let live'. The new climate of professionalism has had a calming effect on Wallid as well as everyone else. He is preoccupied with the business opportunities created by the boom in MMA, and talks about himself as a promoter and businessman. Last year he co-promoted a big MMA event in the Amazon, Jungle Fight, with Antonio Inoki, a well-known Japanese pro wrestler and politician, and he plans to hold more Jungle Fight events – maybe in Japan or even China – as well as develop his new team. It's as though he used to be a private fighting from the trenches, but now he's promoted himself to the rank of a general organising large troop movements away from the front line.

'Before, I'm so crazy, you know what I mean? I challenge everybody, I fight, I wanna war. Now I just want war when you want war with me. If you wanna war with me, let's go to war.'

He doesn't want to give the wrong impression, though. He doesn't want it to be thought that he has mellowed too much.

'Don't think, "Oh, Wallid is a nice guy." No, I'm a tough guy, you know what I mean? I'm a crazy guy.'

Actually, Wallid appears to be uncertain on this last point, and oscillates between considering himself crazy and more normal.

'No, I'm another guy right now. Before I be crazy, man. Before I always wanna fight somebody, I always wanna say I gonna beat you. If the guy beat me, OK, I don't care, but I go over. This is my main thing, you understand? I have the heart. This nobody can buy.'

I take his photo outside. He makes sure to change into a Brasil Dojo T-shirt to garner publicity for his new team.

Without prompting, he snaps into a series of tough-guy poses.
He stands frowning with fists cocked. He stands frowning with
arms folded. He stands frowning with his arms out and his
head tipped to the side a little. The frown is a big part of his
look.

I arrange to meet Joe outside Gracie Barra after training. We
have to meet outside the academy rather than inside because
we intend to effect an illicit transaction. I need a new kimono
and Joe has sourced a Koral-brand one at a good price through
a Jiu-Jitsu contact. The problem is that Gracie Barra has a new
policy that says everyone who buys a new kimono has to buy
one through them – and it has to have Gracie Barra team
patches. But by nature I don't like uniforms and I don't want
to wear team colours either as I consider myself a neutral. Joe
and I sit at a table outside Juice Co. He places the Koral
kimono in a bag under the table. I need to try the kimono on to
see if it fits, but we don't want to be seen by anyone senior from
the academy while we find out.

'How should we do this?' I ask him.

'Oh fuck it,' he says. 'This isn't a drugs deal.'

He takes the kimono out of the bag and passes the jacket
over. I try it on. It seems to fit well.

'Does it look like it fits to you?' I ask Joe.

'Yeah, it does. It looks good.'

I take the jacket off.

'Put it in your bag just to be safe,' says Joe.

It's a good thing I do, because afterwards we're eating in
Guaranamania when Carlinhos and Marcio come and greet us
on their way to the sushi restaurant upstairs. I smile nervously
as Carlinhos slaps me on the shoulder. This must be how drug
mules feel when they pass through Customs.

I try the jacket and trousers on properly back in my room.
They're a perfect fit. I look at myself in a mirror. Koral is one of
the best brands. It feels good to be wearing a pukka piece
of Brazilian Jiu-Jitsu kit. Up till now I've been making do with
an old judo outfit, and for the first time I feel like I really look
the part. I tell Joe this when we've reconvened at Juice Co the
next day.

'Did you sleep in it?' he asks, laughing. 'Did you knock one off in it?'

I look forward to blooding the new kimono on the mats and bring it to a Friday evening session at Gracie Barra. Strangely, everyone is wearing surf shorts. No one else appears to have brought their kimono. Arroz is taking the lesson.

'Arroz, is this a kimono class?'

'No,' he says. 'From now on it's without kimono on Friday.'

MRVT suffers another round of defections. This time more than ten MRVT team members leave for Gracie Barra. Among them is Ximu, one of their best prospects. It's a huge blow for MRVT. I visit the Flamengo gym one morning and speak to Roberto Leitao Snr. As before, he puts on a brave face.

'Ximu phoned me last night,' he says. 'He said the training no good. They don't' – he holds his arms up – 'fight.'

'So maybe he wants to come back.'

'I don't think Marco and Pedro accept,' retorts Roberto.

Pedro Rizzo is at the gym. He is MRVT's best fighter and is well known worldwide in MMA. His contract has run out with the UFC and he now intends to fight in Japan, perhaps in Pride. Pedro has a hard and sour pugilist's face. He likes to kick the legs of opponents – a strategy that originates from Thai boxing. The idea of being kicked by Pedro's legs is too painful to contemplate. Taken together his quad and hamstring muscles are the size and shape of a young child swinging in a hammock.

'I'd hate to be kicked by Pedro,' I tell Roberto.

'Even the guys that beat him go to the hospital,' he concurs.

'Why's that?'

'Because of the leg kicks.'

Roberto points to the part of his own leg where Pedro aims – just above the knee.

'If the guy's wearing wrestling boots, terrible,' he says.

'Why?'

To explain, Roberto acts out the scenario. He demonstrates how, if Pedro's opponent is not wearing boots, their leg moves when it's kicked, which, with an engineer's eye, he points out means they absorb less of the force. But if they make the

mistake of wearing wrestling boots, their leg is more bolted to
the floor, with the consequence that it will have to absorb more
of the power in the kick.

After a light training session, Pedro sits and chats with the
other fighters in the middle of the mat. I approach him and ask
about his leg kicks.

'Where do you aim for?'

'The ligaments here,' he says, touching his own thigh just
above the knee. 'I try to break the femur.'

'Is it true that your opponents have to go to hospital after
fighting you?'

'Yes, nearly always.'

'Why?'

'The muscles break here,' he says, pointing to the spot above
the knee again. 'After his fight with me, Kevin Randleman had
to have surgery because there was a hole in the muscle.
Because of that, he had to go down a weight category.'

'How do you feel about putting someone in hospital?'

'I don't go to kill, just to fight.'

He touches his nose: 'I've had my nose broken, too. It's a
sport.'

It is troubling to hear Pedro talk about breaking opponents'
legs. Again, as when Babalu said he would kill his opponent if
the referee did not stop the fight, I'm not sure whether it is
meant literally. Maybe Pedro uses the idea of breaking the leg
as a visualisation technique to ensure he kicks with maximum
power. But whether he intends to injure his opponents or not,
he says he does injure them – in one case he claims to have
done permanent damage by tearing the muscle.

I don't like the idea of a fighter going out to intentionally
injure an opponent. There are other aspects of MMA that are
unsettling. For one thing, Ze Mario being defeated in his Pride
fight with a knee to the head on the ground. Kneeing someone
in the head on the ground is a dishonourable thing to do,
whether the rules allow it or not, and it is also a technique that
requires little skill – though there is skill in getting into the
position where you're able to execute the technique. MMA
rules can be too liberal and pander too much to a wish to see

fights contested under as close to street conditions as possible.

A theory has been forming in my mind for some time that instead of inventing something bigger and better when you combine fighting arts to create MMA, perhaps you end up with something smaller and worse. Rules that allow hitting make a lot of grappling technique redundant. The crude but effective strategy of 'ground and pound' makes it unnecessary to pass the guard, a complex skill upon which Gracie Jiu-Jitsu is founded. A lot of Gracie Jiu-Jitsu technique is negated anyway because it relies on being able to hold the material of a kimono. Wrestling is abbreviated too. In amateur wrestling, you close and tie up with an opponent – in other words you take a hold of him, and he takes a hold of you. However, many wrestling tie-ups are made redundant by MMA rules, because your opponent can simply hit you if you are close. You are typically restricted to having to shoot for your opponent's legs from a distance, which is difficult to do without telegraphing your intention. Some takedowns place you in danger of being choked and are therefore risky. Many throws, particularly those where you turn your back to an opponent, are virtually out of the question because they also put you in too much danger. Nearly all the techniques for turning an opponent onto his back are irrelevant too, so the net effect is you end up having to throw away large swathes of grappling skills.

When I think about wrestling's relationship with MMA, I sometimes feel like the father of a daughter, Wrestling, who is unsure whether her brash new boyfriend, MMA, is entirely suitable for her. MMA supporters would counter that this is a distinct new sport with its own techniques and an ethic based on what works in reality, and that combative truth is more important than anything else. There is a lot of validity in that argument, but one of the advantages of ritualising fighting by including rules that disallow striking is that you create conditions in which fine skills can flourish and grow.

One afternoon I sit with Joe at a table outside Juice Co and we discuss the issue of how the rules of MMA negate a lot of technique. He thinks the same way too. On the other hand, we both agree that boxing is one art that could blossom within MMA competition. The variety of techniques open to bare-knuckle pugilists is far greater than the stereotypical jab, cross, uppercut and hook of modern boxing. Bare-knuckle fighters can hold and hit, strike with parts of the hand other than the knuckles, and they don't have big puffy gloves to hold in front of their faces, which means they have to be cagier in defence.

The MMA rules should encourage fighters to learn and refine skills unknown within boxing. Having boxed and witnessed bare-knuckle fights back in England, Joe knows all about the subject. He stands to demonstrate a pet boxing technique that he reckons would be useful in MMA. He jabs with the elbow unconventionally high, exposing his ribs. He asks me to stand too and take a stance. A pair of women in gymwear at a nearby table, drinking *cafezinhos*, look over quizzically. Joe doesn't notice them.

'I'll do it again,' he says. 'Then you throw a short right to my body and then a hook to my head.'

Before I can counter with the right-hook combination, Joe follows through from the jab with a shoulder butt that knocks me off-balance. My upper and lower teeth smack together uncomfortably.

'I've won six or seven fights like that,' says Joe. 'I used to ask me dad, "How did you jab, Dad?" He said, "Until they fell down, Son." He said. We should work on that technique next Saturday. You don't mind being banged in the face, do you? We're both ugly, so it doesn't matter.'

The story goes that Top Team fighter Allan Goes ended up in a coma after a fight against Alex Stiebling in Pride two years ago. Next time I'm at the Top Team gym I approach Allan, who is sitting on a bench and reading a magazine. He has powerful convex shoulders, and the back of his head and neck align from crown to collar. A large crucifix is tattooed on his right upper arm, and his surname is written on the tricep.

'Sit down on this side – I don't hear so good in one ear,' he says.

I ask Allan about the coma story. He says that it is untrue. Furthermore, he is upset that people tell this story because his career has been jeopardised as a result. He says he was hit flush on the chin, but the problem – whatever the problem was supposed to be, which I can't quite fathom from his account –

was not physical but emotional. He felt under a lot of pressure at the time of his fight against Stiebling. He'd lived the life of a playboy and had just had two children, by two different women, who were born at about the same time. He suddenly had to grow up and take responsibility for looking after his children. That responsibility weighed heavily on his shoulders during the fight.

'Today I'm psychologically way better, because I left the kid inside me behind and got together with the man.'

Allan recently fought in HEAT in Natal on the same bill as Carlao. His opponent was Ximu. He took the fight partly to prove to the world that nothing was wrong with him, but it ended in an unfortunate controversy and did nothing to help his career. Ximu tapped to Allan from an armlock but said he had actually stopped fighting at the time because the referee had called for the fighters to break a moment beforehand. Allan questions whether the referee really did call 'break' and says he heard nothing, so how could Ximu. But the referee said he did call 'break'. Whatever the truth, the fight did nothing to help Allan re-establish his career. He walked out the ring in disgust at the referee who duly awarded the fight to Ximu.

Allan used to be a leading MMA fighter. One of the sport's pioneers, he fought professionally for the first time in 1995. At the height of his career he was a regular in Pride. There is even a PlayStation 2 game, Pride FC, with Allan as a character. Now he is 32 and he hasn't fought in top-flight competition since he fought Stiebling. He lived in the States until recently but has returned to train with Top Team in Rio to try to get back on course. He is deeply frustrated by the state of his career. He speaks at length with raw emotion about his predicament, the damaging rumours about his health and how he has resolved to grow up, be a man, and support his children. He takes his responsibilities very seriously nowadays, he says.

'I born in the ghetto,' says Allan. 'I don't want to see my kids end up in the *favela*.'

'You're from a *favela*?'

'Yeah. I born in *favela* Dona Marta, one of the biggest.'

This comes as a surprise. Jiu-Jitsu is still predominantly a pursuit for those from better economic backgrounds, though within the last ten years the picture has started to change. Rio's *favelas*, or shanty towns, are ruled by gangs of drugs dealers. The gangs fight one another for control of the drugs trade, which is conducted through points on the outskirts of the *favela*, each of which is called a *boca-de-fumo*. The violence can be shocking. People are frequently killed in crossfire, or during the shooting when the police storm in to try to catch gang members.

'I used to wake up in the morning and sometimes couldn't even go home, because the drugs dealers were fighting. You cannot go home, you've got to wait. Many times I slept at the house of a friend who don't live in the ghetto. When I was young I never hang in my neighbourhood. My daddy go, "OK, after school you go to club, you go to your buddy's house, you do Jiu-Jitsu, you finish Jiu-Jitsu, you do basketball. Do whatever but don't hang here."'

'So Jiu-Jitsu kept you away from danger in the *favela*?'

'Jiu-Jitsu saved my life really because was through Jiu-Jitsu that I got away from this.'

'Was it important to be able to fight in the *favela*?'

'That was the reason I start fighting. My grandfather taught me some position to defend against the older children, because when I was ten years old the kids with thirteen or fifteen years pick on me and kick my ass. I was also a kid with a lot of attitude. One time I go back home and cry. My dad goes, "Hey, what's up?" I say, "A guy kick my ass." He say, "He kick your ass? Let's go back there. You're gonna kick his ass now." I go, "No, Dad, he's *thirteen*." We went back there, I fought the kid, I punched him, he punched me, and he kicked my ass one more time, because he was older.

'But my father was always saying, "Don't run away from him. Always fight him any time he wants, because that way he never gonna pick on you again. He gonna think twice." He go, "Never cry in front of anybody. You go to your bed and cry by yourself, OK. Don't cry in front of him or me. Fight him. Doesn't matter if you kick ass or you get your ass kicked – doesn't matter."'

'He didn't want you to cry because it's a sign of weakness?'

'Because he thinks I have no reason to cry. If it hurts you, so what? You take a pill, medicine, you feel better. You crying because you feeling the hurt. You must not let this control you. My father thinks if he pick on you one time and you don't do anything, he gonna pick on you again. That's the law in the *favela*. If he pick on you' – Allan punches his own hand – 'knock him out. Even if he kick your ass, you go, "OK, are we done?" He says, "We're done." He gonna respect you for ever and you never fight again.'

I ask Allan whether his parents still live in a *favela*. He says not any longer. He bought them a house just outside one. He now wants to take them out of the neighbourhood altogether and is building a new house for them in Barra. He talks about his nephew, who is disabled – can't walk – and lives with his parents.

'He's a beautiful kid, a really nice guy.'

Tears well up in Allan's eyes. They are tears of frustration at his own predicament as much as anything else.

'For me it was very difficult dealing with this. My nephew keep me strong. He said to me, "Uncle, don't stop fighting, man. I love to see you fighting."'

Tears run down Allan's cheeks. He wipes them away with his fingers.

'Because when all these bullshit rumours went around I go, "That's enough – I've had enough." My nephew looked in my eyes and said, "I need you to fight, I love to see you fight. Why you no fight any more? Keep fighting, don't stop, don't stop." He made me come back.'

Allan composes himself again.

'Sorry to cry, man,' he says.

'No, don't apologise. There's no shame in crying. If that's how you feel, that's how you feel.'

He gets up and walks towards the door. I watch him leave, moved by his emotional honesty. Before he reaches the door, he thinks of something else to say and returns. He is smiling now.

'You know my dad said to me, "Hey, Allan, you've done well. You've come from the ghetto and now you're part of a video game."'

He laughs and leaves.

★

Allan offers to show me around the *favela* that his parents once lived in and now live near. First we go for something to eat. Allan parks the car outside a juice bar and restaurant in Barra, and we sit at a table on the pavement. His presence instantly creates ripples. People recognise him and come over to talk. It feels good to be out with a celebrity.

'Do you get a lot of attention from women?' I ask him.

'Oh yeah,' he says. 'Women really love fighters. Especially women in Barra. Women in Barra really love fighters. They check your ears to see if you're one.'

We eat beef sandwiches and chips, and down a couple of juices. Two women sitting at an adjacent table get up, smile at us and leave.

'Did you see them smile at us?' I ask.

'Yeah, man. When we were looking for a place to sit they gave us a hand signal to go and sit with them.'

We head back across town to Allan's apartment in Laranjeiras. Allan gets changed, gives his three-year-old son a shower and brings him with us to visit his parents. We drive into a tunnel, come out the other side and take a turn-off to the *favela*. When we're close, Allan winds down the dark window on the driver's side and tells me to do the same.

'You've always got to do this so that people can see you – otherwise they get suspicious. Don't be frightened if you see people carrying machine guns.'

He parks the car near his parents' home and we go inside. Allan's disabled nephew is sitting in front of a TV screen playing a video game on an old Sega console. His wheelchair is folded up behind him. Allan lifts his nephew's hands up to form a boxer's guard.

'Defend, defend, defend, defend!' he says, as he throws light slaps that rattle against his nephew's forearms.

They both laugh and enjoy the ritual greeting. The house is small and homely – pink walls, knick-knacks, lots of photos. Allan's parents are watching television. I sit and talk to them while a group of relatives and friends assemble to accompany us on our walk round the *favela*. We leave the house and go down a graffiti-addicted street of old buildings with rotting wooden shutters and blocks of small, boxy flats. Allan points to two parts of a nearby hillside. Red Command control one side and Third Command control the other, he says. These are rival drugs gangs.

'Do you know the people who run the gangs, Allan?'

'Yes, but they change all the time. They get killed.'

We turn down a side-alley next to a church that looks like an aircraft hangar, then take a route that loops upwards through the heart of the *favela*. We climb steep concrete steps, and stop to chat to people on street corners. Eventually we arrive at an open area. A steady stream of preaching emanates from a church.

'Don't worry, but we're gonna pass some guys with machine guns now,' says Allan. 'The church is here, the drugs dealers are there. They live side by side.'

Ahead of us two men sit on a low wall while another pair stand chatting to them. The light is failing, but it looks like one of them is holding the butt or muzzle of a weapon. We walk towards them, but as we get closer I realise that they are not gang members but road workers. What I took for a weapon is actually a tool handle.

'Don't look now,' says Allan. 'The drugs dealers are the guys over there with the machine guns.'

He's referring to another group up ahead, one of whom is wearing a bandana. We don't go near the dealers, but instead peel away onto a path that leads back down the hillside. An old lady comes up the steps. The others in the group stop to talk to her.

'When Red Command fight Third Command this is where the shooting happens,' says Allan. 'That lady they're talking to speaks to the gangs. They really respect old ladies. She's lived here maybe thirty years or more. She tries to create a peace. She tells them, "Look, this is not good. All this shooting with children around is not good."'

At the bottom of the hillside we meet a road.

'You see that line?' says Allan, pointing to a dark band of tarmac. 'The police never come any further than there.'

Cars flow into the *favela*. I catch myself wondering how people living here can afford to own decent cars and also wondering where they park them, because I haven't seen any garages, then chastise myself for a lack of street savvy as it dawns on me that the cars are being driven by wealthy

Cariocas who come here to score drugs. This is the entrance to a *boca-de-fumo*. It's like a drive-thru restaurant. Customers drive in, place an order, pay, pick up marijuana or coke, then leave. It is incomprehensible for a European that entire neighbourhoods are ruled by crime gangs who openly conduct drugs deals and walk around carrying machine guns, but the authorities have no presence here. *Favelas* are states within the state. The police occasionally make raids, then leave. When they do go in, they go in shooting and innocents are frequently the victims of crossfire as the drugs dealers and police fight it out. By taking the road of Jiu-Jitsu, Allan found a way to get out of the *favela*. Jiu-Jitsu was his lifeboat in a sea of poverty and sporadic violence – and through Jiu-Jitsu he has also rescued his mother and father.

'The responsibility of taking my parents away from there really weighed heavily on me,' reflects Allan, during the drive home. 'Sometimes, in fights, I lost my focus because I was thinking about this – about getting my parents out of the favela.'

You would have thought *favelas* are a perfect breeding ground for fighters. Like Allan, *favela* kids have to be tough to survive. They need to be able to learn to handle themselves in physical situations. As they get older, few decent opportunities are available to them. They might typically end up with a low-status, low-paid job such as taxi driver, petrol pump attendant, waiter or security guard. Under such circumstances, you would expect thousands of young *favela* kids would want to emulate Allan and escape both the ghetto and the tyranny of dead-end jobs by fighting professionally.

Now that MMA has become a global sport and the top fighters are paid big purses, talented fighters from the slums have the chance to make a good living from fighting abroad – just as Brazilian footballers can make a good living from playing in Europe, although there is a long way to go before fighters will make the kind of money that footballers can. The fact is, though, that whether or not a market exists for Jiu-Jitsu in Rio's *favelas*, there is virtually no supply. Yet Jiu-Jitsu could find a much-needed sense of mission and purpose by reaching into poor communities. It has the capacity to be a positive force in that it can give children, youths and men a structure and order in their lives. In *favelas* it can fulfil the archetypal social role of ritualised fighting sport by helping males channel their masculine energies down a course of honest effort and achievement, and steer them away from the temptations of crime, drugs and alcohol.

An instructor nicknamed Tata has a club in Rocinha, the largest *favela* in Rio. I've been phoning him every few days to see whether it's safe to visit. A drugs gang leader recently escaped from prison and police believe he is hiding in Rocinha. Hundreds of armed officers have been flooding into the *favela* to try to snatch him, and Tata's academy has therefore been closed for the time being.

I call Tata again. He says it should be OK now. I meet him at a newspaper booth behind Fashion Mall in Sao Conrado, near his apartment block.

'So it's no longer dangerous to go in?'

'It's dangerous at night but not in the day.'

'Has anyone been killed?'

'A drug dealer was killed yesterday, and a woman was killed in crossfire during the weekend.'

We drive the short distance to Rocinha, which is located on a hillside. It is something to behold: a broad landslide of small boxy homes cascades down the hill and comes to a petrified halt by the main freeway. Large pylons stride manfully up the hill beside it. Perhaps 300,000 people live here in all. Tata parks the car not far from the foot of the hill. The vehicle visibly rises when he gets out. He is a large man – 20 stone or more. We cross the road and go up some stairs. Tata puts his head through a hole in a flimsy locked door and whistles for someone to come down and open it. We cross roofs and pass lines of drying clothes until we reach the small academy, which is also on a rooftop. After Tata has taken the class, he talks about his reasons for founding the school.

'How can I explain? It's like Greenpeace – you know what I'm saying?'

Tata has three Jiu-Jitsu academies including this one. The other two are in wealthy areas. He founded the Rocinha club after a student from the *favela*, nicknamed Baby, came to train at his school in Sao Conrado. Tata later visited Baby's home.

'Like, how can I explain the size? The apartment was the size of two small cars. There was him, four brothers and his mum, who slept on the floor in front of the refrigerator. I started to cry about the situation. I was very sad about this. Was the first time I came inside a house in Rocinha. It changed my life, you know what I'm saying? I said to Baby, "I'm gonna help you."'

He opened a school in Rocinha and used students' fees to buy a better place for Baby and his family to live in. Students no longer have to pay fees and the club receives support from sponsors.

Tata outlines the kinds of difficulties Jiu-Jitsu faces in the *favela*. To start with, students can't afford kimonos. Families tend to be large. A family of, say, six will have a combined monthly income of about 500 reais, or £100. A kimono costs 120 reais, which represents a sizeable chunk of their income. If you train regularly you need at least two kimonos – one to wear while the other is in the wash – and they wear out quickly. Fortunately benefactors have donated kimonos that the students can use for free.

A less surmountable problem arises when students reach the age of 18–20 and finish high school education. They often have to decide between Jiu-Jitsu and going out to earn a living, because it's difficult to do both. If they work, says Tata, they typically have to put in between 10 and 12 hours a day, including bus travel, so they arrive home too late for Jiu-Jitsu class. Tata calculates that about 80 per cent of his students have to stop because of work. But he is battling on with his philanthropic venture. Eventually he would like to open more clubs in other *favelas*.

'Jiu-Jitsu is gonna change because the poor kids are hungrier for success,' he says. 'They wanna be someone, they wanna be a champion.'

Baby, the student whose living conditions inspired Tata to establish the academy, is at the gym today. As fireworks pop off deep in the heart of the *favela*, he crawls belly-down across the mat and mimes holding an automatic weapon. It's his way to explain that the fireworks are being let off by drugs gang look-outs to warn of police movements. Baby is now a brown belt instructor, and Tata plans to help set him up as a Jiu-Jitsu teacher in the States. Jiu-Jitsu could be his passport out of the ghetto and away from the crossfire for good.

Allan can't train because of a rib injury. He lies on a crash mat at the Top Team gym and acts as a human alarm bell for the sparring fighters. He calls time to end their bouts with a loud slap of the mat and a piercing whistle. When the training session is finished, a fighter nicknamed Chocolate and I get in Allan's car and he drives us over to his apartment. Chocolate is well built and tattooed, but wears an incongruous pair of black-framed glasses like you would expect a media professional or architect to have. He comes from the north of Brazil. Allan talks about Chocolate in English, which Chocolate doesn't understand.

'When he first came to Rio he had glasses that looked like the bottoms of bottles. He has an accent. He talks like in the States someone would talk who comes from Alabama. I had to tell him, "Lose your accent, man. The chicks here don't like that accent. Get some different glasses and a tattoo. Chicks like tattoos."'

Back at Allan's apartment, the maid cooks us rice and beans with chicken. After lunch Allan sits at a table and signs grading certificates for students who train at his Jiu-Jitsu schools in the States. When he's finished, the three of us take the lift down to the underground carpark and get back in the car. Allan wants to take us to a waterfall in Horto, which is not far away.

We sit in traffic. Allan winds down the windows and plays samba on the stereo. Carnival is coming. Allan chops out the rhythm with his hands in front of the steering wheel and sings. His energy is infectious. He is a constant orchestrator of uplifting moods. Everything about him is full-bodied, to the maximum, and emotionally honest. He sings when he feels like singing, he cries when he feels like crying. He has a natural exuberant charisma that makes you want to be around him.

Allan parks on the edge of the jungle at Horto and we get out of the car.

'I'm going to find a snake for you to hold,' he says.

I'm unsure whether he is being serious or winding me up. I think he is serious.

'Look, Allan, I've had dengue fever, malaria twice and a tropical disease the doctors didn't even know the name of that nearly killed me. The last thing I need in my life right now is to be bitten by a snake.'

'No problem,' says Allan, laughing. 'If it bites you, you will only have fever for forty minutes. Just take two aspirins and the fever will go. I keep aspirin in the car. You'll be fine, man.'

A feeble waterfall is nearby.

'The waterfall I want to take you to is higher up and hidden,' says Allan. 'We're gonna have to climb.'

The three of us stand and scrutinise a ridiculously steep and muddy path tangled with sinewy roots and branches. A sign warns against using the route.

'We'll take this path,' says Allan.

'You must be joking.'

He is not. Chocolate is on my side, so Allan finds another route that is hardly any easier, and we pull ourselves up by tree-trunks and roots. Both Chocolate and I wonder what we've let ourselves in for. We thought we'd signed up for a gentle walk, not a challenging climb without proper equipment. Allan is on point and keeps looking under roots and rocks for snakes. I follow behind him, while Chocolate follows behind me, and continually cracks jokes in Portuguese. We scramble up steep slopes and walk along narrow precipices from where a fall would lead to serious injury. Eventually we reach the waterfall.

'Go into the waterfall and you'll receive a blessing,' says Allan. 'Drink the water and make a wish.'

I strip down, get in the pool and stand under the falling water. It pummels my head and body, and the sensation is incredible. I make a wish, and come out feeling light and smiley. Allan takes his turn and says a prayer. Worried about treading on broken glass, Chocolate decides not to go in. We dry ourselves and sit for a while, then take the adventurous route back down. At one point we have to take a lunging step from one rock to another across a gorge created by the mountain stream. There's a sheer drop to the bottom. Allan goes first, then it's my turn. I look down and instantly feel my body go numb. A fall would be fatal. I study how the gap varies in distance and decide to step across at a point where the distance is greater yet the fall would be serious but probably not fatal. Allan watches from the other side.

'Don't step there,' he says. 'Come here.'

He directs me to the narrower crossing point from where a fall would be lethal. I focus on the place on the far rock where I'm going to step, but suddenly become aware of how inathletic my body feels. My legs are like lead. I take the step anyway and make it. Chocolate follows. Allan leads us the rest of the way back down to the car.

Chocolate and I can't believe what Allan has just put us through. We both feel like we've survived a dangerous ordeal. At least Allan didn't find a snake for me to hold. Yet I feel closer to Allan for having completed the climb. This, I suppose, is how we bond as men. Intimacy comes through shared action. We never really feel comfortable around one other until we've been through something together. The hike was Allan's test to see how I would react, what type of person I am, as would have been holding a snake. Wrestling, too, is a test that reveals who you really are, and the revelations about personality and character that come through the shared ordeal of wrestling equip men with knowledge that helps them to bond into tight groups, like the Jiu-Jitsu teams of Rio.

It feels good to have passed the test that Allan set, and it feels good to be around him. For the first time in Rio I feel the electricity of what it is to be a monkey gaining acceptance into a troop he'd like to join.

Glossary

Boca-de-fumo: drugs-selling patch.
Cafezinho: small, strong black coffee.
Creonte: name given to traitors.
Futevolei: ball game played over a volleyball net in which players use techniques allowed in football.
Kimono: Jiu-Jitsu suit. Like a judo outfit.
MMA (Mixed Martial Arts): the term most widely adopted to describe the new wave of no-holds-barred fighting.
Vale Tudo: no-holds-barred style of competition.

PART VII

England
2004–2005

Chapter 17

Grudge Fight

News comes of a fight over an issue of honour scheduled between two Brazilian Jiu-Jitsu instructors. Ironically, it will occur on a pier in Portsmouth, not in Rio. Joe and I are at an Internet centre in Shopping Downtown when we come across the story on a MMA website. The protagonists, Roberto Atalla and Alex De Souza, got into an argument on an Internet chat forum, sfuk.net. It degenerated into a bitter row and the pair intend to settle their differences by fighting no-holds-barred, which is the traditional way of resolving disputes over honour between Brazilian Jiu-Jitsu fighters. Joe is familiar with both Roberto and Alex, and has no doubts about who will win.

'Roberto's a psycho,' he says, admiringly. 'He'll batter Alex in under a minute.'

I'm less concerned about who wins and more interested in whether the fight can help the pair to resolve their differences. The idea that a new respect can be forged between men through fighting is archetypal and finds expression in everything from the ancient Sumerian story of Gilgamesh and Enkidu to the tale of how Robin Hood meets Little John. I wonder how far its bonding power reaches, and whether it has the capacity even to transform men who hate each other, such as Roberto and Alex, into friends. The idea of a rapprochement is also on Joe's mind.

'After he's lost in under a minute, I hope Alex doesn't hug Roberto and want to be his best mate and be a black belt under him,' he says.

'But that would be OK if the fight lasted ten minutes and he gave a good account of himself, don't you think?'

'Yeah, if it lasted ten minutes, but it won't.'

Back in London I track down Roberto Atalla. He is in his early thirties, and has a worn and weathered face. He teaches Jiu-Jitsu at a small basement gym at the School of Oriental and African Studies. After a class, we go to a Brazilian restaurant on Oxford Street and sit at a table near the window. Roberto gives his account of the events leading up to the challenge. He says he arrived in London about seven months ago and used to train in Rio. He responded to a thread on sfuk.net about where to find good Jiu-Jitsu training and posted that it's best to learn from a black belt, who will have more expertise and usually be a better teacher than lesser-ranked instructors. (Roberto himself is a black belt; it normally takes about eight years of dedication to reach black belt level.)

Alex De Souza, a brown belt who teaches in Bournemouth, read the post and phoned Roberto to complain. He said it was bad for the business of lesser-ranked Jiu-Jitsu instructors such as himself. Roberto countered that he was talking about training in the context of London only and that he understood that in some parts of the country, such as Bournemouth, the choice of instructors is limited so the same rule does not apply. He and Alex spoke for about an hour, says Roberto, and he thought they ended the conversation on friendly terms and with Alex agreeing with him. He went online the next day to discover a new post from Alex.

'It was this big,' he says, holding his hands a foot apart horizontally.

Alex was antagonistic towards him, says Roberto. Among other things, he wrote that sometimes brown belts can be better instructors than black belts, which Roberto interpreted to mean Alex was suggesting that he might be better at teaching than him. Roberto challenged Alex on the forum to a Jiu-Jitsu match at a forthcoming tournament, but Alex didn't accept.

'He tried to make irony with me,' says Roberto. 'He tried to be funny.'

Roberto was so annoyed that he provoked Alex by posting a message insulting him in Portuguese. Among other things, he accused him of being a coward. Alex reacted angrily and upped the ante by challenging Roberto to fight under Vale Tudo rules. Roberto accepted. They eventually agreed to fight on the bill of Full Contact Fight Night, a MMA event that will be held in Portsmouth in April.

What offended him most, says Roberto, was that Alex was friendly to him on the phone, but rude on the chat forum. If Alex felt they still had differences to resolve, he should have talked to him directly, he maintains, not bad-mouthed him in public on the Web. He sees the fight as a lose–lose situation. If he wins, he will have beaten someone he considers inferior – and there's no glory in that. If he loses it would be terrible for his reputation, which he is trying to establish in the UK.

'I have to win in a way that I prove to everybody in this country that not only is Alex bad, but also I am good. I'm not fighting him to prove that I am better than him any more, because I know I'm better than him. I want to go there and show people that without proper Jiu-Jitsu you are never going to do any good in the MMA ring.'

Roberto has no experience of fighting under MMA rules, though he says he used to fight in the street when he was young.

'Before I discovered Jiu-Jitsu I was not the guy you know today. I was someone who wanted to prove myself, so I had this attitude of confronting anybody, no matter what size and stuff.'

As proof, he points to a scar on his forearm that came from a beer bottle, and one on his forehead from a club.

Predictably Alex De Souza's version of events differs from Roberto's. I phone him during the week before the fight. His voice drips with indignation and a sense of grievance. He used to train in Jiu-Jitsu back in the north of Brazil, but stopped

training when he first came to the UK in 1996, he says. Four
years later he decided to resume training, but there was no one
practising Jiu-Jitsu in Bournemouth to work out with, so he
started his own club. It became popular, so when he gave up a
restaurant job he began to teach professionally. It wasn't his
original intention to be a Jiu-Jitsu instructor – that's just how
things worked out. He says he has never sold himself as the
best Jiu-Jitsu practitioner around, yet his club is thriving. He is
now well established in England, unlike Roberto who has been
here for less than a year yet wants to dictate to everybody in the
Jiu-Jitsu community.

'He always likes to give advice as if he is Yoda, the wise man
from *Star Wars*.'

Alex says Roberto said in a post that if a black belt moves
into town any lower-grade instructors should move out of his
way to let the higher-grade teach (the posts have since been
deleted, so it's impossible to verify the accounts of either
party). He phoned Roberto after he'd read it. He came away
from their conversation thinking he had convinced Roberto
that Brazilian Jiu-Jitsu instructors needed to work together in
the UK and avoid treading on one another's toes, but that
Roberto then posted the next day repeating his unrecon-
structed view that black belt instructors are superior. His
description of how the rest of the disagreement unfolded
mirrors Roberto's. He was deeply offended by the abuse in
Portuguese. Unlike Roberto, Alex has fought before under
MMA rules – four times.

'But this is probably my most important fight. I go in there
as an underdog. If I lose, it's fine. All people will say is, "Well
done, Alex, you took up a fight against a big guy." But if he
loses I don't think he will ever teach a seminar here again.'

'Do you expect to win?'

'I expect to win.' He laughs. 'I'm gonna destroy him. That's
what's gonna happen.'

After I've spoken to Alex, I think about what it is precisely
that is fuelling this feud. Essentially it is a territorial dispute.
Both protagonists are fighting for a resource, Jiu-Jitsu students,
and both feel that their reputation and the livelihood that
follows from maintaining that reputation are at stake. Both feel
that their ability to teach is being called into question in front

of an audience whose respect they need if they are going to thrive as instructors. The very public nature of the feud has inflamed it. Because the disagreement escalated on a chat forum, neither Roberto nor Alex was able to back down without losing face in front of the people they need to impress.

On the day of the grudge match I stand drinking in Bar Blu with Andrew, a photographer who will take pictures of the event. The venue, Southsea South Parade Pier, is just over the road. It's fitting that the fight will be held on a pier – as though a grudge match under Vale Tudo rules is an exotic import from Brazil that must first be offloaded onto a jetty where it can be held under quarantine until it's been properly assessed. We like their coffee and we like their footballers, but I wonder whether this new Brazilian import will be judged suitable to allow onto the mainland proper.

The weigh-in is at the bar. Neither Alex nor Roberto need to make a particular weight, but I hope they will show their faces anyway. Grant Waterman, who will referee all the bouts, stands holding a plate of food in one hand and fork in the other. He is co-promoter of the event, and says he plans to give Roberto and Alex an extra incentive.

'They don't know this yet but I'm going to go into their changing rooms and offer them an extra fifty quid for a knockout.'

Roberto arrives and comes over to talk.

'Should I have music to intimidate my opponent or that I like?' he asks.

'That you like. Your opponent won't even hear it. He'll be so focused on what is about to happen.'

He goes over to speak to someone.

'He's shaking,' says Andrew. 'You notice that? His hands are shaking.'

Roberto returns. I ask him how he thinks the fight will end.

'Keep it to yourself, but I think I'll finish with an elbow' – he elbows the palm of his hand to illustrate – 'or a rear naked choke.'

Inside the venue, yellow fight programmes await the audience on each chair. The hall quickly fills with a few

hundred people or more. Queues form at the bar for drinks
and portions of chips. I find Alex standing in a far corner and
introduce myself. He wears a red tracksuit and black beanie,
and says he feels confident though sounds nervous. Shaolin,
one of the top MMA fighters in the world, has come over from
Brazil to be his cornerman and sits quietly behind a desk
nearby selling MMA merchandise. The promoters intended to
keep Roberto and Alex well away from one another before the
fight to prevent hostilities breaking out early, but Roberto and
his faction have taken up position at an alcove table not far
from Alex. I go over to Roberto and ask him whether he has
spoken to Alex so far this evening.

'We exchanged a look. I said you won't be laughing for long,
motherfucker.'

One of Roberto's Brazilian students returns to the group
with a T-shirt he has just bought from Shaolin. Roberto barks
at him in Portuguese. He feels his student is supporting Alex in
an indirect way. I recognise the words 'T-shirt', 'return' and
'now'.

There are nine fights on the bill. The grudge match will be
its climax. Just before the bouts start, I go and sit on the stage
near the ring. During the opening fight, I am transfixed by the
raw hate and aggression of a group of spectators sitting nearby
in a front row. They shout 'Go on Ashley, knock 'im awt!' and
'It 'im!' and rise together from their seats in one reactive wave.
Unfortunately for them, Ashley is trapped in a triangle-choke
and passes out rather than tap. The doctor is called into the
ring. During his post-victory celebration, Ashley's opponent
approaches the side of the ring where Ashley's fans sit. One of
them rises, shouts 'Wanker!' and delivers the auxiliary hand
signal from a combative crouch.

The fighters in the early bouts have one gear. They rush
across the ring at each other like two people rushing from
opposite ends of a corridor to use the same centrally located
fire escape during a serious blaze. They give the audience what
the audience wants to see: proverbial, good old-fashioned tear-
ups. I wondered beforehand where Vale Tudo would locate
itself within English culture and tonight it is being welcomed
with open arms by the council estate demographic and
anglicised. The compere uses an English dialect reserved for

ring announcers: 'We have a unanimous decision-*ah*' and 'In the red corn-*ah*'. The ring girls wear hipster pinstripe trousers, G-strings, bikini tops and porn actress heels.

'All our ring girls are lapdancers, *obviously*,' explains the compere.

After each bout, he says a little something about how both protagonists were 'warriors', and the ring girls award each fighter a trophy. It's the British working-class equivalent of the Dukawa tradition of girls rubbing ground guinea corn on the heads of wrestlers. The compere also tells the audience that they can have their photos taken with the ring girls during the intermission.

'Both topless and nude-*ah*, I have to say.'

For which there is no parallel in traditional Dukawa culture.

I leave ringside and find the upstairs room where Roberto is doing his final preparations. Chairs and tables have been cleared out of the way to create a space in which to warm up. Roberto is working his ground and pound. A pad-holder lies underneath him. Roberto practises hammering the pad-holder's lower ribs and whacks the pads with his elbows. His strategy is going to be to take Alex down, then punish him with punches and elbows to the ribs and face.

A cheer comes from the venue hall downstairs. One of Roberto's faction enters the room and shouts, '*Bora, bora, bora!*' ('Go, go, go!') Two fights have ended quickly, he explains. There are only two more before Roberto is on. Instantly there is more urgency in Roberto's movements. He paces up and down. One of his cornermen tells him to breathe deeply and slowly. I go back downstairs and watch for a few moments as Alex warms up on a mat in a back room. In contrast to Roberto he appears relaxed and is casually skipping. Shaolin sits on a chair with his legs extended and watches as if at the beach. I make my way back to the hall and just catch seeing Grant, the referee, return shirtless from outside to cheers from the audience.

'It all kicked off here a moment ago,' explains Andrew.

Grant took it upon himself to leave the ring and personally eject an unruly member of the audience from the venue.

The time comes for the main event. Alex De Souza enters the hall to Amazonian music. He removes his beanie to reveal a

surprisingly voluminous mop of blond curls. Roberto enters
wearing a hoodie to loud, crashing music. He looks dangerous,
focused and impatient, like someone who wants to commit a
premeditated murder to a tight predetermined schedule. He
wears a Flamengo football top under his blue kimono, which is
poignantly tied with a black belt, and strips down to surf
shorts. The fight is scheduled for three ten-minute rounds.
When it starts, Roberto takes it to Alex. The pair clinch in the
corner, then Roberto artfully throws Alex to the ground. Alex
lies under Roberto with his legs wrapped around him – closed
guard. Roberto pounds his ribs and throws elbows. Alex goes
for an armlock. There's a big cheer as he straightens Roberto's
arm. This could be the end. It would be hugely embarrassing
for Roberto not only to submit to Alex but also submit to a Jiu-
Jitsu technique. Yet though his elbow is possibly injured,
Roberto refuses to tap.

He slips out of danger and gets behind Alex, who is now the
one in trouble. Roberto wraps his legs around Alex's body and
goes to strangle him. It should be simple. He should be able to
finish the fight here, but Alex frustrates Roberto's attempts to
sink his arms around his neck. Eventually, Alex disentangles
and spins so that he is in Roberto's guard. He headbutts
Roberto, which is against the rules. Grant stops the fight and
stands the pair up. Alex taunts Roberto, who answers with a
punch that staggers him. Sarcastic laughing comes from
Roberto's corner. Alex falls back to the guard, and Roberto
tries to bludgeon him in the face with forearms and elbows.
Alex gives a defiant finger to Roberto's cornermen.

At the start of the second round, Roberto comes out with a
look that says he intends to disembowel Alex. He takes Alex to
the ground at will and throws more punches. One of Roberto's
cornermen drums on the ring apron and shouts, 'Punch,
punch! Elbow, elbow!' A counter chant goes up of 'Alex, Alex,
Alex, Alex.' Alex connects with a kick to the head. By the end of
the round, after twenty minutes of intense and bitter fighting,
Roberto has been by far the most active and aggressive of the
two, but by the same token he must have punched himself out.
He can only be fuelled by hatred at this point. He sits in his
corner and pours water over himself, while Alex is fresh
enough to stand. Alex doesn't appear to have any cuts, though

his blond locks are dyed with blood. His hair looks like a mop used to clean an abattoir floor.

In the third round Roberto follows the same strategy of taking Alex down and trying to bludgeon him. It is strange that he has not tried even once to pass Alex's guard. He said he wanted to demonstrate the effectiveness of good Jiu-Jitsu, yet he has utilised little Jiu-Jitsu so far. Alex drums on Roberto's buttocks, both to indicate how ineffective Roberto's attacks have been and to insult him. I sense there is not going to be a rapprochement tonight. Near the end of the round, Alex knees Roberto, who momentarily appears to be in trouble.

The fight ends inconclusively, and goes to a judges' decision. The judges rule it a draw. Both fighters make a speech. Alex gloats over the draw and over the fact that Roberto's face is mashed up, while Roberto is more gentlemanly and thanks the audience.

Minutes later, Andrew and I make our way to see Roberto in his dressing room. He is sitting on a chair, leaning forwards and trying to comprehend what has just happened. His face is cut, bruised and puffy. His cornermen and faction stand around him. Profoundly exhausted and possibly in shock, Roberto remains silent for long interludes between questions that betray his disorientation.

'I don't even remember what happened, really,' he says.

'You beat him up for three rounds,' reassures one of his cornermen.

'Was it a draw?' asks Roberto a little later, and after another silence: 'It's finished? No more rounds?'

He sits in a mellow state of concussed contemplation while his faction move around him, hyper and kinetic, pacing up and down, punching their palms with their fists. They can't believe the judges' decision and think it's a fix. Their anger at the fight's outcome, their frustration, needs a release, a scapegoat. I sense they may turn on me, the outsider. One of the cornermen asks Andrew to leave. He asks me to go too, but I'm determined to stay unless Roberto himself tells me to leave, so I ignore him.

Roberto slumps to the floor, lying face up, with his right arm out straight – a half-crucified pose. One of his team applies ice wrapped in a T-shirt to his face and right elbow, which was damaged by the armlock.

'Did I lose, guys?' he asks.

'Roberto, you hammered him,' is the firm comeback.

Alex slips away from the venue. We later speak on the phone. He is even more defiant than before. He laughs at the suggestion that he was hurt and says Roberto did not land any blows. All the blood was Roberto's, not his, he says. He and Roberto will never resolve their differences. It would be best if they simply forgot about each other.

The fight was physically and emotionally brutal but also powerful and mesmeric. Andrew and I left the venue so hyped up that it was difficult to come down. Sadly, though, there has been no resolution. Roberto and Alex failed to find a new respect for one another in the ring. They did not shake hands and make up. Legend and folk tale found no distant echo on a Portsmouth pier.

During the week following the grudge match, the online cognoscenti discuss it at the sfuk.net website. The consensus is that it was an incredible but bad-natured thirty minutes of combat. Alarmingly, Grant posts that there were small pieces of human flesh left on the canvas afterwards. No one seems to know why Roberto and Alex grew to detest each other in the first place.

'[*I*] still find the root of this beef a bit baffling,' writes someone styling himself Miaghi Carioca. 'It all kinda sprung from nothing.'

Chapter 18

The Fall II

Late winter snow is falling. I wrap up warm and take a train from London to Redhill then walk to my old school, Wray Common, situated in a cul-de-sac among detached houses. In the playground are red bins, netball posts and courts but no children. A light is on in a classroom but it is empty. In moments of reflection during the trips to India, Mongolia, Australia, Nigeria and Brazil, I often re-enacted dramas from my childhood on this now empty stage as I tried to understand why I would later become so obsessed with wrestling and the life of the body.

I was a pupil at Wray Common from the ages of five to eleven. Back then I lived through my body. As children, we played cowboys and Indians, war games, hide and seek, marbles and football. They were games, but the feelings they engendered were authentic and vivid. The years between the ages of about six and eleven were a deeply masculine period of my life – more masculine, in fact, than much of my adulthood. As children we were preoccupied with heroism, warfare, sport, competition and creating bonds with one another through experience and action. We had a finely tuned sense of hierarchy forged in breaktime interaction and games, particularly football.

I loved playing football and was vice captain of the team. I was an attacking force in playground matches, but clammed up and became overdefensive in games against other schools. A boy called John captained the team and was also top dog in our year. He was the first to have an England number 7 shirt like Kevin Keegan's, and one of the first to have a skateboard and a digital watch. He understood exactly what the teacher was talking about in the sex education class when I didn't have a clue. At one point John had a girlfriend called Katie who had dark hair and blue eyes and who I thought was the prettiest girl in the world. The dominant athlete won the princess back when we were nine.

My first experience of fighting was against John. I came across him beating up another boy in the cloakroom. I intervened without really knowing what to do and John shoved me out of the way and into the jutting corner of the wall next to the toilet cubicles. My head cracked open. The profuse bleeding shocked the bullying to an end. I went to hospital for stitches and enjoyed picking bogeys of black, congealed blood out of my hair for a couple of days afterwards. Even though I came off badly, it felt good to have been in a fight and have a scar to show for it. Later, when we were older, John and I fought again, this time on the playing field. He must have thrown me, tripped me perhaps, because I remember that he sat on my chest and hit me in the face until someone intervened to stop it.

I didn't throw one punch in both these fights. I was psychologically hobbled by a dislike of causing pain. From an early age I despised myself if I hurt anyone. My fear of hurting other people was so strong it even overrode my desire to protect myself. Somehow, from somewhere, I absorbed the idea that I had to be a good person and that good people did not hit others – even if that meant almost offering myself as a sacrifice to a bully. While I was growing up, I thought you only fought when you were angry and that anger was always bad. I remember watching Muhammad Ali box on TV, the stare-off before the first round, and how I thought Ali was about to fight his opponent because he had insulted Ali's sister, which, having a sister myself, was the only reason I could manufacture to make sense of the fact that they were about to hit one another.

I walk the couple of miles to Reigate Grammar School, and stand and consider the school buildings from the opposite side of the road. I did well at Wray Common and my teacher said it would be a waste for me to go to the local comprehensive. I took the entrance exam to the grammar and won a part scholarship. I was there for five years from the age of twelve to nearly sixteen and grew to hate the place. Wray Common had been a warm and friendly state school, but the grammar was unnecessarily disciplinarian and had pretensions to be a public school. We were organised into houses and had to wear caps in the first year and do Latin. We referred to the masters as 'Sir' and they referred to us by our surnames. We studied hard – the days of fun and play were over.

A friend once said that he saw his body as a shopping trolley – just something to carry his brain around in – an image that neatly sums up an attitude characteristic of our age. It was at the grammar that it really began: the demotion of our bodies from instruments through which to live and express ourselves, to shopping trolleys in which to carry the brain. We sat at wooden desks scarred with initials etched by bored students with compass points, and pored over books or copied notes from the blackboard. Ostensibly we learnt physics and chemistry and history and French, but we were also being taught how to sit passively at desks for hours on end during the best parts of the day without complaint – a lesson that would equip us for the middle-class desk jobs to come. We were far too physically inactive at a time when it's natural for boys to be active, and far too intellectual when it's natural for boys to be physical. It was here that the body was really cowed and tamed. Whenever I hear the fact repeated that girls do better than boys at school, I think of how that may well be true, but that part of the reason is surely that modern mass education is fundamentally anti-male in that it gives little attention to the cultivation of the virtues of the body, or learning through experience and action.

I look in at the grammar's playground and classrooms. The

school has a mellower aura than it did twenty-five years earlier. The ugly air-raid shelter and toilet block are gone. There is a new wing of happier-looking classrooms. The old main building still has a malevolent air about it though – something to do with the pointiness of the roof and big window. The few children around look happy. There are girls in grammar school uniform too. When I was at the school a few girls were introduced into the sixth year, like creatures tentatively let loose into the wild in small batches to see whether they would survive.

Sometimes the chant 'Fight! Fight! Fight!' would go up in the playground and a crowd would form around the two protagonists. I was so excited by fighting that I literally couldn't watch. Though I had absorbed the idea that fighting was wrong, I was also fascinated by it. I wanted to want to fight. As we grew older, how hard you were, or how hard you weren't, became bigger and bigger issues. By the age of fourteen we had divided into tribal groups based around taste in music: mods, new romantics, metallers. We drank in pubs and at parties as soon as we could – there was nothing much else to do.

Once I went to a party and got drunk and said something stupid on the pavement outside as I was leaving. In the presence of a group of mods, I said, 'I could have any mod.' I don't know why. A mod headbutted me and threw a fast combination of punches that cut and bruised my face. Someone said afterwards that he boxed. As reasons go for fighting back, being punched in the face and headbutted rate as good ones, yet I didn't. The headbutt caught me too high, so I didn't go down. I didn't cower either, or say anything, just stood there defiantly, sobering up fast yet incapable of hitting back through inhibition. Even after heavy provocation, I couldn't use my fists. Fighting inhabited a psychological territory I just couldn't enter. In my fear of anger and fighting I embodied a certain spirit of our age – a deep suspicion and dislike of male violence. Yet though violence is often bad and anger is often destructive and inappropriate, fighting is neither always a form of violence nor always the product of anger. There are good reasons to fight – such as in self-defence or to protect others – and boys, youths and men have a natural urge to test themselves in physical contests against one another that can take the form of ritualised fighting.

When I was young, I didn't realise this last category of action existed. I thought all fighting was the same – the violent product of anger. For years I was stuck with this misunderstanding. This is why I would eventually fall for wrestling: it so sweetly resolved what I thought was an irresolvable paradox in that it allowed me to fight hard but without hurting. It made the impossible possible, and enabled me to do something I dreamt about yet grew up believing was taboo.

When we were boys, our culture should have offered us ways, such as wrestling, which is part of England's heritage – part of the heritage of men the world over – to express our need to fight in a positive way. Instead, during the teenage years, during the testosterone-underpinned adolescent years when we needed to be tested and to come to know and express ourselves as males in a physical body, we predominantly sat at desks and were filled with information as a prelude to entering the office world. We were encouraged to allow the body, which is beautiful and flexible, to degenerate into something rigid and mundane, like a shopping trolley. But our innate desire to fight and test ourselves physically had to go somewhere. Luckily, years later, mine flowered into a passion for wrestling.

I take the alleyway down to Reigate town centre and find the entrance to the rugby fields beyond the Blue Anchor pub. A security fence and Barratt's sign indicate that housing is about to be built on the site. The building in which we used to change is boarded up but hasn't been knocked down yet, if that is the intention. The fields are still there, too, beyond a hedge. The grammar's sports facilities are elsewhere now.

I remember the chatter of boot studs on the changing-room floor, and the apprehension I felt before a rugby match, which I associate with the hiss and smell of Ralgex spray, and I remember the warm-up of cycle-pedalling our arms in the air and running on the spot. The grammar school's games masters ruled that football was for girls and we had to play rugby. It was their idea of a manly game. I played fullback or inside centre for the 'A' team and was a half-decent player. In particular I was good at tackles, the wrestling-like moments. I loved to come across field and nail wingers trapped against the touchline – especially if they came from toff schools and their parents were watching. I revelled in the man-against-man physical element of rugby. I couldn't fight in the playground, but I enjoyed the licence to compete hard on the rugby pitch under clearly defined rules. This is what we needed more of at school: combative contact sport.

But we needed to learn to play rugby in the right empathetic environment from teachers who could mentor us through the feelings and issues that sport can engender. For me, those would have included pre-match trepidation, the fear of losing face by playing badly and an exaggerated sense of personal responsibility for the performance of the team as a whole. In the absence of wrestling, rugby would have been a good tool through which to begin to develop and understand ourselves as men, but playing rugby was rarely a pleasure, because of the attitude of the masters. They were severe and disciplinarian and effectively forced us to play whether we wanted to or not. They wanted us to win but never really showed us how. Playing rugby was all about bringing honour to the school and had nothing to do with enjoyment or your development as a human being.

When I was fifteen I got a Saturday job at Woolworths. One dinner-time I approached the table in the canteen where the rugby masters, Mr Reid and Mr Jones, were sitting and told them I wasn't going to play rugby any more, as Saturday fixtures clashed with my new job. By this time I had had enough of rugby anyway. The Saturday job was just a good excuse to stop playing. I was a fifth year but sometimes played for the lower order sixth-form teams and would always be the smallest player on the pitch, which meant I kept getting hurt and injured as I couldn't shirk tackles as a matter of pride.

It was a big thing to assert yourself against the rugby masters. Mr Jones was a peculiar-looking man whose face puffed up like a sunfish when he got angry, as he frequently did. When I told him I was giving up rugby, he was derisory but didn't explode. He told me not to come back to the grammar school the following year if I wasn't prepared to play for the team. I didn't, and instead went to the state sixth-form college down the road, which was a revelation because the teachers treated you like a human being.

Rugby felt like it was just another weapon in the teachers' armoury for the subjugation of pupils, which was a big shame. Probably many people have similarly alienating experiences with sport at school and end up shunning it for the rest of their lives as a consequence. After my unhappy experiences with rugby, I turned my back on physical pursuits and concentrated on academic education. Going to university would be my ticket out of the stagnant suburbs.

I didn't return to physical training until I was nineteen or twenty and took up weight-training then martial arts. But now that I think about it, it would be women who would guide me back to the path that leads through the body. Like Dukawa men, I was teased by girls. Janet, my first girlfriend at university, did Tae Kwon Do and said she reckoned she could beat me up in a fight. We half-jokingly had a play fight one night. Whether she proved her point or not, I don't remember, but I felt some shame because I knew there was truth in what she said – and that made me think about taking up martial arts. Nicky, another girlfriend, once compared my physique unfavourably with a friend of mine's, which provoked me to try weights. Women were pulling the strings – as they always have and always will.

I turn round and head towards the station. I've seen enough of my old school haunts. According to the station timetable there won't be a train to Redhill for nearly an hour. It is still snowing heavily and I am soaked through. I order a cab at a taxi booth and get into conversation with the driver during the ride to Redhill.

'What brought you back here today?' he asks.

'I thought I'd just come down for nostalgia reasons, really, and to visit the places where I went to school.'

I don't tell him the full story – that I came back to help close one chapter of my life so that another could open. I don't say that I am about to return to Brazil, hopefully to live, because Brazil is a country that celebrates the life of the body, unlike England. I don't say that living in Brazil will be an act of reluctant defiance against England, my country, a country that I love yet which conspires against those who want to live through the body and makes no place for wrestlers.

In moments of pessimism I wonder whether history will

record that I came from one of the last generations of wrestlers in England, whether we will go down as England's last wrestlers, though in more optimistic moments I reflect that every boy born will feel the same urge to fight that wrestling can answer, so maybe all is not lost. Nature wants us to wrestle whatever nurture and culture do between them to stop us. No, we're going to keep wrestling – and I'm going to try to get back into it, even if, at thirty-seven, I don't feel quite the same degree of passion as I did in my twenties.

Perhaps I'll teach again. Maybe that's how I can rekindle the connection: teach and do my bit to ensure wrestling has a future. It's been nearly ten years since I trained seriously. My health problem robbed me of my peak years as a wrestler and I've often felt tormented – even ashamed – by the fact that I never really proved myself, but you have to accept what fate brings and there is no point in continuing to feel bitter. And perhaps good came out of the illness. It diverted me towards doing something that may ultimately turn out to be more beneficial for the greater cause of wrestling than concentrating on my own career would have been: had I been fit and healthy, I probably would have been too preoccupied with my own training to have made this journey.

The taxi passes the grammar school.

'I went to that school,' I say to the driver. 'I hated it. The teachers acted like they hated the pupils. It was only many years later that I realised there were actually schools where teachers liked and empathised with pupils, and vice versa.'

The driver chuckles. 'I think all schools were like that back then,' he says. 'I gave a lift to the wife of a teacher of mine recently. She asked me whether her husband had ever given me the slipper. There weren't many boys that he hadn't slippered, to tell the truth. I told her I got slippered a couple of times. He used to keep three slippers and he would ask you which one you wanted to be slippered with – though it didn't make any difference in terms of pain.'

'Right. It's only later on in life that you realise your teachers were probably living out strange sexual perversions. What school were you at?'

'Woodhatch.'

'That was a tough school. We also had a teacher, a music

teacher, who used a slipper. I think it was a slipper, or maybe it was a rugby boot – I'm not sure which. Another teacher used to throw at you that thing they used to use to wipe the chalk off the blackboard – I've forgotten the name. I also have a vivid memory of an angry teacher chasing a boy while trying to hit him with a chair he was holding above his head. I don't know what the boy had done to annoy him.'

We both laugh at the image. In the absence of wrestling, perhaps that's where our desire to fight went: into provoking and upsetting the teachers.

Notes

Chapter 2   The Fall
p. 9 *The Gene LeBell special.* My name for the Closed Three-Finger Grip. See p. 16, *Grappling Master*, Gene LeBell (1992).

p. 15 *Written by EJ Harrison and published in 1934,* Wrestling *sat waiting for me on a basement shelf of a secondhand bookshop on the Fulham Road.* The book was 'published under the auspices of W (Billy) Wood', a well-known wrestler at the time, but was actually written by EJ Harrison.

p. 16 *'Most styles of wrestling can be practised on the greensward,'* wrote EJ. Harrison (1934) p. 25.

Chapter 3   The Whole World Loses Something
p. 33 *Described by one newspaper as a 'gigantic Galician', Zbyszko was much heavier than Gama.* This description comes from *The Times*, 12 September 1910, which reported that Gama weighed a little over 14 stone and Zbyszko was 3 stone 12 ounces heavier. However, *The Sportsman* (12 September 1910) said the weight difference was smaller – about a stone and a half – which is nonetheless significant.

p. 33 *Zbyszko realised he had no chance of winning and every chance of losing if he stood and fought, as sooner or later he would be thrown on his back and pinned.* The bout was contested at the

Stadium, Shepherd's Bush on Saturday, 10 September 1910. It was hyped unjustifiably as being for the Catch-As-Catch-Can championship of the world. The match was stopped due to poor light after about two and a half hours. Gama attacked most, according to all reports, while Zbyszko used passive tactics and was on his feet only three times. It is difficult to turn and pin a wrestler who passively hugs the mat like Zbyszko did, especially if he is heavier, and it didn't make for an entertaining contest. *The Sportsman* called the fight 'surely the dullest big match of modern times' and reported that Zbyszko crawled about the platform 'generally with the Indian hanging onto his loins' while the crowd chanted 'Get up Zbyszko, get up Zbyszko!' *The Times* correspondent reported that Gama was vastly superior in 'open play', in other words during the brief lulls when both wrestlers wrestled from standing – but not well versed enough in ground-wrestling to find a way to deal with Zbyszko's mat-hugging tactic. (All newspaper reports from Monday, 12 September 1910.)

p. 34 Comprehensive Asian Fighting Arts *included a brief outline of an Indian wrestler's daily schedule. The amount of exercise catalogued was incredible.* See Draeger and Smith (1980) pp. 147–9.

Chapter 5   A Tight Loincloth
p. 72 *I ask Mahendra to relate how his grandfather came to kill a lion.* Hari Narayan Singh encountered the lion in about 1880. Though extremely rare by then, lions were, and are, native to India. Today, the nation's last remaining population lives at the Sasangir Wildlife Sanctuary in Gujarat.

Chapter 6   Giant
p. 105 *The wrestlers wear. . . small jackets cut to leave the chest exposed.* Variations of the following story are commonly told to explain the odd shape of the jacket. A woman once disguised herself as a man, entered Naadam and won. She was found out afterwards, and ever since then the wrestling jacket has been cut to leave the chest exposed so that female entrants are easy to detect and bar.

p. 113 *The connection between herding and wrestling runs deep. . .*
It can also be seen in the culture of the Nuba of the Sudan. In
The Last of the Nuba (1976), Leni Riefenstahl reports that
wrestlers go to live at a *zariba*, a place usually a few miles from
the village where cattle are kept (pp. 101–3). In effect a *zariba*
doubles as a herdsman's and wrestler's camp. At inter-village
competitions, writes Riefensthal, 'wrestlers are identified with
the spirit of their herds of cattle' (p. 132). Women are not
allowed at a *zariba*: the Nuba believe in celibacy to preserve
strength. An obvious reason why cultures might want to have
wrestlers living with their herds is apparent in the story of
Herakles: strong men can protect valuable livestock from
dangerous predators and rustlers. When he is eighteen,
Herakles sets out from the cattle ranch, where he has been
living, and tracks down and clubs to death the lion of
Cithaeron, which has been killing livestock (Graves, 1955, Vol
II, pp. 95–6). He later graduates from protecting livestock to
protecting people.

p. 114 *Krishna, one of the two gods commonly worshipped by
wrestlers in India, spent his youth living among herders.* While he is
growing up, Krishna lives among cowherds of the Abhiras clan
on the banks of the River Yamuna.

p. 114 *Herakles was worshipped by Greek athletes in general and by
wrestlers in particular, and during his youth he too lived among
herders. It is expressly stated in the story of Herakles that he develops
strength, courage and physical stature while living on a cattle farm.*
Graves (1955) Vol II, p. 92.

Chapter 9   Testosterone's Fingerprints
p. 181 *During puberty, testosterone matures males' bodies into
muscular forms instantly distinguishable from the physiques of
females.* For details of the effects of testosterone on the
adolescent male body, see Dabbs (2000) p. 15.

p. 184 *There is also evidence that hinds are attracted to stags that
lead bouts of roaring and have a high roaring rate.* See Andersson
(1994) p. 364.

p. 184 *Though injuries can and do occur, the principal aim is to enter into a shoving contest to see who is strongest, not to eviscerate.* The difference between intention and outcome has to be stressed: with one exception (see below), stags don't intend to wound each other, though that can be the outcome. TH Clutton-Brock and a team of fellow researchers did an extensive long-term study of the behaviour of red deer on the Hebridean island of Rhum (for information about competition between stags, see Clutton-Brock *et al*, 1982, Chapter 6, p. 104). They found that permanent injury, such as loss of sight in an eye and lameness, would sometimes result from a fight, though less debilitating injuries such as antler breakages made up the bulk of the injuries witnessed. A sample of 107 fights, involving 72 different stags, that took place between 1971 and 1976 resulted in only two permanent injuries. However, Clutton-Brock writes that about 23 per cent of stags over the age of five – in other words mature enough to take part in the rut – 'showed some sign of injury during the rut each year and that up to six per cent were permanently injured. Since most stags rutted for three to five years during their lifetime and natural mortality among mature stags was low, this suggested that virtually all stags may be slightly injured at some stage and as many as 20 per cent may sustain permanent injury during their lifetime' (pp. 132–3). Clutton-Brock's team also identified a particular circumstance under which stags would try to stab one another: 'if a stag slipped in the course of a fight his rival would immediately attempt to horn him in the flank, rump, or neck, and there was no evidence of dangerous attacks being inhibited in such situations' (p. 30).

p. 185 *The rule that shoving an opponent from a territory counts as victory is not common in wrestling. . .*There are examples, however, beyond sumo. The Ancient Greeks may have competed under the same rule. 'Greek wrestling also appears to have had a rule that throwing an opponent out of the *skamma* [wrestling arena] counted as victory: it was not a fall, but it meant defeat for the opponent nonetheless' (Poliakoff, 1987, p. 28). The traditional Turkish oil wrestling style has a similar penalty against those who allow themselves to be manhandled – if you are lifted off the ground by your opponent and he is able to walk three steps you lose.

p. 186 *Stags' testosterone levels rise exponentially before the rut and drop exponentially afterwards.* See chart in Clutton-Brock *et al* (1982) p. 106.

p. 187 *Similarly, testosterone levels peak at about twenty, remain near their highest level till a man's late twenties, then begin to decline at more of a pace.* See graph in Dabbs (2000) p. 16.

Chapter 10   Nigeria Welcomes You

p. 196 *According to information posted on the Net, wrestling is an integral part of Dukawa culture, and girls from the tribe choose husbands at wrestling matches.* The post (www.ksafe.com/profiles/p_code4/457.html) is from a Christian evangelical group. In the context of discussing the marriage customs of the Dukawa, the post says Dukawa girls and boys 'meet at the wrestling matches, and a girl is given flour to sprinkle over the head of the boy she chooses'.

p. 212 *The custom of wrestling at funerals that the elders mentioned is fascinating, too, and something I have only read about before in sources from Ancient Greece, such as Homer's* Iliad, *which describes how contests including wrestling are held at the funeral of the dead warrior Patroklos.* The contests consisted of chariot racing, boxing, wrestling, a foot race, armed single combat, throwing a lump of iron, archery and spear throwing (uncontested). For a good translation of this passage of the *Iliad*, see Miller (1991) pp. 1–14.

Chapter 11   Mr Capable of Killing a Cow

p. 232 *There is a scene in Chinua Achebe's* Things Fall Apart *where two families conduct marriage negotiations using short broomsticks to represent how many bags of cowries the groom's family will give for a wife-to-be.* Achebe (2001) pp. 51–3.

Chapter 12   If You Win, People Will Clap

p. 248 *The story represents something greater than I ever really expected to find in Nigeria: it is an account of a practice, apparently common, characterised by the same kind of decisiveness found in animal ruts.* Yet the story is very different from the rutting of animals in one essential aspect: only one of the wrestlers was fighting to win a female. Theresa's brother clearly was not.

Chapter 13   The Primal Underworld

p. 259 *'In the holy dayes all the Sommer the youths are exercised in leaping, dancing, shooting, wrastling, casting the stone, and practizing their shields.* Stow (1603/1908) pp. 91–2.

p. 260 *Stow goes on to write: 'Ye may reade in mine Annales. . .'* Ibid, pp. 94–5.

p. 260 *Stow's* Annales *relate that the contests near St Giles' Hospital took place on Saint James' Day (25 July).* See Stow (1615) pp. 178–9.

p. 261 *St Giles' Hospital used to be around here somewhere. It was established in 1101 by Queen Matilda, the wife of Henry I, as a hospital for lepers.* For information about St Giles-in-the-Fields, see the pamphlet *St Giles-in-the-Fields: Its Part in History,* by Rev Gordon Taylor (1989 edition), available at the church.

p. 261 *Stow. . . refers to a declining tradition of regular tournaments between Londoners and suburbanites held in Clerkenwell on St Bartholomew's Day.* 'In the Moneth of August about the feast of S Bartholomew the Apostle, before the Lord Maior, Aldermen, and Shiriffes of London placed in a large Tent neare vnto Clarken well, of olde time were diuerse dayes spent in the pastime of wrestling, where the Officers of the Citie: namely the Shiriffes, Sergeants and Yeoman, the Porters of the kings beame, or weigh house, now no such men, and other of the Citie, were challengers of all men in the suburbs, to wrestle for games appointed. . . but now of late yeares the wrestling is onely practised on Bartholomew day in the after noone. . . ' (Stow, 1603/1908, p. 104).

p. 263 *Like Pehalwans in India, Greek athletes and wrestlers oiled their bodies – but with olive oil, not mustard – and Greek wrestlers wrestled on earth.* The wrestling cultures of contemporary India and Ancient Greece are remarkably similar. Both wrestlers from Ancient Greece and India worship, or worshipped, gods at their gyms: Greek wrestlers worshipped Theseus, Hermes and Herakles; wrestlers in India worship Hanuman and Krishna. The Greek *palaestra* had both a sand wrestling arena and one of earth, while Indians wrestle on earth at the *akhara*. Ancient Greek doctors thought the earth of the arena could have healing qualities, a view shared in India, where particular ingredients are mixed with the soil because they are believed to have health-giving benefits, and where doctors sometimes recommend that people go to an *akhara* and wallow in the mud to improve their health. Greek wrestlers used a pickaxe to loosen and prepare the wrestling surface; similarly Indian wrestlers use a heavy hoe to dig and loosen the ground. The Greeks considered this to be a valuable exercise in itself, which is also true in India. Massage was a central part of life at the *palaestra* just as at the *akhara*. (See Poliakoff, 1987, pp. 11–14, for descriptions of the Greek training regimen.)

These are striking enough similarities in themselves that cannot plausibly be coincidental and deserve explanation – yet the similarities go far deeper. It would appear that there was a systematic advocacy of celibacy among Ancient Greek athletes just as there is among wrestlers in India. In *The Laws*, which was written shortly before his death, Plato (*c.* 427–347 BC) commends a pentathlete, Ikkos of Tarentum, for keeping celibate during a peak period of training, which he implies was a common practice among athletes (Plato, 1970, pp. 338–9). In an obtuse but revealing reference, the famous physician Galen (b. AD 131, d. AD 201 or possibly later) relates the case of a patient who abstained from sex – so that he can be like an athlete (see Foucault, 1990, pp. 120–1; original source: Galen, *On the Affected Parts*). Ancient Greek sources reveal that celibacy was advocated for the same reason that it is advocated in India: it was believed to preserve strength. The Greek mathematician and philosopher Pythagoras (569–475 BC) was once asked when the best time was to make love. He replied, 'Whenever you wish to be weaker than yourself.' (Diogenes Laertius, 1853, p. 342.)

Aretaeus of Cappadocia, a Greek physician who wrote texts

that survive today and who probably lived in the 1st century AD, wrote: 'For it is this vivifying sperm that makes us men; warm, well-knit, hairy, of strong voice, high mettled, and efficient both to think and do. Those who are men, illustrate it; but they with whom the vivifying seed does not abide, are wrinkled, weak, with squeaking voices, hairless, beardless, and effeminate: eunuchs are a proof of it. So if any man be continent, he becomes powerful, courageous, and strong as a wild animal. They who are temperate among the athletes afford an instance of this; for they who are by nature superior to some others, become much their inferiors by intemperance; and they who by nature are much inferior from continence become superior, and an animal becomes strong from no other source than the seed. Great is its consequence in regard of health, courage, and procreation; Satyriasis frequently ends in this disorder' (Aretaeus, 1837, pp. 122–3). This is a musty translation from the nineteenth century that uses the vocabulary of the day, but if you blow away the dust you uncover the vivid belief that sex weakens strong men and abstention from sex makes weak men strong. (Aretaeus, of course, is partly confusing the role of testosterone with the role of sperm. Testosterone wasn't discovered until 1935.)

For many years, in order to piece together a picture of Ancient Greek athletics, writers and academics have either sat at desks in libraries to pore over fleeting references in ancient texts, or teased meaning from fragmentary archaeological evidence, or looked for clues in depictions of athletics that decorate the sides of ancient pots. All along they could have travelled to India and trained at an *akhara* to intuit what life at an Ancient Greek *palaestra* may have been like. Palaeontologists would kill for the opportunity to study a living dinosaur in its natural habitat; the opportunity that students of Ancient Greek athletics have open to them in India is just as exceptional.

It is sad in itself that *kushti* is in steep decline in India, but as it dies out the world is also losing the last living expression of an athletic culture strikingly similar to that of Ancient Greece and a fascinating possible gateway to that ancient world – which makes the decline even more tragic. There is a cruel irony here. The main patrons of wrestling in India are state organisations, such as the State Bank of India, railways and police force, which operate sports quotas through which they employ athletes from a range of sports on the understanding that they represent the organisation in competition. These organisations are only interested in employing wrestlers who excel at Freestyle. If a wrestler in India wants to make wrestling his vocation, he has to compete for a place on the sports quota of a state organisation and is therefore forced to focus on Freestyle at the expense of *kushti*. Consequently, for pragmatic reasons, Freestyle is taking over from *kushti* in India. Freestyle is an artificial style with time limits, a points system and labyrinthine rules that have evolved to serve the requirements of the modern Olympic movement – which means that *kushti*, the closest living link to the wrestling style practised at the ancient Olympics, is being killed off by a style developed for the modern Games.

Freestyle was a lifeboat for me in England. It was the only honest style practised to any extent. Yet today in India, it is playing the role of a generic global product destroying an ancient local tradition.

p. 263 *Evidence has been found for athletics predating the historic Greek era – such as a fresco of boy boxers discovered on the Greek island of Thera that dates from about 1500 BC. . .* For a photo of the fresco, see Yalouris (1982) p. 21.

p. 264 *The Olympics, which ancient sources said began in 776 BC, were the first and most prestigious.* Scholars have contested the date of 776 BC on the basis of literary sources and archaeological evidence at the site of Olympia. See Hugh M Lee's discussion of the subject, in Raschke (1988), Chapter 7, p. 110.

p. 264 *The Games consisted of athletic contests for men and youths, chariot races and horse races, and contests for heralds and trumpeteers were also added in 396 BC.* The roster of events varied over time. According to Pausanias, the men's athletic events were instituted as follows: the *stadion* was the only event from 776 BC till 724 BC, when the *diaulos* was added. At the next Olympic Games, in 720 BC, the *dolikhos* was held for the first time. Wrestling and pentathlon were contested for the first time in 708 BC, boxing in 688 BC and pankration in 648 BC. The race in armour was instituted in 520 BC. See Pausanias (1979) pp. 217–20.

p. 265 *Boxers did not hit each other with padded gloves but instead punched with a minimum of wrapping to protect their hands, not opponents' ribs and faces.* Boxers usually wore light rawhide thongs until the 4th century BC, then there was a switch to what were called sharp thongs, which had padding across the knuckle and were larger than rawhide thongs and capable of doing more damage. See Poliakoff (1987) pp. 68–75.

p. 265 *Wrestlers were allowed to strangle each other into submission.* I have used Michael B Poliakoff's description of the rules of Ancient Greek wrestling – see Poliakoff (1987) pp. 23–30. The aim was to score three falls. According to Poliakoff, a fall was given when a wrestler's back or shoulders touched the ground, when he was stretched out prone, or when he was tied up in a controlling hold. A wrestler might also submit from a chokehold or joint-lock, and presumably this did not count as a single fall but constituted total defeat. Allowing yourself to be shunted out the arena may have also meant the end of the match.

However, it is impossible to be absolutely certain about the rules of Greek wrestling on the basis of existing evidence, and there is contention over the subject. According to K Palaeologos in Yalouris (1982), there were actually two forms of wrestling at Greek games, a standing style and a ground style (see p. 202), and touching the ground with a knee counted as a fall in the standing style (p. 208), a rule frequently found in other styles, among them Cumberland & Westmorland, sumo and *Mongol Bokh*. Were this true it would mean that Poliakoff is conflating the rules of two distinct forms of wrestling. Finley and Pleket (1976) also believe there was a standing style in which touching the ground with your knee constituted defeat (p. 38), yet they do not say anything about there having been two styles. To explain why references to touching the ground with a knee are common in Greek texts, Poliakoff maintains that it represented a position of danger that might lead to a fall, but did not represent a fall in itself. As Miller (2004, pp. 48–9) points out, illustrations show wrestlers dropping onto a knee to execute a throw, which would suggest going down on a knee did not constitute a fall – though there is a third possibility that it constituted defeat in a standing style but not in a second style that included groundwork, and a fourth that touching the ground with your knee was acceptable in a standing style if it was part of a deliberate, offensive action such as a throw, but counted as a fall if you were forced to do it. Miller maintains there was no ground wrestling at all (p. 46).

Just to add to the confusion, it is worth pointing out that it is highly probable that different styles of wrestling were practised in different parts of the Greek world, and wrestling styles and rules changed over time, so the illustrations of wrestling that survive on pots and references to the sport from ancient sources are not necessarily evocations of the same style, which is an easy assumption to make. On the other hand, even if there were various styles, it is likely that the style, or styles, practised at principal Greek games such as the Olympics would have come to dominate others, as athletes would naturally have wanted to succeed at the festivals that brought them the greatest fame and glory – so this style, or these styles, would have exercised a standardising influence throughout the Greek world.

p. 265 *It appears that by and large pankratiasts did not bind their fists like boxers.* See Poliakoff (1987) p. 56.

p. 265 *The central importance to the Greeks of their combat sports is demonstrated by the fact that they formed the climax of the athletic schedule.* See Golden (1998, p. 20) for the events schedule for 350 BC or thereabouts. According to this running order, the race in armour actually followed the combat events, but it is impossible to imagine that a race that took over 250 years to be integrated into the Games and that would be over in under a couple of minutes (the course was about 385 metres) upstaged the tough and lengthy tests of the combat sports.

p. 266 *Greek athletes competed naked, like wild animals.* There is uncertainty about when the practice of competing naked began. See the discussion in Golden (1998) pp. 65–9.

p. 266 *Three out of the four races at the Olympics were sprints.* The other race, the *dolikhos*, was a middle-distance run of perhaps about 4,625 metres. See Miller (1991) p. 212.

p. 266 *Two out of the three events unique to the pentathlon, the javelin and discus, stressed the upper body development necessary to throw with explosive power. . .* The other pentathlon events were long-jump made with hand-weights, a sprint over the *stadion* distance, and wrestling.

p. 267 *Pausanias writes that, with one notable exception, married women were barred from watching the athletes compete. . . yet unmarried women were not.* He says: 'Virgin girls of course are not barred from watching.' Pausanias (1979) p. 345. For a brief discussion of the subject, see Golden (1998) pp. 132–3.

p. 267 *With one notable exception, married women were barred from watching the athletes compete.* It's interesting to note that the only married woman allowed to watch the Olympics was the priestess of Demeter Chamyne (Demeter of the Ground). Demeter was the goddess of grain and harvests. Perhaps her priestess was present because the Games were held in part as a thanks offering to her for good crops, just as the Igbo used to give thanks to the goddess of the earth and the god of yams at the New Yam Festival, which also featured wrestling.

Wrestling and other sports contests commonly feature at festivals held at, or following, the harvest – a pattern that deserves proper explanation. The ancient Tailtean Games, which were held in what is now County Meath, Ireland, were another example of a summer athletic festival and were also held at the beginning of the harvest. They took place just before and after the Celtic festival of Lughnasad (1 August). Unfortunately, information concerning the Tailtean Games is sparse. According to legend, they were instituted by the god Lugh to mourn and commemorate the death of his foster-mother, Tailltiu. One ancient source says the Games began in 1420 BC, and they were certainly still going more than two thousand years later, as poems were specially composed for festivals held in AD 885 and 1007. A small local version of the event was still being held at the site at the end of the eighteenth century. In their heyday, the Tailtean Games were a huge gathering. The historian PW Joyce describes them as corresponding with the Olympic, Isthmian and other games of Greece, and says people from the whole of Ireland, as well as Scotland, attended (see Joyce, 1913, Vol II, pp. 438–9). Joyce quotes a source who, writing about the festival of 1169, says the horses and chariots of those arriving at the Games formed an unbroken queue of more than six miles. What's particularly interesting about the Tailtean Games is that they had an explicit marriage dimension. According to Joyce, young people from all surrounding areas came to the fair with their parents to look for partners. Bachelors and maidens were kept apart while their parents made negotiations, and if a marriage was agreed the ceremony was performed at a particular spot. The Tailtean Games were just one of many manifestations of Lughnasad celebrations. Lughnasad was Christianised and became known as Lammas Day. It was turned into a Christian thanksgiving festival. Therefore an interesting question is whether the wrestling tournament held on Lammas Day in Westminster in 1222, documented by John Stow in his *Annales* (see p. 260), represented the survival in the Christian era of an ancient pagan custom of holding sports competitions at this time.

In Japan, sumo matches used to be held at shinto shrines and were dedicated to the gods in the hope of securing a good harvest. Korea apparently has a harvest festival, Chu Sok, at which Ssireum, a traditional Korean wrestling style, is a principal feature. The festival is commonly referred to as correlating with Thanksgiving in the States.

Mongolia also has thanksgiving festivals during summer. Ceremonies are commonly held at *ovoos* to thank the spirits of nature for good pasture and weather. These ceremonies are followed by horse-racing and wrestling. While in Mongolia, I briefly investigated *ovoo* worship ceremonies and was told that the wrestling and horse-racing were merely an entertainment and had no ritual significance. However, presumably the Tibetan Buddhists, who established their religion in Mongolia only as recently as the late sixteenth century, inherited *ovoo* worship ceremonies from the religious culture that preceded them. It's possible, therefore, that they retained the ceremony and the wrestling and horse-racing that characterised it but curbed the role of the latter two activities. Perhaps wrestling was demoted from something with ritual significance to mere entertainment in the process. See also note referring to p. 270, on p. 375.

p. 267 *These young women, known as* parthenoi, *would have been aged between about eleven and fourteen years old and physically mature but not yet married. Greek girls married early – from the age of about fourteen onwards – so these were eligible young women.* See Reeder (1995) pp. 14, 21 and 32.

p. 267 *It may have been that the Greeks allowed unmarried girls to watch for the same reasons that the Dukawa have unmarried young women at their wrestling festivals: so that athletes could demonstrate their manliness in front of women who would both admire them and be in a position to marry.* There is further evidence to bolster the argument that the Games may have descended from a type of human rutting behaviour: the idea that winning a manly contest is a route to winning a bride is encapsulated in a central story told to explain the foundation of the Olympics; and a deity with a temple at the Altis was a goddess of marriage.

According to a key legend, the Games were established by the hero Pelops after he won the hand in marriage of a princess, Hippodaemia, by beating her father, King Oenomaus, in a chariot race. Before Pelops succeeded, many suitors had failed and paid for their failure with their lives at the hands of the king. Pelops' tomb was located at Olympia within a precinct dedicated to him, and his bones were kept elsewhere on the site in a bronze chest. There was also a pillar said to be the last remaining part of Oenomaus's house, which was supposedly destroyed in a fire started by one of Zeus's lightning bolts. One legend said Pelops established the Games to give thanks for his victory over Oenomaus, while another said he established them as funeral games in order to purify himself following the king's death (Pelops arranges for the king's chariot to be tampered with and Oenomaus is killed when it crashes). The grounding of the story at Olympia demonstrates its central importance in the explanatory framework for the ancient Games – a status confirmed by the fact that the scene at the beginning of the chariot race was carved on the front pediment of the temple of Zeus, the centre of gravity of the Altis.

The precinct also contained a temple for Hera, the wife and sister of Zeus. Hera was the Greek goddess of marriage – and according to Pausanias this role may have been emphasised at Olympia. In a passage describing Hera's temple, he writes: 'Every four years the sixteen women weave a robe for Hera and the same women hold Hera's games. The games are a running match between virgin girls.' The event was a sprint and it took place at a different time from the men-only Olympics. Pausanias gives two explanations for the origins of the race – and one is that they were first held by Hippodaemeia to give thanks to Hera for her marriage to Pelops. See Pausanias (1979) pp. 245–6, for a description of the Games and the legends describing how they came about.

p. 268 *Pindar eludes to this dimension when he writes that Telesikrates competed, 'While maidens watched, and in silence each one wished/You, Telesikrates/Were her dearest husband, or her son.'* See Pythian IX, For Telesikrates of Kyrene, Winner in the Race in Armour, Pindar (1985) p. 91.

p. 268 *The ancient Olympics. . . were held in July or August.* In fact all but one of the principal Ancient Greek athletic festivals were always held during summer. The Olympic Games, Pythian Games, Nemean Games and Panathenaic Games were all convened during the summer months, while the Isthmian Games were held in spring or early summer. See Golden (1998) pp. 10–11. The Pythian Games were sacred to Apollo and held every four years at Delphi from either 586 BC or 582 BC. The Nemean Games were sacred to Zeus and held every other year; they were first held at Nemea, then at nearby Argos from 573 BC. The Isthmian Games were sacred to Poseidon and took place every other year at Corinth from 582 BC onwards. The Panathenaic Games were held in Athens. Originally they were held every year, then in 566 BC or 565 BC a big four-yearly festival was also instituted.

p. 269 *Females are present but don't take an active part in these physical contests.* Women do compete in the archery contests at Naadam in Mongolia, but this is not really the type of physical contest I have in mind. Furthermore, archery is the least popular event at Naadam, and in some festivals, such as the Naadams I saw in Khovsgol, it plays no part at all.

p. 270 *Maybe the* [Mongolian wrestlers'] *eagle dance, title-singing and hat-wearing also originated as tactics to intimidate rivals and impress those watching.* There are even closer parallels between the aggressive display behaviour of chimpanzees and Mongolian wrestlers. Alpha male chimps walk in an exaggeratedly slow and heavy manner, and their hair stands on end to make them look bigger (see de Waal, 1998, p. 78). Similarly, the eagle dance communicates a sense of lumbering mass and power, and – as already mentioned – the hats make wrestlers look taller and more imposing. If wrestling does represent the refinement and ritualisation of a type of human rutting behaviour, it is likely that the natural intimidatory display behaviour of humans would also have been ritualised alongside it and have entered the modern era as formalised preludes to wrestling bouts.

p. 270 *There is enough evidence of a recurring pattern in the deep structure of these gatherings, and there are enough similarities between this recurring pattern and the idiom in which other species rut, to suggest that these summer athletic festivals may well be the various descendants of the same ancient form of human rutting behaviour. . .* Were the human rutting theory to be correct, you would anticipate a whole group of factors to conspire to create and support the behaviour. In particular, you would expect male behaviour to be complemented by female behaviour. For instance, you might anticipate a summer peak in ritualised competition between males to be matched by a peak in female fertility. Tournaments would logically be held at a time when females either once were, or still are, most capable of conceiving.

There is evidence that both fits this idea and may help to explain why tournaments are routinely held after harvesting. Through studying the Lese people of the Ituri Forest in the

Congo, Peter Ellison, a leading researcher in the field of understanding the evolution of female reproductive biology, has found good evidence that the ability to conceive is governed by food availability. The Lese eke out a marginal existence, and food supply can vary wildly. Ellison has discovered that conceptions reach a peak when food is at its most abundant after the harvest and plummet during periods of hunger. He makes a strong case that there is a causative relationship and food availability governs ovarian function – in other words, when Lese women have enough food to meet their energy requirements they are more able to conceive than when they do not. If this is a principle that operates in general, and if a proposed human rutting behaviour evolved among groups like the Lese who were also subject to extreme annual variations in food availability, this may help explain why tournaments routinely occur at a time of greatest food abundance: women are more likely to conceive. See Ellison (2001) pp. 198–201.

p. 270 *It is also documented that Nuba tribes in Sudan hold inter-village wrestling tournaments during the dry season after the harvest, but it is not known whether these have any marriage dimension.* See Riefenstahl (1976). Wrestling is a hugely significant part of Nuba life. Like the Dukawa, the Mesakin Quissayr tribe of the Nuba, who live in the south-western corner of the Nuba Mountains in Kordofan, Sudan, and whose life Riefenstahl documents, grow guinea corn as their staple crop. If there is a good harvest, many inter-village wrestling competitions are held afterwards during the dry season. According to Riefensthal, whole villages will walk distances of up to 25 miles for them. Wrestling festivals are times to renew bonds with friends and acquaintances. 'For the people as a whole, these larger wrestling contests are the only important occasion when many villages come together,' writes Riefenstahl. 'It is in so doing that they renew and strengthen their contacts, and revitalise the idea of the unity of the whole people' (p. 135).

pp. 270–1 *Today's humans are not currently understood to follow a seasonal rutting behaviour, but some primates, such as ringtailed lemurs, squirrel monkeys and rhesus macaques, do have a seasonal breeding season. However, none of the apes, including chimpanzees and gorillas, our closest evolutionary relatives, is currently believed to follow any seasonal pattern.* See Dixson (1998) p. 389.

p. 271 *Research undertaken by a team in Denmark and published in 2003 found that testosterone levels in male subjects peaked in June and July, and fell in winter and early spring.* See Andersson *et al* (2003); 27 male subjects were studied over a 17-month period by the team from Copenhagen University Hospital.

p. 271 *Similarly, a small Dutch study published in 1976 reported that testosterone levels reached a near-peak in August and reached their maximum level a little later in the year in October.* See Smals *et al* (1976). Plasma testosterone levels of 15 male subjects were measured at three-monthly intervals from April 1974 to April 1975 by a team from the University of Nijmegen, Netherlands. Testosterone levels were high in July, reached a slightly higher level to peak in October, and low in January and April.

p. 271 *However, a large-scale study of military veterans, undertaken by American testosterone researcher James Dabbs, showed a different picture: levels troughed in late spring and early summer, and peaked in late autumn and early winter.* See Dabbs (1990); data from 4,462 military veterans from all over the States, aged 32–44, was taken over a 16-month period and studied.

p. 274 *Male northern elephant seals tip the scales at more than three times the weight of their female sweethearts.* See Andersson (1994) p. 117. Males fight for females at beach gatherings during a three-month reproductive season. Only a few males get to mate.

p. 276 *The human rutting theory gives a strong explanation for the enduring importance of winning in the wrestling cultures of India, Mongolia and everywhere else. An implication of the theory is that losing really used to be the tragedy for males that they often think of it as.* Testosterone research offers intriguing evidence that something profound is going on when men win. Studies consistently show that winners enjoy an immediate rise in their testosterone level, while losers suffer an immediate fall whether they are wrestling or playing chess (see Ellison, 2001, pp. 266–9; Dabbs, 2000, pp. 89–90). As testosterone level also modulates libido, it would be interesting to know whether the immediate rise in the testosterone level of the winner also produces an immediate increase in virility or interest in sex – to the winner the spoils – though the current thinking is that libido does not vary as long as testosterone level remains within the normal range.

p. 277 *Among males of the great ape species, only humans and chimpanzees have indeed found a way to collaborate.* Males of both species live together in the same group, which is in stark contrast to those of other great apes – a dominant male silverback gorilla will not usually tolerate another mature male in his troop, while male orang-utans are fairly solitary and hostile towards one another when they do meet.

p. 277 *Both chimps and men within the same group fight in a ritualised way. . .* See de Waal (1998) pp. 104–5. Chimpanzees usually use a 'special kind of controlled fighting', says de Waal, who has studied chimp behaviour at Arnhem Zoo. Males confine attacks to biting each other's extremities – usually a finger or foot – and less frequently the shoulder or head. De Waal also sees a connection between such fight ritualisation and male-bonding.

Afterthoughts

India

Sadhana: During the interview with Mahendra Singh, the grandson of lion-killer Hari Narayan Singh, I didn't understand what Mahendra meant when he talked about wrestling as a *sadhana*, and I thought at the time that Pinku's translation of the term as 'practice' was not that helpful (see Chapter 5, p. 75). However, I later realised that this was a fair translation. The word *sadhana* is frequently used in a spiritual context and refers to the discipline or practices followed to attain a spiritual goal. When he referred to wrestling as a *sadhana*, I think Mahendra meant that it not only involves a hard schedule of daily practices, but I believe he was also trying to express the idea that wrestling training has the perfume of a spiritual journey and brings spiritual dividends.

Wrestler versus Lion: The tale of how Hari Narayan Singh came to kill a lion was not the only such story I came across while in India. Bachau Sardar, a strong man, renowned *lathi* man and sometime wrestler from the Yadav caste, is well known in Varanasi for having killed a man-eating lion in 1920. I tracked down and interviewed descendants of Bachau Sardar, including a son, who live in a village just outside the city and just beyond the campus of Banaras Hindu University. The family said that the lion wandered into the village and everyone ran away from it except Bachau, who tried to hit it with his *lathi*. The lion jumped up and placed its paws on his shoulders, and Bachau threw it to the ground where he pinned it while villagers beat it with *lathis*. The family related how Bachau then broke its back by pulling its front paws back while driving his knees into its spine.

In order to verify the story, I tracked down a 98-year-old man called Fuchai Dada Yadav who lived near where the incident happened. Though he didn't see the incident first-hand, Fuchai Dada, too, said Bachau threw the lion to the ground, but his account differed in that he said both the lion and Bachau Sardar were beaten unconscious by the group of people that quickly formed around the two in order to whack the animal to death with sticks. His account suggested that the description of how Bachau broke the lion's back was an embellishment. Furthermore, though he saw the dead animal and described it as about the length of a bed, Fuchai Dada couldn't be sure whether the man-eater was actually a lion or tiger. Given that he almost certainly could not read or write and had probably never visited a zoo in his life, his inability to say for sure what type of big cat he had seen briefly nearly 80 years before was quite understandable.

Bachau Sardar was a bodyguard for Mohan Mahedev Malvi, the revered founder of Banaras Hindu University, and was hacked to death in 1925 during a dispute with locals over land upon which Malvi wanted to build the university. Bachau Sardar's descendants said that he bravely stood up to his murderers, who were armed while he himself had no weapon. As Bachau Sardar was a brave and noble man, a simple temple has been built for him in the village where he lived. In the centre of the temple is a large conical-shaped shrine, called a *chearo*. Painted orange, it looks like a giant lipstick. Villagers make *puja* at the temple, and ask for Bachau's help and protection. This, in itself, is remarkable: here is an example of people worshipping a strong man renowned for his bravery as though a god.

Interestingly, the ancient writer Pausanias gives an account of a similar practice. He mentions that Theogenes, a boxer and pankratiast from the Greek island of Thasos who lived in the early 5th century BC, was worshipped by Greeks and non-Greeks alike, and that he was said to be able to cure diseases (Pausanias, 1979, p. 317). A shrine to Theogenes has been discovered on Thasos by archaeologists. Here is yet another example of the resonance between Ancient Greek and Indian culture (see note pp. 365–8).

The Sperm Stigmata Story: The story of semen erupting from the body of Bishember Chobe (see Chapter 5, p. 82 onwards) was predicated on a gross misunderstanding of what semen is and where it is stored – a misunderstanding underwritten by Ayurveda. In interview, Galu Chobe said he'd seen semen leak from Bishember Chobe's toe during surgery (p. 90). While in Maturah, I also spoke to an old wrestler, Madanuwa Phatak, who served Bishember when he was a boy, and he had a different version of events. He said that semen leaked from Bishember Chobe's body through cuts between his fingers and toes. Thakure Chobe, too, believed that the semen had erupted from Bishember Chobe's feet (p. 84). My guess is that Bishember Chobe had some kind of health condition that cracked and broke the skin of his hands and feet leading to a seepage of body fluids that looked like semen. Maybe, when people saw this discharge, they put two and two together to make five: they concluded that as Bishember was such a fierce advocate of *brahmacharya*, the fluid had to be semen bursting out of his body.

Mongolia

Wrestling Tibetan Buddhist monks: Some time after I visited Mongolia, a friend drew my attention to a book, *Adventures of a Tibetan Fighting Monk*, which gives a brief description of the subculture of strong men and sports at Tibetan Buddhist monasteries in Tibet. The book tells the story of Tashi Khedrup, a Tibetan who was born in about 1937 and later fled from the Chinese invaders. Khedrup became a Dob-Dob, a special category of monk known for their strength and courage. For sport and exercise, Dob-Dobs would run, wrestle, and carry and throw heavy stones. The most important competitive sport they practised, says Khedrup, was long-jumping off a raised ramp. Dob-Dobs did not study the Buddhist teachings to the extent that other monks did. Instead they were employed as bodyguards and used as a kind of monastery police, and also played the oboe and long trumpet at ceremonies. A responsibility of the young and strong Dob-Dobs was to make and serve tea – which resonates with the anecdote Governor

Namkhai related about Namkhai Giant in which the champion won a running competition between monks carrying heavy containers of tea (see p. 155). Dob-Dobs cultivated a particular appearance, says Khedrup. They would wear their monks' clothes in a special way, walk with swagger, wear their hair quite long with a curl trained round the left ear and onto the cheek, and blacken their eyes to look fierce. They also tied a red silk scarf just above the elbow of their right arm. Interestingly, the old man Senge whom I interviewed in Tsaagan Uur *sum*, Khovsgol, about the monk-wrestlers of Dayan Deerkh, said wrestlers who won five rounds in the monastery Nadaan were given a red scarf (see Khedrup, 1998, particularly pp. 47–53).

Brazil

Immediately after his Pride fight against Yuki Kondo, Ze Mario Sperry thought he had had Kondo in half-guard when the Japanese fighter kneed him in the face (p. 306). In fact Kondo jump-passed Ze Mario's guard and landed a knee on him. Pedro Rizzo said that Kevin Randleman had to have surgery on his leg after they fought at UFC 26 (9 June 2000), and had to go down a weight category afterwards (see p. 324). However, Randleman fought five months later in UFC 28 (17 November 2000) against Randy Couture in the same weight category as before, heavyweight (93–120kg), so Pedro must have got that wrong. I tried to contact Randleman to ask him whether he was nevertheless badly injured by leg kicks, but he is a very elusive man.

Note: The visit to Richmond Park described in Chapter 9 took place in 2005. I slotted it into that chapter because it made sense to do so in terms of the narrative. Also, Joe is not the real name of my friend mentioned in the Brazil section. I changed his name at his request.

Bibliography and References

Achebe, Chinua (2001) *Things Fall Apart*. London: Penguin (1st edition, William Heinemann, 1958).

Andersson, Malte (1994) *Sexual Selection*. Princeton: Princeton University Press.

Andersson, AM, Carlsen, E, Petersen, JH and Skakkebflk, NE (2003) Variation in levels of serum inhibin B, testosterone, estradiol, luteinizing hormone, follicle-stimulating hormone, and sex hormone-binding globulin in monthly samples from healthy men during a seventeen-month period: possible effects of seasons. *Journal of Clinical Endocrinology and Metabolism* 88(2): 932–7.

Aretaeus (1837) *Of the Causes and Signs of Acute and Chronic Disease*, translated by TF Reynolds. London: William Pickering.

Clutton-Brock, TH, Guinness, FE and Albon, SD (1982) *Red Deer: Behaviour and Ecology of Two Sexes*. Edinburgh: Edinburgh University Press.

Dabbs, James McBride (1990) Age and seasonal variation in serum testosterone concentration among men. *Chronobiology International* 7: 245–9.

Dabbs, James McBride (2000) *Heroes, Rogues, and Lovers*. New York: McGraw-Hill.

de Waal, Frans (1998) *Chimpanzee Politics*. Baltimore and London: The John Hopkins University Press.

Diogenes Laertius (1853) *The Lives and Opinions of Eminent Philosophers*, translated by CD Yonge. London: Henry G Bohn.

Dixson, Alan F (1998) *Primate Sexuality*. Oxford: Oxford University Press.

Draeger, Donn F and Smith, Robert W (1980) *Comprehensive Asian Fighting Arts*. Tokyo: Kodansha International.

Ellison, Peter T (2001) *On Fertile Ground*. Cambridge, MA: Harvard University Press.

Finley, MI and Pleket, HW (1976) *The Olympic Games: The First Thousand Years*. London: Chatto & Windus.

Foucault, Michel (1990) *The Care of the Self*. London: Penguin.

Golden, Mark (1998) *Sport and Society in Ancient Greece*. Cambridge: Cambridge University Press.

Graves, Robert (1955) *The Greek Myths*. Harmondsworth: Penguin.

Harrison, EJ (1934) *Wrestling*. London: Foulsham.

Joyce, PW (1913) *A Social History of Ancient Ireland*. Dublin and Belfast: Gresham.

Khedrup, Tashi (1998) *Adventures of a Tibetan Fighting Monk*. Bangkok: Orchid Press.

LeBell, Gene (1992) *Grappling Master: Combat for Street Defense and Competition*. Los Angeles: Pro-Action Publishing.

Maduka, Chidi T (1996) *Power Mike Who Ruled the World*. Onitsha: Tabansi Publishers Ltd.

Miller, Stephen G (1991) *Arete*. Berkeley and Los Angeles: University of California Press.

Pausanias (1979) *Guide to Greece, Vol II*, translated and introduction by Peter Levi. London: Penguin.

Pindar (1985) *The Odes*, translated and introduction by CM Bowra. Harmondsworth: Penguin.

Plato (1970) *The Laws*, translated and introduction by Trevor J Saunders. Harmondsworth: Penguin.

Poliakoff, Michael B (1987) *Combat Sports in the Ancient World*. New Haven and London: Yale University Press.

Raschke, Wendy J (ed) (1988) *The Archaeology of the Olympics*. Madison: University of Wisconsin Press.

Reeder, Ellen D *et al* (1995) *Pandora: Women in Classical Greece*. Baltimore and Princeton: Trustees of the Walters Art Gallery in association with Princeton University Press.

Riefenstahl, Leni (1976) *The Last of the Nuba*. London: Collins.

Smals, AG, Kloppenborg, PW and Benraad, TJ (1976) Circannual cycle in plasma testosterone levels in man. *Journal of Clinical Endocrinology and Metabolism* 42: 979–82.

Stow, John (1615) *The Annales.* London: imprinted for Thomas Dawson for Thomas Adams.

Stow, John (1908) *A Survey of London, Vol I.* 1603 text with introduction and notes by Charles Lethbridge Kingsford. Oxford: Clarendon Press.

Yalouris, Nicolaos (ed) (1982) *The Olympic Games in Ancient Greece.* Athens: Ekdotike Athenon SA.

Acknowledgements

A big thank-you to my parents for their support during a long and – at times – difficult journey. Thanks to Tim Willis for early encouragement. In India, a particular thank-you goes to Goverdhan Das and the Pandey family, as well as Mr James and Mr Kesri. Mongolia: thanks to Crazy Bob, and Brook and Brandon Kohrt for your company. A special thanks to Agaa, too, for stepping in to help at a difficult time, and to Ouyuntsetseg for your hard work. Australia: thanks go to Larry Papadopoulos for your generous help.

I must thank Frank Salamone and Kirik Jenness for helping me gear up for the trip to Nigeria. A huge thank-you to all the Brothers, Sisters and Fathers who subsequently looked after me while there. In particular, a big thank-you to Father Peter, Father Daniel, Father Jerome and the Okeres – Edwin, Linus and Theophilus. Also, thanks to Father Stephen and Father Gregory in Zuru for your hospitality, and the Gulders and crocodiles. A big thank-you to the staff of Crawley Hospital and St George's in Tooting for helping me to recover after Nige. In Brazil I'd like to particularly thank Luca Atalla for your hospitality and help, as well as Ze Mario Sperry, Carlinhos Gracie, Roberto Leitao Snr, Allan Goes, Carlos Duarte and Tata Duarte.

Special thanks to Judy Silver for your guidance all the way through this trip, and to Han van de Braak, a true doctor. Also, my thanks go to Daniel Collier for helping out at difficult times, and to my readers – Andrew Shaylor, Catherine

Cumming, Patricia O'Kicki, Grant Osman and Brandon Kohrt – for your criticism and encouragement. A big thank-you to William Cook for your sage advice at key moments and to Natalie Fry for the style of your literary criticism. A huge thanks to my agent, John Saddler, and to Hannah MacDonald and Ken Barlow at Ebury Press for your help during editing. I must thank Lucy Edge, too, for the invite.

Particular thanks are also due to EJ Harrison, Agent 47, Sergeant Baker, Toby Lures, A4 paper, salt, and *a familia Torresini*.